"This impressive collection makes an important contribution to our understanding of environmental justice. With a refreshing and original focus on transitions and futures, it is highly recommended for anyone interested in how environmental inequalities are made and sustained, and how, crucially, we might imagine and achieve a more just future."

– Neil Simcock, Liverpool John Moores
University, UK

"This is an impressive volume, with a distinctively critical and international perspective, drawing together fresh voices on the challenges and possibilities of just transitions across different sites and settings. Its multi-scalar, multi-species, and intersectional scope puts it at the cutting edge of contemporary environmental justice scholarship."

– Professor Gordon Walker, Lancaster
Environment Centre, Lancaster University, UK

"This impressive, interdisciplinary collection makes important contributions to the field of critical environmental justice studies in its broad examination of the social and ecological inequities intrinsic to the 'Anthropocene.' Grounded in a wide range of case studies from diverse national contexts, the chapters draw on foundational concepts of spatial and intergenerational justice to analyze the degree to which our go-to 'sustainability solutions' will in fact bring about the *just* transitions they promise. From the complexities of bioenergy justice initiatives in Yucatán, Mexico, to climate transition strategies in Tanzanian forest management policies, to the challenges and prospects of intersectional climate justice organizing in California, the authors provide original and forward-facing assessments of what is needed to move from '(un)just presents to just futures.'"

– Giovanna Di Chiro, Professor of Environmental
Studies, Swarthmore College, USA

ENVIRONMENTAL JUSTICE IN THE ANTHROPOCENE

Through various international case studies presented by both practitioners and scholars, *Environmental Justice in the Anthropocene* explores how an environmental justice approach is necessary for reflections on inequality in the Anthropocene and for forging societal transitions toward a more just and sustainable future.

Environmental justice is a central component of sustainability politics during the Anthropocene – the current geological age in which human activity is the dominant influence on climate and the environment. Every aspect of sustainability politics requires a close analysis of equity implications, including problematizing the notion that humans as a collective are equally responsible for ushering in this new epoch. Environmental justice provides us with the tools to critically investigate the drivers and characteristics of this era and the debates over the inequitable outcomes of the Anthropocene for historically marginalized peoples. The contributors to this volume focus on a critical approach to power and issues of environmental injustice across time, space, and context – drawing from twelve national contexts: Austria, Bangladesh, Chile, China, India, Nicaragua, Hungary, Mexico, Brazil, Sweden, Tanzania, and the United States. Beyond highlighting injustices, the volume highlights forward-facing efforts at building just transitions, with a goal of identifying practical steps to connect theory and movement and envision an environmentally and ecologically just future.

This interdisciplinary work will be of great interest to students, scholars, and practitioners focused on conservation, environmental politics and governance, environmental and earth sciences, environmental sociology, environment and planning, environmental justice, and global sustainability and governance. It will also be of interest to social and environmental justice advocates and activists.

Stacia Ryder is a Post-Doctoral Research Fellow at the University of Exeter, UK.

Kathryn Powlen is a PhD Candidate in Human Dimensions of Natural Resources, Colorado State University, USA.

Melinda Laituri is Professor emeritus of Ecosystem Science and Sustainability at Colorado State University, USA.

Stephanie A. Malin is Associate Professor of Sociology at Colorado State University, USA.

Joshua Sbicca is Associate Professor of Sociology at Colorado State University, USA.

Dimitris Stevis is Professor of Politics at Colorado State University, USA.

Routledge Studies in Environmental Justice

This series is theoretically and geographically broad in scope, seeking to explore the emerging debates, controversies and practical solutions within Environmental Justice, from around the globe. It offers cutting-edge perspectives at both a local and global scale, engaging with topics such as climate justice, water governance, air pollution, waste management, environmental crime, and the various intersections of the field with related disciplines.

The *Routledge Studies in Environmental Justice* series welcomes submissions that combine strong academic theory with practical applications, and as such is relevant to a global readership of students, researchers, policy-makers, practitioners and activists.

Ecosocialism and Climate Justice
An Ecological Neo-Gramscian Analysis
Eve Croeser

Climate Change Justice and Global Resource Commons
Local and Global Postcolonial Political Ecologies
Shangrila Joshi

Diversity and Inclusion in Environmentalism
Edited by Karen Bell

Environmental Justice in the Anthropocene
From (Un)Just Presents to Just Futures
Edited by Stacia Ryder, Kathryn Powlen, Melinda Laituri, Stephanie A. Malin, Joshua Sbicca and Dimitris Stevis

For more information about this series, please visit: www.routledge.com/Routledge-Studies-in-Environmental-Justice/book-series/EJS

ENVIRONMENTAL JUSTICE IN THE ANTHROPOCENE

From (Un)Just Presents
to Just Futures

*Edited by Stacia Ryder, Kathryn Powlen,
Melinda Laituri, Stephanie A. Malin,
Joshua Sbicca, and Dimitris Stevis*

Routledge
Taylor & Francis Group

earthscan
from Routledge

LONDON AND NEW YORK

First published 2021
by Routledge
2 Park Square, Milton Park, Abingdon, Oxon OX14 4RN

and by Routledge
605 Third Avenue, New York, NY 10158

Routledge is an imprint of the Taylor & Francis Group, an informa
business

British Library Cataloguing-in-Publication Data
A catalogue record for this book is available from the British Library

Library of Congress Cataloging-in-Publication Data
A catalog record has been requested for this book

ISBN: 978-0-367-90294-0 (hbk)
ISBN: 978-0-367-90288-9 (pbk)
ISBN: 978-1-003-02360-9 (ebk)

Typeset in Bembo
by Deanta Global Publishing Services, Chennai, India

CONTENTS

FIGURES

TABLES

EDITORS

Melinda Laituri is a Professor Emeritus of Geography at Colorado State University (CSU), USA. She was the founding Director of the Geospatial Centroid at CSU and a Co-director of the Center for Environmental Justice at CSU. Her research focuses on participatory mapping, water resource management, and disaster preparedness.

Stephanie A. Malin, PhD, is an Environmental Sociologist specializing in natural resource sociology, governance, and rural development, with a focus on the community impacts of resource extraction and energy production. Stephanie serves as an Associate Professor in the Department of Sociology at Colorado State University, USA, and is an adjunct Associate Professor with the Colorado School of Public Health. At Colorado State, Stephanie is an award-winning teacher of courses on environmental justice, water and society, and environmental sociology. She is also the author of *The Price of Nuclear Power: Uranium Communities and Environmental Justice* and has published her research in journals such as *Social Forces*, *Environmental Politics*, the *Journal of Rural Studies*, and *Society and Natural Resources*. She completed a Mellon Foundation Postdoctoral Fellowship at Brown University after earning her PhD in Sociology from Utah State University, USA.

Kathryn Powlen is a doctoral candidate in the Department of Human Dimensions of Natural Resources at Colorado State University (CSU). As a human-environment geographer, she draws from land systems science and social science to critically examine environmental governance and social justice in conservation interventions. While pursuing her graduate degree at CSU, she served as the program coordinator for the Center for Environmental Justice.

Stacia Ryder is a Postdoctoral Research Fellow in the Geography Department at the University of Exeter in the UK and a co-founder of the Center for

Environmental Justice at Colorado State University, USA. She received her PhD in Sociology in 2019 from Colorado State University. In addition to recently publishing works focused on environmental justice issues in energy contexts, Stacia has also recently co-edited two special issues on power and environmental justice for the journal *Environmental Sociology*. She plans to continue to advance this theoretical approach in the context of climate displacement and whole community resettlement, and how we can plan and develop policy that will allow for just and equitable transitions for displaced people and communities in the face of the current anthropogenic climate crisis.

Joshua Sbicca is Associate Professor of Sociology at Colorado State University, USA. He is the author of *Food Justice Now! Deepening the Roots of Social Struggle* and a co-editor of *A Recipe for Gentrification: Food, Power, and Resistance in the City*.

Dimitris Stevis is Professor of Politics at Colorado State University, USA. His research focuses on global labor and environmental politics, with particular attention to labor environmentalism and social and ecological justice. He is a Codirector of the Center for Environmental Justice at Colorado State University. He has recently co-edited, with Nora Räthzel and David Uzzell, a special issue of the journal *Globalizations* (2018, 15:4) entitled 'Labour in the Web of Life' and with Edouard Morena and Dunja Krause *Just Transitions: Social Justice in the Shift Towards a Low-Carbon World* (2020). He is a co-author of the Report on the Just Transition Listening Project, organized by the Labour Network for Sustainability (USA) (March 2021).

CONTRIBUTORS

Nino Antadze is Assistant Professor of Environmental Studies, University of Prince Edward Island, Canada.

Attila Antal is Senior Lecturer of Political Science at Eötvös Loránd University Faculty of Law Institute of Political Science, Budapest, Hungary, and Coordinator at Institute of Political History Social Theory Research Group.

Aparajita Banerjee is Postdoctoral Fellow, College of Business, University College Dublin, Ireland.

Sherrie Baver is Professor of Political Science at The City College and The Graduate Center-CUNY. She is also a member of the Latin American and Latino Studies Program at City College.

Matthew J. Burke is Postdoctoral Associate with the Leadership for the Ecozoic project at the University of Vermont Rubenstein School of Environment and Natural Resources and Gund Institute for Environment.

Matt Comi is PhD candidate in Sociology at University of Kansas in Lawrence, USA.

Roberta Cucca is Associate Professor in the Department of Urban and Regional Planning at the Norwegian University of Life Sciences (NMBU).

Caroline Farrell is the Executive Director of the Center on Race, Poverty and the Environment.

Judson B. Finley is Associate Professor of Anthropology in the Department of Sociology, Social Work, and Anthropology at Utah State University, USA.

Michael Friesenecker is a Researcher in the Department of Sociology at the University of Vienna, Austria.

Benjamin Max Goloff is a Senior Campaigner at the Center for Biological Diversity's Climate Law Institute.

Michelle Larkins is an Assistant Professor of Environmental Science and Studies, and the Director of the Center for a Sustainable Society at Pacific University.

G. Thomas LaVanchy is Assistant Professor of Geography at Oklahoma State University, Stillwater, Oklahoma, USA.

Julie A. Lester is a Professor of Political Science at Middle Georgia State University, Macon, Georgia, USA.

KuoRay Mao is Associate Professor in the Department of Sociology at Colorado State University, USA.

Lilia García Manrique is a PhD student from the Economics department at the University of Sussex, UK.

Chaitanya Motupalli is currently serving as the Director of Student Life at the Graduate Theological Union, Berkeley, CA, where he received his doctorate in Ethics and Social Theory.

Rita Vasconcellos Oliveira is a Senior Researcher in the Department of Industrial Economics and Technology Management, Faculty of Economics and Management at Norwegian University of Science and Technology.

Jessica Omukuti is Postdoctoral Research Associate at the Interdisciplinary Global Development Centre (IGDC) at the University of York, UK.

Saptaparni Pandit is currently a PhD Research Scholar at Kazi Nazrul University, Asansol, West Bengal, India.

Isabel Rodríguez Peña is a Professor of Business and Economics at the Universidad Anáhuac Mexico.

Anindya Sekhar Purakayastha is Professor at the Department of English, Kazi Nazrul University, India.

Sarah T. Romano is an Associate Professor of Political Science and Global Studies at Lesley University in Cambridge, Massachusetts, USA.

Matthew J. Rowe is an Assistant Professor in the School of Anthropology at University of Arizona, USA.

Mad Stano is Energy Equity Senior Legal Counsel at the Greenlining Institute in Oakland, California, USA, and lecturer on environmental justice at Berkeley Law.

Nowrin Tabassum is a sessional faculty of Political Science at McMaster University, Hamilton, Canada.

Gabriel R. Valle is an Associate Professor of Environmental Studies at California State University, San Marcos (CSUSM), USA.

Mónica Santillán Vera is an Associate Professor of Business and Economics at the Universidad Anáhuac Mexico and the Faculty of Economics of the National Autonomous University of Mexico (UNAM). She is a Contributing Author of the IPCC Sixth Assessment Report.

Nefratiri Weeks is a PhD student at Colorado State University, USA.

Christine J. Winter is a Lecturer in the Department of Government & International Relations & Post-Doctoral Fellow at the Sydney Environment Institute at the University of Sydney, Australia.

Qiang Zhang is an Associate Research Fellow at the Chinese Academy of Social Sciences Institute of Sociology.

Shimeng Zhou is an Urban and Regional Development Analyst at Sweco, Stockholm, Sweden. She holds an MSc in Nature, Society and Environmental Policy from the School of Geography and the Environment at the University of Oxford, UK.

FOREWORD

Christine J. Winter

Late in April 2017, in the white-hot glare of newly elected President Trump's anti-environmentalism, the Environmental Justice Working Group at Colorado State University hosted an energizing, optimistic symposium. And there it may have lain, a mere moment of engagement, reflection, and combined intellectual enterprise: a few fleeting days of hope relegated to the past. An opportunity afforded those lucky enough to have shared the inspiration. Fortunately, the momentary is converted here, in this book, to a legacy.

In reflecting on the intention of the symposium and this volume, *Environmental Justice and the Anthropocene*, it is worthwhile to reflect on the broader dimensions of *time*. Time would seem a "fact" – indeed a measurable fact. However, within it and the word Anthropocene are a host of values and normative claims. The "facts" of time obscure other dimensions of time, and other-than-Western constructions of time. In imagining justice in the Anthropocene as this volume seeks to do, to forge just relationships with human and nonhuman, living and non-living, ancestors and future generations, it is valuable to examine the very notion of time 'Anthropocene' evokes.

Environmental justice and the Anthropocene challenge the idea of time as a progressive arc. They test the expectation that time past is lesser, something gone, the "now" is fleeting and yet preeminent, and that the future is unfathomable and may be discounted to the demands of the present. Both transcend the present, bear the marks of the past, and expose morally troubling risks to the future.

Embedded within the word Anthropocene are a host of facts, values, and normative claims. Coined as a scientific claim – that earth's geology, biology, and zoology are in this new epoch shaped primarily by human actions – is its "factual" base. The primary value attached to this claim is that that is bad – bad for humans and other living things, bad for the environment, bad for the earth. And the normative claims derive from the notion of bad: humans have a responsibility to address the harms intrinsic to the claim we have entered the Anthropocene. Picking up this book you are entering into a critical examination of these claims of fact, value, and normativity. Your journey will be an exploration across formidable barriers towards a just world: a world in which environmental justice, and within it intergenerational, social, cultural, multispecies, indigenous, and decolonial justice is normalized.

However, the singular "Anthropocene" is neither a singular event nor does it make earth's peoples one. Throughout this book, repeatedly, we find the multiple causes and effects of the Anthropocene are spatially and temporally diverse. There is no "we." "We" are not in this together. The causal agents are the least likely to bear the harmful effects. The causes and effects are spatially and temporally decoupled. They are dispersed in ways that create, exacerbate and recreate inequalities within nations, between nations, across land-, water-, and cityscapes and through time.

In announcing we are in the Anthropocene, geologists and palaeontologists are staking a claim that we have left an epoch – an epoch of climatic and biological stability that supported the rise and flourishing of humans and human enterprise. That epoch, the Holocene, is now gone. Behind us as it were. Lost with little likelihood of return. It has passed. Our present is the beginning of a new epoch – one which will last as long as we can imagine. The suggestion is that the ways we act now can and will impact the nature of that future. Our behaviors will shape the climate, biosphere, and planetary system for the rest of the Anthropocene, perhaps for the rest of time. The time of the Anthropocene then marks out three distinct intervals: prepresent and the end of the Holocene; the present-Anthropocene; and an as yet unimaginable post-Anthropocene. I want to unsettle that structure. To do that I draw from Maori conceptions of time, from my ancestors' engagement with the structures of being-on-earth. In Matauranga Maori (Maori knowledge and philosophy) time may indeed be measurable and momentary and it is also a spirally bound relationship between times. To understand the Anthropocene, then, is to understand it is simultaneously past, present, and future. Within that construct we find fact, value, and normatively are also unsettled and the subjects to whom we owe justice comprehensively human and nonhuman.

We, the Anthropo of the Anthropocene, are multi-temporal beings. We are more than a singular "I." More than a single lifespan. Each of us contains the DNA of ancestors. For me that means Polynesian Pacific explorers who settled Aotearoa New Zealand and formed the iwi Ngāti Kahungunu; and a whole bunch of Anglo folks who also left their home shores to settle in Aotearoa. They are my ancestors. I am a member of their future generation for whom they, their heirs, and their ancestors left the known for new and better lives for themselves and their heirs. I have a son and a daughter. In them live: the same ancestors; their father and his ancestors; and me. And they are my future generation and the potential creators of even more future generations. And soon they and I will be ancestors to new generations. Our ancestors' DNA will live on.

I am, we are, also an amalgam of elements and chemicals. The nitrogen that makes up 10 percent of our bodies was created three seconds after the Big Bang. Ten percent of our bodies is 13.7 billion years old! I am, you are, we are both living now and composed of minerals and compounds drawn from all time. These elements we draw from our food. Our food draws them from the earth; from the places it grows. Those places then become embedded in our bodies during our lives. And it is to the earth system they return as our bodies undergo their daily cycles of removing waste, growth, and renewal until our living form finally dies. We are chemically ancient and renewing simultaneously.

And there is more still. We are not a single being. The human body is a host to micro-biota on whom we depend – our microbiome. Distinct in and on each of us, we are the time of each of these organisms too. 'We' might continue, but these communities within and on us, these components of the individual we understand ourselves to be, reproduce and die to different clocks, different life cycles. We are their time and ours simultaneously.

And we contain, we embody the knowledge, learnings, cultures, languages, songs and dances, histories and philosophies of people long gone. A mix of relatives and strangers they live on in our imaginations, intellectual enterprises, and artistic pursuits. Their thinking and ours is drawn from the past, is present now, and will resonate into the future – just as this book is doing. It cannot and does not stand in a moment. It is not and cannot be isolated from its entangled time periods. The past, present, and future are simultaneous.

Time simultaneously past–present–future offers environmental justice in the Anthropocene a multigenerational ethics. From the past is drawn the knowledge and experience of ancestors, and a set of obligations and duties to honor and respect our places, our lands from all time, for all time to ensure future generations – human and nonhuman – flourish.

But the time of geology marks a progression – from the Big Bang to the present. Each era and epoch are marked off, left behind as new earth system features shape the biosphere and geosphere. The movement of time marks a progression from primitive to modern, from single cell to multicellular being. This movement is imprinted in rocks, landscapes, and water bodies. The Anthropocene is then the latest in a series of climatic, biological, and geological processes. It is new, forward-looking, and foreboding. We have left the benign conditions of the last epoch.

However, that blurs what has happened, is happening, and will happen. It is human activity, and more specifically extractivist capitalist activity that takes resources from the earth faster than their replacement rate in the pursuit of profit and growing consumption, that is the signature of the Anthropocene. The epoch signals one primary change to the equilibrium of the Holocene: global air temperatures have risen, are rising, and will continue to rise. Releasing greenhouse gases is the primary cause of rising temperatures. Not all societies are party to these processes, and not all people have benefited. The effects are being felt unevenly across the globe. Woven through the contributions to this book are reflections on the injustice that the least responsible are the first affected and most affected. While the beneficiaries are past or present members of industrialized nations, the most affected will be those not-yet-born – future generations. These are spatial injustices and temporal injustice.

I have reflected here on the way in which the past is embedded in the present and future of the Anthropocene. The carbons released by burning fuels are ancient, billions of years ancient. Carbon, captured by plants and trees, was embedded between layers of sand and mud, weighed down, compressed, and converted to the coal, oil, and gas we now extract. The carbon is at once ancient, modern, and future. It is not lost nor destroyed. It is just that some forms are more benign than others. While contained in the substrate it does no harm. Released as gas it is a force of destruction.

As I prefigured earlier, Maori are a people who walk backwards into the future looking at the past. This volume does just that. Drawing from eons of past knowledge, learning, experience, it is asking: What sort of ancestors do we want to be?

Sydney, Australia
Postdoctoral Research Fellow, Sydney Environment Institute
Lecturer, Department of Government and International Relations, The University of Sydney

PREFACE

Environmental justice in the Anthropocene

Dimitris Stevis

This volume is the result of a symposium titled "Environmental Justice in the Anthropocene," which took place from April 24 to 25, 2017, at Colorado State University (CSU), USA. It is important to acknowledge the history of the grounds on which this symposium took place, so here we draw on the CSU Land Acknowledgement to do so:

> Colorado State University acknowledges, with respect, that the land we are on today is the traditional and ancestral homelands of the Arapaho, Cheyenne, and Ute Nations and peoples. This was also a site of trade, gathering, and healing for numerous other Native tribes. We recognize the Indigenous peoples as original stewards of this land and all the relatives within it. This acknowledgment is the education and inclusion we must practice in recognizing our institutional history, responsibility, and commitment.

The symposium was organized and hosted by the Environmental Justice Working Group in the School of Global Environmental Sustainability and was envisioned as the next step in the work the Group had been carrying out since its inception in 2014. We initially imagined a day-long gathering with a small number of presenters and limited audience. We were excited to receive almost 200 proposals from graduate students, faculty, activists, and practitioners from around the world. Due to this interest, we organized a two-day conference around three themes: multidisciplinary facets of environmental justice, just transitions, and just futures. The final program featured 30 sessions and over 100 presentations and, due to space limitations, we closed registration at 300 people.

In addition to the unexpected numbers of presenters and attendees we were also heartened by the diversity of the presenters and the topics. Geographically presenters came from over 30 countries in the Global North and Global South including politically engaged scholars, practitioners, community members, and activists. The topics collectively interrogated environmental injustice and justice across space and time and amongst humans and between humanity and nature in the Anthropocene – as well as the concept of the Anthropocene.

We were further encouraged by the generous support of a number of departments and units within CSU – including the School of Global Environmental Sustainability, the Office of the Provost, the Office of the Vice President for Research, the Office of International Programs, the Partnership for Air Quality, Climate & Health (PACH), the Water Center, Future Earth, the College of Liberal Arts, the Warner College of Natural Resources, the Departments of Philosophy, Political Science and Sociology. The event was supported by Adapting Canadian Work and Workplaces to Respond to Climate Change, based at York University in Canada, and Acknowl-EJ and EnvJustice at the Autonomous University of Barcelona. This support allowed us to host this event without charging a registration fee and fund the travel expenses of a considerable number of junior scholars, activists, and international colleagues ensuring that the symposium reflected the full range of people that responded to our call.

The breadth and depth of the presentations, as well as the general interest and enthusiasm we witnessed, motivated and informed the preparation and content of this volume. The Symposium helped advance the institutionalization of environmental justice within Colorado State University, morphing the Environmental Justice Working Group into the Center for Environmental Justice at CSU in 2020. Our goal as a center is to make environmental justice a lens through which to explore social life *in* nature, across disciplines and issues areas, while balancing and integrating engaged research, teaching, and practice.

The organization and success of the Symposium helped us establish connections with other environmental justice nodes around the world and led us to propose a rotating global environmental justice conference that is becoming a reality. EJ2019 at the University of East Anglia will be followed by EJ 2021 at the Autonomous University of Barcelona and EJ2022 at Colorado State University. This volume is the result of a successful event, part of a continuing project and a contribution to the promotion and study of environmental justice, an urgent demand of these turbulent times.

PART I

Thinking on the Anthropocence

INTRODUCTION

Just Anthropocene?

Dimitris Stevis, Melinda Laituri, Stacia Ryder,
Kathryn Powlen, Stephanie A. Malin, and Joshua Sbicca

This volume explores environmental justice (EJ) in the Anthropocene by address-ing the contested concept of the Anthropocene, the spatiality of EJ, just transi-tions, and just futures. In this general introduction we provide an overview while the two chapters of the first section delve into the concept of the Anthropocene. Introductory chapters in each of the subsequent three sections address spatial justice, just transitions, and just futures in more detail while summarizing how the various contributions address these themes (Sbicca et al.; Ryder et al.; Powlen et al. all in this volume).

Debates over naming our era "The Anthropocene" are less about whether it is a new geological epoch – although that is also an important issue (Davis 2011; Malin in this volume) – and more about its political economy (Moore 2019). Debates between universalist narratives that privilege an undifferentiated plane-tary totality – whether limits to growth, global environmental change, planetary boundaries, or the Anthropocene – and historical narratives that open up that totality – such as ecological imperialism, Capitalocene, the Plantationocene, or environmental justice – have been competing throughout history and modern environmental politics has not been an exception (Buttel et al. 1990; Stevis and Assetto 2001). For critics, universalist narratives serve to obscure differential responsibility for our predicament and, thus, obligation for getting us out of it (Malm and Warlenius 2019; Malin in this volume).

Even when stemming from the best of intentions, such universalist narratives can suspend democratic debate and fights for justice by obscuring or, worse, dis-missing the views of the exploited and the vulnerable, often in the name of sav-ing the Planet (Swyngendow 2010; Methman and Roth 2012). Environmental justice stands as a guardian against such sacrificial practices, particularly when, as used in this volume, it fuses justice amongst humans and justice between human-ity and nature – what is commonly called ecological justice (Low and Gleeson

1998; Schlosberg 2013), multispecies justice (Celermajer et al. 2020a, 2020b), or the even more inclusive eco-justice, as some of the EJ pioneers called it in the early 1970s (Gibson 2004). From that perspective every social practice is also an ecological practice and every ecological practice a social practice (Taylor 2000; Pulido 2017).

Accordingly, EJ requires that we interrogate space and place – whether addressing the Anthropocene, the Capitalocene, or the Plantationocene – keeping in mind that scale is both the product of historical social relations and a metric of place (Sbicca et al. in this volume; Hollifield et al. 2009). What is the spatial scale, or spatial scales, of a particular disruption, whether ecological imperialism, climate change, toxins, loss of biodiversity, or pandemics? What are the implications of the fact that almost every place in our world has been shaped and reshaped by global divisions of labor throughout time (Grove 1994; Marks 2015; Mann 2011; Hornborg and Martinez-Alier 2016)? Sensitivity to the historical and relational nature of space and place, therefore, also allows us to better understand that temporality is also the product of contestation (Adam 1998; Nixon 2011).

As the chapters here showcase, environmental justice is inherently multi-scalar, and it also complicates scales of time and space. Environmental justice activism began in spaces where weak occupational health and safety practices, toxicants, hazards, and environmental risks like chemical contamination and nuclear waste threatened workers, communities, and other beings (Bryant 1997; Taylor 2000). These contaminations often transcend time, as they can last for hundreds, thousands, or even millions of years (in the case of nuclear). This has important implications for intergenerational justice. At the same time, space can also be transcended and complicated, as these contaminants can move from places where they originated to other spaces through water, air, and human and geological processes.

For these reasons we made spatial justice explicit through a series of case studies that examine the following questions (Figure 0.1): Who and what do we include in our spatial scales – what is their intersectional scope (Young 2006; Malin and Ryder 2018)? Are our local or planetary scales limited to particular people (Hultgren 2015; Whyte 2020) or species and to particular ways of looking at well-being? When we include a subaltern – whether species or humans – do we ask about *its* subaltern (Egan 2002; Sze and London 2008)? Do we care as much about crickets as we do about butterflies? Do we care as much about the immigrants that produce our food as we care about those who attend to our health or fight our wars (Park and Ruiz 2020)?

The transition from existing injustices to just futures is a process which requires properly crafted transitions whereby the means are consistent with the ends (Lohman 2009). The section on Just Transitions broadens the scope beyond energy making it clear that just transitions are necessary across sectors and scales (Ryder et al. in this volume). In examining just transitions EJ prompts us to recognize that all social and environmental injustices are felt locally and

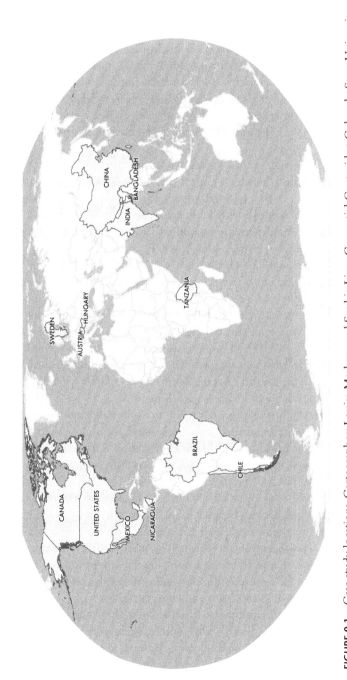

FIGURE 0.1   Case study locations. Cartographer: Louisa Markow and Sophia Linn, Geospatial Centroid at Colorado State University.

by particular people. Like an empire, globalization does not take place in some ethereal space but operates through specific places and people (Dicken 2015). Just transitions, as well as just futures, require that we pay close attention to articulations of scale and scope (Stevis and Felli 2020). This is necessary if we are to avoid the "militant particularism" inherent in some initiatives that while seemingly just or desirable, when viewed within limited spatial or temporal parameters, may actually externalize inequality and injustice (Williams 1989; Gough 2010). For example, "militant particularism" is evident in urban decarbonization policies that do not account for their impacts on coal communities. Just transitions place in front of us the challenge of crafting effective policies that fuse urgency, sustainability, and social justice (Just Transition Research Collaborative 2018; Ciplet and Harrison 2020) rather than privileging one or the other.

Finally, in the section on Just Futures, we consider the elements of an environmentally just world (Powlen et al. in this volume). Who and what visions are included? How can they be fused together in an intersectional manner that challenges structural inequalities (Malin and Ryder 2018; Di Chiro 2020; Ryder 2017; Ryder 2018)? An important question is that inclusion is a necessary but not sufficient condition for environmental justice. EJ encourages analysts and practitioners to ask what the price of inclusion may be, who gets to set the parameters on inclusion and "send out of the invitations," and whether the power relations responsible for injustice are themselves subject to fully democratic participation and deliberation. One of the major mechanisms of power – in addition to force – is the ability of the powerful to fragment, coopt and naturalize inequality (Gaventa 1980; Pulido 2017). EJ prompts us, therefore, to ask whether the powerful are required to be at the table with the full understanding that their power itself is the topic of deliberation and regulation. EJ is not only about empowering the marginalized; it is about weakening the powerful.

For the meaningful inclusion necessary for just transitions to lead to just futures, there has to be a dramatic shift in the world political economy and ecology. These will not come about without contestation – indeed many efforts to curb climate change have been met with resistance by powerful actors such as national governments and the fossil fuel industry. Egalitarian researchers and activists should not be paralyzed by a Manichean choice between transformation or defeat, society, or nature. Neither should they call every change transformational and every non-transformational change a defeat. Difficult as it is, EJ analysts and practitioners must be particularly alert in differentiating between managerial reforms that address crises from structural reforms that allow us to envision and strive for a more egalitarian and ecological world (Just Transition Research Collaborative 2018; Ciplet and Harrison 2020).

A key message of this volume is that EJ is not simply an "add-on" which we can address only after dealing with more existential issues – for those who already experience environmental injustices it is already an existential issue. Its difference from other lines of research and action is not that it adds a normative concern to the study of our world. EJ research can be as systematic and scientific as research in the service of the accumulation of private wealth and, thus, inequality because, in the words of Kristin Shrader-Frechette "we can all be more 'objective' in doing our research but none of us is 'neutral.'" As our volume shows, by centering questions of social inequality and environmental exploitation, we can gather a more accurate understanding of the uneven empirical realities of this epoch, however we may call it.

Robert Cox (1981) argued that "problem solving theories" do not interrogate the world in which we live while "critical" theories ask how that world was created, whom it serves and how it can be made more egalitarian. EJ is a "critical" approach because it calls for research and practice that aims at a more inclusive and realistic understanding of the world, including those accomplishments on whose foundations we can build a more egalitarian and ecological world (Pellow 2018). We fully understand that such a commitment faces formidable and ubiquitous power relations that engender inequality and injustice. Yet, we also know that history is not only a cemetery of despair and sacrifice – although a great deal of it is. It is also a garden of flourishing and hope that we can help reveal and nurture.

References

Adam, Barbara 1998. *Timescapes of Modernity: The Environment and Invisible Hazards.* London: Routledge Press.

Bryant, Bunyan 1997. *The Role of the SNRE in the Environmental Justice Movement.* http://umich.edu/~snre492/history.html

Buttel, Frederick, Hawkins, Ann and Power, Alison 1990. From limits to growth to global change: Constraints and contradictions in the evolution of environmental science and ideology. *Global Environmental Change,* 1(1): 57–66.

Celermajer, D., Chatterjee, S., Cochrane, A., Fishel, S., Neimanis, A., O'Brien, A., Reid, S., Srinivasan, K., Schlosberg, D. and Waldow, A. 2020a. Justice through a multispecies lens. *Contemporary Political Theory,* 19: 475–512.

Celermajer, D., Schlosberg, D., Rickards, L., Stewart-Harawira, M., Thaler, M., Tschakert, P., Verlie, B. and Winter, C. 2020b. Multispecies justice: Theories, challenges, and a research agenda for environmental politics. *Environmental Politics,* 1–22, ahead-of-print

Ciplet, David and Harrison, Jill 2020. Transition tensions: Mapping conflicts in movements for a just and sustainable transition, *Environmental Politics,* 29(3): 435–456.

Cox, Robert 1981. Social forces, states, and world orders: Beyond international relations theory. *Millennium,* 10(2): 126–155.

Davis, Robert 2011. Inventing the present: Historical roots of the Anthropocene. *Earth Sciences History,* 30(1): 63–84.

Di Chiro, Giovanna 2021. Mobilizing 'Intersectionality' in environmental justice research and action in a time of crisis. In Brendan Coolsaet (ed.) *Environmental Justice: Key Issues.* Abingdon, UK: Routledge, 316–333.

Dicken, Peter. 2015. *Global Shift: Mapping the Changing Contours of the World Economy.* Los Angeles: Sage Publications Ltd.

Egan, Michael 2002. Subaltern environmentalism in the United States: A historiographic review. *Environment and History*, 8(1): 21–41.

Gaventa, John 1980. *Power and Powerlessness: Quiessence and Rebellion in an Appalachian Valley*. Champaign, Illinois: University of Illinois Press.

Gibson, William (ed.) 2004. *Eco-justice: The Unfinished Journey*. SYNY Press.

Gough, Jamie 2010. Workers' strategies to secure jobs, their uses of scale, and competing economic moralities: Rethinking the 'geography of justice.' *Political Geography*, 29: 130–139.

Grove, Richard 1994. *Green Imperialism*. Cambridge: Cambridge University Press.

Holifield, Ryan, Porter, Michael and Walker, Gordon 2009. Introduction: Spaces of environmental justice: Frameworks for critical engagement. *Antipode*, 41(4): 591–612.

Hornborg, Alf and Martinez-Alier, Joan 2016. Ecologically unequal exchange and ecological debt. *Journal of Political Ecology*, 23(1): 328–333.

Hultgren, John. 2015. *Border Walls Gone Green: Nature and Anti-immigrant Politics in America*. Minneapolis: University of Minnesota Press.

Just Transition Research Collaborative 2018. *Mapping Just Transition(s) to a Low-Carbon World*. United Nations Research Institute for Social Development.

Lohman, Larry 2009. Toward a different debate in environmental accounting: The cases of carbon and cost-benefit. *Accounting, Organizations and Society*, 34 (3–4): 499–534.

Low, Nicholas and Gleeson, Brendan 1998. *Justice, Society and Nature: An Exploration in Political Ecology*. London: Routledge.

Malin, Stephanie and Ryder, Stacia 2018. Developing deeply intersectional environmental justice scholarship. *Environmental Sociology*, 4(1): 1–7.

Malm, Andreas and Warlenius, Rikard 2019. The grand theft of the atmosphere: Sketches for a theory of climate injustice in the Anthropocene. Ch 4 In Kum-Kum Bhavnani, John Foran, Priya Kurian and Debashish Munshi (eds.) *Climate Futures: Re-Imagining Global Climate Justice*. London: Zed Books.

Mann, Charles 2011. *1493: Uncovering the World That Columbus Created*. New York: Alfred A. Knopf.

Marks, R. 2015. *The Origins of the Modern World: A Global and Ecological Narrative from the Fifteenth to the Twenty-first Century*. 3rd ed. Lanham, MD: Rowman and Littlefield Publishing Group.

Methmann, Chris and Roth, Delf 2012. Politics for the day after tomorrow: The logic of apocalypse in global climate politics. *Security Dialogue*, 43(4): 323–344.

Moore, Jason 2019. Capitalocene and planetary justice. *Maize*, 6: 49–54.

Nixon, Rob 2011. *Slow Violence and the Environmentalism of the Poor*. Cambridge, MA: Harvard University Press.

Park, Lisa Sun-Hee and Ruiz, Steve 2021. Racial minorities in the United States: Race, migration, and reimagining environmental justice. In Brendan Coolsaet (ed.) *Environmental Justice: Key Issues*. Abingdon, UK: Routledge, 224–233.

Pellow, David N. 2018. *What Is Critical Environmental Justice?* Cambridge: Polity Press.

Pulido, Laura 2017. Geographies of race and ethnicity II: Environmental racism, racial capitalism, and state-sanctioned violence. *Progress in Human Geography*, 41(4): 524–533.

Ryder, S.S. 2017. *A Bridge to Challenging Environmental Inequality: Intersectionality, Environmental Justice, and Disaster Vulnerability*. Stacia.

Ryder, S.S. 2018. Developing an intersectionally-informed, multi-sited, critical policy ethnography to examine power and procedural justice in multiscalar energy and climate change decisionmaking processes. *Energy Research & Social Science*, 45: 266–275.

Schlosberg, David 2013. Theorising environmental justice: The expanding sphere of discourse. *Environmental Politics*, 22(1): 37–55.

Stevis, Dimitris, and Assetto, Valerie 2001. History and purpose the international political economy of the environment. In Stevis and Assetto (eds.) *The International Political Economy of the Environment: Critical Perspectives*. Boulder, CO: Lynne Rienner Publishers, 239–255.

Stevis, Dimitris and Felli, Romain 2020. *Planetary Just Transition? How Inclusive and How Just? Earth System Governance* 6: 11pp.

Swyngedouw, Erik 2010. Apocalypse forever? post-political populism and the spectre of climate change. *Theory, Culture and Society*, 27(2–3): 213–232.

Sze, Julie, and London, Jonathan 2008. Environmental justice at the crossroads. *Sociology Compass*, 2(4): 1331–1354.

Taylor, Dorceta 2000. The rise of the environmental justice paradigm: Injustice framing and the social construction of environmental discourses. *American Behavioral Scientist*, 43(4): 508–580.

Whyte, Kyle 2021. Indigenous environmental justice: Anti-colonial action through kinship. In Brendan Coolsaet (ed.) *Environmental Justice: Key Issues*. Abingdon, UK: Routledge, 266–278.

Williams, Raymond 1989. *Resources of Hope*. London: Verso.

Young, Iris Marion 2006. Responsibility and global justice: A social connection model. *Social Philosophy & Policy*, 23(1): 102–130.

1

EXAMINING THE ANTHROPOCENE

A contested term in capitalist times

Stephanie A. Malin

The term 'Anthropocene' carries a good deal of baggage. Really, it has a whole cart full of luggage, packed with a host of disagreements and debates about the term. These debates range from: geological disputes over the accuracy of the moniker compared to much-longer geological periods; other scientific debates over exactly when the Anthropocene period started; and sociological, political, and philosophical debates over the accuracy of the seemingly equal blame for the contemporary crises it places on *all* of humanity.

I will certainly not solve these issues in this introductory chapter. However, I will highlight and encapsulate the debates – and how this term has been productively criticized for its blind spots. All of this will, I hope, point to a path forward. Importantly, the stories we tell matter (Nixon 2014) – mostly because this helps determine how we act on, and interact around, those narratives. Instead of being a point of contention, perhaps the term 'Anthropocene can galvanize and inspire productive solutions to global climate crisis, loss of biodiversity, nuclear contamination, and other traits of this new era.

We have to recognize that the term needs to incorporate the cogent observations about how the word 'Anthropocene' ignores and makes invisible the very real distinctions among people and populations – and their historical contributions, or lack thereof, to our ecological crises (and social ones). Therefore, an environmental justice lens becomes a necessary guide (Nixon 2014).

To preface the impressive and unique chapters in this edited volume, I provide brief overviews of the science behind the Anthropocene era – and some vital, critical responses to its characterization. I pay special attention to our main purpose – to more fully utilize lenses of environmental justice and equity.

Overview of Anthropocene and geological debates

People have long observed that humanity impacts the planet in significant, measurable ways. Since the Agricultural Revolution began about 10,000 years ago, humans have been making marked changes which affect the planet's ecosystems and the more-than-only humans living within them. When Crutzen and Stoermer (2000) first popularized the term 'Anthropocene' about two decades ago, they were not necessarily making groundbreaking assessments that people impact the planet. Nonetheless, the term galvanized thousands of discussions about what it meant and signaled. The way people impacted the planet – the scale, the rapidity, the seeming irreversibility – all of these were importantly drawn out by the word 'Anthropocene.'

These geological debates focus on two central questions. First, whether or not we can identify the Anthropocene epoch as one that is geologically unique and new. They ask: Is this really an epoch that is measurably separate from the Holocene, into which we just entered about 11,000 years ago? After all, as Elizabeth Kolbert observed, the Holocene is 'barely out of diapers' as far as geologic time goes, especially when we consider that the previous Pleistocene epoch took place over about 2 million years and earlier epochs lasted even longer than that. To propose that we have already entered a new geologic epoch can be perceived as controversial and possibly inaccurate or alarmist (Kolbert 2010). Second, if we allow that we have entered a new time period, how do we mark the beginning of that period and the planet's decisive departure from the Holocene?

In the case of the first major debate – whether or not we have entered a new geological epoch – scientists have eased toward agreement that this is, indeed, occurring (Lewis and Maslin 2015b; Zalasiewicz et al. 2010). Nonetheless, elite groups, such as the International Commission on Stratigraphy, the Anthropocene Working Group, and ultimately the International Union of Geological Sciences, continue to debate the specifics – and official designations hinge on their decisions (Meyer 2018; Zalasiewicz et al. 2010). In May 2019, the Anthropocene was designated a new epoch in which human activity is so intensive and has such lasting impacts on the natural world that this era has jolted us out of the Holocene (Subramanian 2020). What a loss.

The Holocene, after all, marks the era that has nurtured human civilizations, at least as we define and understand them currently. Yes, we continue to find evidence that humanity is much older than we thought, and there is growing evidence that settlements and civilization existed well before the Holocene (Childs 2018). Geologically speaking, the Holocene marks a relatively calm period following the last ice age – a time when large-scale civilizations were able to take hold and flourish, when the climate and related weather patterns were fairly predictable, and when we could count on (at least in theory) some normalcy and predictability for daily lives, provision of food, and access to freshwater sources

(Waggoner 1996). The Holocene epoch marks a 'sweet spot' that some humans – and others – got to enjoy, albeit differentially due to the fundamental inequities of early civilization. For example, the large-scale pharaonic water projects of Egypt redesigned waterways built upon slave labor (Worster 1992). However, the Holocene was supposed to be a period of relative comfort, ecological abundance, and stability that allowed us to build grand civilizations (more on the risky outcomes of this below).

It seems, though, that segments of our population have industrialized and capitalized right out of that peaceful Holocene and catapulted all us into this new era – the so-called Anthropocene. Industrialized and capitalist systems – and especially the fossil fuel dependencies our contemporary cultures have developed – have created less predictable, less stable realities. And while scientists and elite professional societies continue to debate, most researchers, observers, and regular people recognize that we live in a fundamentally different era (Carrington 2016; Lewis and Maslin 2015a).

We have indeed accumulated striking evidence that the Anthropocene does in fact mark a new level of environmental change and impact. The sheer scale of human encroachment on all other beings and systems is almost impossible to ignore. The overconsumption of resources, the ways we have altered the earth's surface in the form of megacities and industrialized agricultural systems, the chemicals and biological changes we have introduced onto the earth, and other measurable impacts such as global temperature increases, massive extinctions (Kolbert 2015), and changes to ocean acidity and marine life all mark significant environmental impacts brought on by human systems (Zalasiewicz et al. 2010).

To count as a geologic shift and new era, however, geologists also have to establish changes on a geological time scale – and identify when they started (Zalasiewicz et al. 2010). And this is where some of the key debates remain – defining and identifying the geological strata, as it were, that marks the departure from the Holocene and entry into the Anthropocene. Some perspectives identify the beginning of the Industrial Revolution as this geologic marker, when industrializing societies began to emit and rely on fossil fuels and more massive production systems (Carrington 2016). Other respected voices have a few different markers they identify. Lewis and Maslin (2015b, 2018) identify 1610 and the 'Orbis Spike' as the beginning of the Anthropocene, when we can see the impacts of the first large-scale cross-ocean resettlement by significant numbers of people, signaled by both the exchange of species across oceans and then, by 1610, a massive drop in carbon dioxide levels, likely due to the tens of millions of Native murders and deaths at the hands of settler-colonialists and the diseases (i.e. smallpox) that they brought to the New World.

They also point to another significant marker, a few centuries later – the subsequent accumulation of nuclear fallout from massive nuclear testing, starting in the 1960s, which can be measured in the earth's stratigraphy (Lewis and Maslin 2015a, 2015b). Still others suggest that we can mark the 1950s as a time of 'great acceleration' in the Anthropocene, and some even suggest we should use this more conservative estimate to designate the beginning of the era. Around this time we can observe the measurable presence of nuclear radionuclides and fallout from testing, the presence of plastics and power station pollution, concrete, and even the presence of genetically modified and exponentially increased chicken bones – all marking a new era in which people began to dominate and fundamentally change the world, measurable in stratigraphy (Carrington 2016; Zalasiewicz et al. 2010).

It seems, then, that scientists have attained some (albeit ever-evolving) consensus that we have entered a new era where humanity has caused irreversible and marked ecological change that can be marked in geologic time. But what marks the true beginning of the Anthropocene – that definitive geological marker we need – remains much more under scrutiny and debate.

Key to the issues discussed in this volume lies another debate – one less about geological markers and over-generalized assessments of what 'humanity' has or has not done to defile the 'natural' world. Environmental justice and equity considerations are central to this debate – and mark some of the most relevant and incisive critiques of the term and characterizations of the 'Anthropocene.'

Environmental Justice considerations and critiques of the 'Anthropocene'

The Environmental Justice (EJ) perspective demands attention to the accumulated scientific evidence that we, humans, have disrupted the Holocene. But an EJ perspective demands the recognition that the 'we' refers to a relatively tiny segment of human population and history. After all, industrialization, mega-urbanization, massive and globalized consumption and production systems, losses of biodiversity, extractive industries, fossil fuel addictions, and the chemical, plastic, and other forms of pollution that now inundate the planet – these have been perpetrated by relatively few people, and companies, and a specific, elite economic strata. Record economic inequity has been the reward for many people. As Rob Nixon observes, the changes of the Anthropocene have been accompanied by equally massive and inequitable economic inequality – the yawning gap between the 'haves' and 'have-nots,' or the 'Great Divergence' as he calls it (Nixon 2014). We see this continue to grow today, and we see stark reminders of it amid catastrophes such as the COVID-19 pandemic.

As industrialization and capitalism have overwhelmed the world these systems have largely been imposed upon most of us. And most of humanity, even those of us sitting in comparative comfort in the global North, have not played an active part in defiling the artificially separated 'natural' world. At least, not to the extent that a term like the 'Anthropocene' would suggest – as if this outcome is somehow a given and due to some fundamental flaw or ultimate deficiency of 'human nature.' Instead, economic inequalities and environmental injustices have touched large pockets of humanity across the globe – and this has only gotten worse under neoliberalized systems of governance, as they have spread since the 1980s. As Nixon asserts, and cites from Weardon, in 2013,

> the world's eighty-five richest people – a group small enough to fit into a double-decker bus, in the unlikely event that they would be inclined to take a bus – had a net worth equal to that of fifty percent of the planet's population, the 3.5 billion poorest people.
>
> *(Nixon 2014; cf. Weardon 2014)*

Since neoliberalism became the dominant default governance strategy globally, these outcomes have increased exponentially – alongside their social and ecological ills (Harvey, 2005, 2007, 2016). In this system, private property rights, free trade, de- and re-regulation, privatization of public and ecological goods, financialization of the growing capitalist economy, and deeply reduced social safety nets have become default policy stances – and have allowed wealth to accrue to an infinitesimal sliver of people (Matthews 2017). Via the hegemony of the global North, various powerful and wide-ranging trade agreements, and powerful global lending agencies (such as the World Bank and the International Monetary Fund) requiring nations of the global South to adopt these terms or not receive loans (Goldman 2006) – we have seen the emergence and take-over of a corporate class project. In this system, economic development was the only goal – and ecological and cultural sacrifices were lauded (Harvey 2016).

The ecological stakes have been irreversible and mind-boggling as well. In this short neoliberalized time, roughly, we have seen a biodiversity crisis rapidly accelerate, losing an estimated 60% of the animals on this planet (Carrington 2014, 2018). The industrial systems spread across the globe have also initiated a devastating global climate crisis – due to growing fossil fuel extraction and emissions levels, from which only a handful of people and corporations benefit the most (Klein 2014).

But have 'we' all been driving this train? As should be clear from the above, the answer is no. As Nixon reminds us "Since 1751, a period that encompasses the entire Anthropocene to date, a mere ninety corporations, primarily oil and coal companies, have generated two-thirds of humanity's CO_2 emissions" (2014). To put an even finer point on these inequities, in the neoliberal era, we can name and locate about 100 corporations that are responsible for about 71% of the emissions spewed into our atmosphere since about 1988 (Griffin 2017; Riley 2017).

It seems this is not a problem or condition we can blame on all of humanity, equally – hence the issue of with the choice of the 'Anthropocene' and the erasure it performs as to who is truly responsible for ushering in this epoch. Perhaps the 'Anthropocene' is too imprecise a term, a brushstroke too broad for assessing these massive shifts and for equitably assigning responsibility. The terms 'Capitalocene,' age of 'Fossil Capital' (Malm 2016; Moore 2017; Moore

2018), or even the patriarchal 'Manthropocene' (Raworth 2014) seem to better capture the empirical realities of this marked geologic shift from the Holocene. Other scholars have offered additional conceptualizations and terms for this era, focused on the racialized aspects of colonialism, capitalism, and the eventual result of global climate catastrophe. These include Lewis and Maslin's ideas about the 'Orbis Spike' (2015b, 2018) which coincides with the beginning of global colonialism. Philosopher of science and technology, Donna Haraway, and her colleagues suggest the term Plantationocene, to capture the impacts of colonialism, racialized capitalism, and colonialism starting hundreds of years ago (Haraway 2015; Haraway et al. 2016). Silva reminds us of the complex interweaving of colonialism, racialized capitalism, and their links to the current global climate catastrophe (2018). These terms take on an important power and make us pause for consideration – particularly when we recall the great divergence, where a sliver of humanity has enjoyed an unprecedented increase in wealth, as they have perpetrated multiple existential crises on the rest of humanity and all other beings with whom we share this planet.

Therefore, more accurately, this is a situation where colonizers, imperialists, industrial capitalists, and the uber-elite have taken most of humanity, other plant and animal species, and the planet along with them on their 'wild ride for more.' And the term 'Anthropocene' fails to adequately capture that reality.

Further, as Kyle Powys Whyte adeptly reminds us, a term like 'Anthropocene' makes invisible the experiences of Indigenous and Native populations, which have been dealing with various settler colonial dystopias for hundreds of years (2017). The term may also allow us to romanticize what Indigenous and Native relationships with the land and water looked like in the Americas before the arrival of European colonizers and minimize these cultures' extensive grazing and gardening footprints – although ones far removed from colonial and capitalist systems (Dunbar-Ortiz, 2015). Perhaps, this era of epochal change begins earlier even than the 1600s start suggested by Lewis and Maslin. Using terms like 'Capitalocene,' or perhaps 'Settler Capitalocene,' make these intersecting injustices more visible. These terms provide clear reminders that colonialism, then capitalism and industrialization, then neoliberalism – all these variations on settler colonialism and forcible removal of Indigenous, African, and native peoples from ancestral lands and lifeways have paved the way for the ultimate dystopia, one that some groups have been facing in various forms for centuries (Whyte 2017). This dystopia, this 'wild ride for more,' has now come to a head – with climate crisis, rampant biodiversity loss, and a massive pandemic in the wake of global, unregulated trade and loss of habitats.

This volume problematizes these terms. Indeed, an EJ lens demands we honor these disparities and that we focus on the often marginalized cultures that show us how to build a more sustainable and less extractive world. These perspectives remind us that the collective goal is to find solutions to enormous existential problems. It reminds us that humanity as a whole does not claim equal responsibility – and that solutions that seek to enrich the same capitalist classes will result in similar problems, ecologically and socially. They remind us that the most sustainable and promising solutions are probably not best implemented through radical geoengineering, or greenwashing capitalist practices that still prey on and profit from most people and the planet.

Instead, the EJ lens demands that we see and fight for the just and equitable path forward – which begins with accurately diagnosing the problem. I am offering nothing profound or new here. Just an exclamation point. It is not humanity that can be blamed with a broad brush; it is the way that certain human-created systems (like the capitalist economy, like fossil fuel industries and technologies, like rampant production of plastics and chemicals) have been allowed to take on lives of their own.

The question becomes – how do we move forward with grace and vision, to collectively build a better world for us all? The answers start with reflexivity, humility, and collective productivity that does not use GDP, efficiency, economic growth, and profit as the sole measures of success. Instead, more distributive and regenerative economic and other systems become the goals, indeed the requirements, for survival (Raworth 2017).

The chapters that follow, and many of the other offerings in this volume, help us identify some of these EJ-centered, equitable paths forward. They offer some of the solutions to the very problems created by the 'Anthropocene' and, more accurately, the narrow vision that thoughtlessly uses that term and ignores the variations and nuances in human history, cultures, and lifeways.

References

Carrington, D. (2014, September 30). Earth has lost half of its wildlife in the past 40 years, says WWF. *The Guardian*. https://www.theguardian.com/environment/2014/sep/29/earth-lost-50-wildlife-in-40-years-wwf

Carrington, D. (2016, August 29). The Anthropocene epoch: Scientists declare the dawn of human-influenced age. *The Guardian*.

Carrington, D. (2018, October 30). Humanity has wiped out 60% of animal populations since 1970, report finds. *The Guardian*. https://www.theguardian.com/environment/2018/oct/30/humanity-wiped-out-animals-since-1970-major-report-finds

Childs, C. (2018). *Atlas of a Lost World: Travels in Ice Age America*. Pantheon Press. https://www.amazon.com/Atlas-Lost-World-Travels-America/dp/0307908658

Crutzen, P., & Stoermer, E. (2000). The Anthropocene. *Global Change Newsletter, 41*, 17–18.

Dunbar-Ortiz, R. (2015). *An Indigenous Peoples' History of the United States*. Beacon Press. http://www.beacon.org/An-Indigenous-Peoples-History-of-the-United-States-P1164.aspx

Goldman, M. (2006). *Imperial Nature: The World Bank and Struggles for Social Justice in the Age of Globalization* (59806th edition). Yale University Press.

Griffin, P. (2017). *CDP Carbon Majors Report 2017* (p. 16). CDP (Carbon Majors Database) & Climate Accountability Institute.

Haraway, D. (2015). Anthropocene, capitalocene, plantationocene, chthulucene: Making kin. *Environmental Humanities, 6*(1), 159–165. https://doi.org/10.1215/22011919-3615934

Haraway, D., Ishikawa, N., Gilbert, S.F., Olwig, K., Tsing, A.L., & Bubandt, N. (2016). Anthropologists are talking – about the Anthropocene. *Ethnos, 81*(3), 535–564. https ://doi.org/10.1080/00141844.2015.1105838

Harvey, D. (2005). *Spaces of Neoliberalization: Towards a Theory of Uneven Geographical Development.* Franz Steiner Verlag.

Harvey, D. (2007). *A Brief History of Neoliberalism.* Oxford University Press.

Harvey, D. (2016). Neoliberalism is a political project. *Jacobin Magazine.*

Klein, N. (2014). *This Changes Everything: Capitalism Vs. The Climate.* Simon and Schuster.

Kolbert, E. (2010, May 17). The Anthropocene debate: Marking humanity's impact. *Yale Environment, 360.*

Kolbert, E. (2015). *The Sixth Extinction: An Unnatural History* (Reprint edition). Picador.

Lewis, S.L., & Maslin, M.A. (2015a). A transparent framework for defining the Anthropocene epoch. *The Anthropocene Review, 2*(2), 128–146.

Lewis, S.L., & Maslin, M.A. (2015b). Defining the Anthropocene. *Nature, 519,* 171–180.

Lewis, S.L., & Maslin, M.A. (2018). *Human Planet: How We Created the Anthropocene.* Yale University Press.

Malm, A. (2016). *Fossil Capital.* Verso Press.

Matthews, D. (2017, August 8). *You're Not Imagining it: The Rich Really Are Hoarding Economic Growth.* Vox. https://www.vox.com/policy-and-politics/2017/8/8/161123 68/piketty-saez-zucman-income-growth-inequality-stagnation-chart

Meyer, R. (2018, July 20). *Geology's Timekeepers Are Feuding.* Atlantic. https://www.the atlantic.com/science/archive/2018/07/anthropocene-holocene-geology-drama/56 5628/

Moore, J.W. (2017). The capitalocene part II: Accumulation by appropriation and the centrality of unpaid work/ energy. *The Journal of Peasant Studies,* 237–279.

Moore, J.W. (2018). The capitalocene part II: Accumulation by appropriation and the centrality of unpaid work/energy. *The Journal of Peasant Studies, 45*(2), 237–279. https ://doi.org/10.1080/03066150.2016.1272587

Nixon, R. (2014, March). *The Great Acceleration and the Great Divergence: Vulnerability in the Anthropocene – Profession.* https://profession.mla.org/the-great-acceleration-and-t he-great-divergence-vulnerability-in-the-anthropocene/

Raworth, K. (2014, October 20). Must the Anthropocene be a manthropocene? | Kate Raworth. *The Guardian.* https://www.theguardian.com/commentisfree/2014/oct /20/anthropocene-working-group-science-gender-bias

Raworth, K. (2017). *Doughnut Economics: Seven Ways to Think Like a 21st-Century Economist.* Chelsea Green Publishing.

Riley, T. (2017, July 10). Just 100 companies responsible for 71% of global emissions, study says. *The Guardian.* https://www.theguardian.com/sustainable-business/2017 /jul/10/100-fossil-fuel-companies-investors-responsible-71-global-emissions-cdp-st udy-climate-change

Silva, D.F. da. (2018, October). On heat. *Canadian Art.* https://canadianart.ca/features /on-heat/

Subramanian, M. (2020, May 21) Anthropocene now: Influential panel votes to recognize Earth's new epoch. *Nature.* https://doi.org/10.1038/d41586-019-01641-5

Waggoner, B.M. (1996). *The Holocene Epoch.* https://ucmp.berkeley.edu/quaternary/hol ocene.php

Weardon, G. (2014, January 20). Oxfam: 85 richest people as wealthy as poorest half of the world. *The Guardian.* https://www.theguardian.com/business/2014/jan/20/o xfam-85-richest-people-half-of-the-world

Whyte, K.P. (2017). Our ancestors' dystopia now: Indigenous conservation and the Anthropocene. In *Routledge Companion to the Environmental Humanities*. Routledge Press.

Worster, D. (1992). *Rivers of Empire: Water, Aridity, and the Growth of the American West*. Oxford University Press.

Zalasiewicz, J., Williams, M., Steffen, W., & Crutzen, P. (2010). The new world of the Anthropocene. *Environmental Science & Technology*, *44*(7), 2228–2231. https://doi.org /10.1021/es903118j

2

THE SELECTIVE INVISIBILITY OF OIL AND CLIMATE INJUSTICE IN THE ANTHROPOCENE AND BEYOND

Nino Antadze

Introduction

The September 2019 airstrikes on the oil infrastructure in Saudi Arabia caused one of the most significant disruptions of oil output in recent memory, and the resulting surge in oil prices, has caused widespread fear about oil supplies and prices (BBC News 2019). The anxiety regarding oil prices continued as, several months later, the global COVID-19 pandemic brought oil prices to a record low (Euronews 2020). At the same time, a youth-led global climate strike, which proved to be the biggest climate protest in history, mobilized millions of people worldwide with the demand for climate action (Laville and Watts 2019). These events, happening almost simultaneously, reveal the paradox of living in the Anthropocene: as the negative impacts of climate change become more and more obvious, our societies remain highly reliant on fossil fuels. In fact, carbon emissions reached a record high in 2018 (Harvey 2018). But even more paradoxical is the fact that oil, despite its existential importance for our societies, remains somewhat abstract in our imagination. For those of us not directly involved in the extraction, processing, and transportation of oil, it is impossible to detect it as we usually don't see it, smell it, or touch it. Yet it's there, everywhere and always, invisible but indispensable, with profound material and ethical consequences.

In this chapter I argue that *the invisibility of oil* is an ethically charged phenomenon for two main reasons. First, the material disconnect with oil complements the cognitive-emotional reasons behind the inability to perceive climate change as a moral problem (Gifford 2011; Markowitz and Shariff 2012; Norgaard 2011). Thus, the invisibility makes oil a commodity without clearly articulated and comprehended moral consequences (Hughes 2017) – something that is invisible can hardly be subject to everyday moral judgment. The second reason why the invisibility of oil has profound ethical implications is because oil is *selectively* invisible. Oil is characterized by uneven spatialities of materiality (Balmaceda et al. 2019). For those communities at the forefront of oil extraction, processing, transportation, and disposal, oil is an indispensable part of their everyday material experiences. In those communities oil has visible and tangible consequences, including environmental degradation, livelihood disruption, health impacts, forcible displacement, and human rights violations (Healy et al. 2019). I therefore suggest that creating spaces and moments for physical and/or imaginative encounters with oil may help in converting it from a morally neutral commodity into one having profound normative implications.

In what follows I first discuss the normative implications of the selective invisibility of oil. Next, I draw on the scholarship of new materialism to argue for the necessity to reflect on the materiality of oil in the Anthropocene. I conclude by discussing ways to create physical and/or imaginative encounters with oil.

The selective invisibility of oil and its normative implications

The invisibility of oil, or rather its concealment through a complex network of infrastructure, processes, and decisions, can be rooted in the dominant view of economic development and progress. The premise of this view is the separation of society and nature, wherein nature is understood "as a pure, singular and stable domain removed from and defined in relation to urban, industrial society" (Lorimer 2012, p. 593), and needs to be exploited for the well-being of humans (Taylor 2000). Even though progress has been made and the principle of sustainable development does recognize the interdependence of social, economic, and natural systems, there is still a tendency to delineate and separate society and nature, rather than treat them as inseparable parts of social–ecological systems (Reyers et al. 2018).

In their analysis of human–nature connectedness, Ives et al. (2018) identify five types of connections to nature – material, experiential, cognitive, emotional, and philosophical – and suggest that they are interconnected. The same spectrum can be applied to argue that the types of *disconnect* are also related: the material disconnect with oil makes it much more challenging to establish a deeper philosophical and emotional relationship with the commodity that we depend on. In his ethnographic account of the energy sector in Trinidad and Tobago, Hughes (2017, p. 2) contemplates, "Why do hydrocarbons not inspire disgust – or romance for that matter – among more people more often? To answer this question, one has to measure the subtle effort expended as informed people avoid reflecting ethically or emotionally upon oil." The invisibility of oil further contributes to these efforts by adding to the cognitive–psychological difficulty of recognizing climate change as a moral problem (Gifford 2011; Markowitz and Shariff 2012; Norgaard 2011) and making oil a commodity stripped of normative implications. While for some communities oil's materiality is proximal, real, and consequential for their health and well-being, for many it is invisible, without any immediate material or ethical consequences. The inability to detect oil with the senses encourages us to disengage from the problem, even while knowing about it, and to keep an emotional and ethical distance (Cohen 2001; Norgaard 2011). Thus, for many who consume oil, the origin, route, and process through which oil reached them remains unknown, invisible, and therefore beyond the scope of their moral judgment. This *selectively* invisible quality leads to profound ethical implications.

The uneven spatialities of oil's materiality are driven by the distribution of power and capital within the global fossil fuel–dominant energy regime. Powerful state and corporate players not only make oil selectively invisible by creating "sacrifice zones" (Bullard 1993), which ensure the uninterrupted flow of oil, but also deprive oil of its material qualities and reframe it as "abstracted oil money or abstracted state power" (Balmaceda et al. 2019, p. 11). The strong linkage between corporate and political interests is illustrated by the fact that 12 out of 20 companies that have contributed about 35% of all carbon dioxide and methane emissions since 1965 are state owned (Taylor and Watts 2019).

These actors not only uphold the system that causes the inequitable distribution of environmental harms while making trillions of dollars in profits (Taylor and Ambrose 2020), but they also do so with full knowledge of the disproportionate consequences caused by the production and consumption of oil. For example, it is now well documented that for years ExxonMobile Corporation was engaged in a campaign to mislead the public about the causes and consequences of climate change and ignore the conclusions derived by climate scientists, including those working for ExxonMobil (Supran and Oreskes 2017). In fact, recent findings show that "in the three years following the Paris Agreement, the five largest publicly traded oil and gas majors have invested over $1Bn of shareholder funds on misleading climate-related branding and lobbying" (Influencemap 2019).

The discussion about the role of corporate and state actors in making oil selectively invisible aligns with the recent calls in environmental justice literature to incorporate power dynamics more rigorously in analyzing causes and conse-quences of environmental injustice. Scholars stress the need to analyze broader power structures that underpin environmental inequalities (Pellow 2018), and to employ the intersectionality lens to capture the intersecting and mutually rein-forcing nature of environmental injustices and structurally rooted manifestations of social inequalities (Malin and Ryder 2018; Malin et al. 2019).

Aside from the central actors, the status quo is also upheld because of the exist-ing infrastructure and unchallenged social norms. This intertwined and self-rein-forcing nature of the global fossil fuel–dominant energy regime, which ensures the selective invisibility of oil, is well illustrated by the concept of *carbon lock-in*. Carbon lock-in refers to the path-dependent process that encompasses mutually reinforcing infrastructural, institutional, and behavioral systems, and is resistant to change (Seto et al. 2016). The material side of this intertwined, locked-in system is infrastructure and technologies, which Seto et al. (2016) break down into (a) carbon-emitting infrastructure (e.g., fossil fuel–fired power plants), (b) carbon emissions-supporting infrastructure (e.g., pipelines, refineries), and (c) energy-demanding infrastructure (e.g., buildings, transportation infrastructure). Each element of this complex material system works to ensure a timely, efficient, and abundant flow of fossil fuels in a way that those fuels stay mostly concealed from the majority of society, whose everyday existence largely depends on how well infrastructural carbon lock-in works. At the same time the institutional and behavioral aspects of carbon lock-in strengthen and reinforce the reliance on fossil fuels by linking policy and institutional changes to social and individual behavioral norms. Carbon lock-in enables oil to be a commodity that is "mutable over space and time" (Bridge and Smith 2003, p. 259), thus diminishing the empirical understanding of the materiality of oil in everyday practices. The well-functioning carbon lock-in system makes oil selectively invisible, and this invisibility makes it difficult to disturb the locked-in, fossil fuel–dependent system.

This system is built to make oil selectively invisible and also to make it difficult to track. The supply chain is often not transparent, making it difficult to hold actors accountable for inflicting harm (Healy et al. 2019). The flawless functioning of carbon lock-in comes at the expense of the health and well-being of many communities and people around the globe. Unfortunately, examples abound, such as the infamous Cancer Alley in Louisiana, an industrial corridor with a high concentration of petrochemical facilities (Pezzullo 2003), mostly populated by African American communities; the Indigenous communities in Canada who fight against the "invasive infrastructure" of oil and gas pipelines (Spice 2018); and the vast social–ecological systems of the oil-rich Niger Delta, permeated with violence and pollution (Elum et al. 2016; Nriagu et al. 2016; Peel 2011).

Scholarly discourse has long recognized the disproportionate distribution of environmental harm in vulnerable and marginalized communities. Starting with the emergence of the concept of *environmental racism* (McGurty 1997; Bullard 1983), this scholarly conversation has broadened to include various manifestations of *environmental and climate injustice* (Agyeman et al. 2016; Schlosberg 2013). The more recently emerged interdisciplinary research agenda known as *energy justice* (Jenkins et al. 2016; Sovacool et al. 2017, p. 677; Jenkins 2018) aims to tackle ethical considerations of energy systems by probing into "social and material relations that constitute energy systems" (Partridge et al. 2018, p. 139), and by focusing on the inequalities that accompany the entire energy life cycle, from extraction to final use (Healy and Barry 2017). Along this line of inquiry, Healy et al. (2019, 220) proposed the concept of *embodied energy injustices* "to explicitly consider hidden and distant injustices (upstream and downstream) arising from the extraction, processing, transportation and disposal of energy resources." These types of injustices that manifest themselves throughout the life cycle of oil are often invisible beyond the communities that they scar, and therefore unrecognized in energy-policy decisions (Healy et al. 2019). Yet, for the time being, oil remains one of the most ethically consequential commodities of the Anthropocene, and if we want to move toward "just sustainability" (Agyeman 2008), we need to find a way to encounter oil as a morally charged commodity.

The materiality of oil in the Anthropocene

To discuss the materiality of oil in the Anthropocene, I draw on the scholarship of new materialism, which suggests an immersive coexistence of humans with the non-human realm, including its biotic and abiotic components (Coole and Frost 2010). According to advocates of new materialism, humans are insepara-bly connected to their environment, natural or man-made, and they themselves are "infested by micro-organisms and by the effects of the technical action of humans on the world" (Blanc 2017, p. 139). This condition of inseparable con-nectivity between humans and the non-human world, a condition referred to as "trans-corporeality" (Alaimo 2016, 155; Coole and Frost 2010), views agency in the age of the Anthropocene as being entangled with the nonhuman world. This line of thought relates to Bennett's (2010) argument that we are surrounded by and composed of "vibrant matter," and Haraway's (2016) suggestion to adopt the term *Chthulucene* in order to move the focus from the human as the main actor to other biotic and abiotic elements of the earth as "the main story."

Thus, the new materialist view, which challenges nature–society dualism, postulates that human choices and actions have material consequences for non-humans, making humans responsible for the material transformation they cause in other bodies and the environment (Alaimo 2016; Blanc 2017). As a result, adopting the idea of trans-corporeality has normative implications – it "requires all things to be accountable to each other … continuously responsive to any intra-actions. This conceptual expression suggests that we beings should be held responsible for each material transformation and the exchanges with bodies, sub-stances, and places" (Blanc 2017, p. 144). Pellozzoni (2016, p. 314) sums up the new materialist view of human agency "as disempowered and defective, distrib-uted and assembled with non-human entities – hence also modest, careful and responsible."

The emphasis on the causes and consequences of our interactions with the material world, and their ethical implications, is inseparable from environmental justice discourse. In fact, environmental justice as a concept and a movement emerged because of the recognition that toxic substances were affecting human bodies, and that these impacts were unevenly distributed (McGurty 1997; Taylor 2000; Bullard 1983). Environmental justice scholarship and activism have expanded to include the material manifestations of injustice as they relate to the issues of food, energy, and water (Agyeman et al. 2016). Climate justice claims are also inherently material, because climate change impacts materialize in different forms and in different places. The environmental justice perspec-tive, therefore, is strongly grounded in the premise that "our material lives have power and are invariably connected to the way that environmental injustice is produced, experienced, reproduced, and resisted" (Agyeman et al. 2016, p. 332).

The point about resistance has recently been explored by Schlosberg and Coles (2016), who draw attention to the material side of sustainability, specifically the social movements and grassroots efforts that aim (and have the potential) to change the material relationship between humans and the environment. For example, the work of the communities who are part of the Transition Network is about "reclaiming the economy, sparking entrepreneurship, reimagining work, reskilling themselves and weaving webs of connection and support" (Transition Network 2020). Another example is the proliferation of community-supported agriculture programs, which allow consumers to support local farmers "by purchasing a share of the harvest at the beginning of the growing season" (Canadian Organic Growers 2018). Such movements can be seen as forms of resistance with the goal of "challenging power and creating new collective institutions and food systems that embody sustainable material relationships between human communities and the natural world that supplies our needs" (Schlosberg and Coles 2016, p. 163).

The movements described by Schlosberg and Coles (2016) aim to challenge what are perceived to be unjust and unsustainable practices as well as to rethink the complexities of human–environment interaction involving philosophical, emotional, cognitive, experiential, and material ties (Ives et al. 2018). These different types of connections are not mutually exclusive and, in fact, may affect one another. Therefore, bringing to the forefront of our everyday experiences the material connections with oil can help foster realizations about the large-scale dependence on fossil fuels and the material and ethical consequences this dependence brings. This is important because, as Adam (1998, p. 11) points out, "a large proportion of the processes associated with the most difficult environmental problems tend to be inaccessible to the senses, invisible until they materialise as symptoms." The Anthropocene itself, or rather the fact that it has become obvious – possible to feel and see – is the material consequence of collective actions and inactions, including "human ethical choices" (Lidskog and Waterton 2018, p. 399). Over time invisible processes materialize as environmental problems on different scales, in different contexts, and with disproportionate impacts on some humans and non-humans, but as a result of them, we now live in the Anthropocene.

Encountering oil

If we consider carbon lock-in as a long-term emergency, the necessity and urgency of making this invisible emergency into a material, visible one stems from the pathos demonstrated in Rob Nixon's quote (2013, p. 3):

> How can we convert into image and narrative the disasters that are slow moving and long in the making, disasters that are anonymous and that star nobody, disasters that are attritional and of indifferent interest to the sensation-driven technologies of our image-world? How can we turn the long emergencies of slow violence into stories dramatic enough to rouse public sentiment and warrant political intervention, these emergencies whose repercussions have given rise to some of the most critical challenges of our time?

I would like to propose that the concept of an *encounter* may be useful while searching for answers to the above questions. Wilson (2017, p. 452) theorizes that an encounter is "a distinctive event of relation" that "enact[s] a shift in sensory perception" (Wilson 2017, p. 458) of the material world around us. Here the idea of an encounter strongly aligns with the earlier discussion on transcorporeality and the need to establish a different type of engagement with the non-human living and non-living realms (Wilson 2017). As encounters make us "more responsive to the world" (Wilson 2017, p. 460), their implications may go beyond the specific moment of contact, influencing values and world-views (Valentine 2008). Imaginative or physical encounters with oil and the consequences of its production and consumption can therefore trigger deeper emotional and philosophical connections with this commodity that are often muted because of its selective invisibility (Ives et al. 2018). Such deeper emotional connections can trigger "affective solidarities" (Juris 2008) for those who bear the costs of the selective invisibility of oil, or enhance the emotional basis for long-term action against the proliferation of oil infrastructure (Bosco 2007).

The question then is how to create possibilities for meaningful encounters with oil for those for whom it remains invisible, including what Wilson (2017, p. 462) calls "sustained encounters" – not a one-time event but multiple and even routine occasions. The answer (or one of the answers) may lie in bringing art and literature to the forefront of climate change–related transformations, a recent topic of debate in academic circles (Milkoreit 2017; Galafassi et al. 2018; Westley and Folke 2018; Yusoff and Gabrys 2011). Making oil's materiality relevant through stories and images can influence what Milkoreit (2017, p. 3) refers to as the "socio-climatic imaginary," which implies a vision of the desired future in which "nature is not just a backdrop to social imagination and change; it actively shapes what can be and is imagined."

Artists, writers, and activists have already started this work. For example, Canadian photographer Edward Burtynsky's series of photographs "Oil" depicts landscapes changed by the extraction, refinement, transportation, and use of oil ("Photographs: Oil" n.d.). Most of these landscapes are not familiar to the public visiting Burtynsky's exhibitions. As the photographer explains, "I'm looking for the disconnected landscapes that provide us with the materials we need to live, build, and do everything we do" (Manaugh and Twilley 2012). Another example of making oil visible through photography comes from the renowned Brazilian photographer Sebastião Salgado and his book *Kuwait: A Desert on Fire*. In his signature black-and-white images, Salgado depicts the scenes after Saddam Hussein's forces set oil wells on fire during the Gulf War in the early 1990s. The photos show not only the scale of the inferno and the transformed environment, but also people and animals in the face of the man-made disaster: exhausted fire-fighters soaked in oil and trying to close the gushing oil wells, a shepherd moving its herd while being engulfed in smoke, and a lonely horse standing amid this calamity (*The Guardian* 2016).

The moral significance of oil has also been brought to the forefront by different protest forms in which oil is materialized. On one occasion, in October 2019, Extinction Rebellion activists covered their naked bodies with fake oil at the National Portrait Gallery in London, UK, to protest British Petroleum's sponsorship of the Gallery (Busby 2019; Green 2019). As one of the activists, Eden Rickson, said, "With compassion, we ask you to change. Oil means the end, but art means the beginning" (Green 2019).

Yet another way of encountering oil, or rather the physical and social consequences of its production and consumption, is through so-called "toxic tours," educational and political tools employed by the communities polluted by toxins (Di Chiro 2000; Pezzullo 2007). Such experiential encounters both enable "seeing" oil and provide an opportunity for "an interactive form of sightseeing" (Di Chiro 2000, p. 296). Therefore, they can be effective in bringing to the forefront the moral implications of oil. Toxic tours reveal a physically altered environment as well as human experiences of living in such places, thus diminishing the cultural and physical distance between more privileged tourists and those hosting the tours (Pezzullo 2007).

There certainly are other ways to create physical and imaginative spaces and moments of encounter with oil. They should be explored and encouraged in the public domain as well as in academia by integrating humanities and art more rigorously into our scholarship and teaching (Nightingale et al. 2019; Holm et al. 2015). Creating physical or imaginative encounters with oil can address environmental injustice by making this commodity visible, especially, for those of us selectively distanced from the negative environmental and social impacts of oil. Visibility is not only about a literal ability to see something that is usually concealed, but also about the reflection on the moral implications of uneven spatialities of oil's materiality and our material and ethical connections to this commodity. Such a reflection is necessary in order to imagine a future beyond carbon lock-in which will not replicate the web of inequalities that are characteristic of the present global energy system.

References

Adam, Barbara. 1998. *Timescapes of Modernity: The Environment and Invisible Hazards.* London: Routledge.

Agyeman, Julian. 2008. "Toward a 'Just' Sustainability?" *Continuum* 22 (6): 751–756. https://doi.org/10.1080/10304310802452487.

Agyeman, Julian, David Schlosberg, Luke Craven, and Caitlin Matthews. 2016. "Trends and Directions in Environmental Justice: From Inequity to Everyday Life, Community, and Just Sustainabilities." *Annual Review of Environment and Resources* 41 (1): 321–340. https://doi.org/10.1146/annurev-environ-110615-090052.

Alaimo, Stacy. 2016. *Exposed: Environmental Politics and Pleasures in Posthuman Times.* Minneapolis, MN: University of Minnesota Press.

Balmaceda, Margarita, Per Högselius, Corey Johnson, Heiko Pleines, Douglas Rogers, and Veli-Pekka Tynkkynen. 2019. "Energy Materiality: A Conceptual Review of

Multi-Disciplinary Approaches." *Energy Research & Social Science* 56 (October): 101220. https://doi.org/10.1016/j.erss.2019.101220.

BBC News. 2019. "Oil Prices Soar after Attacks on Saudi Facilities." *Business*, September 17. https://www.bbc.com/news/business-49710820.

Bennett, Jane. 2010. *Vibrant Matter: A Political Ecology of Things*. Durham, NC: Duke University Press.

Blanc, Nathalie. 2017. "The Strange Agencies and the Seaside: (On Stacy Alaimo, 'Exposed: Environmental Politics and Pleasures in Posthuman Times')." *Minnesota Review* 88: 139–145. https://doi.org/10.1215/00265667-3787522.

Bosco, Fernando J. 2007. "Emotions That Build Networks: Geographies of Human Rights Movement in Argentina and Beyond." *Tijdschrift Voor Economische En Sociale Geografie* 98 (5): 545–563. https://doi.org/10.1111/j.1467-9663.2007.00425.x.

Bridge, Gavin, and Adrian Smith. 2003. "Intimate Encounters: Culture—Economy—Commodity." *Environment and Planning D: Society and Space* 21 (3): 257–268. https://doi.org/10.1068/d2103ed.

Bullard, Robert D. 1983. "Solid Waste Sites and the Black Houston Community." *Sociological Inquiry* 53 (2–3): 273–288. https://doi.org/10.1111/j.1475-682X.1983.tb00037.x.

Bullard, Robert D., ed. 1993. *Confronting Environmental Racism: Voices from the Grassroots*. 1st ed. Boston, MA: South End Press.

Busby, Mattha. 2019. "Semi-Naked Activists Protest against National Portrait Gallery's Links with BP." *The Guardian*, October 20, sec. Art and Design. https://www.theguardian.com/artanddesign/2019/oct/20/semi-naked-activists-protest-national-portrait-gallery-bp-sponsorship-fake-oil-extinction-rebellion.

Canadian Organic Growers. 2018. "Canadian Organic Growers » CSA Directories." https://www.cog.ca/home/find-organics/ontario-csa-directory/.

Cohen, Stanley. 2001. *States of Denial: Knowing about Atrocities and Suffering*. Cambridge: Polity; Malden, MA: Blackwell Publishers.

Coole, Diana, and Samantha Frost. 2010. "Introducing the New Materialism." In *New Materialisms: Ontology, Agency, and Politics*, edited by Diana Coole and Samantha Frost, 1–46. Durham, NC: Duke University Press.

Di Chiro, Giovanna. 2000. "Bearing Witness or Taking Action? Toxic Tourism and Environmental Justice." In *Reclaiming the Environmental Debate: The Politics of Health in a Toxic Culture*, edited by Richard Hofrichter, 275–299. Urban and Industrial Environments. Cambridge, MA: MIT Press.

Elum, Z.A., K. Mopipi, and A. Henri-Ukoha. 2016. "Oil Exploitation and Its Socioeconomic Effects on the Niger Delta Region of Nigeria." *Environmental Science and Pollution Research* 23 (13): 12880–12889. https://doi.org/10.1007/s11356-016-6864-1.

Euronews. 2020. "US Oil Prices Plunge below Zero Amid Coronavirus Pandemic." April 20. https://www.euronews.com/2020/04/20/us-oil-prices-plunge-below-zero-amid-coronavirus-pandemic.

Galafassi, Diego, Sacha Kagan, Manjana Milkoreit, María Heras, Chantal Bilodeau, Sadhbh Juarez Bourke, Andrew Merrie, Leonie Guerrero, Guðrún Pétursdóttir, and Joan David Tàbara. 2018. "'Raising the Temperature': The Arts on a Warming Planet." *Current Opinion in Environmental Sustainability* 31 (April): 71–79. https://doi.org/10.1016/j.cosust.2017.12.010.

Gifford, Robert. 2011. "The Dragons of Inaction: Psychological Barriers That Limit Climate Change Mitigation and Adaptation." *American Psychologist* 66 (4): 290–302. https://doi.org/10.1037/a0023566.

Green, Matthew. 2019. "A Crude Performance: Semi-Naked Climate Activists Protest BP Art Sponsorship." *Reuters*, October 20. https://www.reuters.com/article/us-climate-change-britain-gallery-idUSKBN1WZ0K1.

Haraway, Donna. 2016. "Staying with the Trouble: Anthropocene, Capitalocene, Chthulucene." In *Anthropocene or Capitalocene? Nature, History, and the Crisis of Capitalism*, edited by Jason W. Moore, 34–76. Oakland, CA: PM Press.

Harvey, Chelsey. 2018. "CO_2 Emissions Reached an All-Time High in 2018." *Scientific American*, December 6. https://www.scientificamerican.com/article/co2-emissions-reached-an-all-time-high-in-2018/.

Healy, Noel, and John Barry. 2017. "Politicizing Energy Justice and Energy System Transitions: Fossil Fuel Divestment and a 'Just Transition.'" *Energy Policy* 108 (September): 451–459. https://doi.org/10.1016/j.enpol.2017.06.014.

Healy, Noel, Jennie C. Stephens, and Stephanie A. Malin. 2019. "Embodied Energy Injustices: Unveiling and Politicizing the Transboundary Harms of Fossil Fuel Extractivism and Fossil Fuel Supply Chains." *Energy Research & Social Science* 48 (February): 219–234. https://doi.org/10.1016/j.erss.2018.09.016.

Holm, Poul, Joni Adamson, Hsinya Huang, Lars Kirdan, Sally Kitch, Iain McCalman, James Ogude, et al. 2015. "Humanities for the Environment—A Manifesto for Research and Action." *Humanities* 4 (4): 977–992. https://doi.org/10.3390/h4040977.

Hughes, David McDermott. 2017. *Energy Without Conscience: Oil, Climate Change, and Complicity*. Durham, NC: Duke University Press.

Influencemap. 2019. "Big Oil's Real Agenda on Climate Change." https://influencemap.org/report/How-Big-Oil-Continues-to-Oppose-the-Paris-Agreement-3821227 5958aa21196dae3b76220bddc.

Ives, Christopher D., David J. Abson, Henrik von Wehrden, Christian Dorninger, Kathleen Klaniecki, and Joern Fischer. 2018. "Reconnecting with Nature for Sustainability." *Sustainability Science* 13 (5): 1389–1397. https://doi.org/10.1007/s11625-018-0542-9.

Jenkins, Kirsten. 2018. "Setting Energy Justice Apart from the Crowd: Lessons from Environmental and Climate Justice." *Energy Research & Social Science* 39 (May): 117–121. https://doi.org/10.1016/j.erss.2017.11.015.

Jenkins, Kirsten, Darren McCauley, Raphael Heffron, Hannes Stephan, and Robert Rehner. 2016. "Energy Justice: A Conceptual Review." *Energy Research & Social Science* 11 (January): 174–182. https://doi.org/10.1016/j.erss.2015.10.004.

Juris, Jeffrey S. 2008. "Performing Politics: Image, Embodiment, and Affective Solidarity during Anti-Corporate Globalization Protests." *Ethnography* 9 (1): 61–97. https://doi.org/10.1177/1466138108088949.

Laville, Sandra, and Jonathan Watts. 2019. "Across the Globe, Millions Join Biggest Climate Protest Ever." *The Guardian*, September 20, sec. Environment. https://www.theguardian.com/environment/2019/sep/21/across-the-globe-millions-join-biggest-climate-protest-ever.

Lidskog, Rolf, and Waterton. 2018. "The Anthropocene: A Narrative in the Making." In *Environment and Society: Concepts and Challenges*, edited by Magnus Boström and Debra J. Davidson, 25–46. Cham: Springer.

Lorimer, Jamie. 2012. "Multinatural Geographies for the Anthropocene." *Progress in Human Geography* 36 (5): 593–612. https://doi.org/10.1177/0309132511435352.

Malin, Stephanie A., and Stacia S. Ryder. 2018. "Developing Deeply Intersectional Environmental Justice Scholarship." *Environmental Sociology* 4 (1): 1–7. https://doi.org/10.1080/23251042.2018.1446711.

Malin, Stephanie A., Stacia Ryder, and Mariana Galvão Lyra. 2019. "Environmental Justice and Natural Resource Extraction: Intersections of Power, Equity and Access." *Environmental Sociology* 5 (2): 109–116. https://doi.org/10.1080/23251042.2019.16 08420.

Manaugh, Geoff, and Nicola Twilley. 2012. "The Art of Industry: The Making and Meaning of Edward Burtynsky's New Exhibit, 'Oil.'" *Atlantic*, June 19. https://ww w.theatlantic.com/technology/archive/2012/06/the-art-of-industry-the-making -and-meaning-of-edward-burtynskys-new-exhibit-oil/258654/.

Markowitz, Ezra M., and Azim F. Shariff. 2012. "Climate Change and Moral Judgement." *Nature Climate Change* 2 (4): 243–247. https://doi.org/10.1038/ nclimate1378.

McGurty, Eileen Maura. 1997. "From NIMBY to Civil Rights: The Origins of the Environmental Justice Movement." *Environmental History* 2 (3): 301–323. https://doi .org/10.2307/3985352.

Milkoreit, Manjana. 2017. "Imaginary Politics: Climate Change and Making the Future." *Elementa: Science of the Anthropocene* 5: 62. https://doi.org/10.1525/elementa .249.

Nightingale, Andrea Joslyn, Siri Eriksen, Marcus Taylor, Timothy Forsyth, Mark Pelling, Andrew Newsham, Emily Boyd, et al. 2019. "Beyond Technical Fixes: Climate Solutions and the Great Derangement." *Climate and Development*, July 1–10. https://doi.org/10.1080/17565529.2019.1624495.

Nixon, Rob. 2013. *Slow Violence and the Environmentalism of the Poor.* 1. Harvard Univ. Press paperback ed. Cambridge, MA: Harvard University Press.

Norgaard, Kari Marie. 2011. *Living in Denial: Climate Change, Emotions, and Everyday Life.* Cambridge, MA: MIT Press.

Nriagu, Jerome, Emilia Udofia, Ibanga Ekong, and Godwin Ebuk. 2016. "Health Risks Associated with Oil Pollution in the Niger Delta, Nigeria." *International Journal of Environmental Research and Public Health* 13 (3): 346. https://doi.org/10.3390/ ijerph13030346.

Partridge, Tristan, Merryn Thomas, Nick Pidgeon, and Barbara Herr Harthorn. 2018. "Urgency in Energy Justice: Contestation and Time in Prospective Shale Extraction in the United States and United Kingdom." *Energy Research & Social Science* 42 (August): 138–146. https://doi.org/10.1016/j.erss.2018.03.018.

Peel, Michael. 2011. *A Swamp Full of Dollars: Pipelines and Paramilitaries at Nigeria's Oil Frontier.* London: I.B.Tauris.

Pellizzoni, Luigi. 2016. "Catching up with Things? Environmental Sociology and the Material Turn in Social Theory." *Environmental Sociology* 2 (4): 312–321. https://doi .org/10.1080/23251042.2016.1190490.

Pellow, David N. 2018. *What is Critical Environmental Justice?* Cambridge: Polity Press.

Pezzullo, Phaedra Carmen. 2003. "Touring 'Cancer Alley,' Louisiana: Performances of Community and Memory for Environmental Justice." *Text and Performance Quarterly* 23 (3): 226–252. https://doi.org/10.1080/10462930310001635295.

Pezzullo, Phaedra Carmen. 2007. *Toxic Tourism Rhetorics of Pollution, Travel, and Environmental Justice.* Tuscaloosa: The University of Alabama Press.

"Photographs: Oil." n.d. *Edward Burtynsky.* Accessed February 25, 2020. https://www .edwardburtynsky.com/projects/photographs/oil.

Reyers, Belinda, Carl Folke, Michele-Lee Moore, Reinette Biggs, and Victor Galaz. 2018. "Social-Ecological Systems Insights for Navigating the Dynamics of the Anthropocene." *Annual Review of Environment and Resources* 43 (1): 267–289. https:// doi.org/10.1146/annurev-environ-110615-085349.

Schlosberg, David. 2013. "Theorising Environmental Justice: The Expanding Sphere of a Discourse." *Environmental Politics* 22 (1): 37–55. https://doi.org/10.1080/09644016.2013.755387.

Schlosberg, David, and Romand Coles. 2016. "The New Environmentalism of Everyday Life: Sustainability, Material Flows and Movements." *Contemporary Political Theory* 15 (2): 160–181. https://doi.org/10.1057/cpt.2015.34.

Seto, Karen C., Steven J. Davis, Ronald B. Mitchell, Eleanor C. Stokes, Gregory Unruh, and Diana Ürge-Vorsatz. 2016. "Carbon Lock-In: Types, Causes, and Policy Implications." *Annual Review of Environment and Resources* 41 (1): 425–452. https://doi.org/10.1146/annurev-environ-110615-085934.

Sovacool, Benjamin K., Matthew Burke, Lucy Baker, Chaitanya Kumar Kotikalapudi, and Holle Wlokas. 2017. "New Frontiers and Conceptual Frameworks for Energy Justice." *Energy Policy* 105 (June): 677–691. https://doi.org/10.1016/j.enpol.2017.03.005.

Spice, Anne. 2018. "Fighting Invasive Infrastructures. Indigenous Relations against Pipelines." *Environment and Society* 9 (1): 40–56. https://doi.org/10.3167/ares.2018.090104.

Supran, Geoffrey, and Naomi Oreskes. 2017. "Assessing ExxonMobil's Climate Change Communications (1977–2014)." *Environmental Research Letters* 12 (8): 084019. https://doi.org/10.1088/1748-9326/aa815f.

Taylor, Dorceta. 2000. "The Rise of the Environmental Justice Paradigm." *American Behavioral Scientist* 43 (4): 508–580. https://doi.org/10.1177/0002764200043004003.

Taylor, Matthew, and Jillian Ambrose. 2020. "Revealed: Big Oil's Profits since 1990 Total Nearly $2tn." *The Guardian*, February 12, sec. Business. https://www.theguardian.com/business/2020/feb/12/revealed-big-oil-profits-since-1990-total-nearly-2tn-bp-shell-chevron-exxon.

Taylor, Matthew, and Jonathan Watts. 2019. "Revealed: The 20 Firms behind a Third of All Carbon Emissions." *The Guardian*, October 9, sec. Environment. https://www.theguardian.com/environment/2019/oct/09/revealed-20-firms-third-carbon-emissions.

The Guardian. 2016. "Kuwait: A Desert on Fire, by Sebastião Salgado." November 21, sec. Environment. https://www.theguardian.com/environment/gallery/2016/nov/21/kuwait-a-desert-on-fire-by-sebastiao-salgado.

Transition Network. 2020. "What is Transition? | Circular Model & Reconomy." *Transition Network*. https://transitionnetwork.org/about-the-movement/what-is-transition/.

Valentine, Gill. 2008. "Living with Difference: Reflections on Geographies of Encounter." *Progress in Human Geography* 32 (3): 323–337. https://doi.org/10.1177/0309132308089372.

Westley, Frances R., and Carl Folke. 2018. "Iconic Images, Symbols, and Archetypes: Their Function in Art and Science." *Ecology and Society* 23 (4). https://doi.org/10.5751/ES-10495-230431.

Wilson, Helen F. 2017. "On Geography and Encounter: Bodies, Borders, and Difference." *Progress in Human Geography* 41 (4): 451–471. https://doi.org/10.1177/0309132516645958.

Yusoff, Kathryn, and Jennifer Gabrys. 2011. "Climate Change and the Imagination." *Wiley Interdisciplinary Reviews: Climate Change* 2 (4): 516–534. https://doi.org/10.1002/wcc.117.

PART II

Environmental justice as spatial justice

INTRODUCTION

Contextualizing spatial justice

Joshua Sbicca, Melinda Laituri,
Stacia Ryder, and Kathryn Powlen

The spatial dimensions of environmental justice (EJ) are crucial in terms of understanding the uneven distribution of access to water, food, and a safe workplace and home, as well as other burdens and benefits derived from the relationship between humans and their environment. Geography, therefore, matters as it reflects where people live and how inequitable power distributions can produce inequitable landscapes and resource disparities. This section focuses on a series of case studies examining the role of space and place,[1] namely the relationship between physical places and characteristics and their social meaning and context, with a focus on environmental exposure and difference.

Place is space conceptualized as relationships and sets of ongoing encounters. It is dynamic, and shaped by ecology as well as economic, political, and social systems. As Doreen Massey argues, "we need to conceptualize space as constructed out of interrelations, as the simultaneous coexistence of social interrelations and interactions at all spatial scales, from the most local level to the most global" (80). This focus on relation suggests that our social encounters are imbued with where we come from and how scales of social action structure our lives and the places where we live. It is through this encounter that relationships are defined and places change. This change is the product of struggle based on a range of socio-spatial disparities (Walker 2012).

What does it mean to strive for spatial justice? How can we conceptualize the environment and the contemporary longing for greater equity vis-à-vis space? What does it mean to account for the multiscalar global environmental changes shaping human life around the planet? As Edward Soja (2013) notes, spatial justice is an outcome and a process that "can be studied at multiple scales and in many different social contexts" (31). Embedded in this notion is a relational approach to space. If we consider the fact that the Anthropocene operates through and is the outcome of environmental injustice then questions of space are central to any just future for *where* we live, work, and play. These places help us to see differences: different forms of power, inequities, and struggles and different visions for EJ across different geographies. Further, the approaches we use to examine spatial justice are embedded in disciplinary perspectives that may further patterns of injustice. For example, the fundamental tools of geography – maps – have a significant legacy of defining the spatial dimensions of power relationships (Wood 1992; Leuenberger and Iszhak 2020).

This section examines the nuances of a relational approach to socio-spatial conditions. This reflects the fact that as the geographic reach of the study of and fight for EJ has grown, it has become clear that environmental inequities are as heterogeneous as the responses (Martinez-Alier et al. 2016). Communities experiencing local point source pollution, clear cut forests, or land grabbing for industrial agriculture expansion share similarities and differences. Neoliberal capitalism, institutional racism, and colonialism are all common drivers. But how these structural conditions operate in place varies (Pulido 2000; Brenner and Theodore 2002; McKittrick 2006; Whyte 2017). Further, what constitutes environmental injustices can look very different across space, experience, and culture, particularly through Black, decolonial, non-Western approaches to environmental justice (McKittrick 2006; Álvarez and Coolsaet 2020).

Place-based environmental inequities are also sites of resistance. From the local (Agyeman 2005; Sze 2006) to the transnational (Pellow 2007), the networked (Schlosberg 1999), to the activist cell (Pellow 2014), activists and movements work to advance environmental justice. The range of places reveals how power operates everywhere. Boardrooms and backyards, shop floors and shopping malls, underground energy reserves and upper atmospheres, only begin to scratch the surface of where we need to look to understand the incredible reach of elite interests and the terrains of struggle.

Spatial justice across the Anthropocene, Plantationocene, and Capitalocene

The chapters in this section identify an array of EJ concerns that center the relationship between place and broader structural conditions. The diversity of accounts affirms the interconnections between people and their environment, especially the myriad ways in which inequity is spatially produced and maintained, but also resisted. Not only are there many places where EJ is a concern, there are a range of ways that justice is understood vis-à-vis specific forms of extraction and exposure.

Environmental justice has strong historical roots in the experience of racism and class exploitation in the United States (Mohai and Saha 2006; Pellow 2007; Downey and Hawkins 2008; Taylor 2014; Bullard 2018). But environmental justice concerns span the globe over time and space as reflected in these case studies. These concerns are situated in what Karl Marx (1976) referred to as "primitive accumulation." This concept helps make sense of how capitalism emerges by violently enclosing formerly common natural resources and enslaving groups to use them as productive inputs. And as Cedric Robinson (2000) and DuBois (2007[1900] remind us, this is a racialized process. Natural and human wealth are stripped of their social function and transformed into commodities where opportunities are delimited by what DuBois terms the "color line" (2007), a condition that on a global scale has required disciplining nature and racialized people to the violent strictures of plantations (McKittrick 2011). But this is not a spatially isolated practice. By robbing nature and people, racial capitalism undermines its own ability to keep growing. In addition, it produces the body as a politicized space within which contestation and the struggle for freedom and liberation play out. In a word, capitalism produces crises.

Deepening our geographic understanding of these connections, David Harvey (2010) notes that capitalism never resolves its crises, it moves them around in space. To help understand this process, he built on Marx with his notion of "accumulation by dispossession" (Harvey 2004). Synthesized with the realities of racial neoliberalism, we can understand how capitalism has sought new ways to privatize, financialize, and redistribute state resources to the wealthy, and to manage crises through ethnoracial difference (Goldberg 2009). All of this suggests that *capitalism operates through socially differentiated environmental inequality which is inseparable from race, class, ethnicity, and indigeneity, as well as gender, sexuality, and ability.*

While there has always been a global dimension to how rich nations exploit the people and natural resources of poorer nations and peoples (DuBois 1900; Martinez-Alier 1991; Escobar 1995; Watts 2013; Koch et al. 2019), the generalization of Anthropocene, Plantationocene, and Capitalocene conditions is historically distinct (Haraway 2015; Moore 2016; Davis et al. 2019). We live in a time when the reach of the global climate emergency has forced its way into our daily realities, though for some more than others (Beck 2016). We have crossed or are crossing many planetary boundaries deeply entangled in a warming planet. From landscape and climate changes to nitrogen and biodiversity losses, the spaces which are habitable are shrinking.

Humans – especially wealthy white men from countries throughout the global North representing a powerful sociopolitical bloc – have driven destructive ecological changes and insulated their environmental privileges (Foster et al. 2011; Park and Pellow 2013; Sealey-Huggins 2017; Whyte 2017; Koch et al. 2019). The disproportionate negative impacts have fallen on poor people, people of color, and Indigenous people everywhere. Capitalist, colonial, and imperialist historical trends permeate where we live, work, and play. They have transformed our landscapes at every scale imaginable, from our cellular composition to interstellar imagination. We can say that the Anthropocene, Plantationocene, and Capitalocene are a way to understand not just this time, but also this place.

Connecting environmental justice across space and place

Speaking to these connections, the authors in this section draw on conditions in the United States, Hungary, Austria, Mexico, Chile, Canada, Bangladesh, and Nicaragua. Their chapters range from places of relative power and privilege to historically exploited places now on the front lines of socio-ecological change. And in all cases, they illustrate that we cannot take EJ seriously unless we can identify the heterogeneity of spatial relations.

The relations reflect two common themes. First, national and international-level powerful players produce local-level impacts. This scalar relationship is important. Corporations, legislatures, transnational governing entities, and other similar entities concentrate power and use this to extend their reach across and within places. Second, and related, there is pressure on local people to navigate larger scalar processes that they are often unfamiliar with and disadvantaged within. For EJ activists there is the general reality that in order to solve a local problem they must understand and move decision-makers within governing structures. Often this means interfacing with government agency representatives and corporate lawyers in efforts to protect natural and cultural resources.

To specify these general relations, the authors offer analyses of a range of environmental struggles through justice lenses. Their chapters cover energy (Banerjee; Lester; Vera et al.), water (Romano and LaVanchy; Baver), toxic exposure (Antal), mining (Baver), tourism (Romano and LaVanchy), green housing (Friesenecker and Cucca), and explicit forms of resistance (Lester; Baver; Larkins, Perkins). For example, a local pipeline or mine produces immediate impacts for neighboring residents, but to challenge the responsible companies activists must find ways to convince a range of stakeholders of this disproportionate impact, the need for voice and recognition. Activists translate place-based experiences to make new claims for spatial justice.

The authors teach us that not only should we account for different forms of justice, but also that doing so can attune us to why place matters. Common justice considerations include procedural (Banerjee; Lester; Friesenecker and Cucca; Romano and LaVanchy; Baver), distributive (Antal; Lester; Friesenecker and Cucca; Romano and LaVanchy; Vera et al.; Larkins), and recognition (Lester; Larkins) justice. Depending on the conditions one or more of these forms of justice may be important. In some cases, historically marginalized groups are blocked from participating in the political process, which helps perpetuate environmental inequities (Romano and LaVanchy; Banerjee). In other cases, this same kind of opposition may be at play, but due to transnational allies recognizing the claims of local people, pressure can be applied on governments to address local concerns (Baver). These justice lenses help us to see how differently situated stakeholders obstruct or facilitate greater equity, illuminating power struggles over time and through space.

These chapters move beyond this tripartite operationalization of EJ to also think critically about specific EJ sectors, like energy and water justice (Banerjee;

Vera et al.; Romano and LaVanchy; Baver). These subsets of EJ have been critical for detailing the cultural, ecological, economic, political, and social dimensions of natural resources (e.g. timber) and environmental goods (e.g. food). They allow scholars and activists alike to craft analyses and demands that are relevant to particular places and struggles. Moreover, intersectionality and segregation are useful lenses to nuance how EJ issues are enacted and experienced (Larkins; Antil; Friesenecker and Cucca). Beginning from the social position of historically marginalized groups can help center new imaginations and visions that broaden our notions of EJ to consider how place is experienced and contested through an array of intersecting group attributes and experiences (Larkins). Similarly, by identifying patterns of segregation, we can see where environmental inequities and benefits are concentrated and who lives there.

As these chapters collectively show that place is relational, which means that where one lives is produced physically, constructed socially, and often contested. Place matters; geography matters. The intersection of society and environment reflect the multiple struggles that are exemplified by these examples of spatial injustice.

Note

1 We are aware there is an extensive literature on definitions of space and place that reflect the complexity of these terms and the debates surrounding them. This is beyond the scope of this introduction. Refer to Koop, B., and M. Galic, 2017. *Conceptualising space and place: Lessons from geography for the debate on privacy in public.* 10.4337/9781786435408.00007; Devine-Wright, P., 2011. From backyards to places: Public engagement and the emplacement of renewable energy technologies. *Renewable energy and the public: From NIMBY to participation*, pp. 57–70.

References

Agyeman, Julian. 2005. *Sustainable Communities and the Challenge of Environmental Justice.* New York, NY: New York University Press.

Álvarez, L. and Coolsaet, B., 2020. Decolonizing environmental justice studies: a Latin American perspective. *Capitalism Nature Socialism*, 31(2), pp.50–69

Beck, Ulrich. 2016. *The metamorphosis of the world: How climate change is transforming our concept of the world.* Cambridge, UK: Polity Press.

Brenner, Neil, and Nik Theodore. 2002. "Cities and the geographies of 'actually existing neoliberalism'." *Antipode*, 34(3): 349–379.

Bullard, Robert D. 2018. *Dumping in Dixie: Race, Class, and Environmental quality.* Third edition. New York, NY: Routledge

Davis, Janae, Alex A. Moulton, Levi Van Sant, and Brian Williams. 2019. "Anthropocene, capitalocene,… plantationocene?: A manifesto for ecological justice in an age of global crises." *Geography Compass*, 13(5): 1–15.

Downey, Liam, and Brian Hawkins. "Race, income, and environmental inequality in the United States." *Sociological Perspectives* 51.4 (2008): 759–781.

DuBois, W.E.B. (2007) [1900]. The Nations of the World. https://www.blackpast.org /african-american-history/1900-w-e-b-du-bois-nations-world/. January 29, 2007.

Escobar, Arturo. 1995. *Encountering development: The making and unmaking of the Third World*. Princeton, NJ: Princeton University Press.

Foster, John Bellamy, Brett Clark, and Richard York. 2011. *The ecological rift: Capitalism's war on the earth*. New York, NY: Monthly Review Press.

Goldberg, David Theo. 2009. *The Threat of Race: Reflections on Racial Neoliberalism*. Malden, MA: Blackwell.

Haraway, Donna. 2015. "Anthropocene, capitalocene, plantationocene, chthulucene: Making kin." *Environmental Humanities*, 6(1): 159–165.

Harvey, David. 2004. "The 'new' imperialism: accumulation by dispossession." *Socialist Register*, 40: 63–87.

Harvey, David. 2010. *The Enigma of Capital and the Crises of Capitalism*. Oxford: Oxford University Press.

Koch, Alexander, Chris Brierley, Mark M. Maslin, and Simon L. Lewis. 2019. "Earth system impacts of the European arrival and Great Dying in the Americas after 1492." *Quaternary Science Reviews* 207: 13–36.

Leuenberger, C. and I. Schnell. 2020. *The Politics of Maps*. London: Oxford University Press. ISBN: 9780190076238

Martinez-Alier, Joan. 1991. "Ecology and the poor: A neglected dimension of Latin American history." *Journal of Latin American Studies*, 23(3): 621–639.

Martinez-Alier, Joan, Leah Temper, Daniela Del Bene, and Arnim Scheidel. 2016. "Is there a global environmental justice movement?" *The Journal of Peasant Studies*, 43(3): 731–755.

Marx, Karl. 1976. *Capital*, Vol. 1. New York: Vintage.

Massey, Doreen. 1992. "Politics and Space/Time." *New Left Review* 196: 65–84.

McKittrick, Katherine. 2006. *Demonic Grounds: Black Women and the Cartographies of Struggle*. Minneapolis, MN: University of Minnesota Press.

McKittrick, Katherine. 2011. "On plantations, prisons, and a black sense of place." *Social & Cultural Geography*, 12(8): 947–963.

Mohai, Paul, and Robin Saha. "Reassessing racial and socioeconomic disparities in environmental justice research." *Demograph*, 43.2 (2006): 383–399.

Moore, Jason (ed). 2016. *Anthropocene or capitalocene?: Nature, history, and the crisis of capitalism*. Oakland, CA: PM Press.

Park, Lisa Sun-Hee, and David N. Pellow. 2013. *The slums of Aspen: Immigrants vs. the environment in America's Eden*. New York, NY: NYU Press.

Pellow, David Naguib. 2007. *Resisting Global Toxics: Transnational Movements for Environmental Justice*. Boston, MA: MIT Press.

Pellow, David Naguib. 2014. *Total Liberation: The Power and Promise of Animal Rights and the Radical Earth Movement*. Minneapolis, MN: University of Minnesota Press.

Pulido, Laura. 2000. "Rethinking environmental racism: White privilege and urban development in Southern California." *Annals of the Association of American Geographers*, 90(1): 12–40.

Robinson, Cedric J. 2000. *Black Marxism: The Making of the Black Radical Tradition*. Chapel Hill, NC: University of North Carolina Press.

Sealey-Huggins, Leon. "'1.5° C to stay alive': climate change, imperialism and justice for the Caribbean." *Third World Quarterly*, 38.11 (2017): 2444–2463.

Schlosberg, David. 1999. "Networks and mobile arrangements: Organisational innovation in the US environmental justice movement." *Environmental Politics*, 8(1): 122–148.

Soja, Edward W. 2013. *Seeking Spatial Justice*. Minneapolis, MN: University of Minnesota Press.

Sze, Julie. 2006. *Noxious New York: The Racial Politics of Urban Health and Environmental Justice*. Boston, MA: MIT Press.

Taylor, Dorceta. 2014. *Toxic Communities: Environmental Racism, Industrial Pollution, and Residential Mobility*. New York, NY: New York University Press.

Walker, Gordon. 2012. Environmental Justice: Concepts, Evidence and Politics. London, UK: Routledge Taylor & Francis Group.

Watts, Michael J. 2013. *Silent Violence: Food, famine, and peasantry in northern Nigeria*. Athens GA: University of Georgia Press.

Whyte, Kyle. 2017. "Indigenous climate change studies: Indigenizing futures, decolonizing the Anthropocene." *English Language Notes*, 55(1): 153–162.

Wood, Denis. 1992. *The Power of Maps*. London: Guildford Press.

3

ENVIRONMENTAL JUSTICE AND AUTOCRACY IN EASTERN EUROPE

The case of Hungary

Attila Antal

Introduction

There is an expanding discourse on environmental (in)justice as a social problem and racist issue. I will analyze the main notions of these concerns of environmental justice with a special focus on Eastern Europe. One of the earliest approaches concerning environmental justice focused on the inequity in the distribution of environmental bads (Bryant and Mohai 1992; Pellow 2004, 2007). From that standpoint "environmental injustice was about social injustice being manifest in a host of environmental risks and bads" (Schlosberg 2013, p. 47). These environmental problems are characterized as social injustices, which hurt not only poor people but communities of color. Environmental injustice has been framed as eco-racism, so the main explanatory focus of environmental problems was racism. Schlosberg puts it very clearly:

> Environmental justice wasn't simply about establishing the fact that more environmental bads and risks were being put on minority communities [...] The practice, and experience, of racism has been at the heart of environmental justice discourse in the United States.
>
> *(Schlosberg 2013, p. 39)*

The discourse of race and ethnicity are "important aspects in understanding popular environmentalism, but they may not be central in every setting where environmental injustices are present" (Harper et al. 2009, p. 5). Martínez-Alier (2003) cautions against applying "environmental racism" as a universal framework to all environmental injustices.

Nevertheless, there is a broadening environmental justice discourse at the global level. The concept of environmental justice is a broad framework which contains "analyses of transportation, access to countryside and green space, land use and smart growth policy, water quality and distribution, energy development and jobs, brownfields refurbishment, and food justice" (Schlosberg 2013, p. 40). According to Schlosberg (2013, p. 38): "Climate change has pushed environmental justice to more broad considerations of both environment and justice." Climate justice has become one of the main concepts of environmental justice. Several environmental problems which used to be environmental justice questions currently can be seen and interpreted in the climate justice framework.

The environmental justice movement was said to be "a post-materialist movement supported largely by young, white, middle-class citizens" (Harper et al. 2009, p. 5). This approach has mistakenly led a perception that low-income and socially excluded groups are not as interested in the environment as their middle-class, majority counterparts. Doherty and Doyle (2006) argued that there are three major frames in transnational environmentalism: post-colonial, post-materialist, and post-industrial environmentalisms. Martínez-Alier (2003) pointed out the "environmentalism of the poor" which, combining elements of post-colonial and post-industrial environmentalist approaches, addresses the preservation of traditional ecological knowledge and the struggle for environmental justice. The social and environmental aspects go hand in hand, as Michael Löwy pointed out: "The struggle of labor – workers, farmers, the landless, and the unemployed – for social justice is inseparable from the struggle for environmental justice. Capitalism, socially and ecologically exploitative and polluting, is the enemy of nature and of labor alike" (Löwy 2015, p. 90).

Nevertheless, there is a confluence of environmental activism and lessons learned from the US civil rights-based environmental activism which "has fundamentally shifted the discourse on environmental harms toward a more intrinsic or inherent valuation of humans and nature and points to previously untapped possibilities for integration" (Harper et al. 2009, p. 6). Environmental justice advocacy in the United States was based extensively on the civil rights movement and linked to bottom-up, community-based activism. In contrast to the US situation, in the United Kingdom environmental movements are led by environmental organizations with a highly educated staff and international expertise (Harper et al. 2009, p. 6).

In Eastern Europe, post-colonial and post-industrial aspects are found in the environmental critique concerning environmental justice (Harper et al. 2009, p. 5). The environmental and climate justice discourse is influenced by this phenomenon and it is apparent that anti-racism and environmentalism go hand in hand. Harper, Steger and Filčák based their theory on Ladányi and Szelényi's analysis of post-socialist patterns of social exclusion (2005) in Eastern Europe and they argue "that in the case of Roma …, spaces inhabited by low-income Roma have come to be racialized during the post-socialist era, intensifying patterns of environmental exclusion along ethnic lines" (Harper et al. 2009, p. 6).

These are the main approaches to constructing and theorizing environmental justice. Their conclusion is very crucial to deep understanding of the state of environmental justice in Eastern Europe:

> These possibilities could be expressed … through the integration of environmental protection and social inclusion. To date, attempts at such policy integration or activist alliances have been rare; post-socialist policies addressing the conditions of Roma communities have been framed through an ethnic lens as Roma issues, resulting in an ethicized policy silo […]. For mobilizations to be effective, activists … must develop a vocabulary for addressing environmental injustices that is analytically applicable and strategically effective in the context of the European Union and especially at the local and national level.
>
> *(Harper et al. 2009, p. 7)*

The socio-spatial aspects of environmental (in)justice is remarkable on Western and Eastern scales. There is a lack in Eastern Europe of a common and well-established discourse concerning environmental injustices which overlap with environmental and social inclusion fields of thought but it seems to be that the rise of new political autocracies and the climate emergency can establish a new way of thinking.

Environment, democracy, and authoritarianism

Sonnenfeld and Taylor point out: "Paradoxically, environmentalism, like liberalism, does not require democracy. Nor does environmentalism require liberalism. Two decades into the third millennium of the Common Era, environmentalism exists in both liberal and illiberal forms, in democratic and authoritarian settings" (Sonnenfeld and Taylor 2018, p. 517). The superiority of democracy is questionable when considering environmental sustainability outcomes and results. Wurster argues that

> democracy has a clear advantage with regard to weak sustainability … this is not true for strong sustainability … the superiority of the democracies over the autocracies is limited to the solution of area-restricted environmental problems and those that are technically easy to solve. This implies that democracies adapt to, but do not really solve, major environmental problems.
>
> *(2013, p. 89)*

As Wurster states (2013, p. 89), these results in conjunction with strong sustainability do not provide any evidence for the general superiority of autocratic regimes, but it is an important consequence that the environmental crisis of our time cannot be solved just in the framework of democracy.

Authoritarian states do exhibit environmental performance and Eastern Europe provides a suitable place for analysis, given the fact the region had been long associated with political authoritarianism during the communist era. The environmental problems and crises in Eastern Europe have a shared history with the rise of autocracies since the end of the second World War (Gille 2007; Pál 2017; Brain and Pál 2018). The environmentalist approach of Communist regimes was denounced by many scholars, but there is a new rise of investigating "the Communist state's role in the nurture and growth of environmentalism in Eastern Europe" (Pál 2017, p. 3). Pál argues the environmental awareness of the Hungarian Communist regime:

> between the 1960s–1980s, Hungarian environmental attitudes changed considerably. Such a change was effectively nurtured, facilitated and propagated by the state. Public concern over pollution rose and local environmental debates were mostly confined to local media platforms in the 1960s. As a result of societal changes and government sponsored environmentalist propaganda, environmental grew significantly in Hungarian society by the mid-1970s. Communist social and youth organizations incorporated environmental protection into their agenda.
>
> *(2017, p. 231)*

The collective climate and ecological challenge we faced initiated the authoritarian state to elaborate some response to this crisis in China and Southern Asia. This is called environmental authoritarianism and means some kind of "forms of 'good' authoritarianism, in which environmentally unsustainable forms of behavior are simply forbidden, may become not only justifiable, but essential for the survival of humanity in anything approaching a civilised form" (Beeson 2010, p. 289).

The situation is not the same in Eastern Europe despite the authoritarian tendencies. New kinds of authoritarian structures are rising, especially in Hungary and Poland – this is authoritarian right-wing populism (Antal 2017, 2019). I argue that the contemporary authoritarian right-wing regimes in Eastern Europe cannot be seen as environmental autocracies (Beeson 2010; Wainwright and Mann 2018). I argue that these types of autocracies will not be able to answer the environmental emergency raised by the climate and ecological crisis, because they are continuing to distribute environmental injustices to the lower class of the societies (lower-income and homeless people, refugees and migrants).

Environmental injustice issues in Eastern Europe

The IPCC's Climate Change 2014: Synthesis Report warns of extreme weather and climate events, especially the frequency of heat in large parts of Eastern Europe, where heat-related human mortality, decreased cold-related human mortality, and reinforcement of the frequency and intensity of heavy precipitation events will occur (IPCC 2014). Anders et al.'s (2013) investigations reveal that in Central and Eastern Europe the mean annual temperature is projected to increase between 1 and 3 °C until the middle of the century and up to 5 °C by the end of the century (pp. 24–24). This temperature increase will cause several social and political problems across the region. It is predicted that the "European warming will be higher than the global mean temperature increase [...] In the autumn and winter months the temperature change in North and Eastern Europe will be higher (up to 3 °C) compared to South Europe (1–1.5 °C)" (Anders et al. 2013, p. 25). They conclude that

> [f]or all of Central and Eastern Europe a clear temperature rise is visible for the future which is projected to become more distinct at the end of the century. A general pattern is that the projected increase of temperature is highest during summer and lower during winter.
>
> *(Anders et al. 2013, p. 26)*

Analyzing the climate justice problems concerning Eastern Europe it is necessary to show the relevant details about climate change. The maps of *Environmental Justice Atlas* by Environmental Justice Organizations, Liabilities and Trade (EJOLT) highlight the spatial mal-distribution of climate change sources and its impacts. According to the EJOLT *Environmental Justice Atlas* the number of environmental justice problems has grown increasingly in Eastern Europe and some of them have a direct relationship with climate change.

Since the regime changes a new chapter has begun in the environmental history of the post-Communist region. The collapse of Communist regimes revealed the huge environmental and social catastrophe caused by environmental irresponsibility. Unfortunately, the environmental and social systems have not been improved by the new liberal and capitalist systems. The core problems with democracy in this region show a close relationship with the environmental, climate, and social problems. There is a strong connection between social and climate (or environmental) injustices. Moreover, the social problems appear in environmental contexts and the victims do not realize the environmental nature of these challenges that fuel poverty. Therefore, this region suffers from the risk of vulnerability caused by climate change that is relatively high in Eastern Europe compared to other parts of Europe. This can be investigated in a framework of three main climate-related injustices in terms of spatial justice. The first case examines the most vulnerable sociocultural group in this region which is the Roma community. The second one relates to the lower- (and upper-) middle-class group and focuses on energy poverty. The third is the stigmatization of vulnerable groups that include climate refugees, migrants, and homeless people.

The crisis of the Roma population

Environmental injustices concerning Roma people originated in the Eastern European transitions of 1989. Since then, the low-income Roma population in this region has borne the brunt of the post-socialist economic transformation. The Roma minority has been suffering from the following environmental problems and injustices: unequal access to sewage or wastewater treatment; unequal access to household water; unequal access to green space and playgrounds; waste management and illegal dumping; low household energy efficiency and access to fuel for heating and cooking; poor housing quality, access to public infrastructure, and human health resources (Steger 2007; Harper et al. 2009). The harmful effects of climate change (problems with drinking water, floods, and heat waves) have disproportionately affected the Roma minority and will cause environmental and climate injustices theorized as eco-racism. Without a common climate governance structure in Eastern Europe such massive climate and social injustices will cause incalculable damage.

Steger (2007) suggests that the state of the Roma communities and refugees demonstrates the urgency for an environmental justice agenda in Eastern Europe (p. 19). The environmental and climate justice questions concerning Roma people have been investigated in the social justice and racist framework:

> While it is widely known that the Roma experience racial prejudice and discrimination, more attention is needed on how this is reflected in their living conditions and manifested as health problems through the distribution of environmental benefits and harms [...] While Roma take on a disproportionate share of the burden of environmental harms, they are frequently denied the benefits such as access to water and other natural resources.
>
> *(Steger 2007, p. 19)*

The social discrimination towards the Roma community has led to geographical segregation, which is one of the most pressing environmental injustices, in conjunction with spatial justice, which means that they have been confined to the most polluted or high environmental risk areas. Roma communities have insufficient access to environmental goods (such as clean water, sewage treatment) (Table 3.1). Environmental and climate injustices contribute to the devastating social conditions of the Roma people, who cannot exercise the same constitutional environmental rights as the majority of society (Antal 2014).

TABLE 3.1 Percent of Roma population living in households without access to facilities in the dwelling (2002)

	Bulgaria	Czech Republic	Hungary	Romania	Slovak Republic
Running water	45	4	34	65	32
Toilet in the dwelling	75	15	46	65	44
Sewage treatment	51	6	63	62	46
Bathroom in the dwelling	70	12	41	66	37

(*Source*: Steger 2007, p. 20)

There is another side of social and environmental discrimination of Roma communities: "poorly insulated housing and the widespread use of dilapidated woodstoves waste residents' energy resources and also contribute to respiratory ailments in the winter months" (Steger 2007, p. 20). In these segregated areas, it is common that people heat with household and other waste which contributes to the formation of smog.

These environmental burdens endured disproportionately by the Roma people will be increased because of the constantly occurring impact of climate change (Steger 2007, p. 21). This will influence the health records of the Roma communities. The main problem is that there is no shared environmental identity or identity politics in the Roma communities. Harper, Steger, and Filčák (2009) point out that "Roma ... are rarely perceived as 'environmental subjects' by themselves or others although struggles for access to housing and public infrastructure have played a critical role in grassroots organizing in many Roma communities" (p. 7). Nevertheless, this is a huge challenge "since 1989 there has been a push from both Romani activists and the Hungarian state […] to identify and organize Roma as an ethnic group and to target policies towards them," while "many activists and politicians fear that 'ethicizing' political issues of Roma communities marginalizes those issues and promotes stereotypes, but without targeted programs, there is little incentive for members of the majority group to consult or include minorities" (Harper et al. 2009, p. 11). There is a basic need to create a coalition from environmentalist and Roma civil rights activists which can address the racial side of environmental injustices without enhancing stereotypes and creating an environmental discursive or geographical ghetto (Harper et al. 2009, p. 11). Roma communities bear the brunt of environmental and climate inequalities, because they are unable to mobilize social, political, and economic resources (Pellow 2001).

Energy poverty

Fuel poverty represents environmental and climate injustices not only in the marginalized social groups but in the middle class: not all low-income households are fuel poor and there are fuel poor households that do not belong to the lowest income percentiles (Waddams Prince et al. 2006). Fuel poverty refers to the expanding sphere of environmental and climate injustices. According to Tirado and Ürge-Vorsatz,

> [t]he concept of fuel poverty can be located in the broad frame of the lack of or inadequate access to energy services, which refers to the lack access, mostly in developing countries to quality energy services as those provided, for instance, by electricity.
>
> *(2010, p. 4)*

Fuel poverty is about the quality and affordability of energy services and efficiency. It means the inability to afford adequate energy services for the household.

A proposed definition of fuel poverty by Brenda Boardman is an "inability to obtain adequate energy services for 10% of a household income" (1991, p. 201). This definition has been criticized because of the lack of scientific rationality of the mentioned 10%. Tirado and Ürge-Vorsatz suggest that fuel poverty as a concept ought to be framed in more general considerations about poverty and deprivation (2010, p. 4). Fuel poverty is gaining political importance, not just due to climate change, but also due to the increasing energy bills and vulnerable customers, who have everyday trouble paying for their energy consumption.

Tirado and Ürge-Vorsatz state that "[c]onsidering the three factors often considered in the analysis of fuel poverty (energy prices, household income and energy performance of the residential stock), there are concerns about the incidence of this particular type of deprivation" (2010, p. 5.).This is an emerging environmental and climate change-caused deprivation in Eastern Europe. After the regime change in this region the state-owned energy monopolies became privatized. The acceptance of the concept of full-cost recovery tariffs and liberalized energy markets caused higher energy prices. The GDP per capita income of the region's countries is lower than the EU's average. Moreover, "the high energy consumption of the average residential unit is a consequence of the long-time subsidized energy prices and the lack of basic energy efficiency requirements" (Tirado and Ürge-Vorsatz 2010, pp. 5–6).

According to Buzar, these tendencies caused homes to become "prisons" for households unable to properly heat their living space (2007). There are not any standardized measurement frameworks for fuel poverty and no consistent systems for data gathering. Additionally, there is little political discourse about these inequalities. Fuel poverty has become an emerging discourse of environmental or climate justice. The social groups affected by the various levels of fuel poverty are multi-colored and are struggling with the different aspects of fuel poverty. However, there is no group solidarity within the affected groups.

Criminalizing homelessness as environmental injustice

One of the most significant spatial environmental injustice cases caused by the state is the criminalization of homelessness initiated by the Orbán regime. After 2010, the new Hungarian government with a two-thirds constitutional majority tried several times to make poverty a crime. In 2012, the government made a legal regulation in conjunction with the criminalization which was found to be unconstitutional by the Constitutional Court [38/2012. (XI. 14.) AB]. After winning the election in 2018 and again gaining a constitutional majority, the Fidesz-KDNP governing parties overruled the decision of the Constitutional Court and put the unconstitutional resolutions into Fundamental Law. Before the second round of legal solutions, the Orbán regime initiated a hate campaign against homeless people who suffer most from climate change harm. The Seventh Amendment, accepted June 28, 2018, of the Hungarian Fundamental Law ensured the legal bases of the criminalization. The new regulation criminalized homelessness, stating that using public space as a habitual dwelling shall be illegal. The new composition of the Constitutional Court has embarrassingly found the regulation constitutional. This is to say that the most extreme form of housing poverty has been declared as a crime by the constitutional framework, which also means that a serious environmental injustice has been legitimized by the Fundamental Law. This is not just a so-called bureaucratic solution, but an unprecedented aggravation of social and climate injustice. The consequences are unthinkable as people suffering from energy poverty problems are endangered under this constitutional regulation.

Parallel with the constitutional procedure, the governing majority adopted an amendment to the Minor Offences Act, passed on June 20, 2018, and came into force on October 15, 2018, which criminalized homelessness. Under the new regulation, proceedings are instituted against individuals who habitually live in public spaces and who do not discontinue this activity within 90 days of being called upon to do so three times. The act stipulated that no fine may be imposed, but the person concerned must be detained at once for a minor offence. The court may even sentence the perpetrator to custody and his or her assets may even be destroyed. The new regulation undermines human rights, especially the environmental rights of homeless people. That is to say that the constitutional and legal rules are unenforceable and the enforcement of them depends on the police force and judges, given the fact the Hungarian state has no capacity at all to punish those homeless people by mass incarceration. As a result of regulation, the police have been enacting the law and homeless people have adapted to the regulations. They have disappeared from frequented public places in Budapest. This has resulted in many homeless people appearing on the outskirts of Budapest and looking for shelter in the countryside. This marginalization is a huge risk, because these people totally fall out from the social care system. In 2018 and 2019, the authorities were in compliance with the enforcement of strict and unfair rules, but the homeless people have still not returned to frequented urban places.

Conclusions

The three issues analyzed represent the socio-spatial aspect of environmental injustice of people who are socially disadvantaged and spatially segregated. In the era of climate and ecological emergency there are several environmental injustice issues in Eastern Europe which have been caused by liberal democracies. The emerging authoritarian regimes make the situation even worse and more worrisome. The region had been long associated with political authoritarianism, and during the Communist era there were some environmental achievements, but the contemporary new authoritarian regimes do not really care about the environment. There is no officially declared climate emergency in Eastern Europe. Some Eastern European governments are trying to blackmail the European Union by blocking the decarbonization targets, but the societies show that the people do worry about the climate and ecological disaster (Vass 2019).

It seems to be there is a need to (re)enhance the social nature of environmental problems and this will strengthen the environmental consciousness in Eastern Europe. Access to information and social participation can evolve the environmental consciousness which is indispensable in the context of environmental justice. It is also crucial to find the right solution between the under- and over-ethnicized frameworks concerning the ethnical problems caused by environmental and climate injustices. This means broadening racial and ethnic minority groups' participation in ecological activities which can play an important role in transforming ecological attitudes and promoting social inclusion (Mohai 1990).

The discourse of environmental and climate justice in Eastern Europe should be based on environmental identities constructed on ethnical and social solidarity.

> Environmental justice reflects a growing wave of environmentalism as people seek justice in the distribution of environmental benefits and harms. Fundamental to this process is not only the application of distributive and procedural notions of justice, but a widening discourse on what constitutes an environmentalist and environmentalism. Further research on environmental justice […] need to explore the opportunities and barriers to an emergent environmental identity amongst the Roma, and their capacity to generate "new vocabulary" around that identity.
>
> *(Harper et al. 2009, p. 25)*

All this is not facilitated at all by the fact that the state racism of authoritarian regimes across the region has a serious impact on environmental and climate justice.

References

Anders, I., Stagl, J., Auer, I., Pavlik, D. (2013). Climate Change in Central and Eastern Europe. In: S. Rannow, M. Neubert, ed., *Managing Protected Areas in Central and Eastern Europe Under Climate Change*, Springer, Dordrecht, Heidelberg, New York, London: Spinger, pp. 17–30.

Antal, A. (2014). *Strong Constitutional Basis – Weak Environmental Policy. How Could Be the Environmental Policy Unconstitutional? – The Case of Hungary*. Conference paper, 3rd UNITAR-Yale Conference on Environmental Governance and Democracy, 5–7 September 2014, New Haven, USA.

Antal, A. (2017). The Political Theories, Preconditions and Dangers of the Governing Populism in Hungary. *Czech Journal of Political Science*, 14(2), pp. 5–20.

Antal, A. (2019). *The Rise of Hungarian Populism: State Autocracy and the Orbán Regime*. Howard House, Wagon Lane, Bingley BD16 1WA, UK: Emerald Publishing.

Beeson, M. (2010): The Coming of Environmental Authoritarianism. *Environmental Politics*, 19(2), pp. 276–294.

Boardman, B. (1991). *Fuel Poverty: From Cold Homes to Affordable Warmth*. London: Belhaven Press.

Brain, S., Pál, V. (2018). *Environmentalism under Authoritarian Regimes. Myth, Propaganda, Reality*. 1st Edition. Abingdon, Oxon; New York, NY; Routledge: Routledge.

Bryant, B., Mohai, P. (1992). *Race and the Incidence of Environmental Hazards: A Time for Discourse*. Boulder, CO: Westview Press.

Buzar, S. (2007). When Homes Become Prisons: The Relational Spaces of Postsocialist Energy Poverty. *Environment and Planning. Part A*, 39, pp. 1908–1925.

Doherty, B., Doyle, T. (2006). Beyond Borders: Transnational Politics, Social Movements and Modern Environmentalisms. *Environmental Politics*, 15(5), pp. 697–712.

Gille, Zs. (2007). *From the Cult of Waste to the Trash Heap of History. The Politics of Waste in Socialist and Postsocialist Hungary*. Bloomington: Indiana University Press.

Harper, K., Steger, T., Filčák, R. (2009). *Environmental Justice and Roma Communities in Central and Eastern Europe*. Selected Publications of EFS Faculty, Students, and Alumni. Paper 1.

Intergovernmental on Panel Climate Change (IPCC) (2014). *Climate Change 2014: Synthesis Report*. Contribution of Working Groups I, II and III to the Fifth Assessment Report of the Intergovernmental Panel on Climate Change [Core Writing Team, R.K. Pachauri and L.A. Meyer (eds.)]. Geneva, Switzerland.

Ladányi, J., Szelenyi, I. (2005). *Patterns of Exclusion: Constructing Gypsy Ethnicity and the Making of an Underclass in Transitional Societies of Europe*. Boulder, CO: East European Monographs.

Löwy, M. (2015). *Ecosocialism: A Radical Alternative to Capitalist Catastrophe*. Chicahi, IL: Haymarket Books.

Martínez-Alier, J. (2003). *The Environmentalism of the Poor: A Study of Ecological Conflicts and Valuation*. Northampton, MA: Edward Elgar.

Mohai, P. (1990). Black Environmentalism. *Social Science Quarterly*, 71(4), pp. 744–765.

Pál, V. (2017). *Technology and the Environment in State-Socialist Hungary: An Economic History*. Cham, Switzerland: Palgrave Macmillan.

Pellow, D. (2001). Environmental Justice and the Political Process: Movements, Corporations and the State. *Sociological Quarterly*, 42(1), pp. 46–67.

Pellow, D. (2004). *Garbage Wars: The Struggle for Environmental Justice in Chicago*. Cambridge, MA: MIT Press.

Pellow, D. (2007). *Resisting Global Toxics: Transnational Movements for Environmental Justice*. Cambridge, MA: MIT Press.

Schlosberg, D. (2013). Theorising Environmental Justice: The Expanding Sphere of a Discourse. *Environmental Politics*, 22(1), pp. 37–55.

Sonnenfeld, D.A., Taylor, P.L. (2018). Liberalism, Illiberalism, and the Environment. *Society & Natural Resources*, 31(5), pp. 515–524.

Steger, T. (2007). *Making the Case for Environmental Justice in Central & Eastern Europe*. CEU Center for Environmental Policy and Law (CEPL). The Health and Environment Alliance (HEAL). The Coalition for Environmental Justice.

Tirado, S.H., Ürge-Vorsatz, D. (2010). *Fuel Poverty in Hungary. A First Assessment*. Center for Climate Change and Sustainable Energy Policy (3CSEP). Central European University (CEU). https://3csep.ceu.edu/projects/fuel-poverty-in-hungary

Vass, A. (2019). Climate Strike in Budapest Draws Thousands. *Hungary Today*, 30 September. https://hungarytoday.hu/climate-strike-budapest-draws-thousands/

Waddams Price, C., Brazier, K., Pham, K., Mathieu, L., Wang, W. (2006). *Identifying Fuel Poverty Using Objective and Subjective Measures*. CCP Working Paper no. 07-11. Centre for Competition Policy, University of East Anglia, UK.

Wainwright, J., Mann, G. (2018). *Climate Leviathan. A Political Theory of Our Planetary Future*. London: Verso.

Wurster, S. (2013). Comparing Ecological Sustainability in Autocracies and Democracies. *Contemporary Politics*, 19(1), pp. 76–93.

4

NAVIGATING ENVIRONMENTAL JUSTICE IN CHILE

The case of Pascua Lama

Sherrie Baver

Introduction

The environmental justice (EJ) lens is crucial to studying environmental conflicts in Latin America. EJ sheds light on how continuing power differentials and inequities, in this most unequal region in the world, play out regionwide and in the specific case of Chile. This chapter will examine the complex interplay among the country's twenty-first-century environmental governance reforms, transnational NGO networks, international organizations, and Indigenous claims to stop a gold mining project in the high Andes of northern Chile. The goal is to highlight Chile's recent institutional governance changes that activist networks used to end Barrick Gold's quest to undertake what was widely viewed as an environmentally risky venture. The project was initially supported by Chile, a country known for its centuries-long history of extractivism, its centuries-long history of abuses against Indigenous people, and its present commitment to neoliberalism. The endeavor might be seen as a breathtaking example of state technocratic thinking in the Anthropocene, imagining moving glaciers to allow mining to proceed. This project's termination was a rare success for environmental justice and speaks to the potential for success when social activists employ modern procedural environmental governance tools along with linkage to regional and international institutions.

The Pascua Lama case highlights "the geography of injustice." The project involved Barrick, the world's largest gold-mining company and its unusual plan. The mine was to be developed in the Andes at 15,000 feet and as the world's first bi-national mine (the Pascua side was in Chile with the Lama side in Argentina). Furthermore, it would be located in the Atacama Desert, one of the driest places on Earth, and would have involved mining under the region's glaciers, the water reserve for farmers in the nearby Huasco Valley. The following discussion focuses mainly on the small-scale farmers in the valley, who, in the process of fighting the mine, successfully used the new tools of environmental democracy to stop the project. The argument here is that these procedural rights and institutions are important additions to the toolkit of EJ activists. In addition, at least in this case, in the process of pursuing justice, the smallholders regained their ethnic identity as Indigenous Diaguita.

It is reasonable to ask what ultimately stopped Pascua Lama. Was it primarily general environmental concern for glacier destruction or primarily environmental justice concerns? Not surprisingly, different scholars stress different concerns. While Li (2018), Barandiarán (2018), and Haslam (2018) stress the glaciers, and Barrick's proposal to "move" them as the mobilizing force, Urkidi and Walter (2011), Cuadra Montoya (2014), and Chile's *Observatorio Cuidadano* (2016) put more emphasis on the environmental justice dimension. Additionally, the timing of the conflict also played a part in the government's decision to terminate the venture. The Pascua Lama struggle began as Chile was seeking to enter the Organization of Economic Cooperation and Development (OECD). At the same time, another conflict was transpiring involving the more numerous and better organized Indigenous Mapuches in southern Chile over a large-scale energy/dam project, HydroAysén. (While the project was not being built in their territory, the proposed transmission lines and high-voltage towers to carry the energy north to Chile's main population and mining centers would traverse their lands.) Finally, starting in 2012, Chile was promoting its reputation as an environmental human rights leader in the Latin American and Caribbean (LAC) region by promoting the Escazú Environmental Democracy Convention.

What is environmental democracy and why is it a means of pursuing environmental justice?

The three "Principle 10 (P10)" environmental access rights, also known as the pillars of environmental democracy, were first promulgated in the 1992 Rio Declaration (UNCED 1992). Since the late 1990s, these P10 rights, "access to environmental information," "access to participation," and, "access to justice in environmental matters," are globally seen as promoting transparent, inclusive, and accountable governance. Their greatest success to date is the European Union's (EU) 1998 Aarhus Convention, which the EU saw as a way to deepen democracy and sustainability, especially in new Central and Eastern member states. Currently, the push for environmental access rights worldwide is being promoted by several UN-related agencies, including the Economic Commission for Latin America and the Caribbean (ECLAC). ECLAC began working in 2012 on promoting a regionwide Convention for Latin America and the Caribbean, along with The Access Initiative (TAI), a transnational network of civil society groups. Indeed, with Chile and Costa Rica as leaders, the region was successful in negotiating a treaty in 2018, the Escazú Convention, the region's first legally binding Principle 10 agreement (CEPAL 2018).

The three rights require relevant laws and institutions to have meaning. For access to public information in environmental matters, a government would need to have a Freedom of Information Act (FOIA) and an agency that provides the requested information or explains information denials. For the second right, public participation, typically, governments would create an agency that oversees public input in Environmental Impact Assessments (EIAs) for large-scale public and private projects. The third right, access to justice, requires at a minimum, citizen standing in court if the rights to information or participation are denied by a government agency. In lieu of individual citizen suits, nongovernmental organizations (NGOs) also need standing to sue on environmental matters in court, a condition still not recognized globally. Additionally, several countries, including Chile, have adopted specialized environmental courts or tribunals (Pring and Pring 2016).

In this chapter, environmental justice means not only the procedural access rights but more. EJ means the government also makes it possible for relatively equitable employment of these rights by all. For example, if a group of non-dominant language speakers need project information or want to participate in an EIA, the state must provide materials translated into the group's language. Therefore, in the general literature discussing these three procedural rights and justice, scholars recognize not only the distributional dimension of environmental injustice, i.e. the disproportionate harm faced by the poor and minorities (Agyeman et al. 2003) but also the disproportionate abilities of some groups more than others to employ the rights (Foti 2008**).** Both aspects of EJ must be addressed by governments.

Key questions and methods

Key research questions explored in this study are: (1) Why would individual countries (in this case, Chile) adopt Principle 10 access rights and institutions? (2) Once adopted, how are the rights and institutions implemented and what roles can regional and international organizations play in leveraging implementation? (3) Finally, in the case of Pascua Lama, in what way did these access rights and institutions help deepen democracy and contribute to environmental justice?

I mainly used qualitative methods which included semi-structured interviews with 20 government officials involved in environmental issues, ECLAC officials and activists in environmental NGOs in Chile. Also important were scores from the Environmental Democracy Index (EDI), created by the World Resources Institute and TAI to compare countries' implementation of environmental access rights (http://environmentaldemocracyindex.org/. Accessed 7 March 2015). Finally, I trace how these rights were deployed by activist networks and environmental NGOs in the Pascua Lama case.

Institutions of modern environmental governance in Chile

Chile's economy, like others in Latin America, has been tied to natural resource exploitation from its founding to the present. Chile returned to democracy in 1990, after 17 years under a brutal military junta, which had promoted a strict neoliberal development model during its years in power. Elected governments since 1990 have continued a neoliberal economic orientation and intensive resource extraction, an economic strategy that has frequently provoked conflicts. The first task is to examine Chilean environmental governance since the return to democracy in 1990, especially the adoption and implementation of the institutions of Principle 10 rights. Although some minor environmental activism occurred in the 1980s during the years of the military junta, the government's nearly total embrace of a neoliberal ideology, "relegated environmentalism to the margins both culturally and politically (Carruthers and Rodríguez 2009).

While the main concern of center-left *Concertación* coalition, which ruled Chile from 1990 to 2010, was continued economic growth, it also acknowledged some need to improve sustainability. In 1994, it launched its first attempt at a modern environmental framework with Ley (19.300) de Bases Generales del Medio Ambiente (LBGMA), The Comisión Nacional del Medio Ambiente (CONAMA) was established in stages between 1990 and 1994. Still, these initiatives were weak for a country trying to gain international prestige for good governance and economic success and also trying to gain membership in the OECD (OECD/ECLAC 2005). Therefore, it is essential in this analysis also to consider the role of various supranational organizations in pressuring the country to fully modernize its environmental governance.

The first regional organization to consider as pressuring Chile to adopt access rights was the Inter-American Court of Human Rights (IACHR). The IACHR's *Claude Reyes* decision (September 19, 2006), supported the new activism of the Chilean judiciary by finding the plaintiff had been denied the rights of free expression, due process, and judicial protection. The next year, the Chilean Constitutional Court decided in *Casas Cordero et al. v. The National Customs Service* (August 9, 2007), that Chileans had a right of access to information. Thus, given the OECD's requirement of a FOI law for membership, regional and domestic court rulings, and President Bachelet's support, the Chilean government created the Right to Information Law (20.285) in 2009 to be administered by a newly created *Consejo para la Transparencia*.

Following other OECD requirements, the Bachelet administration continued with a comprehensive reform of the country's environmental management, which included adding the two remaining access rights. In 2010, the legislature amended the 1994 General Environmental Framework Law (19.300) with Law (20.417), containing four major changes. It established for the first time: (1) a Ministry of the Environment, (2) an inter-agency Council of Ministers for Sustainability, (3) an Environmental Inspectorate or *Superintendencia* (SMA), and (4) an Environmental Evaluation Service (SEA). Furthermore, the 2010 amendments called for establishing three environmental courts in Valdivia, Santiago, and Antofagasta, which ultimately commenced with Law 20.600 of 2012.

Finally, a brief discussion of Chile and the International Labor Organization (ILO) Convention 169, covering participation rights of Indigenous people in development projects, is relevant. While ILO 169 was first adopted in 1989, it took Chile 20 years to ratify it. By law, the two Chilean government agencies that oversee Indigenous prior consultations (*consultas previas*) are the National Corporation of Indigenous Development (CONADI) and the Environmental Evaluation Service (SEA). In theory, CONADI's task is to provide technical assistance to Indigenous communities (about 1.5 million Chileans identify as Indigenous), while the SEA's remit is to facilitate citizen participation in evaluating the environmental impacts. In practice, however, this division of labor has not been clearly delineated in regulations. I now turn to the place-based conflict, the case study of Pascua Lama to observe environmental rights in practice.

Case study: the Diaguita and Barrick Gold's Pascua Lama Project

Chile's long-running Pascua Lama mining conflict offers a window into understanding the varying importance of its domestic actors and institutions (related to procedural environmental rights) versus regional, transnational, and international actors and institutions, ultimately, in ending the project. Other scholars have examined this unusual case in which Chile stopped the project after 24 years of negotiations and preparatory work between 1994 and 2018. Urkidi and Walter (2011), Cuadra Montoya (2014), and Li (2018), for example, focused on the role of the domestic and transnational social mobilizations, while Barandiarán (2018), paid special attention to activists' concerns about the area's iconic glaciers. Finally, Haslam (2018), focused on what he labeled Chile's competent bureaucracies and independent judiciary to explain the activists' success in stopping the mining project. My contribution is to show that in addition to these factors – unified, mobilized social activists, highly professional bureaucrats, and independent judiciaries – having the rights and institutions of environmental democracy, which are supported by regional and international organizations (e.g. IACHR, OECD), can provide leverage for enforcing these rights.

The Canadian company, Barrick, the world's largest gold mining firm, first began negotiations over its proposed open-pit project in the Huasco Valley of northern Chile in 1994 and broke ground in 1999. The valley, surrounded by glaciers, lies in the Atacama Region, one of the driest areas on Earth. Pascua Lama would not only have been the world's largest gold mining project with its estimated 17.8 million ounces, but also one of the world's largest silver mining projects with an estimated 635 million ounces. Copper and other minerals of smaller quantities were also involved. Soon after the project was announced, opponents began publicizing the threats. First were the typical challenges of any project associated with mining, the threat of toxic waste for the area's soil and water, but Pascua Lama posed extra challenges. This complex mining venture was not only being undertaken at 15,000 feet, but it would be the world's first bi-national project, with the Pascua part of the project in Chile and the Lama part in Argentina. The project was almost immediately controversial because it involved mining under glaciers, the same glaciers essential for the region's water supply. At first, many of the Huasco Valley's roughly 70,000 residents were generally positive about the project thinking mining might bring jobs to the area (Li 2018).

The project's first Environmental Impact Assessment was approved in 2001 by the National Environmental Commission (CONAMA), but by this time, at least some Huasco Valley residents and many environmentalists were deeply concerned about the dangers the mining venture 80 kilometers away from residents' farms would pose to their water supply. While some valley residents were anxious about possible cyanide spills polluting the river water and surrounding soil, the greater fear was of water shortage or drought due to glacier damage. Strikingly, the first EIA submitted to CONAMA did not even mention glaciers, nor did it mention the company's plan to "move" them. The 2001 impact assessment further worried environmentalists, concerned about earthquake threats from mining the glaciers (specifically breaking the ice with dynamite) in an area already prone to earthquakes.

Barrick delayed the project for three years, at least in part due to a decline in gold prices. In 2004, it submitted a second EIA to the Environmental Commissions for an even larger mine. The government again approved the EIAbut without permission to relocate the glaciers. Between 2001 and 2004, environmentalists' outrage over the project began to gain traction. For example, starting in June 2003, and for several years following, local farmers and environmentalists began holding a "March for Water and Life" in Vallenar, the capital of Huasco Province (Bottaro et al. 2014). Additionally, a transnational network of NGOs opposing the project formed, including Mining Watch Canada and Chile's Latin American Observatory of Environmental Conflicts (Urkidi 2010).

A brief overview of the social structure of the Huasco Valley is essential at this point. For the most part, the Huasco valley has as residents both large landowners, mainly producing grapes and other fruit exports on an industrial scale, and small-scale farmers producing for local consumption and personal use. Both types of farmers, as well as representatives of the Barrick Corporation, became voting members of the valley's privatized Irrigator's Association. Both Li (2018) and Barandiarán (2018) highlight that the larger water users, the large-scale farmers and the mining company, had more votes in the Irrigators' Association than the smaller farmers. As negotiations with Barrick continued, a majority of large farmers continued their support for the project, while most smaller farmers viewed the mining project as a direct threat to their livelihood, especially their water. By mid-2005, as the second EIA was being reviewed by the Chilean government, project opposition grew, with Chilean protestors being joined by foreign environmentalists, especially concerned about continuing threats to the nearby glaciers.

The greatest irony of the Pascua Lama case is that Barrick was the dominant actor helping to legalize the Diaguita Indigenous presence in the Huasco Valley. Many small farmers in the valley considered themselves Indigenous Diaguita, although without formal recognition. In 2004, as Barrick prepared to submit its second EIA to the government, the mining firm began a corporate social responsibility campaign to quell local opposition, mainly from the peasant farmers.

Barrick proposed spending $60 million over 20 years on new infrastructure and other projects. While the larger farmers and local business community welcomed the offer, most of the peasant farmers continued in their disapproval, citing risks of water contamination, but also privatization of resources and loss of culture. These smaller farmers, even with their relative poverty, argued for prevention and not compensation from the company with support from foreign NGOs such as MiningWatch Canada and *Observatorio Latinoamericano de Conflictos Ambientales (OLCA)*. While the larger industrial farming interests would benefit from the infrastructure improvements, the peasant farmers, many cultivating ancestral lands, felt continuing marginalization in negotiations with the mining giant. This was due at least in part because of their self-perception as Indigenous Diaguita, even though Chile did not yet formally recognize "Diaguita" ethnicity. In fact, Chile did not recognize any Indigenous ethnicity until Law No. 19.253 (October 5, 1993). According to anthropologist Fabiana Li (2018), by the early 2000s, about 8,000 people in Northern Chile considered themselves Diaguita. At that time, about 260 families within the larger group considering themselves Diaguita and living in the Huasco Valley (about 3,000 residents), organized the Diaguita Hauascoltino Agricultural Community or CADHA.

In 2006, as part of their corporate social responsibility campaign, Barrick began working with CADHA for formal Indigenous recognition from the government. The company had identified the Diaguita as a distinct ethnic group residing close to their proposed project in their first Environmental Impact Assessment in 2001, notably, the first time this designation of indigeneity had been formally associated with this group. In addition to Barrick's $60 million pledged to the entire Huasco Valley community for maintenance, construction, and irrigation infrastructure improvement, some funds became available for supporting workshops to train new generations of Diaguita artisans.

The project's second EIA received government approval in 2006. Local opposition, including the newly designated Diaguita families, claimed there had been inadequate participation by the smaller water users in the $60 million deal, which had been agreed to by the Irrigators Association before the EIA approval (Segarra 2013). The EIA approval could be fought by opponents under domestic law since, in cases of very large projects, such as Pascua Lama, Chile had required public participation in EIAs since 1994. They could not fight as Indigenous opponents, however, since Chile only signed ILO 169 in 2009.

Therefore, in response to the government's project approval in 2006, CADHA submitted its case to the Inter-American Court on Human Rights (IACHR). The Chilean government responded that this complaint had to go through all domestic courts before the IACHR should have jurisdiction. In 2009, the Santiago-based NGO, *Observatorio Ciudadano,* resubmitted the Diaguita's complaint to the IACHR, claiming Chile's lack of prior consultation with the group was a breach of international law. The Inter-American Court declared the petition admissible, since Chile had signed the Convention; the Commission cited violation of the fundamental right of prior consultation (*consulta previa*) among other violations (Aguilar Cavallo 2013).

Between 2007 and 2013, Barrick continued its project preparations: but during these years, the Diaguita brought another case in Chilean courts against the company fearing threats to their water. In 2012, the community's environmental lawyer, Lorenzo Soto, submitted a case on CADHA's behalf in the Regional Appeals Court in Copiapó. The Court's initial reaction was lukewarm; yet after the partial collapse of the wastewater canal system in January 2013, the Appeals Court ordered a temporary project suspension. "Activists pursued a double strategy of monitoring the firm and using every available institutional avenue to report non-compliance and pressuring regulatory state institutions to be more responsive" (Haslam 2018). In August 2013, lawyer Soto turned to the Chilean Supreme Court requesting a complete end to this project. While full termination did not occur in 2013, the Supreme Court upheld the temporary closure of the mine until completion of all environmental mitigation measures demanded by the government's environmental watchdog, the *Superintendencia* (SMA). In March 2014, the country's new Environmental Tribunal ruled that remediation was incomplete and ordered the SMA to reinstate the sanctioning of Barrick. The SMA alleged 25 violations against Barrick and made clear, at least in this case, the government would enforce its regulations. It would not allow mining to begin until its water management system was complete. The SMA's stance signaled that the Chilean executive and judicial branches would at least take the mining venture seriously consider the numerous public concerns.

At the end of 2016, Chile's Environmental Court in Antofagasta gave permission for a scaled-down version of Pascua Lama to proceed. This was again stopped in March 2017 by the Chilean Supreme Court over new water concerns. On January 17, 2018, the above-ground mining venture was permanently stopped by the Chilean *Superintendencia* but the agency lowered its 2013 maximum fine for violations from $16 million to $11.5 million. Violations included major negative impacts on protected flora and fauna, incomplete monitoring of glaciers, and discharge of acidic fluids into a nearby river. Barrick agreed to pay $20 million to the members of the Huasco Community Irrigation Association, first imposed by the Superintendencia in 2013. This fine was in addition to the $140 million accord won by Barrick investors in the U.S. Federal District Court in Manhattan in 2016. That suit involved the Company's concealing problems at the Chilean mine project and fraudulently inflating the company's market value.

In sum, after more than two decades of negotiations and preparations, Barrick seemed to have accepted the end of the Chilean (Pascua) part of the operation. The Argentine (Lama) portion has only one-fifth of the estimated gold deposits of the original Chile–Argentina plan, but Argentina has proved a more amenable partner than normally pro-business Chile.

Analysis

The case of Pascua Lama offers a complex tale of a daring project proposed for the high Andes, a transnational environmental movement that opposed the project, newly created environmental rights and institutions, and a newly empowered Indigenous community that delayed and finally stopped a mining venture after years of negotiation and litigation. Having a mining project cancelled in Chile is highly unusual and the termination should be seen as a victory for determined social activists as well as for environmental rights and institutions. The case was "widely perceived to have put the democratic era institutions to the test" and, ultimately, the democratic institutions passed (Barandiarán 2018).

It can also be seen as a victory for Indigenous rights and environmental justice. The Diaguita were not the key protagonists in the struggle to stop this environmentally harmful mining project. The key protagonists were members of the network of domestic and transnational environmental NGOs, activists primarily concerned about glacier destruction. The small group of Huasco Valley Diaguita joined the large network of environmentalists and later gained support from domestic and foreign Indigenous rights activists for their cause.

It is important to place this mining struggle in its wider context to fully understand the outcome. During the years of the Pascua Lama negotiations, Chile was simultaneously facing a spate of environmental struggles, for example, the RALCO dam case (Carruthers and Rodríguez 2009) and the CELCO pipeline case (Sepúlveda and Villaroel 2012), taking place in Indigenous territory in southern Chile. While both cases provoked great controversy, the government ultimately allowed both projects to continue. Thus, in the following years, the conflict over the massive HydroAysén hydroelectric project in Patagonia (stopped in 2014) and the end of Pascua Lama (ultimately stopped in 2018) were both highly unusual events in the Chilean context.

These four widely covered environmental conflicts were unfolding as the Chilean government was pursuing its much-desired goal of gaining admittance into the OECD. One of the demands of the organization, however, was that Chile needed to create several institutions of modern environmental governance, which it did from 2008 to 2012. Not only did this involve setting up an Environmental Ministry, but it also involved providing citizens with Principle 10 legal rights and institutions, specifically, access to information, participation, and justice in environmental matters. Chile was motivated by both the search for international prestige, showing the leveraging power of the OECD as well as a domestic search for the proper balance between deepening democracy and maintaining a business-friendly environment. Both factors pushed the country to create P10 institutions that function relatively effectively. Having created access rights at home, Chile, along with Costa Rica, began pursuing regional prestige as environmental leaders starting in 2012. (Under the conservative president, Sebastián Piñera, however, Chile has eschewed this role.) Nevertheless, in 2018, the region passed the Escazú Convention to promote environmental democracy rights throughout Latin America and Caribbean; and by the end of 2020enough countries had ratified the Agreement (11) for the Convention to take effect.

Yet even with environmental democracy rights and ILO 169, our optimism must be tempered since several observers argue the country still lacks a truly effective approach for meaningful Indigenous consultations (OECD 2016, p. 28). Chile's approach resembles what Charles Hale (2005) characterized as "neoliberal multiculturalism" or Cesar Rodriguez-Garavito (2011) labeled "ethnicity. gov." By "neoliberal multiculturalism," Hale suggests neoliberal governance today includes limited recognition of collective (Indigenous) cultural rights, but when combined with neoliberal economic policies, these progressive cultural rights are, essentially, neutralized. For Rodriguez-Garavito, "ethnicity.gov," suggests that the ethno-development approach of the International Financial Institutions with their business-friendly version of prior consultations and juridification of ethnic claims has ambiguous effects at best on Indigenous peoples' rights. Seelau and Seelau (2015) conclude that the Chilean government misunderstands what actions trigger Indigenous consultation and that according to both the ILO and Inter-American Court of Human Rights, participation should occur in all phases of planning and implementation of a project.

Conclusion

As we consider Chile's unusual decision at this point in the Anthropocene, it seems that the government stopped Pascua Lama because it was highly environmentally damaging, involved harm to an Indigenous community, and stimulated an oppositional transnational activist network that brought the country great notoriety. This transnational network was made up of opponents motivated primarily by different concerns, either environmental damage to glaciers or harm to Indigenous communities, but both groups were able to work together to oppose Chile's long-held neoliberal vision of development. While the government must work harder to protect the rights of its Indigenous citizens, the argument put forth here is that P10 rights, skillfully deployed, have afforded Chileans, including Indigenous Chileans, a highly unusual victory against the Pascua Lama mega-project. In sum, the case demonstrates that while strong social movements are essential in socio-environmental conflicts, the tools of environmental democracy, as well as activists leveraging aid from regional and international actors, are also necessary to bring about a just outcome.

References

Aguilar Cavallo, G. (2013). Pascua Lama, Human Rights, and Indigenous Peoples: A Chilean Case Through the Lens of International Law. *Goettingen Journal of International Law*, 5 (1), pp. 215–249.

Agyeman, J., Bullard, R.D., and Evans, B., eds. (2003). *Just Sustainabilities: Development in an Unequal World*. Cambridge, MA: MIT Press.

Barandiarán, J. (2018). *Science and Environment in Chile: The Politics of Expert Advice in a Neoliberal Democracy*. Cambridge, MA: MIT Press.

Bottaro, L., Latta, A., and Sola, M. (2014). La politización del agua en los conflictos por la megaminería: Discursos y resistencia en Chile y Argentina. *European Review of Latin American and Caribbean Studies/ Revista Europea de Estudios Latinoamericanos y del Caribe*, 97 (October), pp. 97–115.

Carruthers, D.V., and Rodríguez, P. (2009). Mapuche Protest, Environmental Conflict and Social Movement Linkage in Chile. *Third World Quarterly*, 30 (June), pp. 743–760.

CEPAL. (2018). *Regional Agreement on Access to Information, Public Participation and Justice in Environmental Matters in Latin America and the Caribbean (UN Symbol LC/PUB.2018/8/*)*. Santiago, Chile: ECLAC.

Cuadra Montoya, X. (2014). Nuevas estrategias de los movimientos indígenas contra el extractivismo en Chile. *Revista CIDOB D'Afers Internacionals*, 105 (April), pp. 141–163.

Foti, J. (2008). *Voice and Choice: Opening the Door to Environmental Democracy*. Washington, DC: World Resources Institute.

Hale, C. (2005). Neoliberal Multiculturalism: The Remaking of Cultural Rights and Racial Dominance in Central America. *PoLAR: Political and Legal Anthropology Review*, 28 (1), pp.10–28.

Haslam, P. (2018). The Two Sides of Pascua Lama: Social Protest, Institutional Responses, and Feedback Loops. *European Review of Latin American and Caribbean Studies// Revista Europea de Estudios Latinoamericanos y del Caribe*, 106 (July-December), pp. 157–182.

Li, F. (2018). Moving Glaciers: Remaking Nature and Mineral Extraction in Chile. *Latin American Perspectives*, 45 (5), pp. 102–119.

Observatorio Ciudadano. (2016). *Canadian Mining Projects in the Territory of the Diaguitas Huasco Altinos Agricultural Community in Chile: Human Rights Impact Assessment*. https://observatorio.cl/2199-2/. Accessed 7 March 2020.

OECD/ECLAC. (2005). *OECD Economic Performance Reviews (keep "s"): Chile 2005*. Paris: OECD.

OECD/ECLAC. (2016). *Chile: 2016 Economic Performance Review*. Paris: OECD.

Pring, G., and Pring, C. 2016. *Environmental Courts and Tribunals: A Guide for Policy Makers*. Nairobi: UN Environment.

Rodriguez Garavito C. (2011). Symposium: Struggle, Identity, and the Collective: Ethnicity.gov, Global Governance, Indigenous Peoples, and the Right to Prior Consultations in Social Minefields. *Indiana Journal of Global Legal Studies*, 18, pp. 263–305.

Seelau, L., and Seelau, R. (2015). When I Want Your Opinion, I'll Give it to You: How Governments Support the Indigenous Right to Consultation in Theory but not in Practice. *Cardozo Journal of International Law*, 23, pp. 547–575.

Segarra, M. (2013). Challenging Neoliberalism and Development: Human Rights and the Environment in Latin America. In K. Hite and M. Ungar eds. *Sustaining Human Rights in the Twenty-First Century: Strategies from Latin America*, 1st ed. Washington, DC: Woodrow Wilson Center, pp. 303–340.

Sepúlveda, C., and Villarroel, P. (2012). Swans, Conflicts, and Resonance: Local Movements and the Reform of Chilean Environment Institutions. *Latin American Perspectives*, 39 (4), pp. 189–200.

United Nations Conference on Environment and Development (UNCED). (1992). *Agenda 21, Rio Declaration, Forest Principles*. New York: United Nations.

Urkidi, L. 2010. A Glocal Environmental Movement Against Gold Mining: Pascua Lama in Chile. *Ecological Economics*, 70: 219–227.

Urkidi, L., and Walter, M. (2011). Dimensions of Environmental Justice in Anti-Gold Mining Movements in Latin America. *Geoforum*, 42, pp. 683–695.

World Resources Institute (WRI) and the Access Initiative (TAI). (2015). *Environmental Democracy Index*. Washington, D.C.: World Resources Institute.

5

TOWARDS SOCIO-ECOLOGICAL INCLUSION

Scaling up housing innovation in Vienna

Michael Friesenecker and Roberta Cucca

Introduction

The relation between environmental quality and residential choices and opportunities is a longstanding issue and has consistently affected the distribution of different social groups in the urban context. Throughout history, gardens and parks have always characterized the most affluent parts of urban areas, whereas the most polluted and unhealthy areas have been spaces of spatial segregation for the most deprived social groups. Over the years, numerous studies have reported that minorities or socioeconomically disadvantaged people are exposed to greater environmental harm, being concentrated in areas affected by high levels of pollution. Environmental justice (EJ) scholars and activists have gradually exposed the mechanisms and processes that lead to the residential segregation of low-income groups in contaminated areas (Bullard 1990).

Beside these investigations, more recently, a new research topic is gaining momentum in the EJ literature (Cucca 2020). It focuses on the other side of the coin: the unequal access to beneficial environmental factors such as urban green space, clean air, waterfronts, biodiversity, good aesthetics, and community resources. In fact, cities represent key sites concerning the production and consumption of commodities and transformative technologies associated with the Anthropocene. The unequal distribution of these benefits is strongly connected on the one hand with the self-segregation of affluent groups in urban areas characterized by high environmental standards, such as eco-districts (Caprotti 2014), and on the other with the displacement of low-income groups due to rising housing costs in areas affected by green urban renewal and ecological gentrification (Dooling 2008). Nevertheless, considerable work is still required to build an understanding of how social justice or equity in an urban context is related to climate or sustainability in the Anthropocene. Providing good environmental standards and enhancing local conditions for ecological innovation while also promoting housing affordability and fighting against segregation should represent a priority, but the debate on this issue remains underdeveloped both in the academic literature and in the political debate on housing solutions.

In order to fill this gap, this chapter will explore the socio-spatial implications of innovative housing projects oriented towards sustainability standards by analyzing two case studies in Vienna. The Austrian capital is an interesting case study to understand the relations between green urban renewal and housing affordability. In comparison to many other cities in Europe, in Vienna a very large part of the housing stock is publicly subsidized (social or municipal housing) and a relevant part of the private rental market is subjected to rent control. In this specific context, many housing projects have experimented with new solutions for urban sustainability by promoting bottom-up initiatives and providing ecological innovation in the social housing stock. We will investigate outputs related both to distributional and procedural aspects of environmental socio-spatial justice connected to these housing projects, with a specific focus on housing accessibility, diversity in the composition of the residents and the development of different socio-ecological orientation and practices.

The chapter is organized as follows. We discuss the state-of-the-art of the literature developed on the socio-spatial implications of urban greening followed by a description of the case studies. Finally, we will provide some concluding remarks on opportunities and challenges characterizing these projects in terms of EJ.

State of the art

To better understand the state of the art of the literature developed on the socio-spatial implications of urban greening, two branches of literature are particularly helpful. The first refers to the concept of 'green or ecological gentrification' (Dooling 2008). The process of green gentrification is believed to be initiated by greening initiatives that create or restore environmental amenities (e.g. renewal of parks, waterfront redevelopment, urban retrofitting), drawing in wealthier groups of residents and pushing out lower-income residents, leading to gentrification (Checker 2011). Green gentrification studies emphasize two important trends related to urban justice: on the one hand, inequalities in relation to EJ in terms of the access of low-income groups to the new environmental amenities created through renewal and local innovation; on the other, to growing spatial inequalities due to increasing housing costs in areas affected by sustainability policies, as reported in many studies across the world (Beretta and Cucca 2019).

Another interesting body of literature focuses on the processes of self-segregation of affluent groups in new developments branded as eco-districts and eco-cities. Eco-cities can be seen as a continuation of planning and architectural and design trends that have sought to reconcile nature and the city since the nineteenth century. Nonetheless, they also contain elements that are novel, because the creation of eco-districts has been suggested as a way to combat urban sprawl and associated socio-environmental issues, in particular environmental degradation and spatial segregation. However, the development of eco-districts has been criticized for their high costs and their failure to meet expectations with respect to increased environmental quality (Holden et al. 2015). Moreover, housing and services are often affordable to only a small elite. Consequently, spatial segregation as well as social inequality may increase.

Within the framework of the literature developed on the socio-spatial consequences of greening, this chapter will instead focus on an under-investigated topic: the socio-spatial justice implications of collaborative housing projects oriented to reaching sustainability standards and linking social and environmental innovation. Among these projects, co-housing initiatives are the most popular. They are usually defined as intentional communities in which reducing one's environmental impact and living in a more sustainable manner is an accepted goal (Jarvis 2011), "a type of intentional, collaborative housing in which residents actively participate in the design and operation of their neighborhoods" (Cohousing Association of the United States, CAUS 2014). While there is a developed literature on the potential of these projects in terms of socio-ecological innovation, few investigations have highlighted implications in terms of urban justice.

As regards their innovative potential, urban forms of intentional communities (Metcalf 2012) are often highly innovative as they are based on a bottom-up approach to design and management, mainly oriented towards a de-growth pattern of socio-ecological innovation. Indeed, the trend of reducing environmental impacts has already been identified across a number of studies, highlighting the importance of everyday consumption practices, particularly related to food, the household, and transportation as well as the reduction of Carbon footprints. However, already many studies have illustrated issues related to the socio-spatial justice implications of these intentional communities, not least that despite their aspirations to achieve a socially mixed structure, co-housing inhabitants are predominantly well-educated, middle-income households (Bresson and Denefle 2015). Nevertheless, intentional communities have been perceived in many contexts as opportunities for vulnerable urban areas. Crucial differences among co-housing projects lie in their everyday practices and design features, such as whether to open their common gardens or services to outsiders or not (Ruiu 2014). Local authorities' role has been considered vital in defining different levels of inclusiveness of co-housing through planning practices (Droste 2015). However, local authorities also seem to have learned lessons from the social and environmental practices developed within these intentional communities and have attempted to scale up such innovations as well.

One interesting case study by which to understand the socio-spatial implications of these innovative projects and the potential of scaling up innovations is the city of Vienna. In recent years, the municipal administration has been subsidizing different kinds of housing projects characterized by socio-ecological innovation, sharing a common principle (for example an orientation towards sustainability) but also showing very deep differences in terms of certain management and access procedures. In this chapter we aim to understand the opportunities and shortcomings of these projects in terms of socio-spatial justice by analyzing two different initiatives. The first is a *Baugruppen* project, an international community characterized by a quite radical, self-determined approach to collaborative housing. The second is a social housing project that focuses – among other communal infrastructure – on the provision of urban gardening infrastructure as a stimulus for collaborative housing.

Socio-ecological housing in Vienna

Historically, Vienna's urban development and housing policy is characterized by strong public intervention. Communal infrastructure and collaborative housing were central elements of the early municipal housing estates built during the era of Red Vienna (1922–1934). Although intended to serve social needs, the top-down approach of Red Vienna led to the construction of schools, libraries, green spaces and common washing and laundry rooms. Nevertheless, from a contemporary perspective, this communal infrastructure also enhances access to green space and fosters the sharing of infrastructure and short distances in everyday life.

However, the City of Vienna's current social housing approach picks up this historical legacy under different circumstances. Having withdrawn from the direct construction of municipal housing, social housing is today primarily built by big, limited-profit housing associations (LPHA) and to a lesser extent by nonprofit cooperatives (Lang and Novy 2011). Consequently, Vienna's policy in urban development has increasingly shifted towards a steering role, focusing on land allocation, subsidizing housing construction, and ensuring high-quality standards. To achieve the latter, developer competitions were introduced in 1995, applicable to building lots owned by the City or to projects that exceed the erection of 500 apartments. Until 2009 it was based on economic, architectural, and ecological criteria and aimed to produce social housing with high ecological standards, such as low-energy consumption standards of the building envelope, energy-efficient heating, and the provision of high-quality green spaces at reasonable rents. However, in 2009 the City re-emphasized collaborative housing aspects with the introduction of "social sustainability" as the fourth pillar in developer competitions. This led to a renaissance of top-down planned communal infrastructure, highlighting the provision of socio-ecological housing rather than the participation of residents. Nevertheless, in 2013 some of the developer competitions became a "dialogue-oriented" two-stage form of competition with the goal of integrating the scale of the neighborhood into the planning phase. The first step determines the winners of single building lots, while the second step advances the single projects in relation to other building lots or to the existing infrastructure of the surrounding neighborhood.

In contrast to the long history and top-down approach in large-scale social housing, *Baugruppen* are rather recent phenomena in Vienna's urban development. *Baugruppen* can be broadly defined as associations of citizens that initiate, plan, and (co-)construct self-determined housing for self-use, communitarian services, and collaborative housing. Over the last 30 years, three main types of *Baugruppen* have evolved in Vienna, which differ in their legal status and state support (Gruber and Lang 2018). First, the participatory model is similar to the social housing approach, but future residents actively participate in the planning processes of communal spaces and individual apartments. A limited-profit housing association finances, constructs, and owns the building, while future residents – organized as an independent tenant association – rent apartments and self-organize daily life in communal spaces. Second, the "Autonomous Baugruppe: Wohnheim" receives a specific subsidy, originally meant for dormitories or elderly homes (*Wohnheim*), which enables the self-organized management of the building by tenant associations as "a sort of mini-cooperative" (Gruber and Lang 2018, p. 50). The house is owned and managed by a tenant association comprising all the tenants, who rent individual apartments from the association. The subsidy facilitates the implementation of social and cultural infrastructure thanks to less strict building code regulations. Initially developed during the planning process of Vienna's iconic *Baugruppe* Sargfabrik in the 1990s, this model has become the blueprint for *Baugruppen* in Vienna. Third, inspired by the German *Mietshäuser Syndikat* (Tenement Syndicate), a newly established *Baugruppen* model has recently emerged in Vienna, which radically emphasizes collective organization and collectively owned and financed housing projects (see Gruber and Lang 2018). However, lately more mixed models have emerged, and a clear-cut classification is no longer easy to make. In particular, the financing of *Baugruppen* often relies on a broad mix of bank loans, direct credits, subsidies from the municipality, and major investments of future tenants.

Consequently, *Baugruppen* are rather homogeneous in socioeconomic and sociodemographic terms: usually higher educated groups equipped with sufficient financial capabilities and time feel able to participate in such projects (Temel et al. 2009), whereas new social housing caters more to low- and mid-income groups due to broad income limits (Franz and Gruber 2018). Furthermore, land allocation policies might result in greater socio-spatial divisions, as the construction of new large-scale social housing in urban development areas on the outskirts of Vienna has produced working-class neighborhoods since the 1970s. Only recently has new social housing been constructed on mixed or middle-class-oriented inner-city brownfield sites (such as Sonnwendviertel or Nordwestbahnhof) as well as eco-districts (Aspern). The City has sought to allocate land to *Baugruppen* in these mixed-class developments with the aim of creating viable neighborhoods (Temel and Weiser 2015).

Sharing is caring, or "just" using? Socio-ecological implications of selected co-housing models

In order to compare the socio-ecological implications of the two collaborative housing models, we have chosen two exemplary projects that show a strong ecological orientation, although neighborhood characteristics also contributed to the selection. The *Baugruppe* Wohnen im Grünen Markt (The Green Market) has been chosen because the mixed-use design of workspaces, shops, offices, and collaborative housing in one building offers an interesting case by which to investigate socio-ecological practices. It is located in the inner-city development area of Sonnwendviertel, which is a mixed-use and mixed-class neighborhood (Figure 5.1). The social housing project Auf lange Sicht (In the Long View) has been chosen because, among the provision of other communal infrastructure, urban gardening infrastructure aimed to catalyze collaborative housing. In contrast to the *Baugruppen* project, In the Long View is located in a working-class neighborhood on the southern outskirts of Vienna, mainly characterized by large social housing premises from the 1960s, 1970s, and 2000s.

The Green Market was realized in the form of the participatory model in co-construction with a limited-profit developer. Tenants pay substantial rents and cost contributions, partly because the construction of the building was not subsidized, but costs are comparatively high mainly due to the large number of

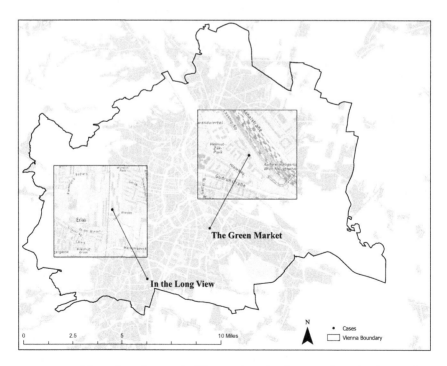

FIGURE 5.1   Map of study area in Vienna, Austria. Cartographer: Louisa Markow, Geospatial Centroid at Colorado State University. Data Source: Esri, Delorme, HERE and basemap.at.

common spaces (Table 5.1). In addition payments for equipment as well as the participatory planning process was paid by the tenants. The Green Market is split into two main areas: 30% representing workspaces and shops on the lower stories and around 70% comprising residential space with 50 apartments on the upper stories (Wohnen im Grünen Markt 2019). The Green Market features a substantial amount of communal infrastructure for collaborative living and for socio-ecological practices, with 350 m² comprising an atelier, a library, a community kitchen, a laundry room, a lounge, a cinema, a sauna, a yoga room, a workshop, a children's playroom, and a youth room. Two rooftop terraces equipped with a playground, beds for urban gardening and relaxing areas constitute 700 m² additional outdoor space for communal use.

As a consequence of the co-planning approach, usage of The Green Market's communal spaces is limited to members of the tenant association because the association rents these spaces from the landlord. To cover these costs, individual renters pay a monthly fee as well as a fee for equipping the communal spaces. Renters are also assigned to co-organize the interior design of one communal space.

The case of the large-scale social housing premises In the Long View consists of 323 subsidized apartments, of which 108 are smart apartments catering to low to mid-income residents with diverse backgrounds. Smart apartments have been introduced to generate more affordable housing as capital contributions – a traditional obstacle to low-income groups – are lowered, while their compact ground floor plans aim to contribute to resource-friendly behavior, too. To compensate for the negative effects of smaller apartments, the City demands social and green amenities. However, In the Long View not only emphasizes compensating spaces, but additionally emphasizes the integrative aspect of urban gardening and communal spaces. However, as this project was planned top-down by architects as well as the limited-profit housing associations supervised by a two-stage developer competition, the location and size of collaborative and compensating infrastructure was already pre-defined at an early stage. Urban gardening infrastructure was implemented on the ground floor as arable spaces for tenants, a terrace with raised beds and common greenhouses for the winter. Moreover, bike storage rooms for 720 bikes, two laundry rooms, four multi-purpose communal rooms including community kitchens and/or playing zones for children, four terraces with different purposes and amenities, extensive public green spaces with edible plants, and a public children's playground are integral parts of the project.

Table 5.1 highlights how the different planning approaches of the selected projects produced different socio-ecological practices. The extensive amount of common spaces in combination with the collective planning process fostered "sharing" and "swapping" as two key socio-ecological practices in The Green Market. First, the co-planning of the communal spaces by the tenants initiated a common understanding of sharing possibilities, leading to smaller individual apartments. Furthermore, the tenant group implemented private car sharing,

TABLE 5.1 Comparison of distributional and procedural aspects of the selected projects

The Green Market	*In the Long View*
Aspects of procedural justice	
High participatory possibilities:	Limited participatory possibilities:
• Co-planning of green and communal infrastructure with architects • Early integration of shared use and swapping scenarios in the planning of communal spaces by future tenants	• Top–down planning of green and communal infrastructure • Participation in organizing the use and equipping after the provision of pre-standardized communal spaces (supported by consultants) • Participatory planning of neighborhood-wide community garden
Aspects of distributional justice	
Housing costs	
• Rent: €11.62/m² • Capital contribution: €700/m² • Association fee: €40 per month and adult • Fee for equipping and planning: approximately €5,000 per adult	Regularly subsidized apartments • Rent: €6.95/m² • Capital contribution: €459/m² smart apartments • Rent: €7.5/m² • Capital contribution: €60/m²
Housing allocation	
• By the tenant association based on reports of individual interviews • Aiming at a sociodemographic mix	• Income limits apply to all apartments • Allocation is split between the City and the developer • Additional criteria for (smart) apartments that are allocated by the City apply
Diversity	
Rather homogeneous:	Rather mixed:
• Higher education backgrounds • Mid- to high incomes • Mostly Western European	• Lower to high education backgrounds • Low to mid-incomes • Diverse immigration backgrounds
Socio-ecological orientation and practices	
• Mixed-use: living and working in one building	• Urban gardening as leading theme: provision of garden beds, glass houses, green spaces with eatable plants, and community garden

(Continued)

TABLE 5.1 (*Continued*) Comparison of distributional and procedural aspects of the selected projects

The Green Market	*In the Long View*
• Sharing of communal infrastructure: community kitchen, laundry rooms, playgrounds, rooftop terraces, workshops, information technology (IT) infrastructure, bike and car sharing, food cooperation • Smaller individual apartments and alternative living arrangements (cluster living) • Reuse: Swapping of everyday objects	• Provision of affordable but ecological individual apartments (smart apartments) including compensating spaces for smaller apartments • (Yet) mainly using rather than sharing the communal spaces: laundry rooms, rooftop terrace, playgrounds, multi-purpose community rooms, sports hall, and gardening infrastructure

Socio-spatial effects

• Access to communal and green infrastructure is limited to a homogeneous group of higher status • Only limited provision of amenities to the wider neighborhood of similar population structure	• Access to communal and green infrastructure for a heterogeneous group of residents • Public green space and communal spaces are also accessible to the wider, working-class neighborhood

Own compilation based on Wohnfonds Wien (2017) and Wohnen im Grünen Markt (2019)

cargo bike sharing, shared IT infrastructure without individual connections, and a food cooperation. Second, swapping and reuse were inscribed into the physical space, enabling the nonprofit swapping, and sharing of books, media, and other everyday objects such as clothes and kitchen utilities. By contrast, the top–down planning approach of In the Long View predefined all common spaces and tenants were not included in the planning phase. To overcome this shortcoming, a two-year lasting participatory process aims to make "dwellers to neighbors" (Wohnfond Wien 2017) and consultant companies support the tenants in organizing the equipping and usage of the common spaces. During this participatory process, the urban gardening infrastructure was allocated to interested households using the "first come, first served" principle. Given the great demand, residents have already been placed on waiting lists. So tenants teamed up and started to collaboratively plant their garden beds. However, a major distinction from the *Baugruppen* example was the use of common spaces other than garden beds. The ecological rationale for sharing gave way to a social rationale, with common spaces used for birthday celebrations, sports activities, and cultural activities as opposed to shared activities in everyday life. In addition, an online booking system through which individual tenants can book rooms for specific time slots hindered the development of sharing practices. Sharing is therefore not (yet) an essential aspect and even though the consultant companies have pursued collaborative aspects such as private car sharing, early meetings have already been postponed due to low interest.

During the planning process of The Green Market, the divide between the workspaces and the residential areas raised questions about the accessibility of communal spaces. As most of the communal infrastructure has been co-planned between the architects and the tenant association, potential entrepreneurs as well as renters who are not part of the tenant association have been excluded from using those spaces. In contrast to the "exclusive" common spaces mentioned above, the *Machhalle* (which literally translates as the "Hall of Doing") is a semi-public space on the ground floor that serves as a place for local everyday supply, a lively neighborhood center and an event location. Attached to this is the *Scala Publica*, which is a semi-public staircase that can also be used as an event location. A forecourt and a (green) playground next to the building open the house up to the pedestrian zone of the neighborhood. The limited accessibility of the common spaces to a rather homogeneous group of higher socio-economic status and the (limited) provision of green amenities to a similar neighborhood compromises the distributive effects of The Green Market, while the collaborative focus on sharing, swapping, and "mixed use" to reduce commuting and leisure mobility positively enhances ecological behavior. By contrast, the collaborative housing approach for the social housing premise is not limited to the building itself. The second stage of the developer competition focused specifically on the integrative planning of five subsidized large-scale developments that form the newly founded neighborhood Erlaaer Flur. As a consequence of this planning approach, each of the five large-scale buildings provide one communal space to the neighborhood, increasing the project's distributive effects. Tenants of the neighborhood are able to reserve a sports hall, a neighborhood kitchen, an atelier/workshop, and a seminar room via an online booking system and can access the rooms via a chip-based system. Nevertheless, the core of this new neighborhood is a neighborhood garden that aims to foster the "community aspects of gardening in large-scale social housing" (Wohnfonds Wien 2017, p. 268). Tenants can participate in the planning and the construction of the neighborhood garden, which will be open to every tenant of the neighborhood and planting will be organized in a collective manner, refraining from "private" beds. Uniquely – even for Vienna – the investment costs of the community garden are financed by a collective fund shared by the neighborhood's five housing associations.

Discussing socio-ecological practices: from whom, for whom?

What can we learn from these two examples in terms of socio-ecological justice? From a procedural socio-ecological justice perspective, the bottom–up planning approach of the *Baugruppen* project generated a substantial amount of communal spaces. In addition, the planning of communal spaces at an early stage enabled tight integration with scenarios of lived socio-ecological practices at later stages of living together. The planned infrastructure is therefore more compatible with smaller apartment designs due to shared spaces, but also sharing and swapping practices in the everyday lives of tenants. These socio-ecological practices are clearly oriented towards a de-growth approach to greening. However, the distributional aspect of socio-ecological justice is rather limited for *Baugruppen*. First of all, the common spaces that allow for environmentally friendly practices are limited to the tenant association. Moreover, the limitation of *Baugruppen* to higher socioeconomic groups and higher educational levels adds up to a rather elitist production of housing and ecological practices.

Nevertheless, the top-down approach of the social housing project shows strong distributional aspects of EJ. Access to environmental green spaces in the selected social housing premises is more equal as social housing in Vienna includes lower and mid-income groups. Furthermore, the efficient use of physical space in the form of compact apartments includes environmentally friendly aspects. The distributional aspects of EJ are also opened up to the wider neighborhood, as the building provides it with public green spaces and communal, social infrastructure. However, aspects of procedural justice are limited to organizational questions of use and equipment after moving into the building. The use of communal and green infrastructure is more important to tenants than sharing and swapping practices. Regardless, the support of consultants seeks to establish such practices, additionally by providing possibilities to participate in the planning of an "iconic" neighborhood garden. The "just" provision and use of amenities are stronger than sharing practices oriented towards de-growth for this model.

In sum, these case studies help to shed light on some relevant aspects of the debate surrounding urban greening and urban justice. The first contribution is related to new research needs emerging in the scientific literature regarding the socio-spatial implications of greening. So far, the debate has primarily focused on the possible negative impacts of urban greening on housing affordability and socio-spatial segregation (Haase et al. 2017). Instead, this chapter has attempted to critically analyze some possible socio-ecological practices that are able to combine urban justice and ecological innovation. The second contribution is related to the literature developed on intentional communities and co-housing practices. The Green Market confirms some criticalities already explored in the literature: these communities may be affected by self-segregation processes, bringing limited distributional benefits in terms of environmental and social justice. However, we agree with Droste (2015) that local authorities are crucial in defining different levels of inclusiveness of co-housing through planning practices. In the case of In the Long View, local authorities have learned relevant lessons in terms of social and environmental practices developed in *Baugruppen* and other kinds of intentional communities. Moreover, they have been able to scale up innovations, using housing policies to provide greater opportunities for inclusiveness and justice.

Although the case study of Vienna represents a peculiar example in the Western European framework due to the legacy of the Red Vienna model as concerns housing policies, it nonetheless illustrates the possibility of developing an alternative, experimental approach to housing production, enhancing our understanding of how socio-spatial justice and environmental justice can be intertwined in the Anthropocene.

References

Beretta, I. and Cucca, R., 2019. Ecological gentrification: A European perspective. *Sociologia urbana e rurale*. Vol. 119, pp. 7–10.

Bresson, S. and Denefle, S., 2015. Diversity of self-managed cohousing initiatives in France. *Urban Research and Practice*. Vol. 8, no. 1, pp. 5–16.

Bullard, R., 1990. *Dumping in Dixie: Race, Class, and Environmental Quality*. Boulder: Westview Press.

Caprotti, F., 2014. Eco-urbanism and the eco-city, or, denying the right to the city? *Antipode*. Vol. 46, pp. 1285–1303.

Checker, M., 2011. Wiped out by the "greenwave": Environmental gentrification and the paradoxical politics of urban sustainability. *City & Society*. Vol. 23, no. 2, pp. 210–229.

Cohousing Association of the United States (CAUS), 2014. *What Is Cohousing?* Cohousing Association of the United States. http://www.cohousing.org/what_is_cohousing [Accessed 28 April 2015].

Cucca, R., 2020. Spatial segregation and the quality of the local environment in contemporary cities. In: S. Musterd, ed. *Handbook of Urban Segregation*. Cheltenham: Edward Elgar, pp. 185–199.

Dooling, S., 2008. Ecological gentrification: Re-negotiating justice in the city. *Critical Planning*. Vol. 15, pp. 40–57.

Droste, C., 2015. German co-housing: An opportunity for municipalities to foster socially inclusive urban development? *Urban Research and Practice*. Vol. 8, no. 1, pp. 79–92.

Franz, Y. and Gruber, E., 2018. Wohnen "für alle" in Zeiten der Wohnungsmarktkrise? *Standort*. Vol. 42, no. 2, pp. 98–104.

Gruber, E. and Lang, R., 2018. Collaborative housing models in Vienna through the lens of social innovation. In: G. Van Bortel, V. Gruis, J. Nieuwenhuijzen and B. Pluijmers, eds. *Affordable Housing Governance and Finance: Innovations, Partnerships and Comparative Perspectives*. London: Routledge, pp. 42–58.

Haase, D., Kabisch, S. and Haase, A., 2017. Greening cities: To be socially inclusive? About the alleged paradox of society and ecology in cities. *Habitat International*. Vol. 64, pp. 41–48.

Holden, M., LI, C. and Molina, A., 2015. The emergence and spread of ecourban neighbourhoods around the world. *Sustainability*. Vol. 7, no. 9, pp. 11418–11437.

Jarvis, H., 2011. Saving space, sharing time: Integrated infrastructures of daily life in cohousing. *Environment and Planning. Part A*. Vol. 43, no. 3, pp. 560–577.

Lang, R. and Novy, A., 2011. Housing cooperatives and social capital: The case of Vienna. *SRE – Discussion Papers*. Vol. 2, pp. 1–46. https://epub.wu.ac.at/3207/ [Accessed 05 March 2020].

Metcalf, B., 2012. Utopian struggle: Preconceptions and realities of intentional communities. In: M. Andreas and F. Wagner, eds. *Realizing Utopia: Ecovillage Endeavours and Academic Approaches*. Munich: Rachel Carson Centre, pp. 21–28.

Ruiu, M., 2014. Differences between cohousing and gated communities: A literature review. *Sociological Inquiry*. Vol. 84, no. 2, pp. 316–335.

Temel, R., Lorbek, m., Ptaszyńska, A. and Wittinger, D., 2009. Baugemeinschaften in Wien, Endbericht 1 Potenzialabschätzung und Rahmenbedingungen. *Studie im Auftrag der Stadt Wien, Magistratsabteilung 50 – Wohnbauförderung, Referat für Wohnbauforschung.* https://www.wohnbauforschung.at/index.php?inc=download&id=5394 [Accessed 17 October 2019].

Temel, R. and Weiser, C., 2015. Baugruppen in Aspern Seestadt. Chronologie einer planerischen innovation. In: Verein Initiative für gemeinschaftliches Bauen und Wohnen, eds. *Gemeinsam Bauen Wohnen in der Praxis. Workshopreihe 2014 über, für und mit Baugruppen in Wien*, pp. 20–29. https://www.aspern-seestadt.at/jart/prj3/aspern /data/downloads/Gemeinsam_bauen_und_wohnen_aspern_Seestadt_2017-07-10 _1507441.pdf [Accessed 05 March 2020].

Wohnen im Grünen Markt, 2019. https://wohnen.gruenermarkt.at/ [Accessed 20 October 2019].

Wohnfonds Wien, 2017. *Bauträgerwettbewerbe 2016. Qualitätswettbewerbe im Wiener Wohnbau.* Wolkersdorf: Wohnfonds_wien.

6

FROM WATER INSECURITY TO WATER INJUSTICE

How tourism produces environmental injustice along Nicaragua's "Emerald Coast"

Sarah T. Romano and G. Thomas LaVanchy

Introduction

The global trends of neoliberalism and anthropogenic climate change interact to produce complex landscapes of environmental injustice (EJ). It is only recently, however, that scholars and activists have expanded EJ frames of analysis to capture the production of environmental injustices in diverse global contexts and in relation to global climate change. This extension has entailed broadening the conceptual underpinnings of EJ to explain new and shifting configurations of injustice. This is particularly relevant to the topic of water and its centrality to the notion of the Anthropocene in that humans are a "major force" in both "disturbing" and "modifying" water cycles in this epoch (Gleeson et al. 2020, p. 1).

This chapter examines tourism as a driver of environmental injustice along Nicaragua's southwest Pacific coast of Tola (see Figure 6.1). Mirroring trends in neighboring Costa Rica, the tourism sector in Nicaragua experienced growth in the 1990s in relation to neoliberal economic reforms that sought to increase foreign investment and jumpstart economic development (Babb 2004). Importantly, an expanding tourism industry has produced new geographies of water insecurity along the coast through reconfiguring the distribution of freshwater to the detriment of local residents (LaVanchy 2017). While tourism inherently affects water use and allocation regimes, the industry's distributional impacts must be understood as embedded within, and affected by, complex ecological, political, and economic contexts.

The case of stark environmental injustice discussed in this chapter confirms the importance of place-based research to reveal and understand varied forms of water-related conflict. Our research found several intersecting contextual factors to be important for understanding how tourism has generated complex geographies of what we call water injustice in both distributive and procedural terms.

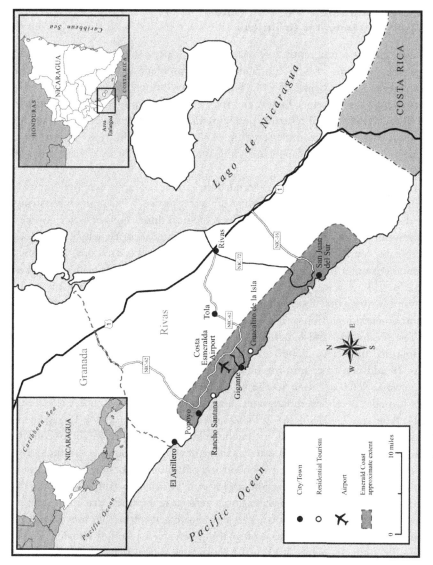

FIGURE 6.1   Map of study area in Nicaragua. Cartography: Michael P. Larson.

These include prolonged drought, the selective implementation of national laws, and local political economies of tourism. Furthermore, exploratory research reveals that local responses to compromised access to freshwater have taken on a largely ad hoc, reactionary character that focuses on obtaining new sources of freshwater rather than resisting resource dispossession. Thus, a key takeaway from this chapter is that responses *to* environmental injustice in Tola do not reflect the pursuit *of* environmental justice. We end the chapter with an exploration of how tourism research can play a role in achieving more just and sustainable expressions of tourism in the context of the climate crisis.

Theoretical framework: from water (in)security to water (in)justice

Climate change is inherently an environmental justice issue – it reflects both vast disparities in terms of who contributes to the problem as well as "the uneven distribution of detrimental effects" (Rasmussen & Pinho 2016, p. 8). Indeed, climate change has introduced a new environmental justice imperative (Stallworthy 2009) to environmental research, policy-making, and activism. The current climate crisis demands an understanding of the equity implications of changing social and physical landscapes, including the production of *water* insecurity, at global and local scales.

In recent years, scholars have extended the concept of environmental injustice to the study of water under the banner of "water justice." Through emphasizing the distributional, procedural, as well as ecological dimensions of water governance, water justice diverges from the concept of water security, which references "acceptable level[s] of water-related risks to humans and ecosystems" and draws attention to water in terms of both quantity and quality for multiple uses (Bakker 2012, p. 914). A water justice framework arguably serves to enrichen the study of water security through placing emphasis on the distributional implications of environmental pollution or resource scarcity.

The production and experience of water injustice typically reflect patterns of injustice in society along social axes including race, ethnicity, gender, and class. In addition to examining inequitable resource distribution, water justice frameworks lend attention to the procedural aspects of justice; in short, who gets to make decisions about water, how, and with what outcomes (Perreault 2014; Romano 2019; Sultana 2018; Zwarteveen & Boelens 2014). Engagement in decision-making – whether via public policy processes, private sector consultations, or community-based water management arrangements – can be highly fraught. Indeed, mere "participation" in and of itself may not empirically constitute the achievement of greater justice (Joy et al. 2014). However, an emphasis on the procedural dimensions of water justice reflects recognition that communities of water users and de facto managers have coalesced into social movements to challenge water policies or decision-making perceived as unjust (Boelens 2008; Perreault 2006; Romano 2012, 2019; Spronk et al. 2012). Struggles for water justice include marginalized actors' demands to engage or participate in decision-making; thus, these efforts must be examined within water justice frameworks.

Tourism has an inherent relationship to issues of water justice in the Anthropocene because it often disrupts the availability, quality, and allocation of water through its (re)shaping of physical and social landscapes. Tourism development and industry operation extract water for cleaning, landscaping, filling pools, and maintaining golf courses, amongst other uses. This extraction and use often produce an inequitable distribution of water, with potentially severe consequences in water scarce regions (Gössling 2001; Rico-Amoros et al. 2009). Dispossession of critical resources like land and water through tourism may be "in situ," meaning it need not physically displace residents in order to constitute a loss of access to resources necessary for lives and livelihoods. Moreover, tourism's production of injustice has discursive dimensions that scholars have described as the violence of *erasing* people and places (Devine & Ojeda 2017). For example, tourism's reshaping of coastal landscapes often includes storytelling and re-naming as erasure or masking of social realities (see, e.g., LaVanchy et al. 2020; Torres & Momsen 2005). Legal frameworks also loom large in the production of injustice. Like other forms of industrial expansion or development, the tourism sector has been facilitated by state policy across national contexts (see, e.g., Bavinck et al. 2017; Borras et al. 2012; LaVanchy et al. 2017).

The variety of responses to resource dispossession constitutes one of the justifications for local, or place-based, examinations of environmental justice. While many instances of resource grabbing and water injustice involve active contestation of how resources are being appropriated, others do not involve an active or highly visible contestation.[1] Hall et al. suggest that local "resistance" to grabbing must be explored in a context and case-specific fashion to reveal "*differentiated impacts* and *variegated political reactions*" (2015, p. 468, emphasis in original).[2] Moreover, a lack of visible reaction does not mean conflict (or injustice) is absent in a given context. Houdret defines conflict simply in terms of a misalignment of interests among local water users (2012). We adopt this understanding as a recognition that active contestation or visible violence need not be constitutive components of water conflict. In fact, the stark power differentials that map onto inequitable access to water in Tola help to explain why much conflict is latent as opposed to overt.

Tourism and water injustice along the "Emerald Coast"

Much of the development along the southwest coast of Nicaragua would be described in the tourism scholarship as residential or "quality" tourism. In contrast to "mass" tourism, quality tourism has described low density, second home communities with substantial landscaping, as well as swimming pools and golf courses. The two largest gated communities along the coast are Guacalito de la Isla and Rancho Santana (see the map in Figure 6.1). The former was developed by a Nicaraguan businessman and caters mostly to wealthy Nicaraguans, while the latter represents the investment vision of U.S.-owned magazine *International Living* to attract wealthy visitors from around the world. Although the term "quality" suggests a positive connection to the environment, this residential model of tourism has been shown to consume more water per capita than its counterparts (Rico-Amoros et al. 2009), especially in regions with distinct dry seasons, whereby landscaping can only be sustained with considerable irrigation.

Residential tourism in coastal southwest Nicaragua is driving an inflated demand for water that intersects with local groundwater hydrology and national water laws to produce inequitable resource distribution. Regarding local hydrology, the absence of local surface water means nearly all freshwater needs are met with groundwater, which is abstracted from hydrogeologically complicated and poorly understood aquifers (LaVanchy & Taylor 2015). Moreover, while most tourism developments pump large volumes of water from deep wells for their operations, much of the local population draws water manually from shallow, hand-dug wells to meet daily needs. Many residents' wells have incurred saline intrusion or have dried altogether. In social and political terms, different abilities to extract water mirror power differentials with respect to local water access.

While tourism thus independently impacts water's local distribution, our research found prolonged drought, the selective implementation of national laws, and local political economies of tourism as intersecting contextual factors that help explain how tourism has generated water injustice in Tola.

Prolonged drought

Taken alone, prolonged drought in Nicaragua has compounded the spatial challenges associated with water supply. Nicaragua has "abundant" freshwater resources (Castillo Hernández et al. 2006); however, water is not distributed evenly in this small Central American country of 5.9 million people (area of 130,370 km^2). Some regions receive annual rainfall in excess of 4,500 mm (e.g., coastal east), while others receive less than 800 mm (e.g., mountains west) (Webster et al. 2001). What this means in practice is that Nicaragua's supply of freshwater is often mismatched with demand. Moreover, and reflecting global patterns, reasons for this mismatch often transcend physiological parameters. That is to say, situations of water "insecurity" are not always defined by the physical amount of water available via natural processes, but are more often the result of a convergence of issues that reflect power, race, gender, political, and economic systems (Cole & Ferguson 2015; Jepson 2012; LaVanchy 2017).

Anthropogenic climate change in the form of prolonged drought contributes a global dimension to the production of local water injustice. Specifically, tourism has converged with drought to exacerbate local water injustices. While reflecting a *disproportionate* water footprint, tourism's initial growth in Tola during the early 2000s coincided with years of above-average rainfall, which sufficiently recharged aquifers tapped to meet the growing demand for water. This perceived abundance of water, coupled with an absence of government oversight, produced a general assumption by tourism developers that an ample supply of groundwater was available to support whatever demands the tourism industry might have. In reality, tourism's longer arc of growth coincided with prolonged drought that dramatically reduced aquifer recharge, led to increased demands for irrigation, and ultimately produced conflict over a dwindling supply of water. LaVanchy et al. (2017) documented these effects and note that the layering of prolonged drought with the high rate of tourism abstraction presents obstacles to assessing empirical data – and leveraging data to work towards water justice – because it is difficult to assign culpability for water insecurity.

Nevertheless, it is clear that tourism and drought together have (re)shaped the socio-physical landscape along the Pacific coast through fundamentally altering the availability, quality, and distribution of water for residents. Rather than recognize their role in the production of water insecurity, gated residential communities have obfuscated the impacts of prolonged drought and continued to promote sales through drawing on imagery and language of a verdant, tropical coast. In practice, resorts must budget a large amount of their total water needs to create year-round green landscapes to draw and satisfy customers. This can exceed 50% of daily water usage for many resort communities (LaVanchy 2017). Certainly, industry's promotion of this coastline as "pristine," "exotic," "undiscovered," and "virgin"[3] makes invisible not only non-tourist residents themselves, but also the ways in which these residents are losing access to water to meet daily needs. This narrative also exists in tension with the dry-tropical forest southwest landscape that experiences an annual dry season where trees lose their leaves and the landscape assumes earth tones – the antithesis to the "Emerald Coast" moniker constructed by the tourism industry.

Selective implementation of national laws

National legal frameworks, which mediate the effects of tourism and drought, contribute to shaping water justice issues in Nicaragua, i.e., who has access to water, who does not, and who gets to decide (Gentes 2011; Ravnborg 2016; Romano 2019). We refer to selective implementation to describe the uneven ways national laws have been enforced by government officials, in effect producing inequitable outcomes. A key example of this is the *Ley General de Aguas Nacionales* (General Water Law of National Waters, or Law 620). Passed in 2007, Law 620 outlined a legal framework for the development of Nicaragua's freshwater resources with an emphasis on sustainable and equitable use and conservation (Articles 1–2). Towards these ends, the law mandated a new National Water Authority to create and maintain water budgets for each of the 21 watersheds across Nicaragua, as well as Basin Organizations to manage and monitor water use and Basin Committees to provide voice for all users within the watershed. To date, none of the watersheds in southwest Nicaragua has a budget or requisite organizations and committees, leaving the door open to distributive as well as procedural injustices.

Simultaneously, via Laws 306 and 495, the national government has promoted and incentivized the tourism industry. In the context of Law 620's weak enforcement, the industry has carried out the de facto privatization of large sums of freshwater along the coast in Tola. Neglecting the on-paper concept of "water budgets," the industry extracts water at rates that are both ecologically unsustainable and socially unjust. Issues of political will intertwine with the government's capacity to regulate the implementation of laws – the risk being that laws work to the detriment of the most vulnerable water uses. For instance, Law 620's Article 19, which allows government officials to declare of "public utility" any water sources needed for drinking and domestic use, leaves up to political discretion the reallocation of resources away from profit-seeking ends towards more essential uses, as well as less economically and politically powerful users.

Local political economy of tourism

As the tourism industry has grown, Tola residents have experienced its double-edged impacts, including negative distributional and procedural impacts in terms of water access and decision-making power, respectively. Regarding potential benefits, some residents have found employment within the sector. Limited data exist to quantify the actual number of jobs available to local populations; however, the uptick in job opportunities can in part be captured by the dramatic increase in motorcycles and taxi services over the past few years to support the movement of residents to and from work at resorts and gated communities. Although finding employment in the sector is "voluntary," it may mask "wide power differentials and complicated processes of societal change [that] interfere with people's choices" (Van Noorloos 2011, p. 88). In other words, while the impetus for tourism expansion has included job opportunities, residents' perceptions of their employment would need to be examined in order to draw conclusions regarding how "adverse" or "favorable" this employment and related conditions have been in practice (Borras et al. 2012).

For example, a striking tension lies in the fact that some employees have lost their personal water sources owing to the operations of their employers. Several interviews revealed that men working in landscaping roles for gated tourist communities use copious amounts of water in their work, all the while knowing that their shallow wells at home were dry and that their children were unable to bathe for lack of water. Each employee drew a direct connection between the volume of water needed for landscaping and the drying of their wells. Although some resorts within the industry recognize general (and drought-induced) water insecurity within surrounding communities and are willing to contribute to problem-solving, their efforts have been neither sustainable nor equitable. This was evident in one resort's donation of (limited) bottled water to a local health clinic to be disbursed free of charge to residents meeting certain health criteria. Not only does this intervention not promote water justice in terms of a redistribution of water resources, it also makes a barely perceptible contribution towards increasing water security for residents more broadly in the area, including employees and their families.

An intersecting political economy of *water* in Tola matters for this story of injustice as residents are largely responsible for securing their own access through wells on private property. New wells are expensive and typically require nongovernmental organization (NGO) and/or governmental financial contributions. However, external support for water projects is not guaranteed; moreover, it is typically ad hoc and dependent upon residents' advocacy for new water projects. Furthermore, maintenance of small-scale water systems can be prohibitively expensive for rural communities of users. Industry is at an advantage in terms of the ability to extract and use water, related to the ability to afford infrastructure and its maintenance.[4] This relates to the stark economic inequalities between residents and resort owners. For one example: Guacalito de la Isla is a US$500 million gated community, replete with villas, water purification system, luxury spa, and "world-class" golf course.[5] In contrast, the average monthly salary for local households is US$160–$200 per month, with the minimum wage for workers in hotels, restaurants, and transportation estimated at 7,282 *córdobas* (US$217) a month (Calero 2018). Many non-tourist residents have seasonal occupations that include fishing, but oftentimes pursue multiple sources of income. Low income, seasonal wage economies combined with the tourism industry's high usage of water resources challenges residents' ability to secure access to potable water.

In addition to vast economic disparities and respective power differentials between residents and the tourism industry, tourism communities along the coast are likewise characterized by significant social disparities within the non-tourist population. In the community of Gigante, for example, local demographics reflect a population of Nicaraguan and immigrant residents (in addition to numerous transient tourists). As water has become increasingly scarce, who can pay for access to water comes into view as a distinct water justice issue. Wealthier residents, such as those owning restaurants or small-scale tourism operations, can afford to dig new wells in the context of scarcity. This proved the case at the height of severe drought in 2016 and 2017 as several residents (both Nicaraguan and immigrant) paid to have new wells dug. In some cases, new plots of land (as small as 4m × 4m) were targeted for water potential and purchased solely for the purpose of well construction. These disparities reflect local water injustices in terms of who can pay to secure a water source – and hence assure water access – and who cannot.

Responding to water *insecurity* or water *injustice*?

How have non-tourist residents responded to this landscape of water injustice in Tola? Taking into account interviews and observations across five years (2012–2017), we found less of an effort to redress the distributional inequities produced by the tourism industry, and more one of seeking to secure water access. That is, despite an unmistakable context of environmental injustice, the discourse and actions of residents in Tola reveal little active pursuit of water *justice*.[6] Specifically, we found that responses to compromised water access have taken on a largely ad hoc, reactionary character reflecting attempts to secure access to new water sources. In one sense, this is surprising, given Nicaragua's revolutionary legacies of social activism and a vibrant civil society, including in relation to water politics and policies as of the mid-2000s (see, e.g., Avendaño 2004; Kreimann 2010; Romano 2012). In another sense, however, the limited "resistance" to the tourism industry's severe impacts on water resources likely reflects the power differentials between resort owners and operators and residents. Conflict stems from disparate interests inherent in the relationship between local wage labor and those of a profit-seeking industry supported by large amounts of capital (Van Noorloos 2011). Furthermore, dependence on the tourism industry for employment complicates claim-making (Walker 2012) in response to drying wells. Water security is likely "safer" and "easier" to pursue than water justice.

Overall, our exploratory research confirms findings in the literature that responses to water injustice are variegated (Hall et al. 2015). In Gigante, we observed few examples of *collective* efforts to *contest* the inequitable effects of the tourism industry. (In one notable example, some residents did explicitly name the tourism industry's disproportionate water usage when visiting the local government office to discuss local water scarcity issues.) However, there have been several efforts in pursuit of water *security*, including those discussed above. For instance, residents collaborated with the Texas-based NGO Living Water in 2016 to construct a new well in an area where many had gone dry. Unfortunately, due to the low aquifer output, the well was equipped only with a hand pump to provide drinking water for 10–15 households. In response, nearby residents solicited money from residential tourists to tap into the low-yield well with a gravity-fed water system in an effort to expand access, but the attempt ultimately failed as the result of insufficient water, fractured leadership, and limited technological understanding and resources.

In addition to assessments of power differentials, the limited role of NGOs and multilateral agencies in supporting the collective action of residents in Tola matters for understanding the response to water injustice. Previous research has demonstrated that forms of bridging and bonding social capital have been important for supporting the activism of residents as water users and managers (Romano 2017). In Nicaragua, nongovernmental and multilateral organizations have played a central role in promoting rural access to water and sanitation since the 1970s, and since the mid-2000s, some of these same domestic and international actors began to support – via bridging social capital – organized water users' forays into collective activism in the sector (Romano 2019). Extra-local support towards building the political knowledge and capacities of water users' associations called CAPS (Potable Water and Sanitation Committees) has contributed to rectifying water injustices in other places in Nicaragua.

One striking example can be found in CAPS' leveraging of Law 620's Article 19 (i.e., the provision allowing eminent domain over water resources). This case involved, ironically, the former president of the state water company, ENACAL, Ruth Selma Herrera, who was also an active leader in anti-water privatization organizing in the mid-2000s. When Herrera refused to cede access to a water source on her property to the community of La Chocolata in San Ramón, Matagalpa, in 2010, active conflict ensued. Organized residents collaborating with ADEMNORTE and CIC Batá, Nicaraguan and Spanish NGOs, respectively, protested the denial of water access outside of the mayor's office and the regional capital's environment division office, effectively pressuring public officials to declare the water source for public use (Romano 2019; SIMAS 2010). Overall, resisting and seeking to redress water injustice is challenging; but, it is also context-dependent, and not impossible. Moreover, grassroots resistance is not the only avenue for pursuing justice, something we explore further in the conclusion.

Conclusion: towards water just futures

Against the backdrop of anthropogenic climate change, a growing tourism industry in Nicaragua has detrimentally affected water availability and quality for local residents. While the promotional imagery of tourism development suggests otherwise, drought and large-scale tourism produce a perfect storm of water injustice when coupled with a political–legal context that falls short of ensuring just decision-making and distribution of resources. Drought, legal frameworks, and political economies of tourism each can be understood as independent drivers of water injustice; however, drawing attention to their *convergence* is important towards documenting and understanding the place-based production of environmental justice. Furthermore, this complex landscape of environmental injustice in many ways transcends the particular, speaking to universal problems and growing crises in the epoch of the Anthropocene.

Can tourism be more sustainable? Can it be just? As Devine and Ojeda contend, tourism's practices and effects "can be unmade" (2017, p. 614). However, there is no clear or singular pathway towards justice. Achieving water justice entails not only reallocating resources, but also changing societies' underlying structures of power. Hence, rectifying water injustices writ large means confronting a highly complex and intractable *set* of problems. To take one: tourism cannot be more sustainable and just without also addressing the multiple crises inherent in climate change, another "wicked" social problem in terms of its complexity. In global terms, the connections between climate change and water security are not lost on (most) leaders and policy makers. However, action on climate change has fallen short of global promises, itself a reflection of the difficulty of redistributing resources and reconfiguring power at a large scale.

Some hope may lie in pursuing *place-based justice* alongside the "laying bare" (Salazar 2017) of tourism's place-based *in*justices. This is not to say that pursuing local justice is necessarily easier than pursing global justice. However, the entry points, we argue, may be more visible and accessible. To emphasize our role as scholars and researchers, this starts with supporting the documentation and analysis of the production of injustice. Our role in pursuing more just futures also must come in the form of direct sharing of research findings via language and format-appropriate publications (see, e.g., Romano 2016). It also can and should include face-to-face presentations to research participants and other issue stakeholders as a means to engage, educate, and empower in and at the site(s) of research. Regarding the tourism industry in particular, research engagements can furthermore involve "critical analyses" of business practices, shared with operators (Salazar 2017, p. 707), as author LaVanchy has done in Tola in tandem with groundwater monitoring for resorts. In terms of scholarship, we can support strengthening the conceptual underpinnings of EJ frameworks through continued interdisciplinary work bridging relevant frameworks. This involves, for example, connecting the interrelated concepts of water security, water justice, environmental justice, and water grabbing, amongst others that together help reveal configurations of injustice. While none of the above creates water justice in and of itself, they are starting points that, crucially, do not rely on those actors most complicit in the production of injustice as the source of change.

Notes

1 Tourism development often constitutes a form of both land and water "grabbing" because of its appropriation of resources and simultaneous resource dispossession from socially and economically marginalized actors (Boelens 2015; Mehta et al. 2012; Borras et al. 2012).
2 Land grabbing is akin to water grabbing as means to appropriate resources away from local residents through legal, semi-legal, or illegal means.
3 See resorts' websites including Guacalito de la Isla (www.guacalitodelaisla.com/), Rancho Santana (https://ranchosantana.com/), and Surf Ranch Hotel and Resort (www.surfranchresorts.com/2016/05/Emerald-Coast-Nicaragua.html).
4 See also Houdret (2012) on farmers' differential abilities to pay for irrigation in Morocco and the resulting production of inequity between small and large farms.
5 See www.guacalitodelaisla.com/.
6 We agree with other scholars that local conceptions of justice matter and undergird the need for context specific environmental justice research (Joy et al. 2014; Zwarteveen & Boelens 2014). While our research did not examine local notions of justice, we emphasize the inequitable distribution of water as constituting a local water *in*justice.

References

Avendaño, N. 2004, *Nicaragua: el proceso de la privatización del agua*, Ediciones Educativas, Diseño e Impresiones S.A., Managua.

Babb, F.E. 2004, 'Recycled Sandinistas: From Revolution to Resorts in the New Nicaragua', *American Anthropologist*, vol. 106, no. 3, pp. 541–555.

Bakker, K. 2012, 'Water Security: Research Challenges and Opportunities', *Science*, vol. 337, pp. 914–915.

Bavinck, M., Berkes, F., Charles, A., Esteves Dias, A.C., Doubleday, P.N., & Sowman, M. 2017, 'The Impact of Coastal Grabbing on Community Conservation – A Global Reconnaissance', *Maritime Studies*, vol. 16, no. 8, pp. 1–17.

Boelens, R. 2008, 'Water Rights Arenas in the Andes: Upscaling Networks to Strengthen Local Water Control', *Water Alternatives*, vol. 1, no. 1, pp. 48–65.

Boelens, R. 2015, 'Water Justice in Latin America: The Politics of Difference, Equality, and Indifference', *Inaugural Lecture*, University of Amsterdam, 21 May. Viewed 09 March 2020, http://www.cedla.uva.nl/20_research/pdf/Boelens/R.Boelens-Water_Justice_in_Latin_America-The_Politics_of_Difference_Equality_and_Indifference.pdf

Borras, S.M., Franco, J.C., Gómez, S., Kay, C., & Spoor, M. 2012, 'Land Grabbing in Latin America and the Caribbean', *The Journal of Peasant Studies*, vol. 39, pp. 845–872.

Calero, M. 2018, 'Estos son los nuevos salarios mínimos en Nicaragua a partir del 1 de septiembre', *El Nuevo Diario*, 16 August.

Castillo Hernández, E., Calderón Palma, H., Delgado Quezada, V., Flores Meza, Y., & Salvatierra Suárez, T. 2006, 'Situación de los recursos hídricos en Nicaragua', *Boletín Geológico y Minero*, vol. 117, pp. 127–146.

Cole, S., & Ferguson, L. 2015, 'Towards a Gendered Political Economy of Water and Tourism', *Tourism Geographies*, vol. 17, no. 4, pp. 511–528.

Devine, J., & Ojeda, D. 2017, 'Violence and Dispossession in Tourism development: A Critical Geographical Approach', *Journal of Sustainable Tourism*, vol. 25, no. 5, pp. 605–617.

Gentes, I. 2011, 'Políticas hídricas, institucionalidad compleja y conflictos transfronterizos en Nicaragua', in R. Boelens, L. Cremers, & M. Zwarteveen (eds.), *Justicia Hídrica: Acumulación, Conflicto y Acción Social*, Agua y Sociedad, 15, Serie Justicia Hídrica.

Gleeson, T., Wang-Erlandsson, L., Porkka, M., Zipper, S.C., Jaramillo, F., Gerten, D., et al. 2020, 'Illuminating Water Cycle Modifications and Earth System Resilience in the Anthropocene', *Water Resources Research*, doi:10.1029/2019WR024957

Gössling, S. 2001, 'The Consequences of Tourism for Sustainable Water Use on a Tropical Island: Zanzibar, Tanzania', *Journal of Environmental Management*, vol. 61, pp. 179–191.

Hall, R., Edelman, M., Borras, S.M., Scoones, I., White, B., & Wolford, W. 2015, 'Resistance, Acquiescence or Incorporation? An Introduction to Land Grabbing and Political Reactions "From Below"', *Journal of Peasant Studies*, vol. 42, no. 3–4, pp. 467–488.

Houdret, A. 2012, 'The Water Connection: Irrigation, Water Grabbing and Politics in Southern Morocco', *Water Alternatives*, vol. 5, no. 2, pp. 284–303.

Jepson, W. 2012, 'Claiming Space, Claiming Water: Contested Legal Geographies of Water in South Texas', *Annals of the Association of American Geographers*, vol. 102, no. 3, pp. 614–631.

Joy, K.L., Kulkarni, S., Roth, D., & Zwarteveen, M. 2014, 'Re-politicising Water Governance: Exploring Water Re-Allocations in Terms of Justice', *Local Environment*, vol. 19, no. 9, pp. 954–973.

Kreimann, R. 2010, 'The Rural CAPS: Ensuring Community Access to Water', *Revista Envío*, June, p. 339. https://www.envio.org.ni/articulo/4197

LaVanchy, G.T. 2017, 'When Wells Run Dry: Water and Tourism in Nicaragua', *Annals of Tourism Research*, vol. 64, pp. 37–50.

LaVanchy, G.T., & Taylor, M.J. 2015, 'Tourism as Tragedy? Common Problems with Water in Post-Revolutionary Nicaragua', *International Journal of Water Resources Development*, vol. 31, no. 4, pp. 765–779.

LaVanchy, G.T., Taylor, M.J., Alvarado, N.A., Sveinsdóttir, A.G., & Aguilar-Støen, M.A. 2020, *Tourism in Post-revolutionary Nicaragua: Struggles over Land, Water, and Fish*. Springer Nature, Cham, Switzerland.

LaVanchy, G.T., Romano, S.T., & Taylor, M.J. 2017, 'Challenges to Water Security along the 'Emerald Coast': A Political Ecology of Local Water Governance in Nicaragua', *Water*, vol. 9, p. 655.

Mehta, L., Veldwisch, G.J., & Franco, J. 2012, 'Introduction to the Special Issue: Water Grabbing? Focus on the (Re)appropriation of Finite Water Resources', *Water Alternatives*, vol. 5, no. 2, pp. 193–207.

Perreault, T. 2006, 'From the Guerra de Agua to the Guerra de Gas: Resource Governance, Neoliberalism, and Popular Protest in Bolivia', *Antipode*, vol. 38, no. 1, pp. 150–172.

Perreault, T. 2014, 'What Kind of Governance for What Kind of Equity? Towards a Theorization of Justice in Water Governance', *Water International*, vol. 39, no.2, pp. 233–245.

Rasmussen, M.B., & Pinho, P.F. 2016, 'Introduction: Environmental Justice and Climate Change in Latin America', *LASA Forum*, vol. XLVII, no. 4, pp. 8–12.

Ravnborg, H.M. 2016, 'Water Governance Reform in the Context of Inequality: Securing Rights or Legitimizing Dispossession?', *Water International*, doi:10.1080/0 2508060.2016.1214895.

Rico-Amoros, A.M., Olcina-Cantos, J., & Sauri, D. 2009, 'Tourism Land Use Patterns and Water Demand: Evidence from the Western Mediterranean', *Land Use Policy*, vol. 26, pp. 493–501.

Romano, S.T. 2012, 'From Protest to Proposal: The Contentious Politics of the Nicaraguan Anti-Water Privatization Social Movement', *Bulletin of Latin American Research*, vol. 31, no. 4, pp. 499–514.

Romano, S.T. 2016, *De la gestión de recursos al activismo social: los CAPS y la gobernanza del agua rural*, Edisa, Managua, NI.

Romano, S.T. 2017, 'Transforming Participation in Water Governance: The Multisectoral Alliances of Rural Water Committees and NGOs in Nicaragua', *International Journal of Water Resources Development*, vol. 35, no. 3, pp. 430–445.

Romano, S.T. 2019, *Transforming Rural Water Governance: The Road From Resource Management to Political Activism*. University of Arizona Press, Tucson, AZ.

Salazar, N.B. 2017, 'The Unbearable Lightness of Tourism…As Violence: An Afterword', *Journal of Sustainable Tourism*, vol. 25, no. 5, pp. 703–709.

SIMAS. 2010, *El agua es propiedad de las Comunidades y no de los funcionarios del Gobierno*. http://www.simas.org.ni/noticias/962/el-agua-es-propiedad-de-las-comunidades-y -no-de-los-funcionarios-del-gobierno/

Spronk, S., Crespo, C., & Olivera, M. 2012, 'Struggles for Water Justice in Latin America: Public and "Social-Public" Alternatives', in D.A. McDonald & G. Ruiters (eds.), *Alternatives to Privatization: Public Options for Essential Services in the Global South*, Routledge, New York.

Stallworthy, M. 2009, 'Environmental Justice Imperatives for an Era of Climate Change', *Journal of Law and Society*, vol. 36, no. 1, pp. 55–74.

Sultana, F. 2018, 'Water Justice: Why it Matters and How to Achieve it', *Water International*, vol. 43, no. 4, pp. 483–493.

Torres, R.M., & Momsen, J. 2005, 'Gringolandia: The Construction of a New Tourist Space in Mexico', *Annals of the Association of American Geographers*, vol. 95, no. 2, pp. 314–335.

Van Noorloos, F. 2011, 'Residential Tourism Causing Land Privatization and Alienation: New Pressures on Costa Rica's Coasts', *Development*, vol. 54, no. 1, pp. 85–90.

Walker, G. 2012, *Environmental Justice: Concepts, Evidence and Politics*, Routledge, New York.

Webster, T.C., Waite, L., & Markley, B. 2001, 'Water Resources Assessment of Nicaragua', US Army Corps of Engineers, Mobile District and Topographic Engineering Center, 122 pp.

Zwarteveen, M.Z., & Boelens, R. 2014, 'Defining, Researching and Struggling for Water Justice: Some Conceptual Building Blocks for Research and Action', *Water International*, vol. 39, pp. 143–158.

7

JATROPHA BIOENERGY IN YUCATÁN, MEXICO

An examination of energy justice

Aparajita Banerjee

Introduction

Affordable and accessible energy is critical to human development and economic growth. Research supports the hypothesis that high energy consumption facilitates high economic growth (Omri 2014). In many parts of the world, people continue to live in energy poverty due to inaccessibility and unaffordability of energy. Energy poverty plagues 1.1 billion people worldwide and 38% of the world's population predominantly in the global South use highly pollutive unprocessed biomass fuel for cooking and heating (IEA 2017). Making all forms of energy affordable and accessible to all can help people to access modern healthcare, education, and communication and eventually eradicate poverty.

Providing affordable energy to all is challenging. Fossil fuels, predominantly used as cheap fuel to produce energy, emit large quantities of greenhouse gas emissions (GHG). Atmospheric accumulation of GHGs exacerbates global warming. The climate impact of fossil fuel used since the first Industrial Revolution is one of the many negative externalities of social and economic systems that have affected the natural and environmental systems so much so that some call the current geologic time the Anthropocene (Ribot 2014). Many of the worst human abuses and ecological disasters are associated with fossil fuel extraction (Watts 2006). One solution to these problems is the deep decarbonization of the economy, meaning that all forms of energy are derived from renewable energy completely replacing fossil fuels.

Increasing renewable energy as part of the energy mix of a country is complicated. Transitioning to low-carbon energy production is predominantly contingent on government policies (Sovacool 2009). Using different policy tools like tax exemptions and subsidies, governments can promote renewable energy or nurture a nascent renewable energy sector. Other tools like funding research and development to develop efficient, affordable, and accessible renewable energy technologies are also used to make it lucrative for national and international entrepreneurs to invest in renewable energy projects (Haas et al. 2004). It is increasingly common for federal, regional, and local governments to facilitate land acquisitions for renewable energy projects, especially in the global South (Yenneti et al. 2016).

Humans differ in terms of agency, power, opportunities, capabilities, and vulnerabilities, and the probability of one group exploiting the other is common. Arguably, the Anthropocene is currently shaped mostly by those who are more powerful and resourceful than others. Such asymmetries and inequalities entrenched in disproportionate geographical development are getting further reinforced by low-carbon transition plans (Bridge et al. 2013). Frequently, instances are emerging where large-scale land acquisitions for green and clean energy production are negatively impacting small-scale farmers, pastoralists, indigenous populations, and others who have access to public or communal lands predominantly in the global South.

In parallel, political challenges in the global South are reducing spaces for democratic decision-making and participation for citizens while restricting civil society to safeguard and monitor human rights violations, even those espoused in international agreements or domestic laws (Osaghae et al. 2013). Views of marginalized communities directly impacted by new energy projects remain unheard of in decision-making processes. They lack enough political power to ensure that their problems are represented in policymaking forums (Sovacool and Dworkin 2014). As a result, stories of dispossession, dislocation, and disenfranchisement of marginalized communities are being reproduced even in clean and green energy projects. However, as Adorno points out, "it is not technology, which is calamitous, but its entanglement with societal conditions in which it is fettered" (Adorno 2000, p. 161). Given this, the critical questions are, how can we use renewable energy technologies to heal the socio-environmental damages of fossil fuel energy? How to ensure clean, accessible, and affordable energy that is socially, economically, and ecologically just and sustainable for all?

Perhaps, one way of addressing this is to increase collective understanding of how "green" lifestyle choices pursued by environmentally conscious consumers may not be sustainable throughout the supply chain. Indeed, "green credentials" can be promoted by corporations involved in large-scale mechanized agriculture to validate the extermination of traditional agriculturalists from their land, converting them into proletariat workers employed in the same plantations that replaced their farms in the name of environmental benefits (Fairhead et al. 2012, p. 238). Arguably, this awareness is especially critical in developed nations where historically, the real cost of their development has been borne by the global South, making some countries the worst performers in socio-economic and environmental indicators. With the global push towards low-carbon energy transition, any perpetuation of resource and environmental injustices must be identified and rectified.

This chapter examines the impact of bioenergy development, a "green" fuel, on local communities in Yucatán, Mexico (Figure 7.1). This story demonstrates how exclusionary, top–down, decision-making processes are designed to benefit the corporates while failing to ensure the long-term sustainability of the projects and, in turn, affecting the lives and livelihood of rural communities. The case provides a context for the argument that externally owned and controlled low-carbon energy projects can create dispossessions and disruptions in embedded communities. As low-carbon transition should aspire to provide energy justice, the study indicates some of the challenges in achieving energy justice, especially in developing countries. Finally, a case is made that low-carbon energy projects should not be presumed as inclusive, democratic, and sustainable by default.

Semi-structured interviews with 120 interviewees, 40% men and 60% women with ages between 20 and 75, conducted in two fieldwork sessions in 2013 and 2016, inform the findings of this case study. Interviews with plantation workers, village heads, and other community leaders provided information about the context and the problems of the plantations, lack of local representation in the process, impacts on livelihoods and way of life, and their own unaddressed energy needs, access, and vulnerabilities. Data from expert interviews, document research, and newspaper articles were used to gather evidence to supplement information about the government policies, implementation plans of federal government agencies, and other details. Contextual secondary data was used to understand demographic composition, income levels, fuel-use, and health conditions.

Tenets of energy justice

Academics interested in fairness, equality, and justice while transitioning to low carbon economy are espousing the concepts of "just transition" and "energy

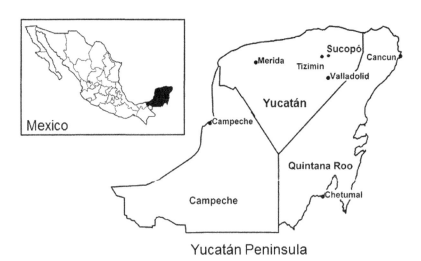

FIGURE 7.1 Map of study site, Yucatán, Mexico.

justice," meaning that such transition should be socially (Goldthau and Sovacool 2012) and environmentally just (Newell and Mulvaney 2013). It is vital to follow a path of just distribution of who gets what share of the benefits or burdens of the transition with a minimal impact on life-sustaining environmental resources (Devine-Wright 2014). Energy justice scholarship aims to develop "a global energy system that fairly disseminates both the benefits and costs of energy services and one that has representative and impartial energy decision-making" (Sovacool and Dworkin 2015, p. 436).

Three tenets of distributive, procedural, and recognition justice may guide energy transition-related decision-making processes (Heffron and McCauley 2014). Distributive energy justice proposes that just energy systems will have all its benefits and burdens distributed equally across all stakeholders. Therefore, to ensure distributive justice, all stakeholders must be engaged in decision-making processes following the tenet of procedural justice. The principle of recognition justice provides that in distributing the pains and gains, no one group of stakeholders is undervalued than any other.

With renewable energy systems using a range of feedstocks and materials, a just energy system implies that the supply chains also adhere to the tenets of energy justice (Heffron and McCauley 2014). Increasingly, research suggests that countries like Denmark, Germany, Australia, and some other developed nations are following tenets of energy justice to an extent. Different stakeholder groups have information about the projects, are aware of their rights and the rights of others. Stakeholders exercise their rights supported by institutionalized participation in decision-making. Companies operating within these spaces function as another stakeholder and abide by the boundaries set by the policies. Therefore, procedural, distributive, and recognition justice related to energy transition entail a democratic system that promotes and makes space for public engagement and deliberation.

In developing countries, public participation in policy decisions is often minimal. Companies can operate in very different conditions where local communities have a minimal role in accepting or rejecting renewable energy projects. The social, economic, political, historical, and cultural realities of these communities often perpetuate inequalities in power, representation, and resource allocation. Local, regional, and national governments facilitate significant land acquisition, mostly public lands, often ignoring how such dispossessions impact the socioeconomic and environmental conditions of the local people. Lacking power, wealth, or resources to rise from their circumstances, communities find alternative livelihoods often depending on the same companies that dispossessed them. Such injustices arise when the state imposes power on local communities acquiring public land in spaces where they live, work, raise their families, and make meaning of life termed as spatial injustice (Soja 2013). These injustices can frequently occur in rural areas as people have negligible sociopolitical power to resist policies that ultimately dislocate them from their common property resources. In this chapter, a case is presented where both energy injustice and spatial injustice are exemplified.

Bioenergy development in Yucatán, Mexico: a top–down approach

Bioenergy is a form of renewable energy derived from organic biomass materials used to produce different types of energy. Bioethanol and biodiesel derived from biomass are used as transportation fuels. In 2008, the Mexican government introduced the Law for the Development and Promotion of Bioenergy (*Ley de Promoción y Desarrollo de Los Bioenergéticos*, 2008) to initiate a bioenergy-based low-carbon energy transition to move away from fossil fuel. Though it set mandatory targets for bioethanol production and blending with petrol in domestic use, such targets were not set for biodiesel. Arguably, this was because biodiesel was to be produced for the international market. At the time, global markets for biodiesel, mainly driven by European countries, were gaining momentum. Biodiesel feedstock crop cultivation was promoted for the export market. In turn, this would revitalize rural economies as some farmers would be able to shift from unprofitable subsistence agriculture. Three federal government ministries, Secretariat of Energy, Secretariat of Agriculture, Livestock, Rural Development, Fisheries and Food, and the Secretariat of Environmental and Natural Resources, were given the responsibilities to provide technical support and financial incentives, and to monitor the overall implementation of the Law.

Drought and pest-resistant Jatropha trees were identified as biodiesel feedstock crops. Jatropha could provide additional re-forestation benefits restoring Mexico's degraded forest lands (Skutsch et al. 2011). The National Forestry Commission provided Jatropha saplings at a subsidized rate. It offered further financial incentives for the first three years while the seedlings grew into trees and produced oil-bearing fruits. Seeing a lucrative opportunity, a Mexican subsidiary of California, USA-based Global Clean Energy Holdings (GCEH) Inc., bought 6,000 hectares of land in Sucopo, Yucatán, in 2009–10. Two other companies with foreign and local joint ownership Kuosol and Lodemo opened smaller plantations in the state near Abala and Muna, planting Jatropha in an additional 3,500 hectares. Agricultural and ranching lands that supported subsistence farming and hay cultivation were bought from local ranchers and farmers.

Before being converted into Jatropha plantations, the land was either communally held by small-scale farmers practicing traditional agriculture or were used as pastures. The state and national governments justified the land-use change as such large-scale plantations in the area can provide benefits like rural infrastructure development, permanent employment opportunities, spin-off jobs, women's empowerment, and the land taxes channeled to develop local education and health care facilities. Additionally, workers would learn new skills in industrially operated agricultural facilities. Therefore, land that provided small-scale farmers with subsistence food production now had substantial commercial potential as Jatropha oil would produce biodiesel, a diesel substitute. The stage was set for a great "green" success story to unfold.

For the initial three years, when the saplings were growing into trees, the plantation companies benefited from government-provided subsidies. The plantations were operating full scale, employing hundreds of local people. Meanwhile, one GCEH plantation was certified by the Roundtable on Sustainable Biofuels (renamed Roundtable on Sustainable Biomaterials in 2013). However, after three years, when eventually the government support for the plantations ended, the companies started firing the workers as the plantations could not produce any biodiesel profitably. In 2013 and 2014, the plantations in the area were closed.

Impacts of energy transitions on local communities

During the time of the research in 2013 and follow-up fieldwork in 2016, rural communities surrounding the plantations had a high degree of marginalization with higher levels of poverty, low rates of formal education, and low average domestic income. The villages had a high concentration of low-income households, low diversity of economic opportunities, poor housing conditions, high dependence on off-grid energy, and below-par mobility and accessibility systems.

People lived in one-room-one-bathroom permanent roof houses built with government aid to protect them from hurricanes frequent in the region. Traditional Mayan houses thatched with palm leaves supplemented as living quarters. Villagers depended on the traditional agricultural practices of growing multiple crops at the same time, known as *milpa*. Many interviewees had some form of land access rights to communally held or *ejido* land around their villages that helped them grow food, mostly corn and vegetables and fodder for livestock if needed. Female family members grew fruit trees and raised pigs, chickens, and turkeys in the land surrounding their houses, also known as *solares*. People heavily depended on the land around them for growing food for subsistence.

Communal land provided biomass for cooking used in traditional and highly pollutive wood-burning stoves. A standard fixture in all the households was a three-stoned traditional cookstove that most interviewees used for cooking. The male members typically collected firewood. A few interviewees had liquid petroleum stoves for emergency use, especially during the rainy season inside their house. To them, wood was a cheap fuel that was almost free to collect other than the opportunity cost of the time spent in gathering. Access to various forms of modern amenities was low. Local transportation was infrequent, villages lacked paved roads to municipal towns, local wells or *cenotes* provided water supply in place of municipal water, and low voltage electricity supply lighted a few bulbs.

Other than working in farms, a few seasonal jobs such as octopus fishing or digging archaeological sites provided livelihood opportunities. Travel time to the tourist centers of Cancun and Playa del Carmen allowed some community youths to occasionally migrate to these places for livelihood opportunities remitting money to their families in the villages.

Given this background, the local plantation jobs emerged as lucrative liveli-hood options, and several farmers sold their rights to the communal land and became plantation workers. Many farm and ranch workers with no land access rights found new opportunities in the plantation jobs requiring similar skill sets. The plantations recruited 500–900 people as semi-skilled and unskilled work-ers from the neighboring villages in the municipalities of Abala, Muna, and Tizimín. During the recruitment, company officials informed the workers that the company would produce Jatropha seeds for biodiesel and provide permanent employment for 15 to 30 years. The wages offered were better than other farm and ranch-based jobs in the region (Banerjee et al. 2017). Local women had opportunities to work in the plantation nurseries, a rare option that helped them to balance both their family commitments and economic independence. Some plantation workers could even afford loans to buy motorcycles that improved transportation options.

The interviewees were mostly unaware of Jatropha or its use in biodiesel pro-duction, especially for export before the companies opened their plantations as no one provided them with any details. They did not participate in any decision-making process associated with Jatropha plantations in the area. Representatives of the companies came to their villages to recruit people *en masse* and were the first to inform them about the company and Jatropha. Given the export potential for biodiesel, they were promised long-term job security. Both men and women working for the companies were paid in the range between 700 and 900 pesos per week and were provided health insurance. These promises converted them to plantation workers as the allure of a steady paycheck was tempting, given their socio-economic conditions.

People knowledgeable about the local agricultural conditions were quick to point out why the Jatropha plantations did not work in the region while inter-viewing. The harsh sunlight in the area, along with fragile topsoil, killed the crops. Expert interviewees expressed that the local phytosanitary conditions were unsuitable for the Jatropha genus introduced locally. The trees were plagued with different diseases, and the use of heavy pesticides further worsened their condi-tions. No test experiments were carried out before converting the land into large-scale plantations. When government subsidies to the companies stopped after the initial three years, no further seeds were planted. As the cost of the upkeep of the existing plants became too high, the companies went bankrupt. Many interviewees reported that labor conditions were violated; accidents were under-reported. Two out of the three plantations did not provide any protective gear to workers spraying pesticides and fungicides. After around five years, the companies left the area, and what remained was 9,500 ha. of land with toxic Jatropha plants with no commercial value. The local water systems were polluted with the pesticide and fungicide run-offs from the plantations. In a follow-up research visit in 2016, it was found that some plantation land remained unsold.

While interviewing in 2013, most of the interviewees were jobless after being fired from the plantations. Some worked on their land if they still had access rights, and the women took care of their families or engaged in small-scale businesses of making hammocks and other handicrafts. Some interviewees mentioned that they were living off the meager severance amount they got from one company due to their abrupt firing or on government welfare payments. As the surrounding land provided them with some food, fodder, and fuel, the little money helped them survive. Others without access to land moved away to tourist areas for jobs or went to work in octopus fishing, archaeological diggings, and ranch work.

Energy justice: a utopia in developing countries?

Though there is a significant focus on energy justice in the low-carbon transition literature, the findings of this case study draw attention to multiple challenges in achieving "just transition," especially in developing countries. Energy transition is not just a technology change from fossil-fuel-based systems to low-carbon energy systems. New land needs to be acquired; new supply chains need to be created. It is improbable to isolate new spaces and processes from the people living around them and their social, economic, political, cultural, and historical realities. Researchers suggest that the interconnections between energy justice and spatial justice need to be considered (Yenneti et al. 2016).

The Yucatán Jatropha for biodiesel case was driven by the federal government policy on low-carbon transition; government agencies were involved in implementation following a top-down approach. From the beginning, the government decided that biodiesel would not be used for domestic blending but mainly for export with farming communities benefitting from the plantation jobs. Implicitly the government assumed that the private companies owning the plantations would create new roads for transporting their raw materials and create local economic opportunities, thus improving many of the conditions falling under government responsibilities. Therefore, many of the government obligations were outsourced to the externally owned private companies. In return, the federal agencies were provided with Jatropha saplings and supported the companies for three years under a reforestation program.

The private companies saw new opportunities in this bioenergy policy to invest money in projects producing "green fuel" that had a burgeoning market in the European countries. Support from the national government helped them in acquiring cheap lands in rural areas and establishing plantations. The considerable labor required to create a plantation by removing vegetation, preparing the soil, planting Jatropha saplings, and other activities came very cheaply from surrounding communities. Expenditures on maintaining health and safety conditions could be curtailed due to the lax labor laws in Mexico where corporatist traditions have eroded labor unions and labor rights (Oliver 2012).

What resulted from this system was that the companies established large-scale plantations without involving locals in decision-making. Instead, they were employed as low paid workers and laborers. As a result, the companies failed to capture and benefit from the traditional knowledge of the local farmers working under local agricultural conditions for generations. Consultation with local communities would have helped in avoiding such costly mistakes. Lack of unions and labor laws placed the workers in very asymmetric power relations with companies. Not surprisingly, workers were quickly fired even after being promised long-term stable jobs. This affected their livelihoods as most sold their land or stopped working on their farms, banking on the new economic opportunity. Many took out loans to make necessary yet expensive purchases such as a motorcycle that would make travel more comfortable in a place challenged by a lack of public transport. With jobs gone, no land ownership, or land-access rights, the pressure of loan repayments drove many workers to move from the security of their community to seek low-wage jobs elsewhere, especially in the highly exploitative tourism sector (Wilson 2008).

Additionally, the government-initiated Jatropha-based low-carbon energy transition plan did not consider the local needs of mitigating the abject energy poverty in rural communities. Gathering biomass is a time-intensive process restricting people to pursue other economic activity. Ironically, the workers who used highly pollutive locally available biomass like tree branches or charcoal in traditional three-stoned cookstoves, went to work in plantations producing feedstock for high quality, low GHG-emitting fuel for the export market. Even liquid petroleum–based daily cooking appliances were unaffordable. Not surprisingly, people suffered from indoor pollution–related health issues.

Arguments can be made that energy justice, is mostly a utopian dream in developing countries, as this case demonstrates. Principles of energy justice like distributional justice were ignored when the plantation companies suddenly closed, making hundreds of workers jobless and changing their way of life. The local communities bore the maximum burden as they first lost access to the public lands sold off to the plantations and later losing their livelihoods as the companies closed. The need for the people to have accessible and affordable clean energy was not recognized from the very beginning when the government focused on supporting Jatropha biodiesel production solely for the export market as domestic blending targets were not set. Jatropha biodiesel was to be produced by exploiting local ecological resources and exported to foreign markets without addressing the abject energy poverty. Tenets of recognition justice were discounted. The impacts on local communities and how they would benefit were promoted by the government. The plantation projects would contribute to "rural revitalization" by creating jobs. Principles of procedural justice were avoided when a top-down approach was followed without considering local communities as key stakeholders.

Instances of rural land being sold to foreign companies are common in developing countries as part of the liberalization policies that began in the 1990s (Zoomers 2010). Little attention is given to the spatial injustices that arise from the massive transfer of land and what it entails for the local communities. Marginalized communities, farmers, pastoralists, livestock farmers often lose access to common property resources like public lands that affect their livelihoods. This may even dislocate local communities when they migrate to other areas in search of alternative livelihoods. National governments also encourage foreign and domestic private entrepreneurship due to the economic opportunities they produce. Job creation is considered the best possible outcome of these policies ignoring the environmental and ecological consequences policy, and the erosion of environmental goods and services are undervalued or ignored. In this case, low-carbon energy transition projects repeat and reinforce the injustices that have been observed since colonial times in developing countries such as land-grabbing (Alden Wily 2012). As this case demonstrates, developing countries can continue to function as peripheral locations providing raw materials for the developed core even while producing "green" biodiesel fuel (Fairhead et al. 2012), while ignoring the domestic energy poverty challenges.

The problems identified in this case study are critical to understanding the challenges for energy transitions, especially in developing countries. Achieving energy justice is challenging due to multiple conditions. Public participation and deliberation spaces are non-existent, marginalized voices are unheard or wilfully ignored, labor laws are not enforced, operational and health safety standards are slack, water contamination from pesticides and other chemicals is not monitored, data of large land transfers are hard to obtain, transparent and accountable institutions are not the norm. Corruption makes it impossible to get any form of legal justice. In this research, even the plantation company that was certified sustainable by the Roundtable of Sustainable Biomaterials, the international sustainability certifying body for biomaterials, was not sustainable as it closed immediately after receiving the certification.

With vast inequalities in how power and representation are distributed, attaining any form of energy justice remains questionable.

Conclusion

Clean energy for all is a requirement globally to mitigate climate change and address energy poverty. Different interest groups will promote bioenergy as a renewable alternative to liquid fossil fuel, especially in countries that have remained in the forefront with a high level of progress in achieving low-carbon energy targets. However, while doing so, it is critical that the same injustices common across the fossil fuel supply chain are not being repeated or reinforced in different forms.

Additionally, it is essential to pay attention that even environmentally beneficial projects can negatively impact communities, especially those that have traditionally remained in socio-economic margins. As they lack the political power to make their voices heard, the chances are that when new energy projects alienate them from their livelihoods or enhance their precarity, their problems will remain. While championing the goodness of "green" energy, it is critical to interrogate and understand how such energy is produced, where it is produced, and how production processes enhance or erode justice components throughout the supply chain. There needs to be increased awareness that "green" is not always clean or the perfect panacea for all problems created due to our fossil fuel consumption. With vast inequalities in how power and representation are distributed, attaining any form of energy justice remains questionable.

References

Adorno, Theodor. *Introduction to Sociology*. Translated by Edmund Jephcott. Cambridge: Polity Press, 2000.

Alden Wily, Liz. "Looking back to see forward: The legal niceties of land theft in land rushes." *The Journal of Peasant Studies* 39, no. 3–4 (2012): 751–775.

Banerjee, Aparajita, Kathleen E. Halvorsen, Amarella Eastmond-Spencer, and Sam R. Sweitz. "Sustainable development for whom and how? Exploring the gaps between popular discourses and ground reality using the Mexican Jatropha biodiesel case." *Environmental Management* 59, no. 6 (2017): 912–923.

Bridge, Gavin, Stefan Bouzarovski, Michael Bradshaw, and Nick Eyre. "Geographies of energy transition: Space, place and the low-carbon economy." *Energy Policy* 53 (2013): 331–340.

Devine-Wright, Patrick, ed. *Renewable Energy and the Public: From NIMBY to Participation*. London: Routledge, 2014.

Fairhead, James, Melissa Leach, and Ian Scoones. "Green grabbing: A new appropriation of nature?" *Journal of Peasant Studies* 39, no. 2 (2012): 237–261.

Goldthau, Andreas, and Benjamin K. Sovacool. "The uniqueness of the energy security, justice, and governance problem." *Energy Policy* 41 (2012): 232–240.

Haas, Reinhard, Wolfgang Eichhammer, Claus Huber, Ole Langniss, Arturo Lorenzoni, Reinhard Madlener, Philippe Menanteau et al. "How to promote renewable energy systems successfully and effectively." *Energy Policy* 32, no. 6 (2004): 833–839.

Heffron, Raphael J., and Darren McCauley. "Achieving sustainable supply chains through energy justice." *Applied Energy* 123 (2014): 435–437.

International Energy Agency. *Energy Access Outlook 2017: From Poverty to Prosperity*. Paris: IEA, 2017.

Newell, Peter, and Dustin Mulvaney. "The political economy of the 'just transition'." *The Geographical Journal* 179, no. 2 (2013): 132–140.

Oliver, Ranko Shiraki. "Mexico's Dilemma: Workers' rights or workers' comparative advantage in the age of globalization." *Pacific McGeorge Global Business & Development Law Journal* 25 (2012): 195.

Omri, Anis. "An international literature survey on energy-economic growth nexus: Evidence from country-specific studies." *Renewable and Sustainable Energy Reviews* 38 (2014): 951–959.

Osaghae, Eghosa E., Arilson Favareto, Ranjita Mohanty, Laurence Edward Piper, Simeen Mahmud, Linda Waldman, Lyla Mehta, Angela Alonso, and Carlos Cortez Ruiz. *Citizenship and Social Movements: Perspectives from the Global South*. London: Zed Books Ltd, 2013.

Ribot, Jesse. "Cause and response: Vulnerability and climate in the Anthropocene." *The Journal of Peasant Studies* 41, no. 5 (2014): 667–705.

Skutsch, Margaret, Emilio De los Rios, Silvia Solis, Enrique Riegelhaupt, Daniel Hinojosa, Sonya Gerfert, Yan Gao, and Omar Masera. "Jatropha in Mexico: Environmental and social impacts of an incipient biofuel program." *Ecology and Society* 16, no. 4 (2011): 1–17.

Soja, Edward W. *Seeking Spatial Justice*. Vol. 16. Minneapolis: University of Minnesota Press, 2013.

Sovacool, Benjamin K. "Rejecting renewables: The socio-technical impediments to renewable electricity in the United States." *Energy Policy* 37, no. 11 (2009): 4500–4513.

Sovacool, Benjamin K., and Michael H. Dworkin. *Global Energy Justice*. Cambridge: Cambridge University Press, 2014.

Sovacool, Benjamin K., and Michael H. Dworkin. "Energy justice: Conceptual insights and practical applications." *Applied Energy* 142 (2015): 435–444.

Watts, Michael. "Empire of oil: Capitalist dispossession and the scramble for Africa." *Monthly Review* 58, no. 4 (2006): 1.

Wilson, Tamar Diana. "Economic and social impacts of tourism in Mexico." *Latin American Perspectives* 35, no. 3 (2008): 37–52.

Yenneti, Komali, Rosie Day, and Oleg Golubchikov. "Spatial justice and the land politics of renewables: Dispossessing vulnerable communities through solar energy mega-projects." *Geoforum* 76 (2016): 90–99.

Zoomers, Annelies. "Globalisation and the foreignisation of space: Seven processes driving the current global land grab." *The Journal of Peasant Studies* 37, no. 2 (2010): 429–447.

8

KEEPING IT LOCAL

The continued relevance of place-based studies for environmental justice research and praxis

Michelle Larkins

Introduction

A familiar quote to the field of environmental studies and planning, is that "space becomes place, when we attach meaning to it" (Tuan 1977, p. 6). Fostering positive place attachment in individuals and communities has become a goal, theoretically connected to behaviors of conservation and stewardship (Grunewald 2003), increased public health outcomes and stronger civic ties (Brown et al. 2003). But what about those communities who are restricted from accessing spaces, or who are encouraged through prejudicial zoning, rampant gentrification, or other oppressive processes to frequent only those spaces deliberately lacking environmental benefits? What do these constructions of space, place, and injustice tell us? Moreover, as researchers examining these phenomena, how do we best acknowledge and incorporate the agentic expressions of community members who are experiencing these forms of environmental injustice, and working against them?

Like the other authors in this volume, I understand space as a social production, dynamic and capable of change, but also vulnerable to decision-makers who embody discriminatory hegemonic values (Soja 2009). The legacies and contemporary impacts of these decisions are in direct conversation with the meta-framework of the Anthropocene (Lewis and Maslin 2015); an epoch of rapid anthropogenic environmental change which has been disparately diffused through (neo)liberal and (neo)colonial structures on certain bodies, communities, and geographies. Apart from its ecological significance, as the environmental justice field reckons with the reality of the Anthropocene, we must continue to draw attention to how *justice*, as conceptualized in our work, reflects whose voices matter, which social locations are visible, and what types of livelihoods are privileged.

To answer this call of visibility and given the spatial and contextual complexity of environmental justice issues (Schlosberg 2013; Szasz and Meuser 1997), attention to scale is vital. Specifically, Pellow (2017) advances the call for more multi-scalar research – spatial and temporal – as one prong of his four-part perspective on critical environmental justice studies, arguing that "environmental threats jump scale" (p. 16), and that imagining just futures depends on understanding these connective tissues. I agree with Pellow and assert that understanding the intricacies and intersections in the local is paramount to acknowledging the plurality of justice claims, the legacies of environmental discrimination, and to meaningfully address the particular manifestations of spatial and environmental injustice impacting people and places (Whyte 2018).

In this chapter, I draw upon an oral history project in the state of Colorado, USA, that examined how intersecting identities of gender, femininity, and place influenced the environmental justice engagement of local women leaders, and to what extent this impacted their work in communities throughout the Rocky Mountain West. I purposively focus on the experiences of seven women leaders working in one community organization to demonstrate the importance of local case studies informed by intersectional frames to investigations of spatial and environmental justice research; and discuss how this approach revealed distinctions regarding the concept of place, and secondly, that access to environmental benefits in this predominantly Latinx community were tightly coupled with experiences of migration and discriminatory discourse at the state/national level. I turn briefly to a conversation of the significance of intersectionality and oral history methods to environmental justice research.

The importance of intersectional frames in environmental justice research

As a field, intersectionality traces its origins to rhetoric within the Civil Rights movement (Collins and Bilge 2016). The scholarly work of Collins (1989) and Crenshaw (1989) used this frame to help illustrate how the structural conditions and forms of oppression faced by black women in the United States could not be reduced simply to an analysis of race, but must be understood as the interstices between race, class, and gender. Suggesting that oppressive practices and discourses connect and contest with subjective identities to produce distinct experiences of (in)justice, intersectionality creates space within research for a multiplicity of standpoints. Problematizing community identities rather than naturalizing them helps to acknowledge different strategies of resistance, the diversity of justice claims (Harrison 2014), and to locate authentic opportunities for social transformation. This is critical to ensuring that researchers do not treat any community disenfranchised by environmental justice as homogenous, an action that may potentially compromise research findings and miss important in-group differences that could explain experience or behavior (Rivers et al. 2010).

Krauss (1993) was one of the first scholars to apply intersectionality to environmental justice issues, linking frameworks of race, class, colonialisms, and gender to women's engagement in toxic waste activism. Later work (Larkins 2018) continues to argue for the synergism between environmental justice and intersectionality, noting that both fields have foundational principles of praxis (Cho et al. 2013). However, intersectionality is not without critique (Davis 2008; Winker and Degele 2011). Its widespread popularity in the academy has sometimes resulted in diluted scholarship; for example, wherein identities are reduced to discrete rather than woven subjectivities, which Collins (2000, 1989) has referred to as intersectionality's ampersand problem. Yet, when rigorously applied – explicitly acknowledging the dialogic between the experiential and structural formations of identity – the production and reproduction of institutions and systems of oppression may be revealed (Martin 2004), contributing to how we examine the mechanisms by which environmental injustice transcends time and space (Pellow 2017; Schlosberg 2013).

Oral histories: enriching environmental justice methods

As completed texts, oral history collections may be thought of as narratives, socially constructed recordings of experiences that operate on varying scalar and temporal levels. The production and dissemination of narratives can privilege one account of history and material relations over another (Gubrium 2005). Thus, there is the potential for oral history narratives from communities or identities who have been previously marginalized to act as counterhegemonic discourse, allowing for an examination by activists and academics into the historicity and systematicity of oppressions – both lenses called for in critical environmental justice studies (Pellow 2017). The development and visibility of new standpoints is needed both within the academy and in more "popular" publics. In addition to these considerations, in this project, oral histories were chosen as a tool to foreground the everyday experiences of the women in these communities as knowledge, their understanding of space and place, and give authorial space to these leaders to construct their identities.

Researchers engaging in this method must consider issues of authorial representation, and the potential risk of essentializing these histories as simple "victory" narratives (Cary 1999). In this instance, narrative texts are mined for emancipatory declarations, or revelations about oppressions that fit theoretical schematics – the "aha" moment. Reflexivity is needed as we look for evidence of transnational injustices, and how they manifest spatially. By incorporating oral histories into multiscalar and critical environmental justice studies, we make room for individuals and communities to name their lived realities and construct a discourse of experience that can help to illuminate the connectivity and materialization of injustice in the local and global. Coupled with intersectional frameworks that include multiple standpoints and variable social locations, oral histories become both investigative tool and social praxis to overcome the problematic past of reductionist research frames.

Community context

The seven oral history interviews included in this piece are a geographic sub-collection from a project that included field sites throughout Colorado and New Mexico, USA. For a period of fourteen months, I traveled between these sites completing homestays and oral history interviews with women leaders who were active in local environmental justice struggles – the majority of these women engaged in work that bridged food and environmental justice frames. The Colorado interviewees range in age from 24 to 44. This cohort of women leaders primarily organized within urban and peri-urban communities of monolingual Spanish speakers, or new Latinx immigrants to the state of Colorado. Self-disclosed relationship history revealed that one woman had a divorced male partner, and that six of the seven women are currently in heterosexual marriages or long-term partnerships; all of the women are mothers. While each of these women are documented US residents, some of the community members they work with are not, and therefore I have made the decision to avoid neighborhood-level place names. Hiding these specific geographies is an attempt to protect the social and physical spaces for these communities, and to shield neighborhood organizations from harassment.

These women self-identified as *promotoras.* For them, this term signifies their advocacy within and for Latinx communities around issues of social and environmental justice. Socially, my time included meals and family events, and in the beginning of my fourteen-month tenure I was often paired with a promotora to facilitate my entrance into community spaces where my identity as a white woman was rightfully questioned. Currently, these women receive an hourly wage for their work (approximately 10–15 hours/week), which is derived from grant funding and foundation support. I completed seven oral histories with this cohort. At the time of data collection, the group was primarily working with three peri-urban neighborhoods on food security initiatives with Latina women (i.e. access, availability, and culturally appropriate food ways), family-based nutrition education, and exercise/mobility for public health. While men are not barred from participation, women were the target stakeholders, given the cultural expectations of women's role in food acquisition and cooking.

Six of the seven promotoras with whom I worked, reside in the neighborhoods described here. Five of these women became promotoras after themselves being recipients of assistance from the group leader, Lisa. Thus, these material conditions inform their community action, and are layered upon their identities (Alkon and Agyeman 2011). The communities these promotoras work within include neighborhoods with some of the highest scores on zip code risk indices as calculated by the Environmental Protection Agency (EPA); including proximity to active Superfund sites, brownfield redevelopment sites, current Toxic

Release Inventory (TRI) polluters, and overall ambient air quality (US EPA 2016). Residents face other vectors of soil contamination, sub-standard housing, and lack of public transportation that limit traditional ideas of environmental benefits such as green space, and contribute to food access inequities which was the primary focus of the promotora network during the fourteen months I engaged with them.

For the State of Colorado, the overall Hispanic/Latino population grew by 41.20% from 2000 to 2010 (American Community Survey 2017), with ethnic concentration in some neighborhoods – including those the promotoras engaged with – as high as 79.39%. Some of these communities are being threatened by planned highway infrastructure projects that would physically separate them from their neighbors, important cultural centers, and in some instances require they relocate (CDOT 2017). Accurate socioeconomic data is difficult to obtain, but triangulation with property values, educational attainment, social service receipts, and programming like Supplemental Nutrition Assistance Program (SNAP) suggest lower socio-economic status for these geographic areas. In addition to the food access concerns addressed by these promotoras, as mentioned, these are communities faced with disparate air quality, soil contamination, lack of public transportation, and continued discriminatory discourse. An interview in the *Gazette*, with an on-the-record statement from former state senator Dave Schultheis (R, 2007–2011) is emblematic of regional hostility that preceded the Trump administration, "People just don't know what kind of negative impact (illegal immigrants) can have. They use our welfare system, use our schools, and take jobs away from Americans" (Phillips 2011). However, in major urban centers such as Denver, Boulder, and Colorado Springs, there are currently city-wide movements to create sanctuary spaces in churches (Colorado is not a sanctuary state) for undocumented residents, in response to recent deportation executive orders. As a region with a complicated historical and contemporary record of tensions between majority (White/Anglo) and Latinx minority populations, connections can be drawn with Guzmán's (2006) findings that most media representations about Latinx people amplify tropes of immigration, sexuality, poverty, and crime.

Compounding the work of the promotoras is the real and perceived risk of US residency denial based on social services access, resulting in some community members avoiding any food access points, in addition to formal programs such as SNAP. At the time of data collection and analysis, a draft executive order (Protecting our Taxpayer Resources by Ensuring our Immigration Laws Promote Responsibility and Accountability 2017) had been released that indicated use of benefits would restrict/deny immigration approval. This has since been codified as the "Inadmissibility on Public Charge Grounds" rule by the United States Citizenship and Immigration Services (2020), and challenges to its legality by immigrant rights groups dismissed by the US Supreme Court (2020). Thus, while there is some social support in localities to create sanctuary spaces in Colorado, it is at odds with discourse and regulatory decisions at the federal level which frame immigrants as a threat to resources (Cisneros 2008). Coupled with the disinvestment in/de-prioritization of the environmental health by public authorities in the physical spaces described above, it becomes clear that these communities experience a nexus of social and environmental inequities which could inform perceptions of belonging and access to resources.

The excerpts below come from interviews conducted over several months to respect respondent's competing time demands, and to give them space to reflect on what more they wished to share. The interviews were conducted in English and/or Spanish depending on the preference of the respondent, and all participants were given a copy of their transcript in their preferred language, as well as a chance to correct or redact any statements.

Place belonging?

Throughout their oral histories, women self-defined race/ethnicity, gender, and place-based identities, and how these intersected in their lives. Some women framed place-based identity as *exclusionary* in their communities, because of their experiences of race/ethnicity discrimination, and how this sense of "not belonging" shaped their engagement strategies. Elsewhere in the environmental justice literature (Brown and Ferguson 1995; Burley et al. 2007; Devine-Wright 2006; Krauss 1993), women's engagement in community action is partially attributed to place-based attachment or community affinities. In the present case, intersectional frameworks allowed for a discussion of how feelings of place exclusions and experiences of racial/ethnic discrimination may inform women's involvement in community-based environmental justice groups, and how they navigate improving resource access for their communities. In the following excerpts, the promotoras discuss insider/outsider dynamics in their geographic communities, and how it has impacted their engagement on behalf of their organization.

Lisa, 44 years old, one of the group founders, discusses her frustration that the American (or Anglo) community does not think Latina women capable of leadership. She articulates her strength, and that of many of the women she works with, through shared experiences of leaving Mexico, feelings of isolation, and lack of "new" community support.

> When my husband left me here, it was like being born again. I did not want to come to the United States; I was really happy in my country. I didn't know the language, I didn't know how to drive. I knew no one. I was unhealthy, the food was no good. I prayed to God to let me live, to be successful, and I would help my community. Now, I tell other women, *if you can run across the border, you can survive anything here.* But it is hard, new immigrants are neglected, and we are good at hiding. So, I know who I am: I'm a strong Latina woman and I don't need people to, you know, label me just because I'm a strong Mexican woman and Americans, unfortunately, haven't seen that. And so, everyone is like, "Where are you from?

What do you do again?" because I lead. You know, they don't understand that part of me.

In contrast, Juliet, 24 years old, speaks of being pushed to the margins in both the Hispanic/Latino and American cultures; something she attributes to having been born in America, though she lived in Mexico for over eight years. While she self-identifies as Mexican, members of her community consider her to be Chicana, which she perceives as an insult. Doubly an outsider, in the excerpt below, Juliet discusses the difficulties she faces when interacting with the constituents of her organization, and with Anglo-Americans in professional settings.

Yes, so in the Hispanic community it's difficult because I consider myself a lot more Mexican than American. I relate more towards the Mexican culture than I ever could to American, just because of – just my lifestyle; just the environment that I'm around. I like it a lot more in the Mexican culture. But it's sad because they don't consider me Mexican because I was born here. So, they will always say Chicana. But to me, Chicana is not a very good word, because I've seen what Chicanos are kind of like. First of all, they don't like to speak the language. They don't like to be considered Mexicans. They don't relate to that culture. And so, I'm like, no, what do you mean? Like, we're the same. But they don't consider me the same. So, it's curious because in the Hispanic community I have to defend myself as a Mexican. And in the American community, I still have to defend myself as a Mexican, but then I also have to say, you know what, I understand everything you're – like where you come from, because at the end of the day I grew up here as well, so I have both. And so, it's difficult because you do defend yourself in both areas.

Yasmin, 27 years old, shares similar experiences to Lisa – feelings of isolation, fear – and despite her commitment to this community – place as exclusionary.

Every time I was using my four walls. I never know that I have a world close to me. You know, I was, like, in a little room and I never get out. Because I was really afraid … Everybody look at me like what she's doing here. And I say, okay, just breathe. Nothing's going to happen. I try to stand up really … I really want the people see me that I am strong. They think that because I'm Hispanic or Latino, that I'm nothing. The women I work with, I don't want them to feel that if you get out somebody's going to arrest them and take them back to Mexico. Things like that, yes. That's what I want. I want to be – I want to see in the future healthy and strong women.

Victoria, 36 years old, described a sense of security and belonging in her Colorado neighborhood; however, she also notes she has never lived elsewhere since immigrating from Mexico at 16. She recognizes feelings of fear and exclusion when working with members of her community regarding food insecurity and nutrition.

> Well, I'm safe, because I live in a Hispanic community. And if I go to the store, I'm always going to see a Mexican or whatever. You know. I never been in other – I haven't ever been in another – like, another neighborhood. There's a lot of families … they still have a lot of needs. They don't know – why is free? Because nothing is free. Are you guys going to charge later, or how this work? Because I think we never have something really free [laughter]. They are still afraid. Like me in the beginning – I think they still afraid, for many reasons. But I think it's working on it. We're still working on it. Yes.

I share these experiences not to draw theoretical connections to literatures outside the scope of this chapter, but to demonstrate why as environmental justice researchers we need to practice intersectionality in our work. The women above share a race/ethnicity and gender identity, but have very different experiences of belonging to the Latinx community that intersects with place. For Juliet, insider/outsider dynamics are at play within the Mexican community she identifies with, as well as with her engagement with the "American" community. She speaks of relating more to the Mexican culture, but her birthplace excludes her from full acceptance. Lisa, on the other hand only feels like her authentic self when she is engaging with the Latinx community, personally or professionally. American culture is something to be survived. Interestingly, both women speak of needing to defend and/or prove themselves. Moreover, Yasmin feels physically and socially isolated, but is working to overcome it to be a strong leader for her community. Victoria's sense of belonging is strongly tied to her residency in her ethnic neighborhood.

Taken together, these narratives suggest that gender and race/ethnicity are not a clear determinant of their experiences, illustrating how critical it is that we treat communities heterogeneously. Further, it demonstrates the continuing necessity for deep, local case studies in environmental justice works that problematize the intersections of identity and place – especially as we seek to enact culturally informed praxis and work toward some of the community benefits of positive place attachment. Understanding place as exclusionary is part of how these women engage with their community, and part of how they advocate for/ design programs to redress food injustice and create new socio-physical spaces for solidarity in their communities.

Politics of access

In addition to navigating different experiences and attachment to *place*, ability to access healthy food, to frequent food pantries, and to travel to food distribution locations was constrained for the promotoras and their representative communities. The reason most frequently cited was the difficulty in obtaining an appointment for a driver's license for persons going through the immigration process, the fear of repercussion for driving without one to food locations, and the lack of public transportation options in these neighborhoods.

Yasmin, a promotora and mother of two shared her fear of driving to work, but described it as a necessity because of the lack of public transportation servicing her neighborhood, the freeway structure that divides communities, and her dedication to the organization.

> Because I was really afraid about the police; about the all kind of things that we have, that we think that are going to happen if we going to get out, you know. And I remember that I don't drive on the freeway. If you notice, it's too far to here to the office. And I got to take two freeways to get there. So, I was so afraid. And the first time I said okay, (Yasmin), you've got a job. You want to do this, you have to go alone. Oh, when I get on there I was shaking like jelly. It was so, so scared because, you know, I don't have a license. If the police stop me, what I going to do?

Yasmin's concern was echoed by many of the promotoras, and again in group meetings with the families they served. Addressing food injustice in this community would require in part, regulatory changes to licensing laws (most respondents indicated an over six-month wait time, and that was for those willing to visit a state agency), and/or advances in transit equity. In the short term, neither of these options seems likely. Delaney (2015) articulates a persuasive case regarding the difficulty of rectifying transit-related spatial injustices, citing that many campaigns fall short, given issues of measurement and planning mechanisms in the courts. To his analysis, I would add the complexity of new migrants with precarious residency status interacting voluntarily with regulatory agencies.

Lisa, the formal leader of the Colorado promotora network describes her community as "good at hiding." As a result, many of their programs focus on food and grocery distribution in sanctuary spaces within neighborhood walking distance, group carpooling, or even delivery. This distinction is important; on the surface these programs would seem to be associated with community members not having access to reliable transportation. However, the oral histories reveal that many families do have a car, but fear traveling on busy roads (perceived to have more traffic cops) lest they be cited for a traffic violation which in the most extreme case could result in deportation. Instead, the focus of these programs is to create a geography of access that limits fear of apprehension, and to create food access points within "safe" community spaces that do not require identification/disassociated from federal benefits (i.e. SNAP). Public transit equity would be a partial, but incomplete, solution to the disparate access to nutritious food for this community. Without requisite attention to the complexity of local communities, remediation of environmental injustice is unlikely to be comprehensive, and could cause greater harm to some marginalized communities.

Concluding thoughts

I opened this chapter by asking as environmental justice scholars who are committed to praxis and visibility, how do we authentically represent the agency of the communities we work with? Reasserting these commitments, and being mindful of representation is paramount as scholars navigate research in the Anthropocene. Global action is swiftly needed; however, so too is a recognition that the devaluation of people and ecosystems was never random – the disparities of this epoch were intentional. This recognition helps to ground the ways in which the Anthropocene is embodied in local spatial injustices, and how communities counteract them.

As an intersectional local case study, this work revealed how exclusion based on place and race/ethnicity may differentially inform women's involvement in environmental justice action, how they approach resource access for their communities, and critically, that decisions to improve physical access to environmental benefits had to reckon with impacts of discriminatory discourse/behavior toward Latinx communities occurring at the state and federal level. Merry (2005) suggests that when scholars begin to work on questions of social justice, the borderland between science and activism is breached; and that by studying these issues, our work becomes part of an external activist narrative. As scholars answer Pellow's (2017) call for more multiscalar approaches, the continued importance of local studies that illuminate how spatial and environmental injustice is manifested, what is needed to remediate those effects, and what just futures must be comprised of, cannot be understated.

References

Alkon, A.H., and Agyeman, J. 2011. Cultivating the fertile field of food justice. *Cultivating Food Justice: Race, Class, and Sustainability*, MIT Press. pp. 331–347.

American Community Survey. 2017. https://www.census.gov/programs-surveys/acs

Brown, P., and Ferguson, F. 1995. Making a big stink: Women's work, women's relationships, and toxic waste activism. *Gender & Society* 9, no. 2: 145–172.

Brown, B., Perkins, D.D., and Brown, G. 2003. Place attachment in revitalizing neighborhoods: Individual and block level analysis. *Journal of Environmental Psychology* 23, no. 3: 259–271.

Burley, D., Jenkins, P., Laska, S., and Davis, T. 2007. Place attachment and environmental change in coastal Louisiana. *Organization & Environment* 20, no. 3: 347–366.

Cary, L.J. 1999. Unexpected stories: Life history and the limits of representation." *Qualitative Inquiry* 5, no. 3: 411–427.

CDOT - Colorado Department of Transportation. 2017. Annual Report. https://www.codot.gov/library/AnnualReports/cdot-official-annual-reports/2017-annual-report

Cho, S., Crenshaw, K.W., and McCall, L., 2013. Toward a field of intersectionality studies: Theory, applications, and praxis. *Signs: Journal of Women in Culture and Society* 38, no. 4: 785–810.

Cisneros, J.D. 2008. Contaminated communities: The metaphor of "immigrant as pollutant" in media representations of immigration. *Rhetoric and Public Affairs*, 569–601.

Collins, P.H. 1989. The social construction of black feminist thought. *Signs: Journal of Women in Culture and Society* 14, no. 4: 745–773.

Collins, P.H. 2000. Gender, black feminism, and black political economy. *Annals of the American Academy of Political and Social Science* 568, no. 1: 41–53.

Collins, P.H., and Bilge, S. 2016. *Intersectionality*. Cambridge: Polity.

Crenshaw, K. 1989. Demarginalizing the intersection of race and sex: A black feminist critique of antidiscrimination doctrine, feminist theory and antiracist politics. *The University of Chicago Legal Forum* 1989: 139.

Davis, K. 2008.Intersectionality as buzzword: A sociology of science perspective on what makes a feminist theory successful. *Feminist Theory* 9, no. 1: 67–85.

Delaney, D. 2015 Legal geography I: Constitutivities, complexities, and contingencies. *Progress in Human Geography* 39, no. 1: 96–102.

Devine-Wright, P. 2006. Rethinking NIMBYism: The role of place attachment and place identity in explaining place-protective action. *Journal of Community & Applied Social Psychology* 19, no. 6: 426–441.

Gruenewald, D.A. 2003. The best of both worlds: A critical pedagogy of place. *Educational Researcher* 32, no. 4:3–12.

Gubrium, J. 2005. Introduction: Narrative environments and social problems. *Social Problems* 52, no. 4: 525–528.

Guzmán, I.M. 2006. Competing discourses of community: Ideological tensions between local general-market and Latino news media." *Journalism* 7, no. 3: 281–298.

Harrison, J.L. 2014. Neoliberal environmental justice: Mainstream ideas of justice in political conflict over agricultural pesticides in the United States. *Environmental Politics* 23, no. 4: 650–669.

Inadmissibility on Public Charge Grounds Final Rule. United States Citizenship and Immigration Service. 2020. https://www.uscis.gov/news/fact-sheets/public-charge -fact-sheet

Krauss, C. 1993. Women and toxic waste protests: Race, class and gender as resources of resistance. *Qualitative Sociology* 16, no. 3: 247–262.

Larkins, M.L. 2018. Complicating communities: An intersectional approach to women's environmental justice narratives in the Rocky Mountain West. *Environmental Sociology* 4, no. 1: 67–78.

Lewis, S.L., and Maslin, M.A. 2015. Defining the anthropocene. *Nature* 519, no. 7542: 171–180.

Martin, P.Y. 2004. Gender as social institution. *Social Forces* 82, no. 4: 1249–1273.

Merry, S.E. 2005. Anthropology and activism: Researching human rights across porous boundaries. *PoLAR* 28: 240.

Pellow, D.N. 2017. *What is Critical Environmental Justice?* New Jersey: John Wiley & Sons.

Phillips, D. 2011. Latinos are fastest-growing population in county, census says. *Gazette*. Retrieved 2019. https://gazette.com/news/latinos-are-fastest-growing-population-i n-county-census-says/article_eebd7280-0722-50e7-a3af-e65f66630e70.html

Rivers, L., Arvai, J., and Slovic, P. 2010. Beyond a simple case of black and white: Searching for the white male effect in the African-American community. *Risk Analysis* 30, no. 1: 65–77.

Schlosberg, D. 2013. Theorising environmental justice: The expanding sphere of a discourse. *Environmental Politics* 22, no. 1: 37–55.

Soja, E., 2009. The city and spatial justice. *Justice Spatiale/Spatial Justice* 1, no. 1: 1–5.

Szasz, A., and Meuser, M. 1997. Environmental inequalities: Literature review and proposals for new directions in research and theory. *Current Sociology* 45, no. 3: 99–120.

Tuan, Y. 1977. *Space and Place: The Perspective of Experience*. Minnesota: University of Minnesota Press.

US Environmental Protection Agency. 2016. https://www.epa.gov/toxics-release-inventory-tri-program

Whyte, K.P. 2018. Indigenous science (fiction) for the Anthropocene: Ancestral dystopias and fantasies of climate change crises. *Environment and Planning E: Nature and Space* 1, no. 1–2: 224–242.

Winker, G., and Degele, N. 2011. Intersectionality as multi-level analysis: Dealing with social inequality. *European Journal of Women's Studies* 18, no. 1: 51–66.

9

DETERMINANTS OF HOUSEHOLD ELECTRICITY CONSUMPTION IN MEXICO BY INCOME LEVEL

Mónica Santillán Vera, Lilia García Manrique, and Isabel Rodríguez Peña

Introduction

Improving household energy services (electricity and modern technologies and fuels for cooking and heat) has positive effects on education, health, and employment opportunities, demonstrating a direct link between energy and development (AGEEC, 2010; IBRD, 2017; Karekezi et al., 2012; Reddy et al., 2000; United Nations, 2015). Thus, there is a growing interest in improving energy for all, considering several aspects: access, environmental sustainability, affordability, reliability, security, among others. Most research and policies have focused on promoting better energy conditions to the sectors that suffer energy poverty (lack of energy access and/or undesirable consequences of the use of energy like health problems, pollution, etc.). Walker and Day (2012) considered energy poverty as a distinct form of inequality and as a problem of distributive injustice. We think that it is necessary to broaden the analysis of disparities in energy access and use – which often mirror inequalities in income – contributing to the conceptual underpinning of energy justice.

Within the framework of environmental justice, energy justice imposes an important paradox to disentangle. Considering the most basic definition of energy justice, i.e. "distribution of benefits and burdens," gives a glimpse of the problem. Energy can hardly be defined as a benefit or a burden because, even though it may look like a benefit, the reality is that it is just a means of how a good is obtained (electricity, thermal comfort, hot meal). For this reason, it is called energy services, and as such, it is necessary to guarantee an equal distribution of these services (Sovacool et al., 2014). The importance of distribution takes a central position in understanding energy justice as a principal component of environmental justice. The concept of energy justice is extensive, including such variate issues like decentralization, access, sustainability, gender inequalities, marginalized regions, and institutional instability (Lacey-Barnacle et al., 2020). According to Jenkins et al. (2016), energy justice applies justice principles to energy policy, energy production and systems, energy consumption, energy activism, energy security, and climate change.

Focusing on inequalities on energy consumption of Mexican households, research has identified that the household income level plays a significant role in energy consumption: there is a direct but not linear relationship between energy expenditure and income level and/or between energy consumption (in physical terms) and income level (Cruz Islas 2012; Jiménez and Yépez-García 2017; Navarro 2014; Rosas Flores 2011; Rosas Flores et al. 2010; Sánchez Peña 2012). Also, research using descriptive statistics (Franco and Velázquez 2017), logistic regression (Cruz Islas 2012), ordinary least squares (OLS) and Tobit models (Rodríguez Oreggia and Yépez García 2014), and polynomial regression (Jiménez and Yépez-García 2017) identified that sociodemographic factors, dwelling and equipment characteristics are determinants of the varying energy consumption levels in Mexican households.

Distinguishing what factors are important drivers of energy consumption at high-, medium-, and low-income levels could be useful to design strategies and policies focused on a certain type of consumers. In this context, the objective of this paper is to identify the main drivers of household electricity[1] consumption by income level in Mexico in 2016 through a quantile regression model (Koenker and Bassett Jr 1978) using the Household Income and Expenditure Survey (*Encuesta Nacional de Ingresos y Gastos de los Hogares*, ENIGH). Our hypothesis is that the determinants of electricity consumption levels are heterogeneous among income levels. In low-income households, economic aspects such as income and electricity price limit electricity consumption, while low energy-efficient equipment increases electricity consumption. In high-income households, the electricity consumption level is inelastic with respect to economic factors, high energy-efficient equipment limits electricity consumption, and high saturation of equipment[2] increases electricity consumption.

An initial approach to electricity inequality in Mexico 2016

We make an initial approach to electricity consumption inequality in Mexico using data of the 2016 ENIGH through descriptive statistics. This survey is representative at the national and state levels for urban and rural locations, its sample size is 70,311 households, and its expanded sample is 33,462,598 households (INEGI 2017). For this analysis, we classified the households by income deciles according to their current income,[3] and we discussed the statistics at three levels: income, location (urban or rural), and states.

In 2016, 99.5% of Mexican households had access to electricity (INEGI 2017). Lack of access to electricity was more common in deciles, locations, and states that structurally face more poverty: 48% of the households without electricity access were concentrated in the lowest income decile, 70% in rural locations, and almost 36% in three states of the country (Veracruz, Oaxaca, and Mexico State) that are classified within the five states with the highest population in poverty (Table 9.1). This situation is concerning because in the long term lack of access to electricity could exacerbate poverty, inequality, and social exclusion in the country.

Public service was the main form of electricity access (99.4%). Households with low incomes and in rural locations presented the highest participation in solar panels (Table 9.1). This situation is related to the difficulties of expanding the main electricity grid to the most geographically isolated areas with low population density, which limits the supply of public service in these areas and favors mini-grids and off-grid systems, such as solar panels. Additionally, this situation reflects a low scope of power distributed generation, a policy that aims to boost clean distributed generation at households that have high-consumption household tariffs (*Tarifa Doméstica de Alto Consumo, DAC*),[4] which are mostly high-income households.

Regarding economic aspects, we only considered the households that reported electricity expenditure greater than zero in the ENIGH, hence the new sample size is 62,470 households and the expanded sample is 29,571,038 households. Table 9.1 shows that household electricity expenditure was directly related to household income levels, while the proportion of income allocated to pay electricity bills was inversely related to household income levels. Electricity expenditures increased as household income was higher (271 vs 1,359 Mexican pesos quarterly in the first and tenth deciles, respectively). The weight of electricity expenditures on the household budget decreased as household income was higher (3.4% in the first decile vs 1.0% in the tenth decile). Even though household electricity tariffs are subsided by the Mexican government – except DAC tariffs – and the proportions of income to pay electricity are small, it could be that some households pay low bills because they do not satisfy all their electricity needs and cannot afford to spend more money.

According to location, Table 9.1 shows that the average quarterly electricity expenditure per household was higher in urban locations than in rural ones (699.5 vs 385.7 Mexican pesos, respectively), and the proportion of income to electricity expenditure was a little lower in urban locations than in rural ones (1.8% vs 1.9%, respectively). Although the average electricity expenditure in urban households is significantly higher than that in rural households, in recent years there have been increasing energy poverty problems in urban areas of Mexico and Latin America (García Ochoa 2014; Kozulj 2009). This phenomenon could be explained by the migration of poor people from rural to urban areas, who do not meet better life conditions automatically and often form poverty belts on the periphery of the cities, where they suffer, among other things, energy poverty.

At the state level, households located in states with hot weather in the North of Mexico (Sonora, Sinaloa, and Baja California) spent more money on electricity and allocated a higher proportion of their income to pay electricity bills than the rest of the country (Table 9.1). This situation could be explained

TABLE 9.1 Distribution of lack of electricity, electricity expenditure/income ratio, and type of electricity access (%)

Decile / Location / State	Distribution of Lack of Electricity (%)	Type of Electricity Access (%)				Electricity Expenditure		Electricity Consumption
		Public Service	Private Plant	Solar Panel	Other Sources	Household Quarterly Average (Mexican Pesos)	Proportion of Household Income (%)	Household Quarterly Average (kWh)
1st Decile	48	98.5	0.1	0.5	1.0	271.0	3.4	245.3
2nd Decile	19	99.1	0.2	0.1	0.6	351.1	2.5	323.2
3rd Decile	11	99.3	0.1	0.1	0.5	391.9	2.1	354.8
4th Decile	9	99.1	0.1	0.1	0.7	452.1	1.9	406.2
5th Decile	6	99.6	0.1	0.1	0.3	519.8	1.8	460.9
6th Decile	3	99.5	0.1	0.1	0.3	571.1	1.6	503.6
7th Decile	2	99.7	0.1	0.0	0.2	647.2	1.5	551.1
8th Decile	1	99.6	0.2	0.0	0.1	744.7	1.4	609.2
9th Decile	0	99.7	0.2	0.0	0.0	903.2	1.3	696.0
10th Decile	0	99.8	0.1	0.0	0.0	1,358.7	1.0	816.9
Urban Loc.	30	99.6	0.1	0.0	0.3	699.5	1.8	550.2
Rural Loc.	70	98.5	0.2	0.5	0.8	385.7	1.9	330.9
Mexican states with the highest lack of electricity, electricity expenditure and electricity consumption	Veracruz (16) Oaxaca (10) Mexico State (9)					Sonora (1,987.7) Sinaloa (1,418.5) Baja California (1,398.4)	Sonora (4.8) Sinaloa (3.8) Baja California (3.2)	Sonora (1,841.2) Sinaloa (1,432.5) Baja California (1,124.9)
Total or Average	**100**	**99.4**	**0.1**	**0.1**	**0.4**	**634.2**	**1.8**	**504.6**

Data based on the 2016 ENIGH (INEGI, 2017).

by air conditioning usage. In 2016, 33% of the Mexican households placed in hot regions used air conditioning, but not all households could afford to pay for air conditioning. Although the North and the South of the country present high temperatures, using air conditioning is more frequent in the North than in the South because North households have a higher income than South households, as well as the contrasting lifestyles between them. Meeting cooling demand in hot Mexican regions is a big challenge as many of the dwelling units do not use building designs that keep indoor temperatures down (CONUEE, 2016).

Finally, we analyzed the household electricity consumption in physical units (kWh) by income, location, and state levels. Given that there is no official disaggregated information on household electricity consumption in Mexico, we estimated it following the methodology applied by Santillán (2019) and using data of electricity expenditure reported in the ENIGH (INEGI 2017), the average price of electricity by tariffs (SIE 2019), and electricity users by tariff and municipality (CFE 2018). We found that there was a direct relationship between income and electricity consumption, urban locations consumed more electricity than rural ones, and states in the North of the country consumed more electricity than the rest of the country (Table 9.1). These trends were like electricity expenditure ones. However, electricity consumption changes were not directly proportional to electricity expenditure changes because of several electricity tariffs. The most evident decoupling between electricity expenditure and electricity consumption was at the high-income deciles. This situation is related to DAC tariffs, which are mainly paid by high-income households (more than 50% of the DAC tariffs are placed in households at 9th and 10th deciles).

Quantile regression (QR) model

Given the relevance of income inequality on household energy consumption levels, we used a quantile regression (Koenker and Bassett Jr 1978) to determine the drivers of household energy consumption by income level. This model is more appropriate than the ordinary least squares (OLS) model for analyzing quantile information. A quantile regression may be viewed as an extension of classical least squares estimation of conditional mean models to the estimation of an ensemble of models for several conditional quantile functions (Koenker and Hallock 2001). The QR does not assume that the disturbances are normally distributed, which is convenient, using microdata from survey information that often has heteroscedastic disturbances, i.e., variance of the errors are not constant in the whole sample.

For the purpose of this paper, we estimated both the OLS and the QR in order to contrast them and analyze the differences between the average coefficients of OLS and QR with income distribution. For both methodologies, we used the microdata from the 2016 ENIGH, considered the households that reported electricity expenditure greater than zero, and used the Stata 14 software.[5] We established the natural logarithm (ln) of electricity consumption as a dependent variable and three sets of independent variables. For this model we have 59 covariates, plus an intercept. Table 9.2 shows the operationalization of independent variables, their expected sign, and their expected interquantile

TABLE 9.2 Covariates of the model

Covariates	Operationalization	Expected sign /Expected interquantile tendency
Economic factors		
Income (ln)	Estimated variable	+ / decreasing
Electricity price (ln)	Estimated variable	− / decreasing
Socio-demographic factors		
Household members	Number of household members	+ / stable
Gender of household head	1=female, 0=male	neutral / stable
Education level of household head	1= Less than High School	(reference category)
	2= High School	+ / decreasing
	3= Some College	+ / decreasing
	4= College Graduate	+ / decreasing
	5= Postgraduate	+ / decreasing
Age of household head	Years of the household head	+ / decreasing
Type of locations	1=urban, 0=rural	+ / rising
Dwelling and equipment		
Number of rooms	Number of rooms	+ / decreasing
Usage of gas	1= use gas; 0=not use gas	neutral / stable
Usage of biomass	1= use biomass; 0=not use biomass	− / decreasing
Ownership of air conditioning	1= with air conditioning; 0= without air conditioning	+ / rising
Ownership of heating	1= with heating; 0=without heating	+ / rising
Incandescent lightbulbs	Number of incandescent lightbulbs	+ / decreasing
Energy-efficient lightbulbs	Number of energy-efficient lightbulbs	+ / rising
Appliances: refrigerator, microwave, washing machine, digital TV, analog TV, computer, fan	Number of appliances: refrigerator, microwave, washing machine, digital TV, analog TV, computer, fan	+ / rising
★Years old of the appliances: refrigerator, microwave, washing machine, digital TV, analog TV, computer, fan	1= without appliance	(reference category)
	2= 0–5 years old of the appliance	+ / rising
	3= 6–10 years old of the appliance	+ / rising
	4= 11–15 years old of the appliance	+ / stable
	5= 16–20 years old of the appliance	+ / decreasing
	6= more than 20 years old of the appliance	+ / decreasing

★ Given that not all observations don't report the aging years old of all appliances all because not all households own appliances. For that reason, we set an extra category to identify households without appliances and took it as a reference category.

tendency. Our expectations of sign and tendency are based on a literature review and descriptive statistics previously exposed.

The OLS model was estimated using the following equation:

$$\ln q_i = \beta_0 + \beta_1 \ln x_{1i} + \beta_2 \ln x_{2i} + \beta_3 x_{3i} + \beta_4 x_{4i} + \ldots + \beta_{59} x_{59i} + \varepsilon_i$$

Where q_i is the household electricity consumption and x_{ki} are the values of the covariates before described. Then we computed the quantile regression using the following model:

$$\min_\beta \left[\sum_{i \in \{i: y_i \geq x_i \beta\}} \theta \left| y_i - x_i \beta_\theta \right| + \sum_{i \in \{i: y_i < x_i \beta\}} (1-\theta) \left| y_i - x_i \beta_\theta \right| \right]$$

Where θ is the quantile estimated, y_i are the observed values from the sample, x_i is the vector of independent variables and β_θ is the value minimizing the expression. We estimated the model for the quantiles $\lambda = 0.10$, 0.25, 0.50, 0.75, and 0.90.

Results and discussion

We limit the discussion and graphical presentation of these results to only a few of the covariates, mainly to those covariates that are statistically significant ($\alpha =$ 0.10) and that present a wide contrast between OLS and QR estimations. For Figures 9.1–9.6, each of the plots have a horizontal quantile scale and a vertical scale that indicates the covariate effect. The solid curves represent the quantile regression estimates. The shaded grey areas depict a 90% pointwise confidence band for the quantile regression estimates. The dashed lines show the ordinary least squares estimate of the conditional mean effect. The two dotted lines represent conventional 90% confidence interval for the least squares estimate.

Household income level showed a direct relation to electricity consumption (Figure 9.1), electricity price presented an inverse relation to electricity consumption (Figure 9.2), and both covariates presented a decreasing interquantile tendency. The effects of changes in economic factors (household income and electricity price) were more intensive on the electricity consumption of low-income households than high-income households, i.e., electricity consumption was more elastic in low-income households.[6] As we can see by the contrast between OLS and QR in Figures 9.1 and 9.2, the conventional least squares confidence interval did a poor job of representing this range of disparity, mainly regarding electricity price. For Mexico this is an important topic since income distribution is highly heterogeneous.

For the rest of the coefficients discussed here, it is important to keep in mind that the coefficients estimated of numerical variables indicate the relative change of a one-unit change of the covariate on electricity consumption, holding other

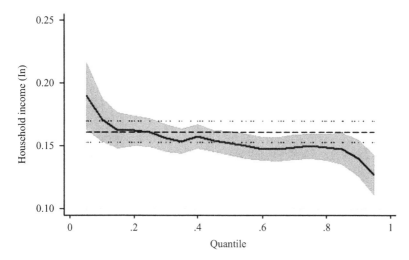

FIGURE 9.1   Ordinary least squares (OLS) and quantile regression (QR) of household income.

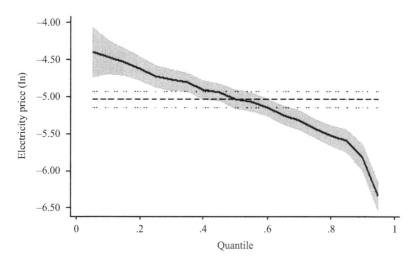

FIGURE 9.2   Ordinary least squares (OLS) and quantile regression (QR) of electricity price.

covariates fixed. For dichotomic variables, the coefficients estimated indicate the relative change in comparison to the reference category of the covariate on electricity consumption holding other covariates fixed. Each coefficient could be multiplied by 100 in order to obtain the percentage change or semi-elasticity.

The number of household members had a direct effect on the electricity consumption level, with a reduced effect in high-income households and a changing interquantile trend (Figure 9.3). Electricity consumption was lower in households with more educated household heads, without high interquantile contrasts, and with a relatively good fit to OLS confidence interval. The age of the household heads did not have a relevant effect on electricity consumption (coefficients=0). Households placed in urban locations consumed more electricity than rural ones, and this effect was higher in low-income households, but the differences were not very large and the distribution was within the OLS confidence interval (Figure 9.4).

The number of rooms had a direct impact on household electricity consumption and the interquantile tendency was stable and within the OLS confidence interval. Usage of gas had a direct relationship to electricity consumption, while usage of biomass had an indirect one. These coefficients could be explained by the modern and traditional equipment of the households. If a household uses gas, it has a higher probability of consuming more electricity because of its modern equipment, and vice versa for the case of biomass. The interquantile tendency for gas usage was decreasing. Ownership of air conditioning was the covariate with the highest coefficient in the dwelling and equipment group of variables, and it presented a rising interquantile tendency that clearly contrasts with OLS (Figure 9.5). At the λ=90, if a household had air conditioning, its electricity consumption rose 68%.

The number of appliances was directly related to electricity consumption (except washing machines and computers), but it was not statistically significant for all appliances nor for all quantiles. The number of lightbulbs did not affect electricity consumption (coefficients=0). In contrast, the number of refrigerators has a direct and larger effect on the electricity consumption of high-income households (coefficients statistically significant at λ=75 y λ=90). Also, Figure 9.6

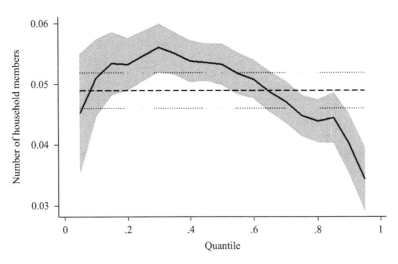

FIGURE 9.3 Ordinary least squares (OLS) and quantile regression (QR) of number of household members.

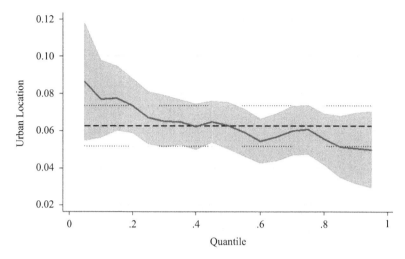

FIGURE 9.4   Ordinary least squares (OLS) and quantile regression (QR) of type of location (rural/urban).

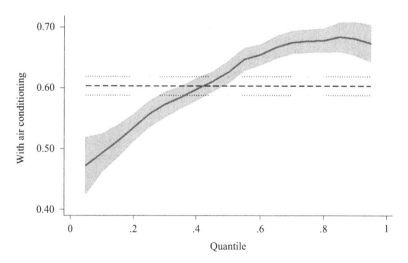

FIGURE 9.5   Ordinary least squares (OLS) and quantile regression (QR) of ownership of air conditioning.

shows that the interquantile estimates of the number of refrigerators are not in line with the average OLS. The interquantile estimates demonstrate how refrigerators are appliances with heterogeneous consumption given a certain household income. The number of analog TVs had a positive coefficient and a decreasing interquantile tendency. The number of fans had a U-inverted interquantile tendency. Regarding the number of computers, we consider that it requires more research to explain the inverse relationship to electricity consumption.

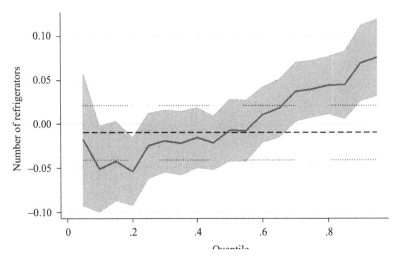

FIGURE 9.6 Ordinary least squares (OLS) and quantile regression (QR) of ownership of number of refrigerators.

The coefficients of the age of the appliances were positive because the reference category represents households without an appliance. The interquantile tendencies were diverse; this diversity is not regular according to the age of the appliances. We expected certain interquantile tendencies (Table 9.2) assuming that high-income households have newer appliances that are more energy-efficient, thus reducing their energy consumption. But the coefficients of the age of appliances do not increase very much between the modern appliances (0–5 years old) and the old ones (more than 20 years old), which could be related to the wider capacity and new functions of modern appliances. Among all the appliances analyzed, only the age of refrigerators and washing machines was statistically significant at most categories (α=0.01).

These observations require more research and discussion. With the implementation of the Minimum Energy Efficiency Standards since the 1990s, it was expected decreased electricity consumption would result due to more energy-efficient appliances (Martínez & Sheinbaum, 2016). However, this expected change has not been significant and household electricity consumption has increased in absolute terms. This increase may be explained by a higher saturation of appliances (Escoto Castillo et al. 2016) and a higher capacity of the modern appliances that limit the expected decreasing energy consumption (Davis et al. 2014). These responses are known as rebound effects[7] (Hertwich, 2005). For developing countries, rebound effects could be more pronounced than in developed countries (Gottron, F. & Resources, Science, and Industry Division 2001). For Mexico, Gopal et al. (2014) estimated that the rebound effect is 11% for refrigerators and televisions, and 24% for air conditioners.

Conclusions

We applied a quantile regression model (Koenker and Bassett Jr 1978) in order to identify the drivers of household electricity consumption by income level in Mexico using the 2016 ENIGH. The results can be divided into three groups: economic, sociodemographic, and dwelling and equipment factors. Regarding economic factors, we found a direct relation between income level and electricity consumption and an inverse relationship between electricity price and electricity consumption. Regarding socio-demographic factors, the households in urban locations consumed more electricity than rural ones, mainly low-income households. The number of household members had a direct relation to electricity consumption. Electricity consumption was lower in households with the more educated household heads. Finally, regarding dwelling and equipment characteristics, household electricity consumption was higher when the dwelling was bigger. The number of appliances was directly related to electricity consumption (except washing machines and computers), but it was not statistically significant for all appliances nor for all quantiles. The number of refrigerators influenced electricity consumption. The number of analog TVs had a positive coefficient. The number of fans presented a U-inverted interquantile tendency.

In conclusion, the quantile regression model for household electricity consumption in Mexico does prove that the determinants of electricity consumption levels are heterogeneous among income levels. In low-income households, economic aspects such as income and electricity price limit electricity consumption, so that a change in these variables affects electricity consumption significantly. In contrast, in high-income households, the most relevant aspects are the equipment of dwelling and saturation of appliances. This result opens alternatives to manage energy consumption. At high-income households, tempering the number of appliances may be an option to reduce energy consumption without affecting life conditions within a framework of energy justice. Information disclosure on household energy consumption patterns is emerging as a procedural mechanism for tackling distributive injustices (Jenkins et al. 2016).

These results demonstrate the complexity of energy justice. First, it is clear that at the lowest distribution of income there should be a better allocation of resources in a way that low-income households can satisfy their energy needs. On the other hand, at the highest distribution of income, there is a concentration of resources that allows a higher demand for electricity. Although more resources can signify more efficient appliances, the rebound effect results in a higher demand of electricity. As a service, energy should be available equally to everyone but as people become more affluent, their energy consumption increases, resulting in a contradictory outcome: higher social welfare but higher negative impact in the environment (Sovacool et al. 2014).

Energy transition must take into consideration questions of energy justice to ensure that policies, plans, and programs guarantee fair and equitable access to resources and technologies (McCauley et al. 2019). Energy inequality and energy poverty are relevant under a broader definition – that of energy justice. For this case study, income levels are determinant as are spatial variables (urban vs rural) and gender related variables (head of household). For future research it will be relevant to control for these variables in a more explicit way, given the impact on the overall results.

Notes

1 We limited the analysis of household energy consumption to household electricity consumption in order to obtain more accurate conclusions about just one type of energy.
2 Following Rosas Flores et al. (2011), saturation is defined as the number of appliances per household.
3 The quarterly average household income (in Mexican pesos) from the 1st to the 10th deciles were the following: 8,166; 14,206; 18,917; 23,553; 28,811; 34,836; 42,431; 53,380; 72,033; 168,838.
4 DAC tariff is applied to households with high electricity consumption and is not subsidized by the Mexican government.
5 Stata is a complete and integrated statistical software package that provides data analysis, data management, graphics, simulations, regression, and custom programming.
6 Given that we used natural logarithms for these variables, the estimated coefficients are elasticity values that represent the percentage impact of a change of 1% of the covariate on electricity consumption holding other covariates fixed.
7 As defined by Sorell (2007): "Improvements in energy efficiency encourage greater use of the services which energy helps to provide."

References

AGEEC, Advisory Group on Energy and Climate, 2010. *Energy for a Sustainable Future.* Nueva York: UN Secretary-General's Advisory Group on Energy and Climate Change.

Escoto Castillo, A., Sánchez Peña, L. & Pérez Guardián, G., 2016. Hogares y energía eléctrica en México. *Revista Espinhaço| UFVJM*, 5 (2), pp. 30–43.

CFE, Comisión Federal de Electricidad, 2018. *Usuarios y consumo de electricidad por municipio (a partir de 2018).* https://datos.gob.mx/busca/dataset/usuarios-y-consumo -de-electricidad-por-municipio-a-partir-de-2018/resource/38b7a514-78c2-4355-9 ed0-d6ac72722952 [Accessed 25 agosto 2018].

CONUEE, Comisión Nacional para el Uso Eficiente de la Energía, 2016. *Estudio de caracterización del uso de aire acondicionado en vivienda de interés social.* Ciudad de México: CONUEE-GIZ.

Cruz Islas, I.C., 2012. *Determinantes socio-demográficos del consumo de energía en los hogares de México, en el marco de la Estrategia Nacional del Cambio Climático.* México: Tesis de Doctorado, El Colegio de México.

Davis, L.W., Fuchs, A. & Gertler, P., 2014. Cash for Coolers: Evaluating a Large-Scale Appliance Replacement Program in Mexico. *American Economic Journal: Economic Policy*, 6(4), pp. 207–238.

Franco, A. & Velázquez, M., 2017. Una aproximación sociodemográfica al consumo de energía de los hogares mexicanos, 2014. In: *La situación demográfica de México 2016.* Consejo Nacional de Población, Ciudad de México, pp. 159–181.

García Ochoa, R., 2014. *Pobreza energética en América Latina.*, Santiago de Chile: Comisión Económica para América Latina y el Caribe (CEPAL).

Gopal, A.R., Leventis, G. & Phadke, A., 2014. Self-Financed Efficiency Incentives: Case Study of Mexico. *Energy Efficiency*, 7(5), pp. 865–877.

Gottron, F. & Resources, Science, and Industry Division, 2001. *Energy Efficiency and the Rebound Effect: Does Increasing Efficiency Decrease Demand?* Library of Congress, Congressional Research Service.

Hertwich, E.G., 2005. Consumption and the Rebound Effect. *Journal of Industrial Ecology*, 9(1–2), pp. 85–98.

IBRD, International Bank for Reconstruction and Development, 2017. *Sustainable Energy for All. Global Tracking Framework. Progress Toward Sustainable Energy.* World Bank: Washington, DC.

INEGI, Instituto Nacional de Estadística y Geografía, 2017. *Encuesta Nacional de Ingresos y Gastos de los Hogares 2016*, México: Instituto Nacional de Estadística y Geografía (INEGI), .

Jenkins, K. et al., 2016. Energy Justice: A Conceptual Review. *Energy Research & Social Science*, 11, pp. 174–182.

Jiménez, R. & Yépez-García, A., 2017. *Understanding the Drivers of Household Energy Spending: Micro Evidence for Latin America.* Washington, DC: Inter-American Development Bank.

Karekezi, S., McDade, S., Boardman, B. & Kimani, J., 2012. Chapter 2 - Energy, Poverty and Development. In: *Global Energy Assessment - Toward a Sustainable Future.* Laxenburg: Cambridge University Press, Cambridge, UK and New York, NY, USA and the International Institute for Applied Systems Analysis, pp. 151–190.

Koenker, R. & Bassett Jr, G., 1978. Regression Quantiles. *Econometrica: Journal of the Econometric Society*, 46 (1) (Jan., 1978), pp. 33–50.

Koenker, R. & Hallock, K., 2001. Quantile Regression: An Introduction. *Journal of Economic Perspectives*, 4, pp. 43–56.

Kozulj, R., 2009. *Contribución de los servicios energéticos a los Objetivos de Desarrollo del Milenio y a la mitigación de la pobreza en América Latina y el Caribe.* Santiago de Chile: CEPAL, Naciones Unidas.

Lacey-Barnacle, M., Robison, R. & Foulds, C., 2020. Energy Justice in the Developing World: A Review of Theoretical Frameworks, Key Research Themes and Policy Implications. *Energy for Sustainable Development*, 55, pp. 122–138.

Martínez, S.A. & Sheinbaum, C., 2016. The Impact of Energy Efficiency Standards on Residential Electricity Consumption in Mexico. *Energy for Sustainable Development*, 32, pp. 50–61.

McCauley, D. et al., 2019. Energy Justice in the Transition to Low Carbon Energy Systems: Exploring Key Themes in Interdisciplinary Research. *Applied Energy*, 233–234 (1 January 2019), pp. 916 –921.

Navarro, J.C., 2014. *Energía y equidad en México: tendencias en la distribución del ingreso y el gasto en energía 1968–2008.* México: Tesis de Maestría, UNAM.

Reddy, A.K. et al., 2000. Energy and Social Issues. In: *World Energy Assessment: Energy and the Challenge of Sustainability.* Washington, DC: UNDP, pp. 39–60.

Rodríguez Oreggia, E. & Yépez García, R.A., 2014. *Income and Energy Consumption in Mexican Households.* The World Bank Latin America and the Caribbean Region Energy Unit, Policy Research Working Paper 6864, May 2014.

Rosas Flores, J.A., 2011. *Evolución del consumo y gasto económico de energía en el sector residencial (urbano-rural) mexicano 1996–2006.* Ciudad de México: Tesis de Doctorado, UNAM.

Rosas Flores, J.A., Sheinbaum, C. & Morillon, D., 2010. The Structure of Household Energy Consumption and Related CO2 Emissions by Income Group in Mexico. *Energy for Sustainable Development*, 14, pp. 127–133.

Rosas Flores, J.A., Rosas Flores, D. & Morillón Gálvez, D., 2011. Saturation, Energy Consumption, CO_2 Emission and Energy Efficiency from Urban and Rural Households Appliances in Mexico. *Energy and Buildings*, 43, pp. 10–18.

Sánchez Peña, L., 2012. El consumo energético de los hogares en México. *Coyuntura Demográfica*, No. 2, México: Sociedad Mexicana de Demografía.

Santillán, M., 2019. *La demanda de bienes y servicios de los hogares por nivel de ingresos y las emisiones de CO2: el caso de México 1990–2014*. Ciudad de México: Tesis de Doctorado en Economía, UNAM.

SIE, Sistema de Información Energética, 2019. *Información Estadística*. Ciudad de México: Secretaría de Energía (SENER).

Sorell, 2007. *The Rebound Effect: An Assessment of the Evidence for Economy-Wide Energy Savings from Improved Energy Efficiency*.

Sovacool, B.K., Sidortsov, R.V. & Jones, B.R., 2014. *Energy Security, Equality and Justice*. New York: Routledge.

United Nations, 2015. Resolution A/RES/70/1. Transforming our world: the 2030 Agenda for Sustainable Development. In: Seventieth United Nations General Assembly, New York, 21 October 2015. New York: United Nations. https://undocs .org/A/RES/70/1

Walker, G. & Day, R., 2012. Fuel Poverty as Injustice: Integrating Distribution, Recognition and Procedure in the Struggle for Affordable Warmth. *Energy Policy*, 49, pp. 69–75.

10

ENVIRONMENTAL JUSTICE AND THE SABAL TRAIL PIPELINE

Julie A. Lester

Introduction

One of the challenges in the Anthropocene is meeting increasing demand for affordable energy while minimizing environmental harms. Energy projects, such as natural gas pipelines, may increase affordable energy production but at an environmental cost. While greenhouse gas emissions from natural gas pipelines are lower than other sources, such as coal, there are still negative environmental effects from the drilling and transportation of natural gas through pipelines (Union of Concerned Scientists 2014). Increased greenhouse gas emissions contribute to climate change and may have an impact on the energy sector, such as threats to infrastructure due to rising sea levels, an increase in demand created by increasing temperatures, and increasing costs of energy production (United States Global Change Research Program 2018). Climate change also threatens ecosystems and may lead to cultural and economic changes in communities, especially those that may have a strong economic dependence on agriculture and natural resources (United States Global Change Research Program 2018).

Communities face numerous challenges related to climate change, including the impact of siting decisions for energy projects that may cause a disproportionate negative impact on human and environmental health, especially in environmental justice communities. In response, individuals and groups (stakeholders) interested in the outcome of the United States government's decision-making process for new energy projects have mobilized to vocalize their opinions on projects.

Through a consideration of comments submitted during the public comment period, statements at public meetings and protests, and lawsuits filed by stakeholders, this research will provide information about how stakeholders framed environmental justice claims during the Sabal Trail pipeline's approval and construction process.

The Sabal Trail pipeline

While energy companies have invested in clean energy to mitigate the challenges of climate change in the Anthropocene, many have also expanded on existing infrastructure to meet consumer demands in an affordable manner. In July 2013, Florida Power and Light awarded a contract to Sabal Trail Transmission, LLC (Sabal Trail) for construction of a 515-mile natural gas pipeline that, once complete, would connect to an existing pipeline in Alabama, cross south Georgia, and terminate in central Florida (Florida Power and Light 2013). The Sabal Trail pipeline, part of the larger Southeast Market Pipelines project (SMP), would provide over one billion cubic feet of natural gas daily to help meet the demands for affordable and reliable energy as approximately 68% of Florida's electricity is produced with natural gas (Watkins 2013). The pipeline was unanimously approved by the Florida Public Service Commission in 2013 and, once approved, Sabal Trail commenced the pre-filing process with the Federal Energy Regulatory Commission (FERC) (Penn 2013).

Sabal Trail focused on the economic benefits the pipeline would provide, such as the creation of over 5,000 jobs and more than $200 million going into local economies, but opponents were skeptical (Sabal Trail Transmission, LLC, n.d.a). Over several months, open houses and public scoping meetings were held to provide information about the construction process and to discuss issues relevant to the preparation of the environmental impact statement (EIS) submitted in 2015. The United States Environmental Protection Agency (EPA) expressed concerns about the EIS and, after those concerns were addressed by the company, the EIS was approved in December 2015 and the FERC issued the certificate of public necessity in early 2016 (Sabal Trail Transmission, LLC n.d.b).

In 2016, the Georgia General Assembly passed legislation to refuse easements to drilling under five rivers and, after a court challenge, the company was granted permission to drill under or across the rivers (Sheinin 2016; Chapman 2016). Multiple lawsuits were filed by landowners and environmental groups throughout the approval and construction process. The Georgia Water Coalition (2016) included the pipeline on their "Dirty Dozen" list and protest activity ramped up in late 2016, especially in Florida. While these protest activities had support from a variety of pipeline opponents, there was concern that the protests were too late to make a difference as one opponent commented, "Florida is late to the party ... It would have been nice to have this two years ago" (Cordeiro 2017). Construction continued in spite of the protests and, in July 2017, the pipeline began operation (United States Energy Information Administration 2017).

Framing environmental justice claims

Scholars have recognized the importance of language and issue framing in politics and policymaking, as frames are used by policymakers and the public to understand issues and make decisions about policy action (Zundel 1995). Walker (2012, p. 4) defined framing as

> a notion that recognizes that the world is not just "out there" waiting to be unproblematically discovered, but has to be given meaning, labelled and categorized, and interpreted through ideas, propositions and assertions about how things are and how they ought to be.

As stakeholders submitted written comments and spoke in opposition to the pipeline, many of their claims were framed as environmental justice concerns. In this case, environmental justice claims appeared to be framed around three types of justice as stakeholders attempted to influence the decision-making process: procedural justice which focuses on the decision-making process and the actors involved in that process, distributive justice which focuses on the distribution of benefits or harms, and justice as recognition which considers what actors are "given respect and who is and isn't valued" (Walker 2012, p. 10). While environmental justice scholarship has focused much attention on distributive justice, a consideration of the relationship between the three types of justice may be necessary to address environmental justice issues with greater success (Schlosberg 2007; Bell and Carrick 2018).

Procedural justice, which draws on participatory and deliberative democracy, focuses on how decisions are made, which stakeholders are involved, and how they may influence the decision-making process (Schlosberg 2007; Walker 2012). Public participation in the decision-making process is crucial in a democracy and it has been vital to the environmental justice movement (Schlosberg 2007). The U.S. EPA (n.d.) defines environmental justice as "the fair treatment and meaningful involvement of all people regardless of race, color, national origin, or income, with respect to the development, implementation, and enforcement of environmental laws, regulations, and policies." While the EPA's definition highlights the importance of participation, institutional barriers of segregation and discrimination have created challenges for some seeking power in the policy-making process (Bullard 1993). In this case, procedural justice is applied through the formal decision-making process used by the government to grant permission for pipeline construction and the methods through which a variety of stakeholders worked to influence the outcomes of that process including public meetings, public comment periods, protests, and legal action.

As part of the pre-filing process, Sabal Trail held 31 open houses and 13 public meetings to discuss issues in preparation of the draft EIS. Over 1,000 comment letters and 199 verbal comments were received from over 600 affected landowners, 12 governmental agencies (federal and state), six members of Congress, five non-governmental organizations, and four Native American tribes (Federal Energy Regulatory Commission 2015b). After the draft EIS was submitted, 10 additional meetings were held and 154 verbal comments, 137 letters, and a petition with over 3,700 signatures were received (Federal Energy Regulatory

Commission 2015b). Common themes in the comments included concerns about environmental justice issues, such as negative health and economic impacts on environmental justice communities, and concerns about ecological health, such as threats to air and water quality, in the areas affected by pipeline construction (Federal Energy Regulatory Commission 2015c). Many of the comments were framed to highlight procedural, distributive, and recognition claims important to discussions about environmental justice. Public comment periods and meetings were important as they allowed stakeholders opportunities to participate in the decision-making process, but it does not appear that they significantly influenced the outcome.

Stakeholders also used protests to express their concerns and some protest activities occurred around the same time frame as the Dakota Access pipeline conflict and the Standing Rock protests. At a Florida community meeting and solidarity protest for Standing Rock, many attendees first learned about the Sabal Trail pipeline even though it had been planned for years. As one local resident observed, "this is similar to the Dakota Access pipeline in that most people had no idea that this was in the public interest to look at until it was already approved" (Schweers 2016). Acts of protest and civil disobedience occurred at construction sites in Florida, including an event at Suwannee River State Park that forced the park to close due to the high number of participants (Carver 2017). Dozens were arrested at protests for disrupting pipeline construction and one person was killed by law enforcement after shooting at the pipeline then leading law enforcement on a high-speed chase (Lipscomb 2017; Nelson 2017; Medina and Caplan 2017). With the support of the Seminole Tribe of North Florida, protest camps were established for water protectors and Lakota Sioux elders offered help in organizing and counseling individuals to establish "Standing Rock, Florida" (Stop Sabal Trail Pipeline 2017; Melton 2017). The protests brought attention to issues related to pipeline construction, but some opponents criticized the actions as occurring too late (Cordeiro 2017). While the protests did not successfully end pipeline construction, they did disrupt the process. Power in environmental justice movements may come from the ability to disrupt, not necessarily the ability to reform the system (Benford 2005).

Courts have been used as an avenue to protect environmental justice communities from environmental harms and, in this case, stakeholders used the judicial system in attempts to protect communities and the environment. Alabama and Georgia landowners reported that representatives of Sabal Trail were harassing them, trespassing on their property, and did not pay just compensation for land taken for pipeline construction (Whitehead 2016; Brinkmann 2016; Chapman 2016). While some landowners settled with the company, others took their fight for just compensation to court and won larger settlements than those initially offered (Caplan 2018a; Caplan 2018b). Regional and national environmental groups, including the WWALS Watershed Coalition, the Gulf Restoration Network, the Sierra Club, the Flint Riverkeeper, and the Chattahoochee Riverkeeper, used litigation in state and federal courts making claims in several different cases that the impact on environmental justice communities and environmental hazards were not properly analyzed and that the public were not given appropriate opportunities to comment on plans (McKinney 2015; Berman 2016a, 2016b; Williams 2016). While environmental groups were not successful in getting the courts to address environmental justice claims, litigation was successful in recognizing environmental concerns. A D.C. Circuit Court of Appeals ruled that the environmental analysis by the FERC did not effectively address concerns about climate and greenhouse gas emissions and asked for it to reconsider those issues (Gilmer 2017).

Distributive justice "is conceived in terms of the distribution or sharing out of goods (resources) and bads (harms and risks)" (Walker 2012, p. 10). Stakeholders presented evidence of the potential harm the pipeline would create in communities that would receive few, if any, of its potential benefits. Historically, communities of color and low-income communities have been disproportionately exposed to environmental hazards (Bullard 1990; Austin and Schill 1991). Many of these communities are in the southern United States, which has been identified as a "sacrifice zone" (Schueler 1992, p. 45) as there has been a pro-business atmosphere, lenient enforcement of environmental regulations, and leaders that often look away when environmental harms occur (Bullard and Johnson 2000; Wright 2005). Historically, in the South, there has been "a colonial attitude … to prey on folks who are politically and economically weak" (Schueler 1992, p. 45) and that attitude may have led to siting decisions that have had a negative impact on environmental justice communities. Pipeline opponents argued that this project would pose a threat to communities in the pipeline's path and residents in affected communities mobilized to protect their interests.

Environmental justice communities have organized against projects that threatened their neighborhoods and have fought against the "place in blacks' backyards" (PIBBY) phenomenon (Bullard 1990, p. 4) that may occur when making siting decisions. While it was claimed there would not be any disproportionate effects to the census tracts in or within one mile of the path of the pipeline or its associated facilities where environmental justice populations resided, opponents disagreed (Sabal Trail Transmission, LLC 2014). In its evaluation of the project, the FERC was criticized for "cherry-picking data" because of the use of census tract data, which covers a larger area than census blocks (Yeo 2018). In a lawsuit, the Sierra Club and other environmental groups argued that the use of census tract data, was "over-broad" and provided "information contrary to evidence on the actual make-up of the surrounding community" (*Sierra Club, et al., v. Federal Energy Regulatory Committee* 2016, p. 10) but the court sided with the FERC. In response to the draft EIS, the EPA (2015b) expressed concerns about the impact on environmental justice communities but eventually rescinded those concerns which raised questions about "whether the pipeline's powerful investors pulled political strings to get [the] EPA to back away from the objections it raised a few months ago" (Ritchie 2015).

Affected environmental justice communities located in Albany and Dougherty County, Georgia, expressed concerns about the pipeline's route and plans to locate a compressor station "near a disadvantaged African-American neighborhood that has already borne more than its fair share of pollution" as there were "259 hazardous waste facilities, 78 facilities producing and releasing air pollutants, 20 facilities releasing toxic pollutants, and 16 facilities releasing pollutants into the waters" in south Dougherty County (Bishop et al. 2015). U.S. House Representative Sanford Bishop and four members of the Congressional Black Caucus (2015) spoke out on behalf of the communities,

> Sabal Trail's proposed pipeline and compressor station will further burden an already overburdened and disadvantaged African-American community in this area. Sabal Trail's proposed route will go through Albany and Dougherty County and will run through low-income African-American neighborhoods. The proposed industrial compressor station facility would sit right in the middle of an African-American residential neighborhood comprised of two large subdivisions, a mobile home park, schools, recreational facilities, and the 5,000-plus member Mount Zion Baptist Church, a predominantly African-American congregation.

Local residents attended public meetings, submitted comments, and organized protests to defend their neighborhood. They expressed concerns about how the neighborhood would be affected by the negative impacts of the pipeline and compressor station, especially noise and air pollution complaints (Fletcher 2015). Property owners were concerned that property values would decline, and many were unable to relocate for economic reasons (Whitehead 2016). In her observations about the injustices she saw with pipeline construction, one resident stated that she wanted "to let the folks at (Spectra Energy) know that what they're doing is not going to be like taking candy from a baby. It's going to be like trying to take candy from a Flint River 'gator'" (Fletcher 2015). Distributive claims were prevalent in comments from those living in affected environmental justice communities.

Another environmental justice claim, justice as recognition "is conceived in terms of who is given respect and who is and isn't valued" (Walker 2012, p. 10). In addition to recognizing people that may be affected by environmental justice issues, the environmental justice frame may be expanded to consider nature (or nonhuman life) and how human decisions may affect nature (Schlosberg 2007). Taking a broad approach to include both humans and nature in environmental justice frames reminds decision makers that ecological health and human health are interconnected (Collin and Collin 1998). In this case, pipeline opponents focused on how the pipeline would threaten human health, but they also expanded the environmental justice frame to recognize potential environmental harms to speak out on behalf of preservation of natural resources and local habitats.

Recognizing the threat to a community already burdened with human and environmental health hazards, local governments including the city of Albany and Dougherty County, Georgia, passed resolutions against pipeline construction (McKinney 2014). Governmental leaders questioned why the needs of local residents were not taken into as much consideration as concerns about wildlife and accused the company of running the pipeline through their communities because it was the most economically advantageous route even though an alternate route would have less impact on neighborhoods (Federal Energy Regulatory Commission 2015c; Dorsey 2015). When a representative from Sabal Trail stated that one area considered for the pipeline's route was not selected because of the "beautiful homes" in that area, a county commissioner asked if the company viewed the homes in her district as "less desirable" and expressed that she wanted to ensure that "the beauty of the homes is not a consideration when ... making a decision on the route this pipeline would take" (Fletcher 2013).

As the Sabal Trail pipeline would cross environmentally sensitive areas in Georgia and Florida, opponents voiced concerns about how the pipeline would threaten natural resources. While pipeline construction would threaten wetlands, forests, and wildlife habitats, such as that for the vulnerable populations of gopher tortoise and Florida scrub jays, significant attention was given to how water resources would be threatened along the pipeline's route (Federal Energy Regulatory Commission 2015a, 2015b, 2015c). Stakeholders understood the threat the pipeline posed to the local environment and fought to preserve important natural resources in their area. As one north Florida resident stated,

> You don't see pipelines going through Yosemite. Well we are just as fabulous as Yosemite. We do not want this pipeline going through this area because just the fact that we are here discussing an environmental impact study shows you that there are impacts to our environment.
>
> *(Federal Energy Regulatory Commission 2015a)*

In southwest Georgia, pipeline construction threatened the city of Albany's public water supply due to its proximity to the city's well field (United States Environmental Protection Agency 2015a). Since 2003, more than 40 sinkholes have formed in the city's well field and it was feared that pipeline construction would lead to additional sinkholes that would further threaten the city's water supply (Bishop 2015). The potential for sinkhole development in Florida was also of concern as 3,750 known or potential karst features were identified within one-quarter mile of the pipeline's route (United States Environmental Protection Agency 2015a). Environmental groups argued it was irresponsible to put a pipeline through areas with karst geology and existing sinkholes because of the threat to drinking water and they did not believe appropriate geologic surveys were completed (Federal Energy Regulatory Commission 2015a, 2015c).

The pipeline would also threaten the Floridan aquifer, the largest aquifer in the southeastern United States, which is the primary source of drinking water for southwest Georgia and also provides approximately 60% of Florida's drinking water (United States Geological Service n.d.; United States Environmental Protection Agency 2015a). At a public meeting in Florida, a local resident stated that she wanted to "stand up for the earth and for clean water" as the pipeline would be passing through an area where the Floridan aquifer was "most vulnerable to contamination" (Federal Energy Regulatory Commission 2015a, p. 18). Another shared similar concerns,

> you're going to put explosive gas under the river. It's not going to work. It's inevitable. We're going to have a leak. It's just a matter of time. Who's going to replace our water … it's just not worth the risk.

(Federal Energy Regulatory Commission 2015a, p. 40)

The recognition of the importance of protecting human and ecological health was expressed by a diverse group of stakeholders.

Conclusion

As communities work to address environmental challenges in the Anthropocene, stakeholders have employed a variety of tactics to influence decision makers. In the United States, projects like the Sabal Trail pipeline go through a review process prior to approval and, in that process, stakeholders have the opportunity to participate in conventional ways, such as public comment periods and public meetings and unconventional ways, such as protests. If stakeholders are not satisfied with the process or the outcomes, they may also use the court system to influence outcomes. These opportunities to participate, important in a democracy, highlight procedural justice and allow for opportunities to learn more about who is involved and how they are involved as well as how decisions are made. Other claims of environmental justice, specifically distributive and recognition claims, are used to influence decision makers and appeared in the narratives of pipeline opponents.

Stakeholders were actively engaged in the decision-making process and used environmental justice claims in framing their opposition. Individuals living in affected communities and their representatives, especially in Georgia, focused much attention on distributive claims which are common in environmental justice controversies. Recognition claims were also an important part of narratives and, in this case, the environmental justice frame was expanded beyond humans to consider the impact on natural resources and ecological health, especially the impact on water resources. While these environmental justice claims were prevalent in comments in letters, meetings, and at protests, it does not appear they had the effect stakeholders desired. In this case, litigation was successful as it required the FERC to reassess data, although it did not stop pipeline construction. Even though pipeline opponents were not successful, this case provides more information about the use of environmental justice claims in decision-making processes by the United States government. The experiences of stakeholders in this case may inform and provide direction to communities facing similar challenges in the future.

References

Austin, R. and Schill, M. (1991) Black, brown, poor, & poisoned: Minority grassroots environmentalism and the quest for eco-justice. *The Kansas Journal of Law and Public Policy*, 69, 69–82.

Bell, D. and Carrick, J. (2018) Procedural environmental justice. In Holifield, R., Chakraborty, J. and Walker, G. (eds.). *The Routledge Handbook of Environmental Justice*. New York: Routledge.

Benford, R. (2005) The half-life of the environmental justice frame: Innovation, diffusion, and stagnation. In Pellow, D.N. and Brulle, R.J. (eds.). *Power, Justice, and the Environment: A Critical Appraisal of the Environmental Justice Movement*. Cambridge: MIT Press.

Berman, J. (2016a) Groups file federal lawsuit to block construction of massive fracked gas pipeline in Alabama, Georgia, and Florida. *Sierra Club*. 17 August. Available from: https://content.sierraclub.org/press-releases/2016/08/groups-file-federal-lawsuit-Block-construction-massive-fracked-gas-pipeline [Accessed: 20 December 2016].

Berman, J. (2016b) Groups demand Federal Energy Regulatory Commission examine climate effects of three state natural gas pipelines. *Sierra Club*. 22 September. Available from: http://www.sierraclubfloridanews.org/2016/09/sierra-club-riverkeepers-file-lawsuit.html [Accessed: 20 December 2016].

Bishop, S.D. (2015) Sabal Trail Transmission, LLC, Docket CP15-17-000. *U.S. House of Representatives*, 29 May. Available from: http://bishop.house.gov [Accessed: 15 December 2016].

Bishop, S.D., Lewis, J., Johnson, H.C. and Scott, D. (2015) Sabal Trail Transmission, LLC, FERC Docket No. C15-17–000. *U.S. House of Representatives*, 23 October. Available from: http://bishop.house.gov/media-center/press-releases/proposed-sabal-trail-raises-Environmental-justice-concerns [Accessed: 15 December 2016].

Brinkmann, P. (2016) Sabal Trail pipeline seizes Florida properties. *Orlando Sentinel*, 12 August. Available from: http://www.orlandosentinel.com/business/brinkmann-on-business/on-sabal-trail-pipeline-lawsuits-20160811-story.html

Bullard, R.D. (1990) *Dumping in Dixie: Race, Class, and Environmental Quality*. Boulder: Westview Press.

Bullard, R.D. (1993) Race and environmental justice in the United States. *Yale Journal of International Law*, 18(1), 319–335.

Bullard, R.D. and Johnson, G.S. (2000) Environmental justice: Grassroots activism and its impact on public policy decision making. *Journal of Social Issues*, 56(3), 555–578.

Caplan, A. (2018a) Sabal Trail ordered to pay landowners more. *Gainesville Sun*, 28 June. Available from: https://www.gainesville.com/news/20180628/sabal-trail-ordered-to-pay-landowners-more [Accessed: 5 January 2019].

Caplan, A. (2018b) Sabal Trail must pay Levy landowners $1.3M. *Gainesville Sun*, 12 November. Available from: http://www.gainesville.com/news/2018/1112/sabal-trail-must-pay-levy-landowners-13m [Accessed: 5 January 2019].

Carver, D. (2017) Hundreds protest pipeline. *Suwannee Democrat*, 14 January. Available from: http://www.suwanneedemocrat.com/news/ga_fl_news/hundreds-protest-pipeline/article_da0e346a-2615-5aaf-a805-7ffb7dde6206.html [Accessed: 1 February 2017].

Chapman, D. (2016) Construction likely to begin soon on Southwest Georgia pipeline. *Atlanta Journal-Constitution*, 18 August. Available from: https://www.ajc.com/news/state-regional-govt--politics/construction-likely-begin-soon-southwest-georgia-p ipeline/mVrxJe98vYWDJSamPJH72I/ [Accessed: 15 December 2016].

Collin, R.W. and Collin, R.M. (1998) The role of communities in environmental decisions: Communities speaking for themselves. *Journal of Environmental Law and Litigation*, 13, 37–89.

Cordeiro, M. (2017) The Sabal Trail pipeline is a 'done deal,' and now central Floridians begin to realize what's about to come through their backyards. *Orlando Sentinel*, 1 February. Available from: http://www.orlandoweekly.com/orlando/the-sabal-trail-Pipeline-is-a -done-deal-and-now-central-floridians-begin-to-realize-whats-about-to-come-thro ugh-their-backyards/Content?oid+2558717 [Accessed: 10 March 2017].

Dorsey, T. (2015) Protests persist against the Sabal pipeline trail. *WALB*, 18 July. Available from: https://www.walb.com/story/29576953/protests-persist-against-the-sabal -pipeline-trail/ [Accessed: 10 March 2017].

Federal Energy Regulatory Commission. (2015a) *Southeast Market Pipelines Project*. Available from: https://www.ferc.gov/CalendarFiles/20151102084555-CP14-554-1 0-01-2015.pdf [Accessed: 20 December 2016].

Federal Energy Regulatory Commission. (2015b) *Southeast Market Pipelines Project Final Environmental Impact Statement: Executive Summary Volume One*. Available from: http://www.ferc.gov/industries/gas/enviro/eis/2015/12-18-15-eis.asp [Accessed: 20 December 2016].

Federal Energy Regulatory Commission. (2015c) *Southeast Market Pipelines Project Final Environmental Impact Statement: Appendix O*. Available from: http://www.ferc.gov/industries/gas/enviro/eis/2015/12-18-15-eis.asp [Accessed: 20 December 2016].

Fletcher, C. (2013) Spectra official discusses natural gas pipeline. *Albany Herald*, 15 September. Available from: https://www.albanyherald.com/new s/spectra-official-d iscussses-natural-gas-pipeline/article_fec4b95b-7100-5145-b898-27b0b23b7058 .html [Accessed: 15 December 2016].

Fletcher, C. (2015) FERC gets an earful from Sabal Trail pipeline opponents. *Albany Herald*, 29 September. Available from: https://www.albanyherald.com/news/2015/s ep/29/ferc-gets-an-earful-from-sabal-trail-pipeline/

Florida Power and Light. (2013) *FPL Selects Sabal Trail Transmission and Florida Southeast Connection to Build New Natural Gas Pipeline System into Florida*. 26 July. Available from: http://www.nexteraenergy.com/news/contents/2013/072613_1.shtml [Accessed: 15 November 2016].

Georgia Water Coalition. (2016) *Dirty Dozen List 2016: Dirty Energy Production Pollutes Georgia's Water*. 16 November. Available from: https://www.gawater.org/wp-con tent/uploads/2016/09/2016DirtyDozenPressRelease.pdf [Accessed: 1 March 2017].

Gilmer, E.M. (2017) Major ruling against FERC shakes up climate law. *E&E News*, 23 August. Available from: https://www.eenews.net/stories/1060059077 [Accessed: 15 October 2019].

Lipscomb, J. (2017) Sabal Trail pipeline will be an environmental and economic disaster, critics warn. *Miami New Times*. March 7. Available from: http://www.miam inewtimes.com/news/Sabal-trail-pipeline-will-be-an-environmental-and-econom ic-disaster-critics-warn-9188468 [Accessed: 15 March 2017].

McKinney, C. (2014) Dougherty county commission goes on record, votes to oppose Sabal pipeline. *WALB*. 27 October. Available from: https://www.walb.com/story/27034245/Dougherty-co-commission-goes-on-record-votes-to-oppose-sabal -pipeline [Accessed: 15 January 2017].

McKinney, C. (2015) Judge rules in favor of Sabal Trail pipeline. *Suwannee Democrat*, 14 December. Available from: https://www.suwanneedemocrat.com/news/judge-r ules-in-favor-of-sabal-   trail-pipeline/article_740afb14-a279-11e5-b732-af40d256 017d.html [Accessed: 5 January 2017].

Medina, C. and Caplan, A. (2017) Shots at Sabal Trail pipeline lead to chase, fatal shooting. *Gainesville Sun*, 26 February. Available from: http://www.gainesville .com/news/20170226/shots-at-sabal-trail-pipeline-lead-to-chase-fatal-shooting [Accessed: 1 March 2017].

Melton, S. (2017) Meet Florida's DAPL: The Sabal Trail pipeline. *Pitt News*, 26 January. Available from: http://pittnews.com/article/116191/opinions/meet-floridas-dapl-sa bal-trail-pipeline/ [Accessed: 1 March 2017].

Nelson, A. (2017) Police remove protestors from inside Sabal Trail pipeline. *WUFT*, 22 February. Available from: https://www.wuft.org/news/2017/02/22/protestors-lodge -themselves-in-sabal-trail-pipeline-one-removed/ [Accessed: 1 March 2017].

Penn, I. (2013) Florida PSC approves third major natural gas pipeline. *Tampa Bay Times*, 24 October. Available from: http://www.tampabay.com/news/business/energy/psc-a pproves-third-major-natural-gas-pipeline/2148909 [Accessed: 15 November 2016].

Ritchie, B. (2015) EPA reverses course on several Sabal Trail pipeline issues. *Politico*, 16 December. Available from: https://www.politico.com/states/florida/story/2015 /12/epa-reverses-course-on-several-sabal-trail-pipeline-issues-029232   [Accessed: 10 January 2017].

Sabal Trail Transmission, LLC. (n.d.a) *Economic Benefits*. Available from: http://www .sabaltrailtransmission.com/Economic_Benefits [Accessed: 20 December 2016].

Sabal Trail Transmission, LLC. (n.d.b) *FAQs*. Available from: http://sabaltrailtrans mission.com/faq2 [Accessed: 16 June 2020].

Sabal Trail Transmission, LLC. (2014) *Resource Report 5 – Socioeconomics*. 21 November. Available from: http://content.sabaltrailtransmission.com/resources/2014-update/R R5_Sabal_Trail_11-21-2014_FINAL.pdf

Schlosberg, D. (2007) *Defining Environmental Justice: Theories, Movements, and Nature*. Oxford: Oxford University Press.

Schueler, D.G. (1992) Southern exposure. *Sierra*, November/December, 43–49, 76.

Schweers, J. (2016) Sabal Trail pipeline cuts through heart of springs country. *Tallahassee Democrat*, 17 December. Available from: http://www.tallahassee.com/ story/news/ 2016/12/17/sabal-trail-pipeline-cuts-through-heart-springs-country/95470950. [Accessed: 15 March 2017].

Sheinin, A.G. (2016) Georgia House defeats bill to grant easements for S. Georgia pipeline. *Atlanta Journal-Constitution*, 22 March. Available from: http://www.myajc .com/news/state--regional-govt--politics/georgia-house-defeats-bill-grant-easem ents-for-georgia-pipeline/YRFU2SQyf5Wr3cSAnHAdmM [Accessed: 15 March 2017].

Sierra Club, et al., v. Federal Energy Regulatory Committee. (2016) Available from: http://blogs2.law.columbia.edu/climate-change-litigation/wp-content/uploads /sites/16/case-documents/2016/20161209_docket-16-1329_brief.pdf   [Accessed: 30 March 2017].

Stop Sabal Trail Pipeline. (2017) *The Seminole Tribe of North Florida Announces the Opening of the Heartland Camps in the Goethe Forest, Levy County, Florida*. Available from: http:// stopsabaltrailpipeline.blogspot.com/p/press-releases.html [Accessed: 15 March 2017].

Union of Concerned Scientists. (2014) *Environmental Impacts of Natural Gas*. Available from: https://www.ucsusa.org/resources/environmental-impacts-natural-gas   [Accessed: 29 February 2020].

United States Energy Information Administration. (2017) *Florida's Sabal Trail Pipeline and Associated Natural Gas Pipeline Projects Begin Service*. Available from: https://www.eia.gov/todayinenergy/detail.php?id=31972 [Accessed: 1 July 2019].

United States Environmental Protection Agency. (2015a) *Draft Environmental Impact Statement for the Proposed Southeast Market Pipelines Project*. Available from: https://www.epa.gov [Accessed: 20 December 2016].

United States Environmental Protection Agency. (2015b) *Proposed Southeast Market Pipelines Project*. Available from: https://www.epa.gov [Accessed: 20 December 2016].

United States Environmental Protection Agency. (n.d.) *Environmental Justice*. Available from: https://www.epa.gov/environmentaljustice [Accessed: 20 July 2019].

United States Geological Service. (n.d.) *Aquifer Basics*. Available from: https://water.usgs.gov/ogw/aquiferbasics/floridan.html [Accessed: 10 March 2017].

United States Global Change Research Program. (2018) *Impacts, Risks, and Adaptation in the United States: Fourth National Climate Assessment, Volume II*. Available from: https://nca2018.globalchange.gov/ [Accessed: 20 February 2020].

Walker, G. (2012) *Environmental Justice: Concepts, Evidence, and Politics*. London: Routledge.

Watkins, M. (2013) Contracts for natural gas pipeline through Florida gets initial ok. *Ocala Star Banner*, 24 October. Available from: http://www.ocala.com/news/2013 1024/contracts-For-natural-gas-pipeline-through-florida-gets-initial-ok [Accessed: 15 January 2017].

Whitehead, S. (2016) Sabal Trail pipeline plows through Southwest Georgia, local opposition. *Georgia Public Broadcasting*, 15 September. Available from: http://gpb news.org/post/sabal-trail-pipeline-plows-through-southwest-georgia-local-opposit ion [Accessed: 5 January 2017].

Williams, M. (2016) Environmental groups file lawsuit against Sabal Trail pipeline. *WALB*, 18 August. Available from: http://www.walb.com/story/32792325/envir onmental-Groups-file-lawsuit-against-sabal-trail-pipeline [Accessed 20 December 2016].

Wright, B. (2005) Living and dying in Louisiana's 'Cancer Alley'. In Bullard, R.D. (ed.). *The Quest for Environmental Justice: Human Rights and the Politics of Pollution*. San Francisco: Sierra Club Books.

Yeo, S. (2018) Are the feds cherry-picking data to force pipelines through vulnerable communities? *Pacific Standard*, 7 June. Available from: https://psmag.com/environ ment/feds-cherry-picking-data-to-force-pipelines-through-vulnerable-communi ties [Accessed 15 July 2019].

Zundel, A. (1995) Policy frames and ethical traditions: The case of homeownership for the poor. *Policy Studies Journal*, 23(3), 423–434.

11

INJUSTICES IN IMPLEMENTING DONOR-FUNDED CLIMATE CHANGE RESILIENCE PROJECTS IN BANGLADESH

North–South dichotomy?

Nowrin Tabassum

Introduction: Anthropocene and environmental injustice

Anthropocene is understood as a geological time period in which the population of the world is experiencing an irreversible *impact* of *human activities* on the environment (Stromberg 2013, para. 6). Human activities differ across different geographical locations throughout the world and thus the impacts are highly variable. In the discussion of climate change, excessive carbon emissions from fossil fuel industries of the global North are considered the cause of global warming and subsequent suffering of the global South, particularly, in cases of climate change-induced sea-level rise, frequent and increased numbers of cyclones, drought, and water scarcity. For Malm and Hornborg (2014), "as of 2008, the advanced capitalist countries or the 'North' composed 18.8% of the world population but were responsible for 72.7% of the CO_2 emitted since 1850" (p. 64). This situation creates an injustice towards the global South due to problems not produced by them. The severity of injustice is multiplied when the North takes advantage of the South's sufferings through binding the latter in unequal treaties in the name of climate change-related projects and policies. The following example of Bangladesh is a very good example of such a treaty.

How do environmental justice workers understand and respond to the injustices created by anthropogenic climate change and the subsequent actions of the global North? According to Tokar and Gilbertson (2020),

> climate justice advocates are united by a profound understanding of the disproportionate impacts of global climate disruptions on those who have contributed the least to excess emissions of carbon dioxide and other greenhouse gasses. They also share a common analysis of the shared institutional and political roots of the climate crisis and the numerous other injustices

faced by peoples around the world, with origins in the centuries-long historical legacy of colonialism.

(p. 3)

From this context and as a chronicler of environmental justice workers, I share and analyze the climate change-related injustices in Bangladesh.

Injustices and discrimination in Bangladesh

According to academic/nonacademic publications (i.e., Biermann and Boas 2010; Docherty and Giannini 2009) and official documents of the Intergovernmental Panel on Climate Change (IPCC) (i.e., 1990 IPCC First Assessment Report, the 2001 IPCC Third Assessment Report), the World Bank (i.e., 2000 Bangladesh Climate Change and Sustainable Development), and the government of Bangladesh (i.e., 2005 and 2009 Bangladesh National Adaptation Plan of Action (NAPA), Bangladesh is considered one of the most vulnerable countries in the world to anthropogenic global-warming-induced sea level rise which submerges land, causes frequent and increased cyclones, with changing patterns of weather that impact the agricultural system. However, the country emits 0.3% of the total global carbon dioxide emissions in the world which is low compared to the rate of emission of the high/medium/low carbon emitting countries (Kunnie 2015, p. 252). China emits 25.8%, the United States 12.8%, the European Union 7.8%, and India 6.7% of total greenhouse gasses in the world (Environment and Climate Change Canada 2020). Therefore, it is one of the countries in the world whose population has an extremely low carbon footprint but whose population is less responsible for making the world warmer. However, the population of the country suffers the most from the severe effects of global warming (Biermann and Boas 2010, p 72; Docherty and Giannini 2009, p. 356). Millions of people from the coastal areas of Bangladesh live in an unjust situation in which they suffer from the effects of climate change which were not produced by them but by the excessive carbon emissions of the high carbon emitters, the Western-industrialized countries (Guzman 2013, p. 12).

In 1992, the UNFCCC (the United Nations Framework Convention on Climate Change) labeled high carbon-emitting countries, mainly Western-developed countries, as developed countries. In UNFCCC Articles 3, 4, and 5, these countries are designated to provide funds to climate-vulnerable countries to implement climate change adaptation and resilience projects to curb the effects of climate change. At first glance, this fund-giving activity can be interpreted as the high carbon emitters compensating the vulnerable countries and at the same time recognizing the role and responsibility of developed countries in making the world warmer. However, a closer examination at the process of fund disbursement that includes multiple levels of funds flowing from donors to climate-vulnerable countries reveals specific conditions attached to receiving these funds. This chapter considers the scenario of injustices and multi-layered discrimination towards climate-vulnerable countries that is imposed by the high carbon emitters. The *injustices* and *multi-layered discrimination* reveal that there exists a deep-rooted North–South dichotomy in releasing funds for climate change mitigation.

Funds for climate change mitigation and adaptation are disbursed through international financial organizations, the World Bank, Asian Development Bank (ADB), International Monetary Fund (IMF), and the United Nations (UNFCCC 1992, Article 4). Why the fund-disbursement process includes these financial organizations rather than using bilateral agreements between the donor countries and the recipient countries is unclear. Moreover, the nature of the funds is formulated in a way that: (i) the fund channeling organizations (i.e., the World Bank/ADB) receives a certain percentage of the funds as their service charges, (ii) the World Bank-channeled funds are provided as loans, not grants, (iii) the funds are adjusted with previous loans of the climate-vulnerable countries, which they owe the donors, in a way that the funds are invested in profit-generating projects in order to pay off previous loans to the donor, and (iv) the adaptation/resilience projects are implemented through a co-management approach where organizations within donor countries are contracted.

There are several critical embedded unjust features of these funds. First, the funds are loans to climate-vulnerable countries, making them economically indebted to solving the problem of climate change within their countries. Second, the original goal of the funds is to invest in projects that curb the effects of climate change. However, the funds are used to pay off previous loans owed to donors. Third, channeling the funds via the World Bank/ADB means that some funds are applied as service charges to the channeling organizations. This could be avoided if bilateral agreements between the donor countries and the recipient countries were used instead.

This funding arrangement is representative of the North–South inequalities where Western-developed countries are overwhelmingly responsible for climate-change impacts, yet vulnerable countries of the global South pay through both a degraded environment owing to these changes and economic austerity programs. Western-developed countries representing the global North exercise power over the global South in deciding how funds will be distributed; in what projects those will be invested; and how the funds will be channeled. It is worth noting that the funds are distributed through some international financial organizations (such as the World Bank, ADB, and IMF) which clearly implement a neoliberal political agenda (Bettini and Gioli 2016, pp. 2, 7, 11). Neoliberal rules rely on market forces, encourage free market policies and increased privatization, and discourage interference by governments in market exchanges. These organizations argue that climate vulnerable countries are responsible for taking action against climate change and it is their choice to take the funds from Western-developed countries. This chapter investigates these injustices, multi-layered discriminations, and the North–South dichotomy (inequalities?) in implementing donor-funded climate change resilience projects in Bangladesh.

Donor-funded climate change resilience projects in Bangladesh

Bangladesh is a low-lying and flat riverine country located between the foothills of the Himalayas and the Indian Ocean. Impacts from glacial snowmelt and runoff from the Himalayan mountains coupled with global sea-level rise place Bangladesh in a precarious position. To fight the effects of climate change, the country is nego-tiating in international climate change talks and seeks funds from the high carbon emitter countries to implement projects for climate change adaptation. Bangladesh receives four major funds from donors: the 2008 BCCRF (Bangladesh Climate Change Resilience Fund – $170 million), the 2001 GEF (Global Environmental Facility – $94.7 million), Least Developed Countries Fund (LDCF – $49.8 mil-lion), the 2010 GCF (The Green Climate Fund – $70 million), and the 2010 PPCR (Pilot Programme for Climate Resilience) of the Climate Investment Fund (CIF). The BCCRF has been channeled from the donor countries (i.e., United States, United Kingdom, Australia, Sweden, Denmark, Switzerland, and the European Union) to Bangladesh via the World Bank (World Bank, 2012, para. 3). The UNDP manages GEF's (Global Environmental Facility's LDCF) funds to Bangladesh. The WB, the ADB, and International Financial Corporation (IFC) channel the PPCR's funds from the developed countries to Bangladesh.

The departments of donor countries release the funds to Bangladesh under the fiduciary management of the World Bank, the ADB, and IFC (World Bank 2012, para. 4; Rai and Smith, 2013, p. 12). These departments include: United States Agency for International Development (USAID). the Department for International Development (DFID), the Swedish International Development Cooperation Agency (SIDA), and the German Government Owned Development Bank (KfW).

The BCCRF provides an example of how the funding mechanism works and is representative of how other funds are managed. (The other funds have been released recently; therefore, information about other projects is not publicly available.) The initial amount of BCCRF was approximately USD$170 million. Table 11.1 shows the amounts of funds contributed by donors.

TABLE 11.1 Funds donated to BCCRF by donor countries

No.	Name of the Country	Amount of Money (in USD)
1	Australia	7 million
2	Denmark	1.2 million
3	Sweden	13 million
4	Switzerland	3.4 million
5	The European Union	37 million
6	The United Kingdom	95 million
7	The United States of America	13 million

Source: World Bank, 2012, para. 3.

Donor contributions are not tracked by project and the specific amounts allocated by project remain confidential. In 2016, donors withdrew from the BCCRF and shut down the website due to disagreements over the funding arrangements. Bangladesh protested the funding in the form of loans rather than grants and the large service charges by World Bank (bdnews24.com 2016; Siddique 2016). Although the World Bank claimed that "there are no special conditions attached to the disbursement of the fund by the donors or by the World Bank'", the Bank charges between 4 and 15% service charges (Independent Commission for Aid Impact 2011, p. 13). The BCCRF-funded projects are listed in Table 11.2.

Until 2016, the United Kingdom contributed the highest amount of money to the BCCRF – USD $95 million or £60[1] million (World Bank n.d., para. 3; Independent Commission for Aid Impact 2011, p. 13). The UK channels the funds to Bangladesh through its international development organization, DFID, and the World Bank. Two proposals were accepted for utilizing the DFID funds: Multipurpose Cyclone Shelter Construction Project, and the Construction of the BCCRF Secretariat. According to the World Bank's BCCRF website,[2] the budget for constructing the cyclone shelter is USD$25 million and the secretariat is USD$0.2 million. Some of the rest of the funds were unspent and Bangladesh had to return the unspent money to the British government (McVeigh 2016,

TABLE 11.2 BCCRF funded projects

Project Title	Donors	Grant Amount (USD)
Constructing BCCRF Secretariat	DFID	0.2 million
Urban Flooding of Greater Dhaka Area in a Changing Climate: Vulnerability, Adaptation and Potential Costs (Analytical Activities)	The World Bank	0.5 million
Impacts of Climate Change on Vector-Borne Diseases and Implications for the Health Sector (Analytical Activities)	The World Bank	0.2 million
Detailed Design and Environmental Studies for Construction of Urir Char- Noakhali Cross-Dam (under construction)	Not known	0.7 million
Bangladesh Modern Food Storage Facilities Project (BMFSFP) (under preparation)	Not known	25 million
Solar Irrigation Program – A Green Energy Initiative (under preparation)	Not known	25 million
Agricultural Adaptation in Climate Risk- Prone Areas of Bangladesh (drought, flood, and saline-prone areas)	Not known	22.8 million
Community Climate Change Project	Not known	12.5 million
Climate Resilient Participatory Afforestation and Reforestation Project (CRPARP)	USAID	35 million
Multipurpose Cyclone Shelter Construction Project	DFID	25 million

Source: The World Bank, n.d.

para. 1). The government of Bangladesh had to send back £13 million (McVeigh 2016, para. 2). There are two conflicting explanations about why the funds were unspent and why the funds went back to the United Kingdom. First, according to the 2017 DFID's Annual Report, the delivery of the fund was delayed due to the lack of understanding between the donor and the World Bank (McVeigh 2016, para. 16). The DFID report also stated that the government of Bangladesh was not committed to using the funds and the country governments have high levels of corruption (McVeigh 2016, para. 16).

The Bangladeshi High Commission in London stated that the relationship between the government-fund of Bangladesh and the World Bank soured due to the disagreement about loans versus grants which ultimately drove the donors to shut down the funds (McVeigh 2016, para. 16). The United Kingdom wanted to invest the money in projects with no connection to addressing climate change but to research related to knowledge production of resilience (IIED, n.d., para. 5; ICCCAD, n.d, para. 1). Therefore, Bangladesh did not agree to receive the funds. In addition, the United Kingdom and the World Bank wanted to give the funds as loans with higher interest conditions attached; however, the government of Bangladesh did not agree to take the funds as loans as they preferred grants (McVeigh 2016, para. 5; Adam and Vidal 2010, para. 9).

In addition, international environmental activist groups also became involved.

> Campaigners from the World Development Movement (WDM), Jubilee Debt Campaign and Friends of the Earth plan to protest tomorrow at DFID over the UK proposals. They are also concerned that further payments planned for Bangladesh are loans, the repayment of which they say will force the country further into debt.
>
> *(Adam and Vidal 2010, para. 6)*

Md Shamsuddoha, a campaigner with Justice and Equity Bangladesh, said: "Developing countries are opposing involvement of the World Bank in the management of climate finance because of its long history of imposing economic conditions on developing countries, fuelling unjust debts, and promoting dirty development" (Adam and Vidal 2010, para. 9). There were also demonstrations in the streets in Bangladesh regarding why the WB should be involved in managing the funds (McVeigh 2016, para. 5; Adam and Vidal 2010, para. 9).

In 2016, the disagreement between the parties led the donors to shut down the funds for BCCRF for Bangladesh. This scenario reveals how the United Kingdom and the World Bank exercise power over Bangladesh in deciding how the funds are channeled, managed, and distributed.

While giving climate change resilience funds, the donors attach conditions to Bangladesh that the resilience projects must be implemented in partnership with the organizations, nongovernmental organizations (NGOs), or companies whose origins are in the donor's countries. An example of this kind of fund can be the USAID-funded Climate Resilient Participatory Afforestation and

Reforestation Project (CRPARP). The CRPARP has been implemented under the 1998 Tropical Forest Conservation Act (TFCA), which states:

> The Tropical Forest Conservation Act (TFCA) was enacted in 1998 to offer eligible developing countries options to relieve certain official debt owed the U.S. Government while at the same time generating funds in local currency to support tropical forest conservation activities. In addition to conserving forest and relieving debt, TFCA is intended to strengthen civil society by creating local foundations to support small grants to NGOs and local communities. The majority of TFCA agreements to date have included funds raised by U.S.-based NGOs, a unique public–private partnership.
>
> *(USAID n.d.b, para. 1)*

CRPARP is an attempt to relieve Bangladesh of concessional debts which the country owes the United States and to generate revenues for forest conservation activities. According to the agreement, about USD 7 million would be paid to the United States over the next 19 years (Chemonics International Incorporation, 2001, p. II-1). In addition, as per the condition of TFCA for including US-based NGOs, the CRPARP is implemented by including two US-based organizations: International Resources Group (IRG) and Winrock International (Khan 2013, p. 4). Ecotourism and eco-parks established in the locations of the CRPARP provide revenue from the tourism industry to pay back the loans to the United States. However, ecotourism and eco-parks have no connection with curbing the effects of climate change for which Bangladesh is suffering. The CRPARP serves the economic interests of the United States (i.e., repayment of loans) but it is not clear what the benefit is to Bangladesh in fighting the effects of climate change. This scenario reveals how the United States exercises power over Bangladesh in deciding how the funds will be distributed and what projects will be invested.

Other donor-funded adaptation projects are similarly criticized in Bangladesh. There are concerns about whether the appropriate projects, infrastructure, and technologies are being employed to address climate change. For example, (a) polders and embankments (under construction) are severely damaged by increased attacks of cyclones, coastal flooding, and sea level rise, (b) the coastal afforestation project is not working because most of the plants have been washed away/destroyed by the frequent attacks of cyclones and floods, (c) the saline concentration in the land has increased so much that even saline-tolerant crops cannot survive (Rawlani and Sovacool 2011, p. 860). These projects are not compatible with offsetting the devastating effects of climate change. They are damaged by frequent occurrences of cyclones and floods which impose a double burden on borrowers in Bangladesh. First, the country must pay back the loans that were given for these ineffective projects. Second, the country must seek more funds and technical support to repair the damage from these ineffective projects.

This funding mechanism creates a vicious circle whereby the country becomes increasingly indebted.

This situation provides an opportunity to reflect on the establishment of the Bretton Woods Institutions (the WB and the IMF) which were originally created to provide long-term lending aimed at reconstructing countries after the Second World War and contributing to developing countries after the War (Boughton and Lateef 1995, p. 175; O'Brien and Williams 2016, pp. 175–176). Since the 1970s, these institutions expanded their functions to provide long-term funds to big-budget projects in developing countries such as *sustainable poverty reduction and flood control plans* (see Boughton and Lateef 1995, pp. 123–126, 175–220). However, in the 1980s, the lending practice gave birth to serious debt crises in many developing countries leading to disastrous consequences that included degraded living standards and increasing the numbers of people living in poverty; an example of this is Mexico (O'Brien and Williams 2016, pp. 274–275). The Bretton Woods Institutions' original function has been replicated in releasing climate change funds to climate-vulnerable countries (see Methmann and Oels 2015, p. 60). The funds, instead of offsetting the severe effects of climate change, make the climate-vulnerable countries heavily economically indebted, push people to live in precarious environments, and increase their economic burdens. The international financial organizations and Western-developed countries continue to exercise inequitable power relationships with climate-vulnerable countries.

Suggestions to overcome the injustices, discrimination, and North–South inequalities?

Climate change is a global problem with place-specific impacts. Market solutions to address climate change are driven by international lending institutions of the global North. Climate change has emerged due to excessive carbon emission of fossil fuel-based corporations, located in the North. The onus of blame and responsibility reside with the fossil fuel-based corporations and Northern countries. Thus, it is wrong for Northern countries and international financial institutions (such as World Bank/IMF/ADB) to consider climate-vulnerable countries as responsible for taking action against climate change, but it is an injustice towards them if conditions and increased loan burdens are enforced.

Bangladesh, its state-actors and non-state actors (such as environmental NGOs), are already involved in multiple global climate change–related activism and they demand environmental justice for the country through the polluter pays principle (PPP). The concept PPP has roots in both Western and Eastern philosophy, the core idea being that punishment should rightly pertain to the polluter who caused the damage to the environment, and be expressed in terms of financial penalties intended as compensation for the loss. However, the country's involvement in those kinds of activism does not refer to the injustices regarding unfair lending practices. The author of this chapter believes that the country needs to take part actively in global climate change activism to demand justice against the multi-layered discrimination imposed on the country by unfair lending practices. Scholars may argue what kind of activism can be the best fit for Bangladesh. Tabassum (2019) stated

> Activism can take many forms. It can be violent protests against an unlawful activity, or a peaceful campaign for establishing social and political justice on certain issues ... activism can also consist of sharing knowledge – the knowledge of local sufferings – and connecting that knowledge to global forums of action. The knowledge sharing can educate global forums about who has been suffering in the local areas, what is the reason for their vulnerabilities, how to respond to their sufferings, and who can take what actions in response.
>
> *(Tabassum 2019, p. 81)*

Drawing on this description activism, I suggest that Bangladesh, including its state-actors and non-state actors, should share the information/knowledge of unfair lending practices with the existing global environmental forums and environmental justices of the Anthropocene. Such knowledge sharing would help to spread the information of the lending practices throughout the whole world. The environmental justice groups can create pressure on the World Bank/ADB/IMF and other international donors to review their lending practices and advise that the loans should not be attached to any other previous lending, climate change–related funds should be given as grants not as loans, and climate change–related projects should not be merged with other profit-generating projects; and in order to avoid service charges of international financial organizations, instead of including World Bank/ADB/IMF or any other international organization as media for channeling the climate change-related funds, the donor country should give the funds to the recipient country via bilateral agreements. The pressure of the environmental justice groups can take a strong step to eliminate the unfair lending practices of international organizations.

Notes

1 The conversion rate at the time was US$1=£0.6481 (Independent Commission for Aid Impact, p. 13).
2 The website is: http://siteresources.worldbank.org/SOUTHASIAEXT/Resources /223546-1214948920836/bccrf-projects.pdf. Date accessed January 3, 2019.

References

Adam, D., & Vidal, J. (2010, February 15). Bangladesh rejects terms for £60m of climate aid from UK. *The Guardian*. Retrieved from https://www.theguardian.com/en vironment/2010/feb/15/bangladesh-world-bank-climate-finance. Date accessed 10 January 2010.

bdnews24.com (2016, October 28). *Climate change help should be in aid, not loan, Bangladesh parliamentary panel head says*. Retrieved from https://bdnews24.com/bangladesh/2016 /10/28/climate-change-help-should-be-in-aid-not-loan-bangladesh-parliamentary -panel-head-says. Date accessed 10 December 2019.

Bettini, G., & Gioli, G. (2016). Waltz with development: Insights on the developmentalization of climate-induced migration. *Migration and Development, 5*(2), 171–189.

Biermann, F., & Boas, I. (2010). Preparing for a warmer world: Towards a global governance system to protect climate refugees. *Global Environmental Politics, 10*(1), 60–88.

Boughton, J.M., & Lateef, K.S. (1995). *Fifty years after Bretton Woods: The future of the IMF and the World Bank: Proceedings of a conference held in Madrid, Spain, September 29-30, 1994.* International Monetary Fund.

Chemonics International, Inc (2001, April). *The Bangladesh tropical forest conservation fund preventing and arresting accelerating species loss in Bangladesh.* Washington, DC. Retrieved from http://pdf.usaid.gov/pdf_docs/Pnacq620.pdf. Date accessed November 17, 2019.

Docherty, B., & Giannini, T. (2009). Confronting a rising tide: A proposal for a convention on climate change refugees. *Harvard Environmental Law Review, 33*, 349–403.

Environment and Climate Change Canada (2020) Canadian environmental sustainability indicators: Global greenhouse gas emissions. Consulted on June 23, 2020. Retrieved from http://www.canada.ca/en/environment-climate-change/services/environmen tal-indicators/globalgreenhouse-gas-emissions.html.

Guzman, A.T. (2013). *Overheated the human cost of climate change.* Oxford. Oxford University Press.

ICCCAD (n.d.). *Our partners.* Retrieved from http://www.icccad.net/our-partners/. Date accessed December 25, 2018.

IIED (n.d.). *Ten projects receive funding for research into climate change resilience.* Retrieved from https://www.iied.org/ten-projects-receive-funding-for-research-climate-chan ge-resilience. Date accessed December 25, 2018.

Independent Commission for Aid Impact (2011, November). *The department for international development's climate change programme in Bangladesh.* Retrieved from https://www.oecd .org/countries/bangladesh/49092047.pdf. Date accessed November 26, 2019.

IPCC (1990). *First assessment report. Working group II, policy makers' summary.*

IPCC (2001). *Third assessment report.* Retrieved from https://www.ipcc.ch/site/assets/upl oads/2018/03/WGI_TAR_full_report.pdf. Date accessed June 28, 2018.

Khan, T. (2013). *The project in Bangladesh gas forest and livelihood* (Doctoral thesis). Australia: University of New England.

Kunnie, J.E. (2015). *The cost of globalization: Dangers to the earth and its people.* Jefferson, NC: McFarland & Company, Inc., Publishers.

Malm, A., & Hornborg, A. (2014). The geology of mankind? A critique of the Anthropocene narrative. *The Anthropocene Review, 1*(1), 62–69.

McVeigh, K. (2016, November 10). Climate finance dispute prompts Bangladesh to return £13m of UK aid. *The Guardian.* Retrieved from https://www.theguardian.c om/global-development/2016/nov/10/climate-finance-dispute-bangladesh-returns -13-million-uk-aid-world-bank. Date accessed November 15, 2019.

Methmann, C., & Oels, A. (2015). From 'fearing' to 'empowering' climate refugees: Governing climate-induced migration in the name of resilience. *Security Dialogue, 46*(1), 51–68.

O'Brien, R., & Williams, M. (2016). *Global political economy: Evolution and dynamics.* Palgrave Macmillan, London.

Rai, N., & Smith, B. (2013). *Climate investment funds Pilot Programme for Climate Resilience (PPCR) in Bangladesh- A status review.* IIED Country Report. IIED, London. Retrieved from http://pubs.iied.org/pdfs/10052IIED.pdf. Date accessed November 26, 2019.

Rawlani, A.K., & Sovacool, B.K. (2011). Building responsiveness to climate change through community-based adaptation in Bangladesh. *Mitigation and Adaptation Strategies for Global Change, 16*(8), 845–863.

Siddique, A.B. (2016, June 16). Donors shut down climate fund Bangladesh to lose $50 million. *Dhaka Tribune.* Retrieved from http://www.dhakatribune.com/banglad esh/2016/04/05/donors-shut-climate-fund-bangladesh-lose-50m/. Date accessed November 16, 2019.

Stromberg, J. (2013, January). What is the Anthropocene and are we in it? *Smithsonian Magazine.* Retrieved from http://smithsonianmag.com/science-nature/what-is-t heanthropocene-and-are-we-in-it-164801414/?no-ist, Date accessed June 23, 2020.

Tabassum, N. (2019). International advocacy for climate victims in Bangladesh. *Local Activism for Global Climate Justice: The Great Lakes Watershed,* 81–94. https://www.rou tledge.com/Local-Activism-for-Global-Climate-Justice-The-Great-Lakes-Waters hed/Perkins/p/book/9780367335892

Tokar, B. & Gilbertson, T. (2020). *Climate justice and community renewal resistance and grassroots solution.* Routledge. New York.

UNFCCC (1992). *United Nations framework convention on climate change.* Retrieved from https://unfccc.int/resource/docs/convkp/conveng.pdf. Date accessed December 2, 2019.

USAID (n.d.a). *Asia.* Retrieved from https://www.usaid.gov/where-we-work/asia. Date accessed June 27, 2018.

USAID (n.d.b). *Tropical forest conservation act of 1998.* Retrieved from https://www.usa id.gov/biodiversity/TFCA/tropical-forest-conservation-act-of-1998. Date accessed November 16, 2019.

World Bank (2012, May 22). *Bangladesh climate change resilience fund.* Retrieved from http: //www.worldbank.org/en/news/feature/2012/05/22/bangladesh-climate-change -resilience-fund-bccrf. Date accessed November 30, 2019.

World Bank (n.d.). *List of projects under BCCRF.* Retrieved from http://siteresources.worl dbank.org/SOUTHASIAEXT/Resources/223546-1214948920836/bccrf-projects.p df. Date accessed January 3, 2020.

PART III

Just transitions

INTRODUCTION

Pursuing just transitions: growing from seed to blossom

Stacia Ryder, Kathryn Powlen, and Melinda Laituri

The idea of developing a "just transition" can be traced back to the 1970s and 1980s, emerging out of the USA labor and environmental justice movements to ensure that environmentally desirable transitions did not take place at the expense of affected workers and frontline communities (for a history, see Ciplet and Harrison 2020; Healy et al. 2017; Stevis et al. 2019). While the strategy lost ground in the United States and Canada it was adopted by international union organizations around the turn of the current millennium, with green jobs promoted as a necessary part of any just transition (Healy et al. 2017). This focus on the workforce has been adopted in recent global climate policy agreements, which continue to acknowledge the tensions between jobs and the environment – though they often gloss over issues of power embedded within this JT tension (Stevis and Felli 2016).

Today, conversations around just transitions focus in part on energy sources, carbon emissions, and employment in the fossil fuel industry. McCauley and Heffron (2018), for example, contend that a just transition is a way to shift energy systems away from fossil fuels, decarbonize the energy industry, and move toward clean energy technology and green jobs. In a similar vein, Newell and Mulvaney (2013) suggest that just transitions should move policy and society toward a low-carbon future while accounting for issues of equity and justice – in terms of access to energy, energy poverty, and addressing the livelihoods of those who are currently economically dependent on fossil fuels. In part, the idea of a just transition is that this will be achieved through opening employment opportunities within clean and renewable energy sectors. Yet, increasing employment opportunities in renewable energy is not sufficient to constitute a just transition. As Stevis et al. (2019, 4) note, renewable energy is not innately just, and the sector is "dominated by large corporations who are subject to the same logic of capitalism as fossil fuel corporations." In Chapter 12, Burke suggest that if the emphasis on unending growth and accumulation in the current energy system continues to carry over to renewable and clean energy systems, the result will be an extension of the harmful patterns of extraction and subsequent injustices we see today. We must re-formulate our approach to energy systems – who designs them, who they serve, and how they operate if we are to produce a just transition.

While energy is a crucial component of transitioning to a more environmentally just future, it is not the only piece of this puzzle. The idea of transforming the often-unjust socio-environmental arrangements of our present is not only about moving away from fossil fuels, reducing carbon, and mitigating the impacts of climate change. Across different times, spaces, and scales existing socio-environmental systems could be revolutionized through a transition that emphasizes a more just arrangement for both human and nonhuman actors. In existing research, the concept of just transitions has been applied to "environmental racism, zero waste, energy democracy, mass incarceration and inequitable policing, gentrification, and Indigenous rights and sovereignty" (Ciplet and Harrison 2020: 438). For example, in his analysis in Chapter 19, Valle explores how gardeners deploy convivial labor, contesting capitalistic practices through gardening, providing readers with a concrete example of transition-as-practice. His study of urban home gardens provides us with tools to think about how to opt-out of the current socio-economic system and its restraints, and to instead pursue alternatives which move us toward a just, post-Anthropocenic future.

To transition to a just future means first acknowledging our unjust past and present. We must reflect on the systems of power that got us here, and actively engage in simultaneously challenging them and developing alternatives. This includes thinking on capitalism and growth logics which has led to the continuous pursuit of profit and lifestyles of overconsumption by the wealthy. Coupled with neoliberalism, state co-optation by corporate interests (also known as regulatory capture) has led to unbridled, unregulated industries that have engaged in environmentally degrading practices. These practices disproportionately threaten the health and wellbeing of low-income communities Black, indigenous and other communities of color and resource-dependent communities, particularly those located in the Global South. Further, the pursuit of capitalism cannot be disentangled from settler colonialism and the devastating and lasting effects of the genocide, chattel slavery, resource exploitation and land degradation perpetrated by White Europeans.

In Chapter 14, Omukuti demonstrates how current environmental governance issues are embedded in this colonial past by providing an overview of the history of forest management in Tanzania. She acknowledges the role of colonialism and post-independence policies in shaping forest conservation efforts and subsequently climate policies. She suggests that local forest-dependent communities in Tanzania experience *double injustices*, as they have contributed the least to climate change but are being negatively impacted by climate action policies which restrict their rights to access and use of forests. This case provides an example of why it is crucial we hold the privileged and powerful who have benefitted from these policies accountable, both in terms of reconciling the damage they have already done, and redressing their continued contribution to the present problem. For example, research shows that 100 businesses are responsible for the lion's share (71%) of carbon emissions (Griffin and Heede 2017). When we delineate this responsibility across nation-states, America and Europe are responsible for 53% of historic carbon emissions (Hickel 2020). We must push to establish new systems and structures through which we can hold these companies and countries accountable for the negative impacts climate change is having on the planetary ecosystem.

In this section, there are two predominant threads focused on how we can pursue just transitions. First, we must develop approaches which acknowledge the embeddedness of humans in a global ecological system more holistically. This includes a relational approach which accounts for how other nonhuman components of an ecosystem can act with agency. In Chapter 17, Comi highlights how we might shift from industrial agricultural practices to a more co-produced and environmentally just food production system. More specifically, he writes on materiality and the agency of the "stuff" which makes up the practice of agriculture. He suggests an alternative to the industrial farm model where freeing the farmers starts with "freeing the seed." His contributions build on a recent area of advancement – multispecies justice – which aligns with the notions of plant-thinking that are drawn out by Pandit and Purakayastha in Chapter 21 of this volume.

Another common theme in this section focuses on the necessity of difference. To cultivate interdependence requires acknowledging, encouraging, and valuing difference. This is important in terms of context – as the chapters in this book demonstrate the variation in temporality, spatiality, and scale across environmental (in)justice contexts. This speaks to the need to recognize historically embedded dominant cultures and exclusionary practices, and how these spaces can be transformed into inclusive, legitimate spaces where differences can be acknowledged, valued, and respected. For example, in Chapter 15, Zhou uses a critical lens to examine sustainable practices in Sweden, particularly cycling. She explores how practices like cycling shape a narrative of the model Swedish ecological citizen as an ideal type which can serve to further exclude "other" residents in ethnically diverse communities on the outskirts of Stockholm. She suggests that just transitions must incorporate progressive ontologies of sustainability, urbanism, mobility, and ecological citizenship which accommodate differences.

In discussing the potentialities for just transitions, Farrell and Stano call for a strengthening of our "democratic infrastructure of communities while finding healthy alternatives to our current extraction-based economy." Much like the non-linearity of coalition building Goloff describes in the final section of the book, they trace the forward and backward steps of incorporating just transitions into California's climate policies across both local and state governance scales. Their work shows parallels with the back and forth of effective coalition building Goloff describes in the final section of the book.

To transition is defined as the process of moving from one state to another. We as individuals, society as a collective, and the entirety of the planet exist as constantly in process and motion. Even if processes of just transitions mean we find ourselves achieving the goal of a more just future, there remains a need to continue to work to sustain a just society in a rapidly changing socio-ecological world. Mao et al. begin to describe the constant need for this work in Chapter 13, when discussing how authoritarian state power can exacerbate environmental inequalities to achieve a green transition. They propose that to achieve a just transition in China, authoritarian state environmental intervention should involve *constant responses and adjustments involving multiple stakeholders*, where local communities should be involved in program formulation and implementation oriented toward just transitioning. Constant and careful dialectics, responses, and adjustments will be necessary to carry us all forward toward a just, sustainable future which extends across multiple generations.

A just transition is one that is ripe with contradictions and points of consternation. We must lean into those spaces. The process and change can be incremental, or it can be abrupt. It can often feel like two steps forward and one step back. While a just transition encapsulates a holistic approach (Farrell 2012), it also requires the stitching together of multifaceted, multiscalar efforts reflective of this holistic approach. It needs, as Goloff suggests, room for radical difference. The Anthropocene – a term imprecise and insufficient in its delineation of the role of power and who, precisely, is responsible for getting us here – is itself a transition. How we exist in the Anthropocene is shaped by the conditions which led us here. Simultaneously, how we exist in the Anthropocene has implications for how and when we transition out of it. Precisely how this transition occurs, and the degree to which it exacerbates conflict or creates new opportunities for cooperation will depend on how we plan and enact it. We are not tied to continuing the harmful patterns indicative of the Anthropocene, even as the impacts of climate change, increasing right-wing authoritarianism and a global pandemic loom large in our everyday lives. Spaces for practices, actions, and processes which subvert the status quo, challenge existing systems of power, and deny the need to choose between socioeconomic livelihoods or ecological destruction do exist in our day-to-day lives. Through a just transition which incorporates concerns of recognition, capabilities and participation (see Schlosberg 2007), we can work toward a future epoch we might call the Biospheric Egalitarocene. While perhaps a complicated term, its definition as "the equal right to live and blossom" (Kopnina 2014; Naess 1973:96; O'Sullivan 1987) is more simplistic. In these turbulent times, we must encourage each other to practice radical difference in the face of uncertainty, to continue the world-building work we are all doing, and to develop matrices of resistance (LeQuesne 2019) to state-sanctioned environmental destruction, social inequality, violence, and necropolitics. Together, we must toil to cultivate and nurture a garden where all can live and blossom.

References

Ciplet, D. and Harrison, J.L., 2020. Transition tensions: Mapping conflicts in movements for a just and sustainable transition. *Environmental Politics*, 29(3), pp. 435–456.

Farrell, C., 2012. A just transition: Lessons learned from the environmental justice movement. *Duke FL & Soc. Change*, 4, p. 45.

Griffin, P. and Heede, C.R., 2017. The carbon majors database. *CDP Carbon Majors Report 2017*, 14.

Healy, N. and Barry, J., 2017. Politicizing energy justice and energy system transitions: Fossil fuel divestment and a "just transition". *Energy Policy*, 108, pp. 451–459.

Hickel, J., 2020. Quantifying national responsibility for climate breakdown: An equality-based attribution approach for carbon dioxide emissions in excess of the planetary boundary. *The Lancet Planetary Health*, 4(9), pp. e399–e404.

Kopnina, H., 2014. Environmental justice and biospheric egalitarianism: Reflecting on a normative-philosophical view of human-nature relationship. *Earth Perspectives*, 1(1), pp. 1–11.

LeQuesne, T., 2019. Petro-hegemony and the matrix of resistance: What can standing Rock's water protectors teach us about organizing for climate justice in the United States? *Environmental Sociology*, 5(2), pp. 188–206.

McCauley, D. and Heffron, R., 2018. Just transition: Integrating climate, energy, and environmental justice. *Energy Policy*, 119, pp. 1–7.

Naess, A., 1973. The shallow and the deep, long-range ecology movement. A summary. *Inquiry*, 16(1–4), pp. 95–100.

Newell, P. and Mulvaney, D., 2013. The political economy of the 'just transition'. *The Geographical Journal*, 179(2), pp. 132–140.

O'Sullivan, P.E., 1987. Shallow and deep environmental science. *International Journal of Environmental Studies*, 30(2–3), pp. 91–98.

Stevis, D. and Felli, R., 2016. *Green Transitions, Just Transitions*. Broadening and Deepening Justice.

Stevis, D., Krause, D. and Morena, E., 2019. Reclaiming the role of labour environmentalism in just transitions. *International Union Rights*, 26(4), pp. 3–4.

12

JUST ENERGY SYSTEMS

Five questions and countless responses for regenerative energy communities

Matthew J. Burke

An urgent need to rethink renewable energy futures

Any meaningful response to the Anthropocene requires an energy transition. Whether characterized in terms associated with agriculture, fossil fuels, atomic energy, or human labor, the Anthropocene is meant to describe a time of multiple, widespread, and potentially irreversible breaches of ecological limits. As systems of energy provision and use fundamentally enable these breaches (McNeill and Engelke 2014), the pursuit of a new "age of renewables" (IRENA 2015) is a necessary response to the accumulating disasters and overshoot of the Anthropocene.

Yet there exist different modes of transition, not all of them just (Jasanoff 2018; Morena et al. 2020). To simplify the issue, at least two seemingly contradictory approaches are now promoted for taking renewable energy systems to scale. A first approach, popularized among political and economic elites worldwide, is described as a global energy interconnection (GEI), consisting of large-scale, remotely sited renewable electric generation facilities, ultra-high voltage transnational and transcontinental interconnections, regional and national smart grids, and the supporting global cooperative governing mechanisms (Chatzivasileiadis et al. 2017; Liu 2015). Proposed as a fully developed global energy system by 2050, GEI broadly aligns with three overarching objectives for global energy governance: economic growth, energy access, and environmental sustainability. This pattern of renewable energy development effectively extends an extractivist model of energy provision and use into a new sociotechnical regime, with all its concomitant power dynamics, relations of dominance, and processes of accumulation and enclosure (Angus 2016).

A distinct pathway for transition reprioritizes or outrightly rejects this prevailing set of objectives for modern energy systems. Characterized largely by decentralized and democratic proposals for renewable energy transition, this second approach is termed regenerative rather than extractive (Movement Generation 2016), and exemplified by various actions occurring across all levels of society including community-controlled renewable energy (Creamer et al. 2019), civil society organizations, trade unions, municipalities and others organizing to democratize renewable energy systems (Becker and Naumann 2017), and campaigns to advance globally integrated networks of decentralized, 100% renewable energy regions (Boselli and Leidreiter 2017). Positioning these modes of renewable energy governance as distinct and potentially mutually exclusive trajectories, in view of the resources required for widespread development, underscores the point that renewable energy transition involves not only a shift to renewables, but also a competition among various and innumerable alternatives for renewable energy futures.

This chapter contributes to the understanding and implementation of regenerative energy systems by providing a means to reconsider basic relationships of people to energy, most principally in the context of high-energy societies. The chapter leverages this uniquely prefigurative moment at an early stage of large-scale energy transition as an opportunity to reconsider common assumptions regarding a renewable energy transition – its purpose, functioning, guiding values, and sociopolitical opportunities. As relevant to this volume, the chapter addresses two critical questions. First, how can energy and environmental justice between and among humans and the rest of nature, within and across generations, be achieved in an age of ecological overshoot? And second, what institutional, economic, and governance innovations can be adopted to promote just transitions in the Anthropocene, an inherently unjust period in its capacity to universalize responsibility and response (Davis and Todd 2017; Malm and Hornborg 2014)? The task ahead demands not only shedding the dominance of fossil fuels, but also shedding the fossil-fuel mindset that gave rise to dominant forms of human-energy relations, which remain to a large degree the basis on which renewable energy systems are now envisioned. Efforts to advance an age of renewables, whether centralized, decentralized, or some combination thereof, will likely flounder if they are based on flawed and fossilized foundations and organized around unachievable and unjust outcomes. In short, this project requires new foundations from which to enable renewed human relationships to energy.

To explore these foundations for renewable energy transitions, this chapter follows the authors of *Right Relationship: Building a Whole Earth Economy* (Brown and Garver 2009) in posing five basic questions in search of energy systems in right relationship with the broader communities of life: What is the global energy system for? How does it work? How big is too big? What is fair? How should it be governed? Thinking through these questions helps point toward regenerative energy systems, systems of human energy provisioning and use that exist in right relationship with the whole community of life. Through this exploration, the chapter makes the case that diverse forms of energy must be allowed to enable highly diverse energy communities. An energy community can be thought of as a collective of human and nonhuman beings spatially and temporally enmeshed and interconnected through flows of renewable energy, and the corresponding relationships that emerge from this collective. Thus, while visions for regenerative energy futures must extend globally in order to decisively end the fossil fuel age, this global perspective must simultaneously resist a universalized response. The following section proposes a brief response to each of the above questions, drawing from understandings of renewable energy, integrated social–ecological systems, and energy and environmental ethics. Implications for different pathways are then discussed, concluding with an appeal for broader engagement with these critical questions among varied energy communities.

Energy systems in right relationship

What is the global energy system for?

The energy transition offers an unprecedented opportunity to collectively reconsider the basic purpose of human energy systems. While modern energy systems are in part intended to provide universal energy access and environmental sustainability, in practice these objectives are constrained when they come into conflict with the overarching agenda of economic growth or its derivatives of energy security and energy intensity. Despite attempts at decoupling, global impact of energy use continues to increase even as billions lack sufficient access (Csereklyei and Stern 2015; D'Alessandro et al. 2020; Hickel 2019a; Parrique et al. 2019). The growth agenda of energy systems is failing and deserves to be replaced with a new set of objectives for energy systems.

Developing regenerative energy systems requires recognizing the embeddedness of human economic systems within broader societal and planetary systems. This core perspective draws from ecological economics (Daly and Farley 2011), understanding the economy as a subset of society, which in turn is a subset of the Earth, with materials cycling within and energy flowing through and throughout (Figure 12.1).

From this perspective, renewable energy systems can be understood as technologies for guiding continuous Earthly flows of incoming solar energy and outgoing heat. Human economies are some of the countless ways that life on Earth has developed to capture, make use of, and dissipate low-entropy energy as an ultimate means. In a sense, economies, societies, ecosystems, life itself, may be viewed as diverse means for collecting, using, and dissipating energy and materials. From the perspective of these systems themselves, however, energy and materials are means to other ultimate ends such as longevity and well-being. Energy is thus a means to an end for Earth's living beings, not an end in itself.

To thrive and flourish, all life on Earth must find ways to consistently access primary flows of incoming energy and stocks of cycling materials while safely dissipating waste heat. An energy system in right relationship is one that meets the needs of all members of the Earth community within the means of the planet.

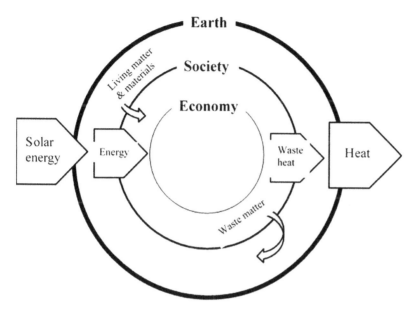

FIGURE 12.1   A Whole Earth Energy System (based on Daly and Farley 2011; and Raworth 2017).

Identifying and meeting these needs of the Earth community through renewable energy systems requires broadened recognition, expanded capabilities, and active and ongoing engagement of diverse energy communities (Baxter 2004; Day et al. 2016; Schlosberg 2013). The core objective of regenerative energy systems then is not growth, rather the achievement of well-being of the whole Earth community within planetary limits, as implemented through social practices of specific energy communities.

How does it work?

Meeting multiple needs of energy communities within the material and energic means of the planet requires a general understanding of how the Earth's energy systems function. Conventional energy systems are structured around spatial and temporal divisions that too often conceal the way modern energy systems work and the damaging social and environmental relationships resulting from their use. Spatially, great distances typically separate extraction, delivery, use, and disposal, as well as the patterns of injustice associated with each of these stages (Bouzarovski and Simcock 2017; Bridge et al. 2013; Fthenakis and Kim 2009; Huber and McCarthy 2017; Vallero 2014). Temporally, fossil energy systems draw from concentrations of ancient sunlight captured by living beings long since deceased, then release the waste from these non-replenishable stocks of high-quality fuels within a very narrow time frame, with consequences spanning generations. Currently, the global energy system provides abundant energy for some and insufficient energy for many (REN21 2017) while exceeding the planet's capacity to absorb new streams of waste. Patterns of energy extraction further compel a universalizing influence evident in the Anthropocene, in which methods of energy development and severed energy relations are replicated worldwide, erasing differences across communities. By contrast, because renewable sources are available in very different forms from place to place, the renewable energy transition opens opportunities for dramatically reducing spatial and temporal gaps, bringing into view the functioning of these systems and the consequences of their use and misuse.

Renewable energy, those forms continuously replenished by the natural environment on a human timescale, include primary sources derived from the sun both directly, such as thermal and photo-electric energy, and indirectly, such as wind and biomass, as well as from other natural movements (Armaroli and Balzani 2011; Ellabban et al. 2014). Globally, this renewable resource potential is enormous, an order of magnitude or more greater than current global energy demand, mostly through direct solar radiation (Desing et al. 2019). However, at a given point in space and time, the maximum flow of solar energy and its related forms is finite, while the density of these flows is substantially less than fossil and nuclear energy (Smil 2015).

Regardless of source, systems of energy require both energy and material inputs and produce waste as losses through energy conversions, typically in the form of heat, as well as material waste (Desing et al. 2019). Although renewable sources are replenishable, their capture, storage, movement, and use require energy inputs and use of living materials and non-living physical matter of the Earth. Materials may be recycled using energy inputs, yet thermodynamics hold that energy cannot be recycled but is rather converted to other forms of energy. These processes of recycling and conversion produce waste. Globally, there has existed a relative balance of incoming and outgoing energy. The influence of factors that change this balance is measured as radiative forcing (W/m^2), where radiative forcing greater than zero W/m^2 produces global warming and forcing less than zero produces global cooling. Most outgoing radiation is absorbed by atmospheric greenhouse gases and the Earth's oceans, contributing to the warming of the planet's surface and atmosphere (USGCRP 2017).

This discussion of energy, while defensible from the perspective of physical sciences, is not intended to exclude other ways of knowing or experiencing energy beyond that of a "resource" for human exploitation (Frigo 2017). Rather, it is intended to accommodate a view of energies as threads that interconnect all living and nonliving phenomena, constituting a human relation to the rest of nature. In the context of right relationships, both an ability to access energy flows and a responsibility to allow the same of other living beings are required. An energy system in right relationship with society and the Earth is one in which energy communities manage to achieve well-being of all members within the common yet limited energic flows, material cycles, and waste assimilative and dissipative capacities of the planet. Understanding these basic processes and parameters then directs attention to questions of physical planetary limits on the one hand, and community needs on the other.

How big is too big?

For genuine ecological well-being, a global renewable energy system needs to operate within the limits of the planet. The climate emergency is a key indicator that current energy systems are failing in this regard. The combustion of fossil fuels and the conversion of forest lands for biofuels are leading sources of greenhouse gas emissions contributing to climate change (Ritchie and Roser 2020). However, climate change is not the only limit currently being tested by modern energy systems. Biodiversity loss, ocean acidification, and water shortages, to name a few, are all partially driven by modern energy use (Algunaibet et al. 2019; Darby and Fawcett 2018). While a shift to systems using solar and wind will undoubtedly reduce the overall negative impacts to the planet, a narrow focus on carbon emissions risks shifting impacts to other planetary catastrophes such as mass extinction. When considering the scale of global energy development in aggregate, including the quantities of energy captured and used, the extent of physical infrastructure, and the pace of development, a variety of potential impacts must be kept in view.

Global development of renewable energy systems must therefore include approaches to recognizing the Earth's physical limits across various measures. The planetary boundaries approach (Steffen et al. 2015) offers a useful way of thinking about the appropriate scale of global renewable energy systems (Algunaibet et al. 2019; Desing et al. 2019; Khan 2019). Planetary boundaries are indicators of sociogenic impacts to key planetary processes. The boundaries define a "safe operating space" within which human societies may safely endure. While nine boundaries provide potentially relevant indicators of planetary limits for modern energy systems, several stand out as most relevant for renewable energy systems. These boundaries include climate change, biosphere integrity, land-system change, freshwater use, ocean acidification, atmospheric aerosol loading, and potential novel entities associated with renewable energy technologies. At a global level, land-system change and biosphere integrity deserve particular attention, given the extinction crisis and loss of habitat that characterize the Anthropocene.

Together, these boundaries offer well-suited indicators for assessing an appropriate scale of modern renewable energy systems, and thus support a move toward right relationship. These limits can be thought of as planetary thresholds or ceilings. These thresholds would constitute the set of planetary limits relevant to energy systems, which when breached will increase the likelihood of undesirable and catastrophic consequences. The boundaries themselves are not immutable, rather they indicate an area of lower risk. For regenerative energy systems, energy communities would seek to meet their needs while preventing the aggregate global scale of energy systems (in both extent and pace of development) from breaching these and other relevant ecological limits.

What is fair?

With these goals, processes, and parameters in view, energy communities can turn to questions of how to define basic needs and how to use energy systems to meet those needs for all. The presently dominant perspective gives priority to increasing energy use, primarily for economic growth and capital accumulation, but also for reducing energy poverty. Beyond a certain point, continued increases in energy demand and economic growth do not contribute to any meaningful gain in well-being, rather they concentrate wealth among the few while undermining the very preconditions for achieving well-being, namely an integrated and resilient natural environment (Clark et al. 2018; Daly 2014). Instead of seeking to decouple growth and consumption from environmental harm, energy communities would decouple human and planetary well-being from the necessity of unending growth. Because global energy demand and economic growth are tightly associated with increasing planetary environmental impact, regenerative energy systems would target community well-being directly, rather than gambling on an agenda of decarbonized green growth. Dispensing with the universal growth imperative implies giving greater weight to distributional equity and justice among all members of the Earth community.

Fairness therefore requires that all communities have the capacity to meet their needs. Before giving weight to conventional notions of energy security (i.e., increasing supply to meet continuously growing demand), meeting community needs through energy systems requires prioritizing sufficient energy sources to achieve a high quality of life. Equitable access to energy must allow the world's poor people, who experience low levels of average per capita energy use, to increase their levels of non-combustion renewable energy use while ensuring that nonhuman members of the earth's communities can meet their energic needs through various natural processes.

These outcomes cannot be accommodated within planetary limits if the world's highest energy users fail to constrain and reduce their overall energy use. Put another way, in the context of existing global overshoot, achieving a good life for all within planetary boundaries is possible only if wealthy societies sharply reduce their biophysical footprints from current levels (Hickel 2019b; O'Neill et al. 2018), including especially the footprint of modern energy systems. Fortunately, beyond a saturation point, there exists little empirical relationship between increasing energy use and further improvements to human well-being, meaning stabilized levels can be targeted without meaningful reductions in measures of quality of life (Burke 2020). In this way, the developed world would seek to decouple their well-being from high levels of energy use (Hickel 2019b). Energy systems and their associated economies would develop so that energy communities can flourish with or without growth (Raworth 2017; van den Bergh 2017). Beyond energy provision, energy systems must also support efforts to ensure that other human and nonhuman needs are met, including access to food, water, shelter/habitat, education, and meaningful work.

Shifting to renewable energy systems offers a key opportunity to redistribute capacity to meet the needs of all. The wide availability of renewable sources can facilitate this redistribution in the present, while a shift to 100% renewables can better ensure that future generations will also have this capacity, as nonrenewable fuel stocks inevitably diminish and their waste exceeds assimilative capacities of the planet. Abandoning the pursuit of endless growth and accumulation (Alarcón Ferrari and Chartier 2017; Alexander and Yacoumis 2018; Brand-Correa et al. 2018; Darby and Fawcett 2018; Kunze and Becker 2015), regenerative energy systems would enable energy communities to use renewable sources to more equitably meet diverse basic needs across all members of the broader Earth community now and into the future.

How should it be governed?

A reoriented approach to renewable energy development opens new opportunities for the governance of emerging and future renewable energy systems. Informed by the above discussion, a foundation for governance of renewable energy systems would involve several key characteristics in practice (Orenstein and Shach-Pinsley 2017). First, governing systems would integrate both top-down and bottom-up initiatives, taking advantage of the strengths of each. Second, governing systems would aim to provide mutual benefit for integrated social–ecological concerns. Third, governing systems would focus on specific outcomes while retaining a more holistic perspective. Finally, energy governance would operate across spatial scales, connecting efforts locally, regionally, and globally.

Addressing these qualities, the notion of a "safe and just operating space" (Raworth 2012, p. 7) demonstrates well the orientation of an energy system governed to achieve well-being of all members of Earth's communities within the limits of the planet (Darby and Fawcett 2018). Raworth represents this space using two concentric rings, one indicating an outer environmental ceiling of critical ecological thresholds, and the other indicating an inner social foundation of basic human needs. This rendering forms a life ring[1] that frames an area targeted for safe and fair economic processes. Operationalizing this life ring concept for the practice of governance of energy systems would require a combination of social and ecological indicators as both ceiling and foundation. As humans are fundamentally interconnected with their natural environment, it is increasingly problematic to draw sharp lines between what constitutes "social" and "environmental" foundations and ceilings. For example, Illich (2013 [1973]) asserts that social ceilings exist for maximum per capita energy use, which when exceeded create social disharmony well before an environmental threshold is reached. In sum, a life ring provides a conceptual tool and approach for governing renewable energy systems (Figure 12.2).

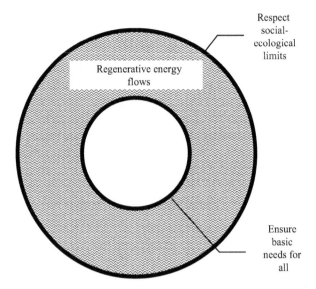

FIGURE 12.2 Energy life ring: conceptual orientation for just energy transitions (based on Darby and Fawcett, 2018, p. 9; and Raworth, 2017, p. 62).

The concept is relevant for top-down and bottom-up initiatives, offers integration of social–ecological systems to guide governance for mutual benefit, places specific issues and concerns within a holistic pattern, and can be adjusted to suit various spatial scales. Accordingly, a life ring provides a focal orientation for the practice of renewable energy governance based on operationalizing a set of metrics relevant to energy communities. The life ring approach allows flexibility for specifying metrics at the local and regional level (Dearing et al. 2014) while integrating globally relevant measures. Application of the energy life ring would require assessments of the points where energy systems threaten to overwhelm planetary thresholds and where they fail to meet basic community needs. Such assessments would become routine practice and constant companions to energy status reports at all levels. The fundamental challenge and objective then for any mode of governance of regenerative energy systems is to achieve well-being for all while respecting planetary limits simultaneously and continuously over time.

Discussion and conclusion

Considering these questions clarifies choices for renewable energy futures. Modes of energy provisioning and use organized around purposes of unending growth and accumulation effectively extend patterns of extraction and their corresponding injustices of the Anthropocene into the renewable age. Systems so oriented will develop by scouring the globe for all available renewable and nonrenewable energy and material inputs needed to connect and feed expanding energy loads, generating at each step waste heat and other harmful outputs, with few clear mechanisms to respect limits, offering growth as its primary response to global inequities, yielding a homogenizing effect physically, technologically, and socially, and further consolidating decision-making processes already severed from their impacts on the ground.

Regenerative energy pathways are preferred for just transitions as the goals of such systems are not the expansion and use of energy as such, rather the provision and attainment of basic needs and community well-being within limits. Regenerative energy systems exist to support life of all forms, using myriad methods for dissipating energy, at levels of throughput sufficient to ensure system endurance. In practice, these questions will require a multitude of responses based on local context, inspiring equally diverse assemblies of energy communities. How these systems will work will therefore vary widely, as diverse energies must generate diverse energy communities. Multiple modes of provision can be tested and adopted as relevant to unique technical and social–ecological contexts, including self-provision, non-monetary provision, market, public, and commons provision, and more. Participation must not be only as a consumer, rather as a member of a community seeking to provide energy to the whole of that community. Thus, the critical choice is not simply which type of energy to acquire, or even from whom, but rather what mode of social structures can best ensure energy for the intended purpose.

Efforts to institutionalize regenerative energy governance globally would begin at the level of local communities and build outward, guided by the energy life ring, leading to interconnected networks of energy communities. This process requires assessing and improving local capacities for energy governance, expanding organizational diversity (e.g., cooperatives, utilities, trusteeships, energy regions) according to local needs and conditions, and reforming and in some cases dismantling existing institutions. For example, the International Renewable Energy Agency (IRENA) could restructure its membership to center on local, municipal, and regional entities and facilitate cooperation among these actors, supporting nested or polycentric structures of renewable energy governance. Goals for energy access could be broadened to include access to ownership and control of technologies rather than simply to energy services.

This approach implies an indeterminate a priori position to energy technologies. Because regenerative agendas begin from needs of local communities, more diverse sets of technologies may be deployed. These technologies would relate closely to needs as identified by the communities themselves; for example, prioritizing increased deployment of off-grid and microgrid solutions or open-source options allowing local repair, maintenance, and development. Technological diversification may help avoid lock-in of infrastructures that fail to support the energy life ring, while better positioning communities to respond to crises and uncertainties. The pace of renewable energy transitions would proceed in a manner attentive to various integrated social–ecological measures. The proportion and date of renewable energy targets would be secondary to the ongoing achievement of ultimate-end outcomes constituting the life ring. This approach also implies decreases in total energy use among the energy-affluent, increases among the energy-poor, and rational, targeted, and decreasing use of fossil fuels, channeling their unique qualities toward genuine needs and replacement technologies, while respecting planetary limits.

Worlds of experimentation and sociotechnical diversity can thus be imagined, employing unique, creative, idiosyncratic, and social–ecologically integrated approaches for capturing, storing, moving, and using renewable energy sources. These approaches rest upon a coherent view of regenerative systems that reorients energy and associated development toward mutual well-being of people and planet. Current practices offer evidence of such approaches already available, including just transition programs, community energy and microgrids, island energy systems, and indigenous-led renewable energy (Burke and Stephens 2017; MacArthur and Matthewman 2018; Morena et al. 2020; Smith and Scott 2018). Beginning at the community level implies less control over energy transition pathways and possibly a messier, flexible approach to sociotechnical development. As such, a variety of decentralized energy transitions would employ many different technologies, financing instruments, organizational forms, and so on, reflecting their social–ecological diversity yet holding a basic commitment to caring for and sharing energy systems designed to achieve well-being for all within the means of the planet.

Accordingly, this chapter seeks to advance a foundation for renewable energy futures through a whole Earth perspective, at once integrating distributed sources of agency, social–ecological responsibility, specific and holistic measures, and multiple scales of governance. More broadly, this work offers an invitation to reconsider common assumptions regarding renewable energy transitions, in an effort to break collective mental and physical dependencies on dangerously inadequate logics of the fossil fuel age and renew human relationships to energy systems. As a core contributor to the disaster and injustice that is the Anthropocene, the age of oil has served to heighten the human disconnect from the rest of nature, enabling self-reinforcing patterns of extraction, while universalizing relations to energy and place. A just transition then not only requires shifting to renewable energy but doing so in multitudes of ways that care for, respect, and give back to the broader communities of life from which these modes of energy arise.

Acknowledgments

This chapter has benefited from comments of the editors and reviewers of this volume, as well as through engagement with the Economics for the Anthropocene program. An earlier version was prepared for the Symposium on Environmental

Justice in the Anthropocene, Colorado State University, 2017. This research was supported by the Social Sciences and Humanities Research Council of Canada, the Department of Natural Resource Sciences at McGill University, the Leadership for the Ecozoic program, and the Gund Institute for Environment at the University of Vermont. The introductory section draws from text published in Burke (2019, pp. 3–4), used here by permission of the author.

Note

1 Raworth uses the term 'doughnut' to describe this concept (as in *Doughnut economics* (2017)) but has also suggested the possibility to use alternative terms, e.g., a life saver (Raworth, 2012, p. 7).

References

Alarcón Ferrari, C., Chartier, C., 2017. Degrowth, energy democracy, technology and social-ecological relations: Discussing a localised energy system in Vaxjö, Sweden. *Journal of Cleaner Production*. https://doi.org/10.1016/j.jclepro.2017.05.100

Alexander, S., Yacoumis, P., 2018. Degrowth, energy descent, and 'low-tech' living: Potential pathways for increased resilience in times of crisis. *Journal of Cleaner Production, Technology and Degrowth* 197, 1840–1848. https://doi.org/10.1016/j.jclepro.2016.09.100

Algunaibet, I.M., Pozo, C., Galán-Martín, Á., Huijbregts, M.A.J., Dowell, N.M., Guillén-Gosálbez, G., 2019. Powering sustainable development within planetary boundaries. *Energy Environmental Science* 12, 1890–1900. https://doi.org/10.1039/C8EE03423K

Angus, I., 2016. *Facing the Anthropocene: Fossil capitalism and the crisis of the earth system.* Monthly Review Press, New York.

Armaroli, N., Balzani, V., 2011. *Energy for a sustainable world: From the oil age to a sun-powered future.* Wiley-VCH Verlag GmbH, Weinheim.

Baxter, B., 2004. *A theory of ecological justice.* Routledge, London. https://doi.org/10.4324/9780203458495

Becker, S., Naumann, M., 2017. Energy democracy: Mapping the debate on energy alternatives. *Geography Compass* 11, e12321. https://doi.org/10.1111/gec3.12321

Boselli, F., Leidreiter, A., 2017. *100% RE building blocks: A practical toolkit for a sustainable transition to 100% renewable energy.* Global 100% RE Campaign, Bonn.

Bouzarovski, S., Simcock, N., 2017. Spatializing energy justice. *Energy Policy* 107, 640–648. https://doi.org/10.1016/j.enpol.2017.03.064

Brand-Correa, L.I., Martin-Ortega, J., Steinberger, J.K., 2018. Human scale energy services: Untangling a 'golden thread.' *Energy Research & Social Science* 38, 178–187. https://doi.org/10.1016/j.erss.2018.01.008

Bridge, G., Bouzarovski, S., Bradshaw, M., Eyre, N., 2013. Geographies of energy transition: Space, place and the low-carbon economy. *Energy Policy* 53, 331–340. https://doi.org/10.1016/j.enpol.2012.10.066

Brown, P.G., Garver, G., 2009. *Right relationship: Building a whole earth economy.* Berrett-Koehler Publishers, San Francisco.

Burke, M.J., 2020. Energy-Sufficiency for a just transition: A systematic review. *Energies* 13, 2444. https://doi.org/10.3390/en13102444

Burke, M.J., 2019. *Energy democracy and the co-evolution of social and technological systems.* McGill University, Montréal, QC.

Burke, M.J., Stephens, J.C., 2017. Energy democracy: Goals and policy instruments for sociotechnical transitions. *Energy Research & Social Science* 33, 35–48. https://doi.org /10.1016/j.erss.2017.09.024

Chatzivasileiadis, S., Ernst, D., Andersson, G., 2017. Global power grids for harnessing world renewable energy, in: Jones, L.E. (Ed.), *Renewable energy integration: Practical management of variability, uncertainty, and flexibility in power grids.* Elsevier, pp. 161–174. https://doi.org/10.1016/B978-0-12-809592-8.00012-3

Clark, B., Auerbach, D., Longo, S.B., 2018. The bottom line: Capital's production of social inequalities and environmental degradation. *Journal of Environmental Studies and Sciences* 8, 562–569. https://doi.org/10.1007/s13412-018-0505-6

Creamer, E., Taylor Aiken, G., van Veelen, B., Walker, G., Devine-Wright, P., 2019. Community renewable energy: What does it do? Walker and Devine-Wright (2008) ten years on. *Energy Research & Social Science* 57, 101223. https://doi.org/10.1016/j.erss .2019.101223

Csereklyei, Z., Stern, D.I., 2015. Global energy use: Decoupling or convergence? *Energy Economics* 51, 633–641. https://doi.org/10.1016/j.eneco.2015.08.029

D'Alessandro, S., Cieplinski, A., Distefano, T., Dittmer, K., 2020. Feasible alternatives to green growth. *Nature Sustainability* 3, 329–335. https://doi.org/10.1038/s41893-02 0-0484-y

Daly, H.E., 2014. *From uneconomic growth to a steady-state economy, advances in ecological economics.* Edward Elgar, Cheltenham Northampton.

Daly, H.E., Farley, J.C., 2011. *Ecological economics: Principles and applications,* 2nd ed. Island Press, Washington, DC.

Darby, S.J., Fawcett, T., 2018. *Energy sufficiency: An introduction.* European Council for an Energy-Efficient Economy, University of Oxford.

Davis, H., Todd, Z., 2017. On the importance of a date, or, decolonizing the Anthropocene. *ACME: An International Journal for Critical Geographies* 16.

Day, R., Walker, G., Simcock, N., 2016. Conceptualising energy use and energy poverty using a capabilities framework. *Energy Policy* 93, 255–264. https://doi.org/10.1016/j .enpol.2016.03.019

Dearing, J.A., Wang, R., Zhang, K., Dyke, J.G., Haberl, H., Hossain, Md.S., Langdon, P.G., Lenton, T.M., Raworth, K., Brown, S., Carstensen, J., Cole, M.J., Cornell, S.E., Dawson, T.P., Doncaster, C.P., Eigenbrod, F., Flörke, M., Jeffers, E., Mackay, A.W., Nykvist, B., Poppy, G.M., 2014. Safe and just operating spaces for regional social-ecological systems. *Global Environmental Change* 28, 227–238. https://doi.org/10.1016 /j.gloenvcha.2014.06.012

Desing, H., Widmer, R., Beloin-Saint-Pierre, D., Hischier, R., Wäger, P., 2019. Powering a sustainable and circular economy: An engineering approach to estimating renewable energy potentials within earth system boundaries. *Energies* 12, 4723. https://doi.org/10.3390/en12244723

Ellabban, O., Abu-Rub, H., Blaabjerg, F., 2014. Renewable energy resources: Current status, future prospects and their enabling technology. *Renewable and Sustainable Energy Reviews* 39, 748–764. https://doi.org/10.1016/j.rser.2014.07.113

Frigo, G., 2017. Energy ethics, homogenization, and hegemony: A reflection on the traditional energy paradigm. *Energy Research & Social Science, Exploring the Anthropology of Energy: Ethnography, Energy and Ethics* 30, 7–17. https://doi.org/10.1016/j.erss.2017 .06.030

Fthenakis, V., Kim, H.C., 2009. Land use and electricity generation: A life-cycle analysis. *Renewable and Sustainable Energy Reviews* 13, 1465–1474. https://doi.org/10.1016/j.rser .2008.09.017

Hickel, J., 2019a. The contradiction of the sustainable development goals: Growth versus ecology on a finite planet. *Sustainable Development* 27, 873–884. https://doi.org/10 .1002/sd.1947

Hickel, J., 2019b. Is it possible to achieve a good life for all within planetary boundaries? *Third World Quarterly* 40, 18–35. https://doi.org/10.1080/01436597.2018.1535895

Huber, M.T., McCarthy, J., 2017. Beyond the subterranean energy regime? Fuel, land use and the production of space. *Transactions of the Institute of British Geographers* 42, 655–668. https://doi.org/10.1111/tran.12182

Illich, I., 2013 [1973]. *Beyond economics and ecology: The radical thought of Ivan Illich*. Marion Boyars Publishers Ltd, New York.

IRENA, 2015. *The age of renewable power: Designing national roadmaps for a successful transformation*. International Renewable Energy Agency, Abu Dhabi.

Jasanoff, S., 2018. Just transitions: A humble approach to global energy futures. *Energy Research & Social Science, SI: Energy and the Future* 35, 11–14. https://doi.org/10.1016 /j.erss.2017.11.025

Khan, F., 2019. Staying within planetary boundaries. *Nature Energy* 4, 260–260. https:// doi.org/10.1038/s41560-019-0380-8

Kunze, C., Becker, S., 2015. Collective ownership in renewable energy and opportunities for sustainable degrowth. *Sustainability Science* 10, 425–437. https://doi.org/10.1007/ s11625-015-0301-0

Liu, Z., 2015. *Global energy interconnection*. Elsevier, Amsterdam.

MacArthur, J., Matthewman, S., 2018. Populist resistance and alternative transitions: Indigenous ownership of energy infrastructure in Aotearoa New Zealand. *Energy Research & Social Science, Sustainable Energy Transformations in an Age of Populism, Post-Truth Politics, and Local Resistance* 43, 16–24. https://doi.org/10.1016/j.erss.2018.05.009

Malm, A., Hornborg, A., 2014. The geology of mankind? A critique of the Anthropocene narrative. *The Anthropocene Review* 1, 62–69. https://doi.org/10.1177 /2053019613516291

McNeill, J.R., Engelke, P., 2014. *The great acceleration: An environmental history of the anthropocene since 1945*. Belknap Press of Harvard University Press, Cambridge, MA.

Morena, E., Krause, D., Stevis, D. (Eds.), 2020. *Just Transitions: Social justice in the shift towards a low-carbon world*. Pluto Press, London.

Movement Generation, 2016. *From banks and tanks to cooperation and caring: A strategic framework for a just transition*. Movement Generation Justice and Ecology Project, Oakland, CA.

O'Neill, D.W., Fanning, A.L., Lamb, W.F., Steinberger, J.K., 2018. A good life for all within planetary boundaries. *Nature Sustainability* 1, 88–95. https://doi.org/10.1038/ s41893-018-0021-4

Orenstein, D.E., Shach-Pinsley, D., 2017. A comparative framework for assessing sustainability initiatives at the regional scale. *World Development* 98, 245–256. https:// doi.org/10.1016/j.worlddev.2017.04.030

Parrique, T., Barth, J., Briens, F., Kerschner, C., Kraus-Polk, A., Kuokkanen, A., Spangenberg, J.H., 2019. *Decoupling debunked: Evidence and arguments against green growth as a sole strategy for sustainability*. European Environmental Bureau, Brussels.

Raworth, K., 2012. A safe and just space for humanity: Can we live within the doughnut? *Oxfam Policy and Practice: Climate Change and Resilience* 8, 1–26.

Raworth, K., 2017. *Doughnut economics: Seven ways to think like a 21st century economist.* Chelsea Green Publishing, White River Junction, VT.

REN21, 2017. *Renewables global futures report: Great debates towards 100% renewable energy.* REN21 Secretariat, Paris.

Ritchie, H., Roser, M., 2020. CO_2 *and greenhouse gas emissions.* Our World in Data. Published online at OurWorldInData.org. Retrieved from: 'https://ourworldindata .org/co2-and-other-greenhouse-gas-emissions' [Online Resource].

Schlosberg, D., 2013. Theorising environmental justice: The expanding sphere of a discourse. *Environmental Politics* 22, 37–55. https://doi.org/10.1080/09644016.2013 .755387

Smil, V., 2015. *Power density: A key to understanding energy sources and uses.* MIT Press, Cambridge, MA.

Smith, A.A., Scott, D.N., 2018. *'Energy without injustice'? Indigenous ownership of renewable energy generation (SSRN Scholarly Paper No. ID 3251922).* Social Science Research Network, Rochester.

Steffen, W., Richardson, K., Rockstrom, J., Cornell, S.E., Fetzer, I., Bennett, E.M., Biggs, R., Carpenter, S.R., de Vries, W., de Wit, C.A., Folke, C., Gerten, D., Heinke, J., Mace, G.M., Persson, L.M., Ramanathan, V., Reyers, B., Sorlin, S., 2015. Planetary boundaries: Guiding human development on a changing planet. *Science* 347, 736–747. https://doi.org/10.1126/science.1259855

USGCRP, 2017. *Climate science special report: A sustained assessment activity of the U.S. global change research program (fifth-order draft (5 OD)).* U.S. Global Change Research Program, Washington, DC.

Vallero, D.A., 2014. Environmental impacts of energy production, distribution and transport, in: Letcher, T.M. (Ed.), *Future Energy* (Second Edition). Elsevier, Boston, pp. 551–581. https://doi.org/10.1016/B978-0-08-099424-6.00025-9

van den Bergh, J.C.J.M., 2017. A third option for climate policy within potential limits to growth. *Nature Climate Change* 7, 107–112. https://doi.org/10.1038/nclimate3113

13

AUTHORITARIAN ENVIRONMENTALISM AS JUST TRANSITION?

A critical environmental justice examination of state environmental intervention in northwestern China

KuoRay Mao, Qian Zhang, and Nefratiri Weeks

Introduction

In the last three decades, China's explosive economic growth has drastically raised the standard of living for most citizens. However, its capitalist turn has also contributed to the global despoliation of natural resources and detrimental environmental harm for its most vulnerable populations. Environmental justice for China's rural populations is especially important in the context of China's multifaceted environmental crises as existing disparities have exacerbated the unequal distribution of economic wealth and environmental harm between rural and urban communities. The Chinese central government has responded to the global challenges of the Anthropocene with multiple environmental regulations and numerous environmental intervention programs to mitigate environmental degradation, natural resources exhaustion, and pollution. China's unique form of environmental governance has spurred a robust academic debate over whether an authoritarian form of state power may be better situated to promote green transition in global sustainability politics (Beeson 2010;; Mao and Zhang 2018). This chapter examines two environmental intervention programs in China to evaluate environmental justice outcomes under authoritarian environmentalism. The first case study analyzes how the Chinese central government responded to desertification in the Shiyang River watershed in Gansu province by regulating groundwater extraction and promoting agricultural adjustments. The second case study analyzes state response to grassland degradation and ecological migration in the Alxa League of the Inner Mongolia Autonomous Region. Our analysis is guided by the following research questions: How have centralized environmental intervention programs addressed northwestern China's environmental and social crises? What are the environmental justice outcomes of top–down implementation of authoritarian environmentalism, and how does the exercise of authoritarian state power shape the equity implications of environmental regulations in China? How might we adapt and modify China's environmental governance approach to a more just and alternative resource management model in the current era of the Anthropocene? Our analysis is guided by a critical environmental justice framework and based on 136 in-depth interviews from farmers, herders, and grassroots cadres as well as government documents, official statistics, and reports from state-owned media in China between 2009 and 2016.

Critical environmental justice and authoritarian environmentalism

Environmental justice (EJ) began as a social movement in the United States seeking to address the unequal distribution of environmental harms affecting communities of color (Bullard 1983; Bullard et. al, 2007; Pellow and Brule 2005; Sze and London, 2008; United Church of Christ 1987) but has quickly expanded to address environmental injustices globally. In recent decades, scholars have proposed that EJ studies expand beyond the distribution of environmental harms to include procedural, recognition, participation, and capabilities concerns (Schlosberg 2004). This expansion has come to include a focus on just transitions in the face of a changing climate. Swilling et al. (2016, p. 6) define just transitions as the combination of two complementary goals within development: "sustainable modes of production and consumption" combined with "high levels of human wellbeing concerning income, education, and health." Just transitions thus depend on a sociopolitical regime that coordinates efforts in sustainable development while expanding human capabilities through "state institutions" and "autonomous publicly accountable institutions" with coherent policy and legislative programs (Swilling et al. 2016, p. 8). As such, a critical environmental justice (CEJ) perspective that incorporates a multi-dimensional and multi-scalar approach to examine how power functions in the Anthropocene is essential to formulate just responses to global socio-environmental crises (Malin and Ryder 2018; Pellow 2018). CEJ research has demonstrated that transnational social movements for EJ must work across diverse geographies and engage diverse geopolitical, symbolic, and cultural scales of governance at the international, national, regional, and local levels (Pulido and De Lara, 2018; Faber 2018; Pellow and Brulle 2005).

Since the formulation and implementation of environmental policies are geographically and historically situated within distinct national contexts and social structures, nation-states differ in their abilities and approaches to regulating environmental and social harms from industrialization and capitalization (Beeson 2010; Pellow and Brulee 2005; Pellow 2018). Approaches to EJ, too, are situated in these different contexts and thus also need to be understood in different conceptualizations outside of Western approaches (Álvarez and Coolsaet 2020).Various approaches raise the question of the optimal use of state power in mitigating contemporary environmental inequalities, given the diverse historical legacies of despoliation from institutionalized practices in different political systems. In China's case, public participation and recognition in environmental governance are distinctive from Western liberal societies as the nation is governed by an authoritarian and centralized state (Xie 2011). The resultant top-down process of environmental governance often referred to as authoritarian environmentalism, is heavily shaped by technocratic elites who use the centralized bureaucratic hierarchy of the authoritarian state to achieve desirable policy outcomes through merit evaluation and the restriction of individual liberties (Beeson 2010; Mao et al. 2020a). An examination of China's top-down environmental intervention not only provides insight on how state power interacts with the distributive and procedural outcomes of environmental governance but also sheds light on how the institutionalized practices of the top-down bureaucracy approach recognition and capabilities concerns in its attempt to achieve a green transition in an authoritarian context.

Environmental inequalities and governance in China

In the last four decades, rapid economic development has generated profound disparities in the distribution of environmental risks and harms between China's eastern and western regions and between urban and rural China (Balme 2014; Liu et al. 2014). Compared with other groups, rural migrants and farmers shoulder a disproportionate share of environmental pollution and natural resource exhaustion and rarely benefit from urban areas' economic growth (Liu et al. 2014; Schoolman and Ma 2012). Environmental victims in China often face significant obstacles to adequate compensation and suffer from the slow violence of political powerlessness at the grassroots level of environmental governance (Mah and Wang 2019; Mao 2018).

EJ research in China has primarily focused on environmental issues related to regional disparity, intergenerational fairness, and the global economic system's detrimental effects on the environment. Notably, Chinese scholars have argued that environmental injustice has mostly resulted from rural/urban differentiation and that grassroots environmental movements have limited impact in alleviating environmental pollution, given the party-state's political dominance (Mah and Wang 2017; Zhang and Barr 2013). Contrary to the rights and movement focus of EJ research outside of China, EJ in China has been redefined as good environmental governance involving institutional and legal practices addressing disparate exposure to environmental harm, unequal access to environmental goods, and meaningful participation in decision-making (Balme 2014; Du 2009; Mah and Wang 2017). The Chinese central government has, in recent decades, established a series of laws incorporating public participation and oversight into its technocratic management of environmental issues. China's "authoritarian environmentalism" has promoted green transition by setting national environmental standards, quantification and zoning of natural resources, and restrictive environmental targets in evaluating bureaucrats (Mao et al. 2020b). The central state often incorporates agricultural structural adjustment into conservation programs and limits public participation within internal channels established by the party-state, assuming that benefits from state-led economic growth can resolve capabilities, procedure, and recognition concerns in EJ (Li et al. 2019; Mao and Zhang 2018; Xie 2011). The following case studies provide insight into how the top-down implementation of conservation programs in northwestern China impeded optimal justice outcomes for vulnerable populations when the centralized state responded to socio-environmental crises generated by the Anthropocene (Figure 13.1).

The Shiyang River integrated watershed management program

The Shiyang River watershed experienced severe environmental degradation in the 1980s and 1990s due to rural development policies encouraging grassland reclamation and groundwater over-extraction (Mao and Hanley 2018). By the early 2000s, more than 40,000 hectares of arable land in the Watershed was lost to desertification and soil alkalization. The environmental crisis and ensuing social instability compelled the Chinese central government to implement the Shiyang River Watershed Restoration Plan (hereafter the Restoration Plan) in 2007, directing $677.1 million to its implementation (MWR and DRC 2007). Framed as the state's resolute response to address the critical national security issue of desertification, the environmental intervention program was jointly designed by the central state's Ministry of Water Resources, the National Reform and Development Commission, and the Gansu Provincial Government. The Restoration Plan imposed scalar pricing for surface and groundwater and mandated agricultural water use reduction, which required agricultural counties in the Watershed to reduce cultivation area by 90.347 hectares. The Restoration Plan aimed to create 70 km^2 of wetland at the terminus of the inland river by 2020 while maintaining an annual gross domestic product (GDP) growth rate of the entire Watershed at 9% between 2003 and 2010 (MWR and DRC 2007). To achieve water conservation and economic development targets, the central government invested heavily in technology and infrastructure promoting agricultural structural adjustments and pushed local farmers to cultivate cash crops. Farmers were also encouraged to work in surrounding cities to increase household non-farm income. The Restoration Plan stated that local governments should respect the autonomy of democratically elected Water Users' Association (WUA) to manage irrigation rights to generate water-saving and equitable rural development. To ensure program outcomes, subnational governments were given tight timelines and quantifiable benchmarks; party officials and grassroots state agents would be severely disciplined if they failed to fulfill the assigned quotas on time (WRB and DRC 2007).

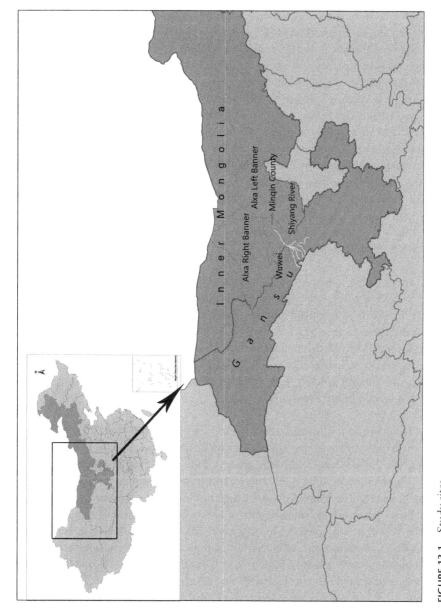

FIGURE 13.1 Study sites.

Unfortunately, the political pressure to achieve a national environmental governance model in the Watershed profoundly undermined distributive and procedural equity in policy implementation. The environmental quotas specified in the Restoration Plan directed that the Watershed's per capita cultivation area be reduced by 44% from 2006 to 2010. Subsequently, state agents arbitrarily shut down water wells and enclosed reclaimed land, violating China's 2002 Water Law and long-standing informal water and land institutions in rural communities. Community resistance was so strong that, by the end of 2009, local governments in the Watershed only achieved a third of the mandated environmental targets. Facing disciplinary reproach from the central state, local governments ordered every bureaucrat to sign target responsibility contracts tying water usage and greenhouse construction quotas to every land slot and farming household. Grassroots state agents would receive severe discipline and salary reduction if their assigned villages failed to fulfill quotas. These stringent deadlines forced local governments to bypass community deliberation and only staff the WUAs with village cadres deeply embedded in the administrative apparatus. The conservation program soon devolved into a fervent political campaign that excluded public participation and elevated policy quotas' fulfillment above all other community concerns regarding implementation procedures and land allocation.

The top-down promotion of horticulture and economic forestry also failed to increase community capabilities for sustainable agriculture as most farmers lacked the necessary capital, training, and labor resources to sustain intensified cultivation. As described by one farmer,

> Some people made money by planting cistanche and licorice. However, they are the ones who already made their first pot of gold from cash cropping before [the implementation of the Restoration program]. These plants take three to four years to mature, becoming a barrier to entry for most farmers. Most of those older than 50 years old also have trouble adapting to the labor-intensive horticulture, and the lack of procurement channels depresses our products' prices. That is why so many greenhouses were abandoned in my township.

Amid the community backlash toward the conservation program, local governments used the access to irrigation water to force villagers to construct greenhouses, build costly drip irrigation systems, and adopt crop choices mandated by local governments. The high costs of constructing and maintaining "water-saving" infrastructure caused the mass desertion of greenhouses and contractual land. Local governments subsequently advocated that abandoned facilities and land be transferred to large-scale operators who would lease the greenhouses from village committees. Under the rationale that increasing agricultural production scale would generate higher resource utilization rates and better fiscal revenue, county governments in the Watershed started to consolidate land owned by small-scale farming households into agricultural and industrial parks to attract outside investment. Local bureaucrats mandated that agricultural subsidies and discounted water pricing be given first to large-scale land leasers and large farm operators to promote high-efficiency and scale-up agriculture. Consequently, many farmers lost their land and water rights and became contracted agricultural workers in industrialized farms.

In 2014, the Gansu Water Resources Bureau announced that the Restoration Plan had achieved its conservation and economic development targets six years ahead of schedule. The conservation program successfully stopped groundwater depletion and created a terminal lake sustained by seasonal releases of "ecological water" from upstream dams (Fan 2018). Nevertheless, the Restoration Plan failed to achieve its original goals to improve equity in economic development and increase community willingness to adopt water-saving agriculture. According to Feng et al. (2015), the intervention program's implementation adversely affected most farmers' livelihoods who expressed they would return to groundwater extraction after the expiration of environmental targets. The conservation program eventually became a state-led rural development project favoring capital-intensive agricultural production and agribusiness owners. The dispossession of land and water resources experienced by small-scale farming households severely weakened community capability to engage in the green transition. A 54-year-old informant remarked,

> the real goal of the conservation program was to remove people and our old way of life from this place. We are the last generation who will stay in this oasis. When we die, there would be no one left to bury our caskets in the dunes.

Ecological migration in Alxa League

Frequent large-scale sandstorms appeared in Inner Mongolia in the late 1990s and early 2000s. The deteriorating natural environment drove local pastoralists into poverty and threatened the air quality of northern Chinese cities such as Beijing (Chinese Academy of Science, 2009). Consequently, the Chinese central government designated the Alxa League of Inner Mongolia as the first "Focus Area" of the national "Converting Pasture to Grassland" (CPG) program in China (BAAH 2002). The environmental intervention designed by central government ministries aimed to reduce overgrazing by relocating pastoral communities from grassland surrounding the Tengger Desert to rural townships, converting pastoralists into settled husbandry and horticulture farmers. From 2002 to 2009, more than $113 million of program funding was invested in the Alxa League to implement the CPG, covering 12,000 km² of grassland in Inner Mongolia (Alxa League Government, 2008). The Alxa Left Banner government designated the Bayanhuode Village as a demonstration village for ecological migration in 2006. The site was designed to house 310 formerly pastoralist households and 90 settled agricultural households in the village before 2006.

By 2010, total state investment in village infrastructure reached $8.6 million as the local government built 294 houses, 350 horticulture greenhouses, irrigation canals, an electric grid, and factory facilities to support the ecological migrant settlement and agricultural restructuring (Alxa Left Banner Government, 2008).

To remove the pastoralists from the grassland and transform them into settled farmers, the local government pledged that each migrant would receive a 60 m² house with water and electricity, a 50 m² livestock shed, and a greenhouse equipped with a rolling blinds machine, straw cover, and mulch films (Alxa Left Banner Government 2008). Besides, relocation guidelines specified that ecological migrants have use rights to the greenhouses for the first five years, after which they could apply for ownership. The guideline also stated that a village-level communist party committee be established to represent the migrants' interests and that local government officials complete the environmental, economic growth, and migration quotas before specified deadlines. As such, nearly all the relocated migrant households in the demonstration village expected to rely on horticulture to make a living.

However, three years after relocation, the migrants still had no access to facilities. Instead, the township government leased the horticulture facilities to agribusiness operators, and the migrants could only work as contracted farm workers with no rights to village infrastructure and water resources. The ecological migrants we interviewed stated that they were shut off from the decision-making process entirely, and local officials unilaterally decided to lease all the village's dairy and horticulture facilities to agribusiness conglomerates. Instead of following the CPG guidelines, the township government assigned 90 of the 400 greenhouses to agribusiness owners lease-free, waiving water and land fees for five years, and 260 greenhouses to the township development park management committee as "state assets" to be rented out to local agribusiness operations at the rate of $286 per greenhouse per year. The last 50 greenhouses were given to local farmers who transferred their landholdings to the township government. To find enough agricultural workers, the township government mandated that, for the first year, all greenhouses be assigned to agribusiness owners, and the ecological migrants were forced to sign farmworker contracts with the corporations in exchange for a wage and training in settled agriculture. As such, the ecological migrants were arbitrarily transformed into farmworkers for agribusiness operators.

Nevertheless, the ecological migrants received no compensation from the agribusiness operators for five months of the contract. After many protests, local officials finally ordered operators to pay each household $147.3 monthly. In exchange, local officials allowed agribusiness owners to operate the greenhouses after the first year, reneging on the relocation guidelines' promises. In 2008, agribusiness owners terminated the lease unilaterally due to the inability to generate a profit. In need of revenue to replace the damaged facilities, local officials briefly assigned the greenhouses to the ecological migrants but insisted that they foot the renovation bill of the greenhouses in addition to paying an annual rent of

$294.5 per greenhouse. Within three months, the township government reneged on its promises again and designated all greenhouses as state assets suitable for outside investment. By 2009, migrants still had no access to promised horticulture facilities and had no means to support their livelihood. As expressed by one informant,

> We depended on the grassland to survive. We followed the government's order and became horticulture farmers. The government promised us that they would build 400 greenhouses for us, but, three years later, they still refused to hand over the facilities. We felt a deep sense of betrayal.

The ecological migrants had no institutional platform to voice their concerns because the local government never formed the village committee to represent their interests. Facing widespread discontent in the local community, local officials stated that

> if they [ecological migrants] want to participate in horticulture, they need to pay rent at the market rate. If they do not have money, they should go back to their places of origin and farm there, given that the grassland would still be there. If they cannot survive here, they should go back.

This statement ran in contrast to the central government's Migrant Settlement Guideline that promised the state would, on average, invest $42,857 to each migrant household for a total investment of $20 million. In addition to issues generated by the dispossession of land resources, the arid land in Alxa could not support settled agriculture because water consumption for cultivation was 500 times that of herding. The exhaustion of groundwater resources in the demonstration village eventually led to many migrants returning to the grassland; less than 10% of the greenhouses were in operation in 2012.

Nevertheless, the return to ranching became impossible when many returnees surprisingly discovered that the Tengger Desert's groundwater suffered severe industrial pollution after they were cleared off the grassland. Many state-owned and private industrial enterprises began using conserved areas as a dumping ground for industrial waste (ME 2015). From 2010 to 2014, media in Beijing reported severe instances of illegal wastewater discharges by regional paper mills and chemical plants. The Chinese central government dispatched an inspection team to the region in 2014 and persecuted eight local enterprises' legal representatives. Nevertheless, this action could not address groundwater pollution. The ecological migrants had no means to apply for compensation as they lost their lease rights when they agreed to the terms for their initial relocation. The authoritarian state's environmental intervention inadvertently worsened grassland conditions, transferred environmental harm, and deprived the ecological migrants of their livelihood.

Discussion and conclusion

The Shiyang Watershed Restoration Plan and the CPG program in Inner Mongolia are good examples of authoritarian environmentalism in northwestern China. The Chinese central government designed both programs and provided substantial financial support for implementation. The central government utilized binding targets, earmarked funding, and ecological zoning in the top–down implementation of intervention programs to improve oversight. Both programs involved state investments in promoting "water-saving agriculture," deemed essential to environmental conservation and poverty alleviation. The central government believed that deliberation within the bureaucracy could ensure equitable access to natural resources and state subsidies. Nevertheless, both environmental interventions from the authoritarian state exacerbated inequalities and environmental injustice experienced by underprivileged rural communities in northwestern China.

Understanding the origins of environmental injustice discussed above requires a multi-scalar analysis to examine environmental intervention programs designed by technocratic elites working in urban China. Both intervention programs intended to address environmental crises threatening urban areas' environmental qualities and national economic interests. Technocrat elites attributed environmental degradation solely to farmers and pastoralists' economic behaviors without considering how the Chinese state-capitalist development model generated urban–rural and regional disparities and incentivized rural residents to pursue short-term economic gains at the expense of the natural environment. Consequently, policy formulation did not adequately consider the economic and institutional constraints local farmers would encounter and failed to recognize local communities' environmental and property rights. Instead, technocratic elites monopolized the definitions of environmental disasters, suitable solutions, policy instruments, and intervention goals. Program implementation became political campaigns to demonstrate the utility and legitimacy of authoritarian environmental governance. Lack of recognition of the causes of environmental degradation combined with the Anthropocene's uneven impacts directly contributed to the unfair environmental, economic, and social burdens local farmers had to shoulder, which exacerbated existing power differentials and inequalities between urban and rural China.

Additionally, the absence of recognition of use rights and public participation fundamentally contributed to severe procedural and distributive injustice in policy implementation. In our case studies, the farmers had no institutional means to challenge local governments' allocation of resources as local bureaucrats completely controlled WUAs and village-level committees, avoiding collaborative deliberation to achieve program timelines imposed by the central government. The subjugation of rural communities turned environmental conservation into state-led rural development initiatives favoring the capitalization of agricultural production. The transition from ecological migrants and subsistence farmers to contracted farm workers dispossessed farmers from access to land and water resources and allowed local governments to shrink public welfare obligations. Subsequently, environmental intervention weakened rural communities' capabilities to deal with environmental degradation and economic precarity while simultaneously exacerbating rural–urban stratification, given that the environmental goods afforded to urban residents originated from the dispossession of local farmers.

Our case studies demonstrate that without considering existing rural–urban disparities and the institutional legacies of natural resources exhaustion, the exertion of authoritarian state power in green transition may worsen environmental inequalities and dispossess the underprivileged rural populace in China. Our findings indicate that a just transition in China requires a multi-scalar examination of how state-led economic development initiatives and the centralized bureaucracy's material interests shape the formulation and implementation of environmental intervention programs. The state's responses to environmental crises primarily relied on plans made by national-level technocratic elites who lived in urban centers and viewed rural communities as regulatory problems to be fixed by arbitrary administrative measures in stringent timelines. Community wellbeing goals of the intervention programs consequently were cannibalized by mandates within the administrative apparatus. "Without the autonomous publicly accountable institutions" (Swilling et al. 2016, p. 8), farmers were left to shoulder the full costs of environmental transitions and economic restructuring in hinterland China, and the plight of local communities eventually contributed to further environmental degradation and injustice. As such, the authoritarian state's needs to maintain its legitimacy may be critical to future just transitions that will ensure sustainable development and community wellbeing. To maintain the intervention programs' effectiveness, the central government may consider building policy feedback channels that are autonomous from local governments' interference. Government-organized NGOs affiliated with national ministries may incorporate community-based perspectives and promote environmental and legal education in rural communities. The inclusion of a semi-official public institution outside the administrative apparatus may counter the technocratic elites' knowledge–power axis and improve participation and recognition in program implementation. Moreover, the newly formed Central Environmental Protection Inspectorate can solicit feedback from marginalized rural residents during anti-corruption campaigns to ensure distributive and procedural justice. Recent state initiatives to transform land tenure to three interrelated rights governing ownership, contractual, and use rights may be expanded to include rural collectives' access to and fair compensation for natural resources, which will empower the newly established environmental courts to consider the environmental rights of rural residents. As such, just transition in China and other illiberal societies will depend on institutional innovations that reconceptualize environmental intervention programs as constant responses and adjustments involving multiple stakeholders in and outside the administrative apparatus.

References

Álvarez L and Coolsaet B (2020) Decolonizing environmental justice studies: A Latin American perspective. *Capitalism Nature Socialism 31*(2): 50–69.

Alxa Left Banner Government (2008) *Action Plan for Migrants Settlement of Demonstration Area of New Rural and Pastoral Construction of Bayanhuode Village of Alxa Left Banner* (Internal document, in Chinese).

Alxa Prefecture Government (2008) *The Implementation of Engineering of Converting Pasture to Grassland in Alxa Prefecture.* http://zwfw.als.gov.cn (accessed October 10, 2019).

Balme R (2014) Mobilizing for environmental justice in China. *Asia Pacific Journal of Public Administration 36*(3): 173–184.

Beeson M (2010) The coming of environmental authoritarianism. *Environmental Politics 19*(2): 276–294.

Bullard RD (1983) Solid waste sites and the black Houston community. *Sociological Inquiry 53*(2–3): 273–288.

Bullard RD, Mohai P, Saha R and Wright B (2007) Toxic wastes and race at twenty 1987–2007: Grassroots struggles to dismantle environmental racism in the United States. *United Church of Christ Justice and Witness Ministries.*

Bureau of Agriculture and Animal Husbandry of Alxa Left Banner (BAAH) (2002) Project Planning for Engineering of Converting Pasture to Grassland on Natural Grassland of Alxa Left Banner. In Material Assembly of Engineering of Converting Pasture to Grassland on Natural Grassland of Alxa Left Banner in 2002.

Du Q (2009) Public participation and the challenges of environmental justice in China. *Environmental Law and Justice in Context*: 139–157.

Faber D (2018) The political economy of environmental justice. In: *The Routledge Handbook of Environmental Justice.* Routledge, pp. 61–73.

Fan X (2018) Harmonious relationship between water and humans: The review of the accomplishments in Minqin County's water reform. *Gansu Daily*, 27, November 18. http://www.minqin.gansu.gov.cn/Item/78397.aspx.

Feng Q, Miao Z, Li Z, Li J, Si J, Yh S and Chang Z (2015) Public perception of an ecological rehabilitation project in inland river basins in northern China: Success or failure. *Environmental Research 139*: 20–30.

Li DX, Sinha PN, Kim S and Lee, YK (2019) The role of environmental justice in sustainable development in China. *Sustainable Development 27*(1): 162–174.

Liu L, Liu J and Zhang Z (2014) Environmental justice and sustainability impact assessment: In search of solutions to ethnic conflicts caused by coal mining in Inner Mongolia, China. *Sustainability 6*(12): 8756–8774.

Mah A and Wang X (2017) Research on environmental justice in China: Limitations and possibilities. *Chinese Journal of Environmental Law 1*(2): 263–272.

Mah A and Wang X (2019) Accumulated injuries of environmental injustice: Living and working with petrochemical pollution in Nanjing, China. *Annals of the American Association of Geographers 109*(6): 1961–1977.

Malin SA and Ryder SS (2018) Developing deeply intersectional environmental justice scholarship. *Environmental Sociology 4*(1): 1–7.

Mao K (2018) The treadmill of taxation: Desertification and organizational state deviance in Minqin Oasis, China. *Critical Criminology 26*(2): 271–288.

Mao K and Hanley EA (2018) State corporatism and environmental harm: Tax farming and desertification in northwestern China. *Journal of Agrarian Change 18*(4): 848–868.

Mao K and Zhang Q (2018) Dilemmas of state-led environmental conservation in China: Environmental target enforcement and public participation in Minqin County. *Society & Natural Resources 31*(5): 615–631.

Mao K, Zhang Q, Xue Y and Weeks N (2020a) Toward a socio-political approach to water management: Successes and limitations of IWRM programs in rural northwestern China. *Frontiers of Earth Science* 14: 268–285.

Mao K, Jin S, Hu Y, Weeks N and Ye L (2020b). Environmental conservation or the treadmill of law: A case study of the post-2014 husbandry waste regulations in China. *International Journal of Offender Therapy and Comparative Criminology* p.0306624X20928024.

Ministry of Environment Protection of China (MEP) (2015). *Notice of Publicized Supervision on Environmental Pollution of Tengger Desert*. MEP No.44 Doc.

Pellow DN (2018) *What is Critical Environmental Justice?* John Wiley & Sons.

Pellow DN and Brulle RJ (2005) Power, justice, and the environment: Toward critical environmental justice studies. *Power, Justice, and the Environment: A Critical Appraisal of the Environmental Justice Movement*: 1–19.

Pulido L and De Lara J (2018) Reimagining 'justice' in environmental justice: Radical ecologies, decolonial thought, and the black radical tradition. *Environment and Planning E: Nature and Space* 1(1–2): 76–98.

Schlosberg D 2004. Reconceiving environmental justice: Global movements and political theories. *Environmental Politics* 13(3): 517–540.

Schoolman ED and Ma C (2012) Migration, class and environmental inequality: Exposure to pollution in China's Jiangsu Province. *Ecological Economics 75*: 140–151.

Sze, J. and London, JK (2008). Environmental justice at the crossroads. *Sociology Compass*, 2(4): 1331–1354.

Swilling M, Musango J and Wakeford J (2016) Developmental states and sustainability transitions: Prospects of a just transition in South Africa. *Journal of Environmental Policy & Planning 18*(5): 650–672.

Zhang, JY and Barr, M, (2013). *Green politics in China: Environmental governance and state-society relations*. Pluto Press.

Chinese Academy of Science (CAS) (2009) The difficult situation of ecology in Alashan Region of Inner Mongolia and countermeasures. *Bulletin of Chinese Academy of Sciences* 3.

Church of Christ Commission for Racial Justice (1987) *Toxic Wastes and Race in the United States: A National Report on the Racial and Socio-Economic Characteristics of Communities with Hazardous Waste Sites*. Public Data Access. (accessed October 10, 2019).

Water Resources Bureau (WRB) and the Development and Reform Committee (DRC) (2007) *The Plan for Comprehensive Improvements in Essential Areas of Shiyang River*.

Xie L (2011) Environmental justice in China's urban decision-making. *Taiwan in Comparative Perspective 3*(2): 160–179.

14

LESSONS FROM TANZANIAN FOREST MANAGEMENT

Justice in environmental and climate policy transitions

Jessica Omukuti

Introduction

Environmental and natural resource management are considered key to enabling the world to respond to climate change (Bonan 2008). Yet, approaches to environmental conservation in developing countries are characterized by historical inequalities, human rights abuses, and colonialism (Verde Selva et al. 2020). This has justice implications for communities in these countries. Effective climate action requires transitions that address these justice implications, as opposed to maintaining and reinforcing them. This chapter discusses how the transition between environmental management and climate change action in Tanzania builds on colonial and post-colonial environmental resource management institutions, the implications of these transitions for environmental justice (EJ) and climate justice (CJ), and pathways forward for achieving a more just climate policy transition.

In Western and non-Western societies, the environment has historically been assigned utility. In non-Western settings, the environment represents spirituality. For example, in some African communities, the environment was linked to nature, the ancestors, and to God (Igboin 2012; Taringa 2006; Conte 1999). However, from the beginning of the nineteenth century, different components of the environment have increasingly been ascribed different values, depending on what is considered important for development and well-being and who informs these valuation processes (Aylward and Barbier 1992). For most of these African communities, colonization formalized environmental valuation based on Western ideals (Nelson 2003), leading to restrictions on access and use of specific resources that were valued by colonial powers. Environmental conservation was pursued primarily for its economic benefits (e.g. income to colonial governments), but also other nonmonetary benefits (e.g. adding/conserving aesthetic value to landscapes) (ibid.). In sub-Saharan Africa, natural resource management and biodiversity conservation were presented as solutions to the perceived problem of environmental degradation (Schabel 1990), with wildlife and forests put under protection and conservation (Lundgren and Lundgren 1982). However, post-independence, current environmental conservation and protection approaches in Tanzania have built on these colonial principles and institutions.

Over the last three decades, the environment has also become critical for responding to climate change. Global pursuit of neoliberal capital has led to unsustainable carbon emissions which has pushed us into the "Anthropocene epoch" (Hursh and Henderson 2011). Among other things, climate change affects environmental functions such as biodiversity distribution (Jewitt et al. 2015). For example, climate change is projected to affect African tourism via changing wildlife migration patterns (Kilungu et al. 2017).

Approaches to responding to the environmental and climate change issues and the links between them reflects commonalities across geographies. For example, in most developed countries, emission reductions are achieved through environment-friendly lifestyles such as cycling, recycling, and use of renewable energy (see Zhou 2021), all of which also generate environmental conservation benefits (Schanes et al. 2016). In developing countries, however, addressing climate change involves a reduction in environmental mismanagement such as deforestation and improvements in urban and coastal planning (Awuor et al. 2008). Consequently, most developing country governments situate roles for responding to climate change within environment departments or ministries (Lasco et al. 2009). Additionally, most civil society organizations (CSO) supporting environmental conservation in developing countries are steadily integrating climate change in their portfolios in support of sustainable development (Scherrer 2009). This highlights the close links between environmental and climate change institutions in developing countries.

Due to the links between environmental management and climate change action in developing countries, stronger environmental management (e.g. waste management) is considered essential for addressing climate change (Ackerman 2000). As such, countries/regions with weak environmental protection laws provide opportunities for enhancing climate action. This enables "bandwagoning," where climate action rides on momentum already created through environmental management debates to generate traction (O'Neill 2019). Existing environmental institutions are therefore leveraged to enable a transition to climate action. However, transitions between environmental conservation and climate action present unique justice implications which must be scrutinized.

This chapter explores the justice implications of building on existing environmental protection policies and institutions to achieve climate action. The chapter asks whether and how just transitions are possible for developing countries that build on existing environmental management institutions to achieve climate action. The chapter provides a historical analysis of forest conservation in

Tanzania to show the evolution of environmental protection and climate action through resource management policies and the emergence of EJ and CJ concerns. The analysis reflects on how societies in developing countries navigate between socio-ecological justice concerns created by the Anthropocene. It further argues that climate change efforts have built on notions of environmental conservation that sustain Western and colonial notions of environmental conservation, thus maintaining and perpetuating these deep-rooted inequalities. This creates double injustices, where local communities that are least responsible for but are adversely impacted by climate change are expected to make livelihood and well-being trade-offs for ecological and carbon capture benefits to limit climate change.

Defining justice in environmental conservation and climate change

EJ in the context of environmental conservation and degradation is focused on the allocation of burden and benefits emerging from environmental resource conservation and protection (Schroeder, 2008). Achieving EJ depends on "how decisions [on sharing of costs and benefits] are made," the actual allocation of costs and benefits and the extent to which "people's way of life are acknowledged or ignored" when making these decisions (Gross-Camp et al. 2019, p. 12). CJ relates to the allocation of costs associated with climate change mitigation and adaptation, through ensuring protection for communities with the least capacity to respond to climate change risks. Debates on CJ have predominantly focused on the international level, where responsibilities for climate change mitigation and adaptation are assigned (Meyer and Roser 2010). However, CJ debates have been extended to intra-state levels, where differential patterns of capacity to respond to climate change are considered when assigning responsibility to addressing climate change (Vanderheiden 2016). These EJ and CJ principles are reflected in Tanzania's colonial, post-independence and current approaches to environmental conservation and climate change action.

EJ in Tanzania's colonial and post-colonial forest conservation

Tanzania's historical approach to environmental conservation is extensively documented in existing literature. Analyses focus on how colonial and post-colonial political environments have impacted environmental conservation policies and actions (e.g. Schabel 1990). Both colonial and post-independence environmental protection actions were generally informed by colonial governance policies. Environmental protection was driven by colonial interests, such as creation of land for commercial agriculture (Campbell et al. 2004) and rangeland protection to promote tourism and sport hunting (Goldstein 2004). Protection efforts regularly alienated local communities who were dependent on these natural resources (Mkumbukwa 2008). This characterized the period of "conservation without representation" (Neumann 1995, p. 364).

Forest conservation was championed by Tanzania's colonial governments for its links to wildlife conservation and the generation of timber products for commercial use (Conte 1999). This was driven by "the need for the state to assume control over forests and woodlands so that they might be managed productively for timber and other forest resources", in turn leading to community displacement for forest conservation (Sunseri 2007, p. 886). Forest conservation regulations consisted of government notices and forest policies. The first national forest policy in Tanzania was developed in 1953 by the British colonial government and built on colonial German government regulations (URT 1998). Large forested land areas were converted into nature reserves and protected areas, with tree plantations replacing some indigenous forests (Conte 1999). This lay the grounds for Tanzania's reputation for forest conservation.

Since then, Tanzania has continued to receive international development finance for forest conservation, e.g. by World Bank and the European Commission (Joint Research Center, 2020). This funding has gradually increased over the last 20 years, specifically been directed towards local level resource management activities (ibid.). This demonstrates the increased national and international interest in forest conservation in Tanzania, accompanied by a proportional increase in donor and (international and local) elite control over forest conservation policy processes and outcomes (Koch 2017).

Post-independence forest management built on colonial environmental resource management policies. After the Arusha declaration in 1967 where Tanzania became a socialist state, all forests were put under the management of the national government (Kihiyo 1998). This resulted in changes in how forests were managed. Although the forestry policy remained the same, limited government capacity to manage these forests coupled with pressures from population growth led to higher rates of defforestaiton (Wily 1999). This was attributed to the reduced gazettement of forest results in comparison to the colonial period which increased pressures on non-gazetted forests (ibid.).

Current environmental management policies in Tanzania were designed to reflect international principles on environmental conservation, such as those in the Convention on Biological Diversity (CBD) and the UN Convention on Climate Change (Goldstein 2004). The 1998 revision of the Tanzania National Forest Policy reflected principles set out in the Rio and CBD conventions (URT 2015). The revised National Forest Policy of 1998 and the Forest Act of 2002 acknowledged the importance of devolved resource governance through participatory and joint forest management (PJFM) and the role of non-government stakeholders, such as communities, in enabling forest conservation (URT 1998). Other policies such as the Land Act and the Village Land Act (both of 1999) supported PJFM by creating provisions for village land managed by Village Councils (VCs) (Kashwan 2015).

PJFM is an approach to devolved forest management that builds on participatory and multistakeholder processes and local governance institutions to ensure secure community land and resource rights and protection of livelihoods of forest-dependent communities (Blomley et al., 2011). Tanzania's PJFM mainly relies on two local institutions – Village Forest Management Committees (VFMC) and VCs – who develop and implement resource management access and use laws. The earlier introduction of multiparty politics in 1993 enabled the development of space for CSO engagement. This resulted in the emergence of many grassroots movements advocating for the protection of community access to environmental resources (Neumann 1995). Through trial and error, some forests in Tanzania went from being government controlled, to joint ownership (with local communities), and finally to being community managed (Wily 1999). Building on these opportunities in the late 1990s, some communities developed by-laws that were based on local customs and local knowledge on resource management for forest conservation.

Assessments on the effectiveness of devolved forest conservation in Tanzania produce mixed results. Some indicate that PJFM reduces local community-driven deforestation and improves local community lievlihoods (Hamza and Kimwer 2007). However, Brockington (2007) notes that limited transparency at the local government level in devolved forest conservation management prevents PJFM initiatives from fully achieving their intended outcomes. Research in communities with PJFM arrangements also find "ambiguous and somewhat negative effects [of decentralization and PJFM] on poverty alleviation and rural livelihoods" (Lund and Treue 2008, p. 23). These inadequate outcomes at the local level are attributed to the tendency of environmental management institutions to prioritize environmental conservation outcomes over social equity and poverty reduction outcomes (Vyamana 2009). This is because these policies are not poverty-centric. For example, Tanzania's forest policies do not "specify the rights of minorities and equitable benefit sharing mechanisms" under the PJFM arrangement (Lund and Treue 2008, p. 24), thereby limiting the use of these policies to address EJ concerns.

The outcome of these gaps in PJFM is a structurally driven forest conservation agenda, where ecological and economic benefits are sought with limited consideration for local-level inequalities or poverty reduction outcomes. This suggests a lack of EJ, as local-level communities bear the unequal burden of environmental conservation (through constrained access to and use of these resources, or sometimes outright exclusion from use) without a corresponding distribution of benefits emerging from the practice of resource conservation. Yet, current approaches to addressing climate change have built on these institutions to enable forest conservation which is expected to accelerate climate change mitigation.

Transitions from forest conservation to climate action

In Tanzania, the transition from environmental conservation to climate change has occurred over the last 20 years. Policies such as the National Adaptation

Plans of Action (NAPA), Nationally Appropriate Mitigation Actions (NAMA), National Climate Change Policy (NCCP) and Nationally Determined Contributions (NDCs) indicate Tanzania's commitment to climate change adaptation and mitigation. Globally, countries such as Tanzania with large tropical forest coverage are considered as potential sites for carbon sinks (Karsenty 2008). However, the development of these sinks is predicated on the presence of appropriate institutional frameworks which determine whether conservation and/or local community well-being outcomes are achieved (Rosendal and Andresen 2011).

To achieve these climate change goals using forest conservation, Tanzania's climate change governance leverages a multi-level institutional framework that engages with local level communities through local environmental management committees (URT 2007, 2012).

Forest conservation in Tanzania is now conducted under a mix of climate change adaptation and mitigation and environmental conservation policies and agendas. Under climate change adaptation and mitigation, forests are seen as providing opportunities for resilient livelihoods as well as the mitigation of greenhouse gas emissions through generation of carbon sinks. Livelihood diversification by forest-dependent communities builds resilience to climate change (URT 2012). Forests, especially mangroves, are also considered important for advancing Tanzania's role to increase carbon stocks and advance global mitigation goals (URT 2018).

The development of REDD and REDD+ (hereafter REDD) in Tanzania illustrates the role that the country's progressive forestry management policies and instutions have played in attracting international attention to Tanzania as a site for climate action through environmental management. Tanzania was chosen by the United Nations REDD program to pilot the REDD mechanism in 2008 (Burgess et al., 2010). PJFM provisions were overlaid with REDD management policies with the expectation that these would produce co-benefits (Khatun et al. 2015). Several REDD projects have since been piloted in Tanzania, with support from international donors such as the Norwegian government.

The emergence of REDD conservation alongside PJFM in Tanzania is characterized by two trends. The first is a move to formalize and strengthen local resource management institutions in accordance with existing resource management policies and regulations which emphasize application of PJFM principles (Peskett 2010). The second is a growth in the number of CSOs supporting forest conservation in Tanzania (Bolin and Tassa 2012). This has resulted in growth of Community Based Organizations (CBOs) networks which link local communities to international institutions, coupled with a failure of REDD initiatives to deliver on CJ expectations.

The increase in local NGOs and CBOs follows an earlier increase of national-level NGOs in Tanzania (Levine 2002). The increase is attributed to: (i) a merger between environment and development at the international and national levels, where NGOs and development organizations are now collaboratively working on both development and conservation (ibid.), (ii) a donor-driven agenda to work with NGOs which has created a demand CSO (Kukkamaa 2008), and (iii) the neoliberal trend in Tanzania, where CSOs emerge to address service delivery gaps left by governments (Dill 2010). Consequently, NGOs and CBOs have become key players in driving environmental conservation and climate change adaptation and mitigation outcomes, specifically those that involve natural resource management. For example, MJUMITA (a network of CBOs) and Forum CC (a network of NGOs) have played significant roles in facilitating environmental conservation and climate change action in Tanzania (Dokken et al. 2014; Navajas and Mkali 2019). Delivery of EJ and CJ hinges on these institutions.

Views on the links between CSO involvement in climate action and environmental conservation in Tanzania are diverse. Some research indicates that there is low CSO engagement in climate change adaptation and mitigation, e.g. in REDD planning, which accounts for the limited engagement of communities in decision-making (Bolin and Tassa 2012). Others question the ability of NGOs and CBOs to address local level inequalities in developing countries (Banks et al. 2015). CBOs involved in natural resource management also fail to deliver on the participation promise (Dill 2010). Donor control emerges from CBO dependence on donor financing (Kukkamaa 2008). This means that the involvement of NGOs in resource conservation in Tanzania is inefficient as it does not automatically guarantee positive benefits for local communities.

Evidence on the unfair allocation of costs for environmental conservation and climate change action is strong. Neumann (1995, pp. 373–374) writes that environmental "protection in Tanzania has for a long time been characterised by patterns of erosion of human rights, economic justice, and political accountability". Irrespective of the goal i.e. whether for environmental management or climate change action, critics argue that forest conservation actions continue to threaten the livelihoods of resource-dependent communities and shift the control of resources from the local level to national and international actors (Beymer-Farris and Bassett 2012). For example, REDD in Tanzania is associated with community displacements, loss of livelihoods for forest-dependent communities, and reduced welfare at the household level (Scheba and Rakotonarivo 2016). Specifically, tenure insecurity is the biggest challenge to the effectiveness of REDD efforts, with some local communities losing out on the REDD benefits or inequitably fostering the costs for forest conservation (Sunderlin et al. 2014).

Double injustices

The concerns raised in the previous paragraphs necessitate a reevaluation of whether it is practically possible to achieve community-centered climate change action through forest conservation. Assessments suggest that forest conservation is incompatible with positive outcomes for local community welfare. For example, REDD critics argue that for forests that mainly support local livelihoods, PJFM cannot be effective in delivering ecological benefits, sustaining local resource uses and enabling carbon capture (Blomley et al. 2017). Instead, trade-offs are likely, where achievement of one objective compromises the other (ibid.). This builds up to *double injustices*.

Double injustices occur when climate change actions build on forest conseravation institutions that have historically been biased against local communities and in favor of national and international interests. First, these actions generate processes that rob local communities of their forest resource use rights. Second, climate change mitigation policies unfairly assign these local forest-dependent communities the responsibility for achieving national and international climate change mitigation goals even though these communities have contributed least to climate change and are particularly vulnerable to climate change risks.

Use of NGOs and CBOs to support climate change adaptation in developing countries highlights how institutions are used to reinforce the deeprooted inequalities that disadvantage local resource-dependent communities. Such policy actions fail to acknowledge that NGOs are political institutions whose relationship with local level communities is mediated by governments and (international) donor institutions. (Ghosh 2009). Most of the conservation work in Tanzania and in sub-Saharan Africa is led by NGOs and international organizations which use funding to advance colonial management principles disguised as community engagement (Nelson 2003). For example, Gezon (2000) notes that increased funding to local CSOs has facilitated their shift in focus from advocacy and activism to implementation and management of conservation activities, which has increased state, NGO and other international organizations' power and influence over resource-dependent communities. Examples from other developing countries also indicate the tendency of NGOs to pay lip service to transformative power issues without actually achieving the results (e.g. Ogra 2012). This means that the increased engagement of CSOs in forest conseavation for climate change action and environmental management advances donor and international actor interests over those of local communities.

The trade-offs emerging from the pursuit of climate action through resource management shifts target outcomes from 'win–win' approaches of forest management (which are initially used to generate buy-in from local communities) to protectionist and reservationist-based approaches, where ecological gains are prioritized over socio-economic gains and poverty reduction outcomes (Mgaya 2016; Vyamana 2009). Centralization of resource management under the veil of decentralization accompanied by further marginalization of local communities is likely to emerge (Benjaminsen and Svarstad 2010). This reflects patterns of inequalities similar to those that informed colonial resource conservation in Tanzania, where forests and other natural resources that were valued for their Western-based are now used to advance climate mitigation goals which address and rectify wrongs committed primarily by developed countries. In this case, the interests of government and other international actors drive actions that are facilitated by NGOs at the local level. Essentially, this leaves local community actors once again in the backseat of decision-making processes that they should be driving.

In summary, Tanzania's climate change solutions that are built on resource conservation are informed by racial discrimination and socio-economic marginalization of local resource-dependent communities. These approaches to climate change action are superficial and advance colonial-based approaches to responding to the Anthropocene, where resource conservation is presented in alignment with economic development and where communities are tasked with rectifying the state–corporate driven mistakes that led to climate change and the subsequent Anthropocene epoch in the first place. In Tanzania, even though forest conservation advances climate mitigation targets, its use of colonial resource management institutions reinforces an ignorance of local community concerns relating to resource rights, tenure and political participation (Neumann 1992). The outcomes are processes that are "seemingly equitable in a sense," but undercut the normative goal of conservation by "creat[ing] a neoliberal economic space for white capital…[which] privileges *only* the elites – state, traditional, private investment, NGOs – while ignoring an important segment of the population – the younger, disenfranchised youth and women or the peasantry" (Singh and Van Houtum 2002, p. 261). This further exposes local resource-dependent communities in the global South to the drivers and impacts of the Anthropocene.

Conclusion: achieving just transitions

Climate change action and environmental and natural resource management are linked. For example, climate change risks are already altering the distribution of natural resources and their use by resource-dependent communities. Countries in the global South, such as Tanzania, have built on environmental resource management institutions to advance transitions to actions that respond to climate change. The historical analysis presented in this chapter highlights Tanzania's unjust transition from environmental conservation to climate action using forest conservation. Absence of EJ and CJ in forest conservation is linked to the persistence of colonial principles in forest conservation. Achieving EJ for forest-dependent communities requires a recognition of local communities' historical dependence on forests, and the harms and missed opportunities caused by the enforcement of forest conservation regulations for environmental management. CJ for forest-dependent communities involves recognizing that these communities have contributed least to causing climate change but have been unfairly burdened with the responsibility for mitigation despite their high levels of vulnerability to climate change risks.

Central to environmental conservation in developing countries are issues of race, poverty, socio-economic and political inequalities, and power (Kepe, 2009). These issues still determine responses to and outcomes from climate change in the global South (Lyons and Westoby 2014). Colonial and post-colonial conservation policies in many African countries reflect unequal power relations between actors, for example between colonial representatives, governments, and communities (Cock and Fig 2000). Historical inequalities shape resource management institutions, which limits their capacity to deliver EJ and CJ outcomes (Dahlberg et al. 2010). Additionally, using colonial conservation policies to define current environmental and climate change action "create[s] … opportunities for territorial claim-making by the post-colonial state and international actors" and "[re-] establishe[s] … the territorial claims of … [developed country] actors in the developing world" (Nelson 2003, p. 261). Addressing the deep-rooted inequalities that drive injustices requires a recognition of the racial biases that informed colonial and post-colonial environmental conservation policies and upon which current climate change action is built. This also requires framing EJ and CJ as dependent upon addressing the unequal allocation of not just benefits but also costs and burdens of environmental conservation and climate action, respectively.

Elimination of these inequalities is a *conditional* requirement for successful transitions that enable both EJ and CJ. This requires that actors abandon the idea that local resource-dependent communities in developing countries can be used to rectify the actions of mass polluters who caused the Anthropocene epoch, while also responding to climate change. This means that any effort that addresses climate change through resource management should first prioritize local welfare and poverty reduction benefits. For example, just transition requires land restitution for dispossessed communities, addressing the drivers of social exclusion and increasing community participation in decision-making (Cock and Fig 2000). This means that assuming that power-sharing approaches such as co-management of resources will generate positive outcomes for local level communities may be naïve at best. Instead, significant shifts in distribution of power are required. As Blomley et al. (2017, p.564) write,

> if protection and sustainable management of forests on village lands is to be strengthened, the current regulations that cede control over harvesting (and disposal of associated revenues) of forests on village lands outside VLFRs with central government has to be addressed and these rights transferred to village governments.

What matters for justice varies across scales, but it is imperative that attention is paid to local scales in EJ and CJ efforts, as communities are usually on the frontlines of the negative effects of harmful policies and practice. Conflicts in countries with histories of environmental conservation such as Tanzania are likely to emerge from "contested visions of what constitutes 'just' environmental management" (Martin et al. 2014, p. 167). This contestation reveals varying preferences for distributive and procedural justice and the need for recognition, e.g. different perceptions of what is just may differ amongst men and women (Woodhouse and McCabe 2018).

Identifying these varying notions of justice is not straightforward in practice. Development involves navigating and balancing diverse needs and interests,

usually scaled across space and time. This means that local community perceptions of EJ and CJ may not reflect sub-national, national, or international goals.
For example, there may be trade-offs between achieving environmental conservation outcomes, sustaining livelihoods, and enabling participatory resource
management (Ribot et al. 2010). These processes can also be costly and extend
beyond the standard time frame of environmental conservation and climate
change responses However, the importance of the local level in achieving EJ
and CJ means that responses to climate change through resource and environmental conservation should integrate processes that neutralize these local level
trade-offs.

References

Ackerman F (2000) Waste management and climate change. *Local Environment* 5(2):
223–229.
Awuor CB, Orindi VA and Ochieng Adwera A (2008) Climate change and coastal cities:
The case of Mombasa, Kenya. *Environment and Urbanization* 20(1): 231–242.
Aylward B and Barbier EB (1992) Valuing environmental functions in developing
countries. *Biodiversity & Conservation* 1(1): 34–50.
Banks N, Hulme D and Edwards M (2015) NGOs, states, and donors revisited: Still too
close for comfort? *World Development* 66: 707–718.
Benjaminsen TA and Svarstad H (2010) The death of an elephant: Conservation discourses
versus practices in Africa. *Forum for Conference Studies* 37(3): 385–408.
Beymer-Farris BA and Bassett TJ (2012) The REDD menace: Resurgent protectionism
in Tanzania's mangrove forests. *Global Environmental Change* 22(2): 332–341.
Blomley T, Edwards K, Kingazi S, et al. (2017) When community forestry meets
REDD+: Has REDD+ helped address implementation barriers to participatory forest
management in Tanzania? *Journal of Eastern African Studies* 11(3): 549–570.
Blomley, T, Lukumbuzya, K and Brodnig, G 2011. *Participatory Forest Management and
REDD+ in Tanzania*. Washington DC. World Bank. 1–24
Bolin A and Tassa DT (2012) Exploring climate justice for forest communities engaging
in REDD+: Experiences from Tanzania. *Forum for Conference Studies* 39(1): 5–29.
Bonan GB (2008) Forests and climate change: Forcings, feedbacks, and the climate
benefits of forests. *Science* 320(5882): 1444–1449.
Brockington D (2007) Forests, community conservation, and local government
performance: The village forest reserves of Tanzania. *Society and Natural Resources*
20(9): 835–848.
Burgess ND, Bahane B, Clairs T, et al. (2010) Getting ready for REDD+ in Tanzania: A
case study of progress and challenges. *Oryx* 44(3): 339–351.
Campbell D, Misana S and Olson J (2004) Comparing the Kenyan and Tanzanian slopes
of Mt.Kilimanjaro: Why are adacent land uses so distinct? LUCID Project Working
Paper 44. Nairobi: Kenya. International Livestock Research Institute(ILRI).
Cock J and Fig D (2000) From colonial to community based conservation:
Environmental justice and the national parks of South Africa. *Society in Transition*
31(1): 22–35.
Conte CA (1999) The forest becomes desert: Forest use and environmental change
in Tanzania's West Usambara mountains. *Land Degradation & Development* 10(4):
291–309.

Dahlberg A, Rohde R and Sandell K (2010) National parks and environmental justice: Comparing access rights and ideological legacies in three countries. *Conservation and Society* 8(3): 209–224.

Dill B (2010) Community-based organizations (CBOs) and norms of participation in Tanzania: Working against the grain. *African Studies Review* 53(2): 23–48.

Dokken T, Putri AAD and Kweka D (2014) Making REDD work for communities and forest conservation in Tanzania. In Erin O. Sills, Stibniati S Atmadja, Claudio de Sassi, Amy E Duchelle, Demetrius L Kweka, Ida Aju Pradnja Resosudarmo and William D Sunderlin (eds), *REDD+ on the Ground: A Case Book of Subnational Initiatives across the Globe.* Bogor Barat: Center for International Forestry Research (CIFOR): 245–260

Gezon LL (2000) The changing face of NGOs: Structure and communitas in conservation and development in Madagascar. *Urban Anthropology and Studies of Cultural Systems and World Economic Development* 29(2): 181–215.

Ghosh S (2009) NGOs as political institutions. *Journal of Asian and African Studies* 44(5): 475–495.

Goldstein G (2004) The legal system and wildlife conservation: History and the law's effect on indigenous people and community conservation in Tanzania. *Georgetown International Environmental Law Review* 17: 481.

Gross-Camp N, Rodriguez I, Martin A, et al. (2019) The type of land we want: Exploring the limits of community forestry in Tanzania and Bolivia. *Sustainability* 11(6): 1643.

Hamza KFS and Kimwer EO (2007) Tanzania's forest policy and its practical achievements with respect to community based forest management in MITMIOMBO. In: Varmola M, Valkonen S and Tapaninen S (eds) *MITMIOMBO – Management of Indigenous Tree Species for Ecosystem Restoration and Wood Production in Semi-Arid Miombo Woodlands in Eastern Africa: Proceedings of the First MITMIOMBO Project Workshop Held in Morogoro, Tanzania, 6th–12th February 2007.* Helsinki: Finnish Forest Research Institute, 24–33.

Hursh DW and Henderson JA (2011) Contesting global neoliberalism and creating alternative futures. *Discourse: Studies in the Cultural Politics of Education* 32(2): 171–185.

Igboin BO (2012) African religion and environmental challenges in post colonial Africa. *Ilorin Journal of Religious Studies* 2(1): 17–38.

Jewitt D, Goodman PS, Erasmus BFN, et al. (2015) Systematic land-cover change in KwaZulu-Natal, South Africa: Implications for biodiversity. *South African Journal of Science* 111(9–10): 1–9.

Joint Research Center (2020) *e-Conservation: Tanzania, United Republic of.* https://econservation.jrc.ec.europa.eu/country/TZ (accessed 22 August 2020).

Karsenty A (2008) The architecture of proposed REDD schemes after Bali: Facing critical choices. *International Forestry Review* 10(3): 443–457.

Kashwan P (2015) Forest policy, institutions, and REDD+ in India, Tanzania, and Mexico. *Global Environmental Politics* 15(3): 95–117.

Kepe T (2009) Shaped by race: Why "race" still matters in the challenges facing biodiversity conservation in Africa. *Local Environment* 14(9): 871–878.

Khatun K, Gross-Camp N, Corbera E, et al. (2015) When participatory forest management makes money: Insights from Tanzania on governance, benefit sharing, and implications for REDD+. *Environment and Planning. Part A* 47(10): 2097–2112.

Kihiyo V (1998) Forest policy changes in Tanzania: Towards community participation in forest management. Reportno. Report Number|, Date. Place Published|: Institution|.

Kilungu H, Leemans R, Munishi PKT, et al. (2017) Climate change threatens major tourist attractions and tourism in Serengeti National Park, Tanzania. In: Leal-Filho W, Simane B, Kalangu J, et al. (eds) *Climate Change Adaptation in Africa: Fostering Resilience and Capacity to Adapt.* Cham: Springer International Publishing AG, 375–392.

Koch S (2017) International influence on forest governance in Tanzania: Analysing the role of aid experts in the REDD+ process. *Forest Policy and Economics* 83: 181–190.

Kukkamaa T (2008) Are NGOs harbingers of democratization in Tanzania? Reportno. Report Number|, Date. Place Published|: Institution|.

Lasco RD, Pulhin FB, Jaranilla-Sanchez PA, et al. (2009) Mainstreaming adaptation in developing countries: The case of the Philippines. *Climate and Development* 1(2): 130–146.

Levine A (2002) Convergence or convenience? International conservation NGOs and development assistance in Tanzania. *World Development* 30(6): 1043–1055.

Lund JF and Treue T (2008) Are we getting there? Evidence of decentralized forest management from the Tanzanian Miombo woodlands. *World Development* 36(12): 2780–2800.

Lundgren B and Lundgren L (1982) Socio-economic effects and constraints in forest management: Tanzania. In: Hallsworth EG (ed.), *Socioeconomic Effects and Constraints in Tropical Forest Management.* Chichester: John Wiley, 43–52

Lyons K and Westoby P (2014) Carbon colonialism and the new land grab: Plantation forestry in Uganda and its livelihood impacts. *Journal of Rural Studies* 36: 13–21.

Martin A, Gross-Camp N, Kebede B, et al. (2014) Whose environmental justice? Exploring local and global perspectives in a payments for ecosystem services scheme in Rwanda. *Geoforum* 54: 167–177.

Meyer LH and Roser D (2010) Climate justice and historical emissions. *Critical Reviews of International Social and Political Philosophy* 13(1): 229–253.

Mgaya E (2016) Forest and forestry in Tanzania: Changes and continuities in policies and practices from colonial times to the present. *Journal of the Geographical Association of Tanzania* 36(2): 45–58.

Mkumbukwa AR (2008) The evolution of wildlife conservation policies in Tanzania during the colonial and post-independence periods. *Development Southern Africa* 25(5): 589–600.

Navajas H and Mkali F (2019) Terminal evaluation of the UNEP–GEF project: Developing core capacity to address adaptation to climate change in productive coastal zones of Tanzania. Reportno. Report Number|, Date. Place Published|: Institution|.

Nelson RH (2003) Environmental colonialism: "Saving" Africa from Africans. *Independent Review* 8(1): 65–86.

Neumann RP (1992) Political ecology of wildlife conservation in the Mt. Meru area of Northeast Tanzania. *Land Degradation & Development* 3(2): 85–98.

Neumann RP (1995) Local challenges to global agendas: Conservation, economic liberalization and the pastoralists rights movement in Tanzania. *Antipode* 27(4): 363–382.

O'Neill K (2019) Linking wastes and climate change: Bandwagoning, contention, and global governance. *Wiley Interdisciplinary Reviews: Climate Change* 10(2): e568.

Ogra MV (2012) Gender mainstreaming in community-oriented wildlife conservation: Experiences from nongovernmental conservation organizations in India. *Society & Natural Resources* 25(12): 1258–1276.

Peskett L (2010) REDD+ benefit sharing in Tanzania. Washington DC: World Bank. 65861, 1-4, http://documents1.worldbank.org/curated/en/488821468313198364/pdf/658610WP00PUBL0ng0and0Carbon0Rights.pdf

Ribot JC, Lund JF and Treue T (2010) Democratic decentralization in sub-Saharan Africa: Its contribution to forest management, livelihoods, and enfranchisement. *Environmental Conservation* 37(1): 35–44.

Rosendal GK and Andresen S (2011) Institutional design for improved forest governance through REDD: Lessons from the global environment facility. *Ecological Economics* 70(11): 1908–1915.

Schabel HG (1990) Tanganyika forestry under German colonial administration, 1891–1919. *Forest & Conservation History* 34(3): 130–141.

Schanes K, Giljum S and Hertwich E (2016) Low carbon lifestyles: A framework to structure consumption strategies and options to reduce carbon footprints. *Journal of Cleaner Production* 139: 1033–1043.

Scheba A and Rakotonarivo OS (2016) Territorialising REDD+: Conflicts over market-based forest conservation in Lindi, Tanzania. *Land Use Policy* 57: 625–637.

Scherrer YM (2009) Environmental conservation NGOs and the concept of sustainable development. *Journal of Business Ethics* 85(3): 555.

Schroeder RA (2008) Environmental justice and the market: The politics of sharing wildlife revenues in Tanzania. *Society and Natural Resources* 21(7): 583–596.

Singh J and Van Houtum H (2002) Post-colonial nature conservation in Southern Africa: Same emperors, new clothes? *GeoJournal* 58(4): 253–263.

Sunderlin WD, Larson AM, Duchelle AE, et al. (2014) How are REDD+ proponents addressing tenure problems? Evidence from Brazil, Cameroon, Tanzania, Indonesia, and Vietnam. *World Development* 55: 37–52.

Sunseri T (2007) "Every African a Nationalist": Scientific forestry and forest nationalism in colonial Tanzania. *Comparative Studies in Society and History* 49(4): 883–913.

Taringa N (2006) How environmental is African traditional religion? *Exchange* 35(2): 191–214.

URT (1998) *National Forest Policy.* Dar es Salaam: United Republic and Tanzania.

URT (2007) *National Adaptation Program of Action (NAPA).* Dar es Salaam: United Republic and Tanzania.

URT (2012) *National Climate Change Strategy.* Dar es Salaam: United Republic of Tanzania (URT), 92.

URT (2015) *National Biodiversity Strategy and Action Plan (NBSAP) 2015–2020.* Dar es Salaam: United Republic and Tanzania.

URT (2018) *Intended Nationally Determined Contributions (INDC).* Tanzania: United Republic.

Vanderheiden S (2016) Climate justice beyond international burden sharing. *Midwest Studies In Philosophy* 40(1): 27–42.

Verde Selva G, Pauli N, Kiatkoski Kim M, et al. (2020) Opportunity for change or reinforcing inequality? Power, governance and equity implications of government payments for conservation in Brazil. *Environmental Science & Policy* 105: 102–112.

Vyamana VG (2009) Participatory forest management in the Eastern arc mountains of Tanzania: Who benefits? *International Forestry Review* 11(2): 239–253.

Wily L (1999) Moving forward in African community forestry: Trading power, not use rights. *Society & Natural Resources* 12(1): 49–61.

Woodhouse E and McCabe JT (2018) Well-being and conservation: Diversity and change in visions of a good life among the Maasai of northern Tanzania. *Ecology and Society* 23(1): 43.

15

IS RENEWABLE POWER REACHING THE PEOPLE AND ARE PEOPLE REACHING THE POWER?

Creating a Just Transition from the ground-up

Caroline Farrell and Mad Stano

The world's supply of fossil fuel is dwindling and a transition to alternative energy production is inevitable. Whether justice is at the center of this transition remains uncertain. Investments in cleaner energy will generate millions of new jobs. Unless a holistic *Just Transition* framework is advanced to support extraction-based communities, workers in the fossil fuel industry will face layoffs, falling incomes, and declining budgets to support vital public services such as libraries, fire services, and other social services. These risks will increase political resistance to effective climate policies. The Trump Administration is defunding climate research, rolling back international climate commitments (Hersher, 2019) and fast-tracking domestic fossil fuel production on federal lands (Solis 2019). These efforts reinforce the fear of what a transition away from fossil fuel means. However, a *Just Transition* framework which works "from the ground up" to transition our economic system and address the needs of the low-income communities and communities of color that have been most impacted by the fossil fuel economy is what is needed to holistically solve our climate crises and improve our communities. A *Just Transition* provides a pathway to mitigate and heal many so-called "externalities" imposed by the Anthropocene era.

This chapter will examine how the Center on Race, Poverty & the Environment (CRPE) and the Committee for a Better Arvin are planning a *Just Transition* in the historic heart of California's oil and gas industry. Similar to many extractive-based economies, taken wealth and resources out of Arvin while remaining one of its largest local industries (Rapier 2015; Morgen 2020). Tied to oil and gas for its economic growth, yet overburdened by its pollution, California reflects the paradox facing many extractive economies around the world. This chapter will discuss how state climate policies and local targeted private investment can improve community health, build community wealth, and create accountable governance systems that benefit low-income communities and communities of color. We will begin by discussing the Environmental Justice Movement's definition of a *Just Transition*. We will then discuss how California's climate policy evolved over the last few years to incorporate elements of a Just Transition Framework. Finally, the chapter will discuss the case study of Arvin, CA, a low-income Latinx community in the heart of the oil and gas industry planning to become 100% fossil fuel free.

What is a Just Transition?

The foundation of the Environmental Justice (EJ) Movement is rooted in a comprehensive analysis of how race and class intersect with economic and environmental benefits and burdens (Principles of Environmental Justice 1991). CRPE bases our work on the reality that low-income communities and communities of color are disproportionately impacted by environmental harms and the lack of environmental benefits. Our comprehensive analysis of the problems with the fossil fuel economy also lends itself to holistic solutions. For us, we need to transition not only to change the way we fuel our economy, but to create a truly just economy. To do this, community residents need to be meaningfully involved in decision-making that affects their health and quality of life (known as procedural justice). This requires us to strengthen the democratic infrastructure of communities while finding healthy alternatives to our current extraction-based economy.

Just Transition is a concept originally developed by the labor movement. Early on, the term Just Transition referred to the false choice between jobs and a clean environment (Kohler 1998). Just Transition has evolved to describe the environmental justice movement's goal to decarbonize our economy and the world with health, equity, and workers and residents' self-determination at the center. It's a framework for holistically building a better world from the ground up toward a regenerative economy. It recognizes and is rooted in lessons from the carbon-based economy – who benefited? Who experienced hardship? Why, how, and most importantly, can we do better? It is a reminder that some places and peoples' economic livelihoods hinge on activities that have a negative impact on the climate and they deserve to be a meaningful part of our climate solutions. It is an invitation to make progress on many problems beyond climate change. It's a concept whose specific elements in practice will vary according to the needs and conditions across communities.

In 2009–2010, the Center on Race, Poverty & the Environment engaged the San Joaquin Valley residents with whom we work in a long-term planning process to define green jobs and help guide the components of a Just Transition. Over the course of eight interactive workshops, community leaders defined what they wanted from a Just Transition:

> They want to live in healthy, vibrant, rural communities where they can
> live, work, [pray] and play free from the threat of environmental harm;

they want to breathe clean air, drink clean water, and have access to economic opportunities that lift their families out of poverty. They want access to equitable and sustainable green jobs, that respect the dignity of workers, provide a living wage and year-round employment, and protect the environment in which people live, work and play.

(Center on Race, Poverty & the Environment 2011)

Residents also acknowledged that to achieve this vision, communities need to be able to meaningfully participate in community planning and decision-making (Center on Race Poverty & the Environment 2011, p. 4). This vision of a just economy that blends environmental health, economic prosperity, and local democracy is part of a larger trend among environmental justice and climate justice advocates.

The California Environmental Justice Alliance created a Green Zones framework to turn overburdened communities from "Red Zones" to "Green Zones." This Green Zones framework involves developing community-driven land use plans, creating policies that reduce pollution in overburdened communities, and investing in environmentally and economically beneficial projects that improve opportunities for the existing community residents (California Environmental Justice Alliance 2015).

Similarly, the Climate Justice Alliance has created a framework that outlines key principles for a Just Transition: understanding the root causes of current inequities to find comprehensive solutions, respecting the rights of oppressed peoples to self-determination, making reparations for past harms, and improving representation so that we have a strong democracy where people impacted are leading us to solutions (Climate Justice Alliance 2010).

In 2019, the California Equity Network expanded on this definition of a Just Transition in its report on the *Four Pillars for a Just Transition* (Cha 2019). The report distils a framework for the Just Transition to four key pillars: strong governmental support, dedicated funding streams, diverse and strong coalitions, and economic diversification. Taken together, the above definitions of Just Transition share several common components: reducing pollution in low-income communities and communities of color, creating economic opportunities that facilitate community ownership in overburdened communities, and improving democratic governance and decision-making. These community-created definitions have informed our advocacy on California's climate policy for almost a decade.

Pushing California's climate policy toward a Just Transition

Over the last decade environmental justice communities and organizations have been successful in transforming California's climate policy to include Just Transition components. As a result, California's market-based climate policy evolved from prioritizing greenhouse gas reductions with some consideration of equity as a secondary goal to a more equity focused Just Transition framework.

When the state passed its landmark climate change bill, AB 32, the Global Warming Solution Act in 2006, the bill set a greenhouse gas reduction target and included provisions to protect public health and provide co-benefits to "disadvantaged communities" as part of implementation. This policy was seen as a way to address climate change as well as the negative health and economic impacts of the carbon economy, especially for low-income communities and communities of color. California climate policy has not met that promise, but since 2006, California has adopted a series of bills which codified many aspects of the Just Transition Framework.

AB 32 set a target for the state to reduce greenhouse gas emissions to 1990 levels by 2020 (Global Warming Solutions Act 2006). The bill also included several measures to ensure activities do not disproportionately impact low-income communities or interfere with air quality standards and efforts to reduce localized toxic air contaminants in communities already impacted by air pollution when including market mechanisms.

Environmental justice (EJ) advocates have long opposed market mechanisms such as pollution trading programs because they allowed polluters who were more often than not located in low-income communities and communities of color to avoid reducing pollution at their facilities by purchasing credits from other facilities that have reduced their pollution elsewhere, thereby creating pollution hot spots in EJ communities.

In 2010, the California Air Resources Board (CARB), the agency charged with implementing AB 32, adopted a market mechanism, specifically cap and trade regulation (CARB 2010). A USC report analyzing the first round of cap and trade compliance reports found a correlation between the largest greenhouse gas emitters, increases in localized air pollution and toxic contamination, and communities of color (Cushing et al. 2016). This confirmed EJ advocates' concerns that AB 32 was not being implemented beyond addressing climate change.

In order to address some of the inequities of cap and trade, the legislature passed SB 535 in 2012 (Global Warming Solutions Act of 2006: Greenhouse Gas Reduction Fund). SB 535 did two important things for EJ interests. First, it required CARB to identify disadvantaged communities in the state. EJ advocates had long recommended the state create a screening tool to identify EJ communities because you cannot reduce disparities if you cannot identify where they occur. Second, SB 535 set aside 25% of money available in the Greenhouse Gas Reduction Fund (GGRF) for projects that provide benefits to disadvantaged communities, and allocated 10% of the available funds to projects located within disadvantaged communities. The legislation linked health and economic benefits explicitly in climate policy and focused on multiple benefits beyond greenhouse gas reductions. However, the EJ movement continued to have significant reservations about the cap and trade system which remained in place and provided the source for the funding for the GGRF. Communities would still be denied pollution reductions, and revenue was not really a solution to that. While problematic, this bill marked an attempt to create climate policy that was specifically beneficial to disadvantaged communities and recognized that focusing only on greenhouse gas emissions missed the opportunity to provide additional benefits.

In 2015, California took another step towards a Just Transition passing SB 350 (Clean Energy and Pollution Reduction Act). This bill required the state to acquire 50% of its electricity from renewable sources and double the state's energy efficiency standards by 2030. In setting this standard, the legislature recognized that there are existing barriers to low-income communities and communities of color accessing renewable energy. The bill required the California Energy Commission to prepare a study examining obstacles to accessing renewable energy, weatherization and energy efficiency programs for low-income and disadvantaged communities. In addition, the bill included measures that combined climate policy with public health, pollution reduction, equity, and workforce development elements in the energy sector while establishing an ambitious renewable energy goal. However, it also presented a setback. Originally, SB 350 included a commitment to reduce fuel use by 50% by 2030. Removing this provision from the final bill signaled that the state was not ready to combine reducing fossil fuel production and use with increased renewable energy production.

Released in 2016, the SB 350 Barriers Study found low-income and disadvantaged communities face many barriers accessing the benefits of renewable energy including, but not limited to, spending three times the percentage of their income on energy costs than other Californians, low homeownership rates, older housing, insufficient access to capital, financial obstacles for small businesses, remote or underserved communities, and so on (SB 350 Barriers Study 2016). California's renewable policies instead largely focus on generation targets, market transformation, reduction of greenhouse gas emissions from a 30,000-foot point of view. These policies, as a whole, do not connect or serve to meet many of the localized problems of the fossil fuel economy in California.

In 2016, the legislature took up extending California's greenhouse gas targets beyond 2020. SB 32 extended California's greenhouse gas reduction targets, requiring that the state reduce greenhouse gas emissions by 40% of 1990 levels by 2030 (California Global Warming Solutions Act of 2006: emission limit). The legislature also passed AB 197 to guide on how ARB should achieve the target. It requires reporting of greenhouse gas emissions, criteria pollutants, and toxic air contaminants from sectors of the economy covered by CARB's climate change regulations (State Air Resources Board: greenhouse gases: regulations). This could help track emission trends and allow the legislature to intervene to reduce localized air pollution in disadvantaged communities. It also requires the Air Resources Board to consider "social costs" when adopting rules and regulations, and prioritize direct emission reductions from greenhouse gas emission sources rather than market mechanisms. Social costs include impacts to public health, climate adaptation impacts, and changes in energy system costs. By factoring in social costs of our carbon-based economy, CARB can capture costs typically externalized by polluters, thus making control technology more economically feasible. It also allows the state to prioritize regulations that achieve multiple benefits moving us closer to a Just Transition Framework.

The legislature passed another bill in 2016 that explicitly set out a Just Transition Framework. AB 2722 creates the Transformative Climate Communities (TCC) Program within the Strategic Growth Council. This was a new approach. The other bills discussed in this article were housed in regulatory agencies dedicated to issues like the Air Resources Board and the California Energy Commission with specific jurisdictions. Housing the program in the Strategic Growth Council is a significant opportunity to broaden the purpose and impact of the program. The Strategic Growth Council also has a broad range of institutional objectives ranging from environmental (improving air and water) to improving public health and equity to strengthening the economy. The Strategic Growth Councils wide purview allows it to be comprehensive in the development of its programs.

Substantively AB 2722, creates a program that will fund "neighborhood-level transformative climate community plans that include multiple, coordinated greenhouse gas emission reduction projects that provide local economic, environmental, and health benefits to disadvantaged communities" (Transformative Climate Communities Program). Unlike other funding opportunities which require applicants to be government entities, TCC funding can be awarded to nonprofit organizations and community development organizations, and must demonstrate multi-stakeholder partnerships with local community-based groups, labor, and workforce development boards at all phases. Projects that receive funding are required to "maximize climate, public health, and environmental, workforce, and economic benefits." The bill also allows the Strategic Growth Council to prioritize funds in communities that have a high proportion of census tracks identified as disadvantaged communities and that focus on communities that are most disadvantaged.

In 2017, the State reauthorized cap and trade, extending it beyond 2020 to 2030 with the passage of AB 398 (California Global Warming Solutions Act of 2006: market-based compliance mechanisms: fire prevention fees: sales and use tax manufacturing exemption). The legislation was a result of deals with the oil industry. However, the state also acknowledged that there were localized impacts from trading. In order to address localized hot spots in environmental justice communities, the state passed AB 617 which set up a framework whereby the Air Resources Board would work with the local Air Districts in the state to establish community-led steering committees to undertake community monitoring for hot spots and emission reduction plans based on existing levels of pollution in overburdened communities. It was seen by some advocates as an important first step in addressing cumulative impacts from existing pollution sources, but it was also seen as a disappointment because rather than setting state-wide standards, it would only focus on 10 initial pilot communities which would receive community monitoring and or emission reduction plans. This resulted in leaving many communities out and waiting for investment.

In 2018, the state accelerated the requirements of our renewable energy production in the passage of SB 100 (De León) which requires 100% renewable energy and zero-carbon electric retail sales to end-use customers by 2045 (California Renewables Portfolio Standard Program: emissions of greenhouse gases). This significant victory reaches only an estimated 15% of our greenhouse gas emissions (GHG Current California Emission Inventory Data, 2020).

Since the RPS standard measures total percentage of electricity sales, in-state oil and fossil fuel production can increase while their percentage of total electric sector sales decreases (Tracking Progress – Renewable Energy, 2020; California Field Production of Crude Oil (Thousand Barrels n.d.). The RPS is an important step toward total energy production from renewable sources, but does not on its own decarbonize our economy.

In 2019, California Governor Gavin Newsom as part of his proposed budget dedicated funding in recognition of "the need for careful study and planning to decrease demand and supply of fossil fuels, while managing the decline in a way that is economically responsible and sustainable." This plan also includes provisions to provide for "apprenticeships and job training in careers that will build a future green economy," and "an emphasis on regions and industries that have been traditionally dependent on fossil fuels, including Kern County" (California Environmental Justice Alliance 2019). This state investment in planning for a Just Transition is considered a real departure from California's climate policy compared to the Brown Administration, yet the Newsom Administration is on track to permit more oil and gas wells in 2019 than the Brown Administration did in 2018 (Ferrar 2019). Environmental justice residents and advocates continued to argue for Just Transition policies in the Newsom administration's various new state administrative venues with little certainty of meaningful state policy changes.

As of 2019, climate and environmental justice advocates have won, and are implementing and pushing several policy solutions to put as much equity as possible into state policies going forward. These solutions seek to decrease fossil fuel production in overburdened communities and prioritize their ability to experience the benefits of the renewable economy. These solutions work to dismantle the capitalist scaffolding in California's renewable energy economy which has historically focused cleaner technological innovations on upper-income "early adopters" instead of low-income environmental justice community residents. These solutions are community-led in policy design, implementation, and evaluation.

In addition to working on state climate policy, Environmental Justice Advocates and low-income communities and communities of color were working on community-identified solutions to ensure policies intended to address climate explicitly benefited low income communities and communities of color. These often took the form of specific proceedings, funding carve-outs of larger programs, or pilot projects.

- AB 693 (Multifamily Affordable Housing Solar Roofs Program SOMAH). In 2017, After years of coordinated environmental justice advocacy, engagement, and activism, the California Public Utilities Commission approved the SOMAH program. The SOMAH program provides financial incentives for installing solar energy systems on multifamily affordable housing. The program will deliver solar power and energy bill credits to affordable housing residents. SOMAH has a program budget of up to $1 billion dollars over ten years. A team of California-based social justice focused nonprofits administer the program with a strong focus on partnering with other community-based organizations for implementation (SOMAH | Solar on Multifamily Affordable Housing 2019).

- AB 523 (Electric Program Investment Charge: allocation) to ensure equity in Clean Energy Investments. AB 523 directs 25% of California Energy Commission Technology Demonstration and Deployment funding for clean energy technologies to projects located in and benefiting disadvantaged communities and an additional 10% to projects located in and benefiting low-income communities. Prior to AB 523 only 14% of funds were going to disadvantaged communities, in its second year of implementation the California Energy Commission (2019) invested 65% of funds into these communities and committed to investing over $60 million dollars to projects in these communities (Stano 2019).

- San Joaquin Valley Proceeding (R.15-03-010). In December 2018, the California Public Utilities Commission approved $56 million dollars for affordable clean energy pilots. San Joaquin Valley communities and residents redlined out of natural gas service led the entire design of fuel switching pilot projects. After years of meaningful community engagement with residents and local community-based organizations, each approved pilot contains community designed beneficial "common elements," like bill savings, tenant protections, workforce development planning, appliance warranties, and continued community engagement (San Joaquin Valley Affordable Energy Proceedings n.d.).

These policies and proceedings provide opportunities for local communities to access the benefits of state climate policy to reform the energy sector. Simultaneously, local communities like the San Joaquin Valley community of Arvin were identifying their own priorities for climate policy in the energy sector and beyond.

On the ground implications for Just Transitions policy: will Arvin lead?

As mentioned above, Arvin, California – a city of just over 20,000 people in Kern County – is one of the communities bearing a disproportionate burden of pollution. Latinx make up 94.1% of the population, with 87.7% of people speaking a language other than English at home. The median household income was $38,314 almost half that of California (Census 2019). Arvin is located 20 miles southwest of Bakersfield, one of the top three most polluted cities in the United States (American Lung Association 2019). Since 1933, Arvin has been an oil town, with many jobs and local funding streams tied to the oil and gas industry. Similar to many extractive-based economies, the oil and gas industry has simultaneously taken significant wealth and resources out of Arvin while remaining one of its largest local businesses. Tied to oil and gas for its economic growth, yet overburdened by its pollution, Arvin reflects the paradox facing many extractive economies around the world. CBA wanted to shift the city's priorities to protect public health.

Poor air and water quality issues prompted residents to organize in 2007. Residents were concerned about local sources of pollution like a large-scale composting facility, local large-scale dairies, and children playing outside when the air quality was poor. They reached out to CRPE for information. While working on air quality issues with the community, they learned that US EPA was reopening a clean-up plan for a Superfund site in Arvin, an old pesticide storage facility that had caused several leaks contaminating the soil in the 1980s. The EPA needed to reopen the clean-up plan because the contamination had migrated offsite and caused the city to close a drinking water well. Residents were outraged. They began to organize a community group, Committee for a Better Arvin, to specifically watchdog the US EPA clean up. The scope of CBA's work has increased considerably as they discover new issues and meet with other community leaders throughout the region. CBA contributed to CRPE's framework for a Just Transition discussed above.

When CBA formed, it created a governance structure and met in a centralized location. They hold meetings every Friday evening to this day. Their meetings are open to the public unless they have some confidential or strategic information to discuss. CBA has created an institution within the community. Residents, who are not members of the group, come to meetings to raise issues and ask for CBA's support at City Council meetings or with the Water District. Local officials such as City Council members or the Police Chief come to community meetings to talk about plans or to answer questions creating new pathways for accountability.

In 2014, CBA began to be concerned about oil and gas in their community. Part of a neighborhood was evacuated because of a gas leak from abandoned pipes transporting oil and gas waste. No one knew the pipes ran under the homes. Residents had felt dizzy and had reported sparks coming out of outlets. When the fire department tested for gas they ordered an evacuation (Bakersfield Californian 2014). CBA and the rest of the community were very concerned. The city was not equipped to respond. Nor was the county. Everyone deferred to the oil and gas company itself to monitor and remedy the contamination.

Since 1933, Arvin has been an oil town, with jobs dependent on the oil and gas industry. Similar to many extractive-based economies, the oil and gas industry has simultaneously taken significant wealth and resources out of Arvin while remaining one of its largest local businesses. Tied to oil and gas for its economic growth, yet overburdened by its pollution, Arvin reflects the paradox facing many extractive economies around the world. CBA wanted to shift the city's priorities to protect public health.

Over the next four years, CBA collected thousands of petitions, worked with community organizers and attorneys to develop strategies to protect public health. They talked about buffer zones or setbacks to create minimum distances between where people live and go to school and oil/gas drilling sites; they talked about improvements to regulations for abandoned wells, and they wanted the city to have greater control over the siting and operation of oil and gas facilities. Specifically, they wanted to update the city's oil and gas ordinance that was created in the 1960s. CBA worked with lawyers to suggest language changes and to make sure the language was legally defensible. CBA members, in their own time, also supported the candidacy of Jose Gurolla for Mayor of Arvin who supported a new health protective ordinance and ran on a Climate Justice platform for Arvin. In 2018, the Arvin City Council approved an update to the city's oil and gas ordinance despite aggressive push back from the oil and gas industry, concerned about the precedent this ordinance would set. This victory is a turning point for communities, who want to protect their health from the negative impacts of deregulated oil and gas industry activity in their towns.

However, CBA's celebration was short-lived. A few weeks after the new ordinance went into effect, the city's Planning Commission voted to grant a permit for four new wells within a couple of hundred feet of residences under the former ordinance. The city reasoned that the application for the wells was filed prior to the new ordinance going into effect. This angered CBA members who had fought so hard for the ordinance. To add insult to injury, the city did not require any environmental review of the proposed project, instead exempting the project under the California Environmental Quality Act's (CEQA) exemptions for small structures. CBA learned about this plan during a City Council meeting it was attending on another matter. CBA elected to sue the city to ensure it complied with the law and lived up to its promise to protect community health. In May 2019, the Kern County Superior Court decided in favor of CBA that the city had violated the law and needed to complete an environmental review of the project. This experience underscored that community residents cannot relax once they win a policy. They must fight every step of the way to ensure it is implemented as intended.

While CBA has been litigating against the city to enforce the spirit of the ordinance to protect public health, it has also been collaborating with the city, indicating the complexity of relationships in community Just Transitions work. CBA supported the city's applications for state funds to electrify public buses and city-owned vehicles as well as build out electric vehicle infrastructure in the city. CBA sees this as an important step to achieving its goal to reduce oil demand, improve transit options, and reduce pollution. Simultaneously, CBA and other groups in the San Joaquin Valley and state-wide allies have been advocating for a state-wide buffer zone of 2,500 feet to build on the 300-foot buffer zone they were able to achieve in Arvin. This is currently a bill – Assembly Bill 345 (A. Muratsuchi) – pending in the 2019–2020 legislative session.

Arvin shows us that community leadership is key if we are to meet our goals for a Just Transition. Arvin is leading the Just Transition by creating local solutions led by local leaders that simultaneously redress the negative impacts of fossil fuels on communities and promotes localized renewable energy innovation and economic opportunities through private and public partnerships. While they may not always be successful, they are also holding their leaders accountable to that vision and challenging the contradictions in California's traditional climate policies head on.

Conclusion

California has created a patchwork of climate policies that can lead to a Just Transition. But, they are also contradictory and can lead us in the opposite direction, toward an unjust transition. Progress is not linear, but continued pressure from community groups has continued to push state and local policymakers forward, even in the face of some setbacks. We have aggressive greenhouse gas reductions targets that depend on market mechanisms to achieve which make it hard to achieve emission reductions where they are most needed, in low-income communities and communities of color. We have 100% renewable energy standards, but we have also been rapidly permitting increased oil and gas drilling in the state simultaneously which increases pollution in disadvantaged communities. While addressing workforce development and training, California's climate policy has not prioritized incubating new community-owned businesses or new ownership models. Similarly, while there is increased civic engagement by low-income communities and communities of color in climate policy that has helped make it more equitable, community solutions are not implemented as mandatory requirements, but rather as a possible outcome for process-based policy. It requires community residents to expend tremendous time and effort at multiple levels of government for the possibility their solutions will be accepted. It requires a prolonged commitment from policymakers and communities to continue to sustain efforts toward a Just Transition and just future.

California's climate journey teaches us we must root climate policy in the communities most impacted by the fossil fuel status quo. These policies must be crafted by communities and their implementation must be community-centered. The inevitable shift from fossil fuels to renewable energy presents communities across the world an opportunity to decrease pollution, improve public health, mitigate climate change, and create living-wage jobs. This opportunity will only become a reality if the communities most impacted by fossil fuels lead the way – not just in designing the policies, but in overseeing and monitoring their implementation. Change is certain. Justice is not. Together, we must continue to build the Just Transition.

References

American Lung Association. 2019. *Most Polluted Cities | State of the Air*. Available at https ://www.lung.org/our-initiatives/healthy-air/sota/city-rankings/most-polluted-cit ies.html [Accessed 12 March 2020].

Bakersfield Californian. Available at https://www.bakersfield.com/mandatory-evacuat ions-in-arvin-neighborhood/article_911d05dc-5930-5db2-a4f7-9cfa1ca6e51d.html [Accessed 12 March 2020].

California Air Resources Board. 2010. *Cap and Trade 2010*. Available at https://ww w.arb.ca.gov/regact/2010/capandtrade10/capandtrade10.htm [Accessed 14 March 2020].

California Air Resources Board. 2020. *GHG Current California Emission Inventory Data*. Available at https://ww2.arb.ca.gov/ghg-inventory-data [Accessed 15 March 2020].

California Environmental Justice Alliance. 2015. *Green Zones*. Available at https://caleja. org/what-we-do/greenzones/ [Accessed 13 March 2020].

California Environmental Justice Alliance. 2019. *Governor Newsom's Budget Sets Stage For A Just Transition From Fossil Fuels*. Available at https://leginfo.legislature.ca.gov/faces/ billNavClient.xhtml?bill_id=201720180AB398 [Accessed 13 March 2020].

California Energy Commission. 2016. *SB 350 Barriers Study*. Available at https://ww2 .energy.ca.gov/sb350/barriers_report/ [Accessed 15 March 2020].

California Energy Commission, 2019. EPIC Highlights. https://ww2.energy.ca.gov /2020publications/CEC-500-2020-009/CEC-500-2020-009-SUM.pdf (2020).

California Energy Commission. 2020. *Tracking Progress - Renewable Energy*. Available at https://www.energy.ca.gov/sites/default/files/2019-12/renewable_ada.pdf [Accessed 15 March 2020].

California Global Warming Solutions Act of 2006: Market-Based Compliance Mechanisms: Fire Prevention Fees: Sales and Use Tax Manufacturing Exemption. Available at https://leginfo.legislature.ca.gov/faces/billNavClient.xhtml?bill_id=2 01720180AB398 [Accessed 13 March 2020].

California Public Utilities Commission. *San Joaquin Valley Affordable Energy Proceeding*. Available at https://www.cpuc.ca.gov/SanJoaquin/ [Accessed 15 March 2020].

California Renewables Portfolio Standard Program: Emissions of Greenhouse Gases. Available at https://leginfo.legislature.ca.gov/faces/billTextClient.xhtml?bill_id= 201720180SB100 [Accessed 15 March 2020].

Center on Race, Poverty & the Environment. 2011. *The Green Paper: A Community Vision For Environmentally And Economically Sustainable Development*. Available at http: //www.crpe-ej.org/crpe/images/stories/featured/green/j6365_crpe_eng_web.pdf [Accessed 10 March 2020].

Cha, J. 2019. *A Roadmap To An Equitable Low-Carbon Future: Four Pillars For Just Transition*. p. 4. Available at https://dornsife.usc.edu/assets/sites/242/docs/JUST_TRANSITI ON_Report_FINAL_12-19.pdf [Accessed 10 March 2020].

Clean Energy and Pollution Reduction Act. Available at https://leginfo.legislature.ca .gov/faces/billNavClient.xhtml?bill_id=201520160SB350 [Accessed 13 March 2020].

Climate Justice Alliance. 2010. *Just Transition - Climate Justice Alliance*. Available at https:/ /climatejusticealliance.org/just-transition/ [Accessed 14 March 2020].

Cushing, Lara J. et al. 2016. *A Preliminary Environmental Equity Assessment of California's Cap-and-Trade Program*. Available at http://dornsife.usc.edu/assets/sites/242/docs/ Climate_Equity_Brief_CA_Cap_and_Trade_Sept20 [Accessed 13 March 2020].

Electric Program Investment Charge: allocation. Available at https://leginfo.legislature
.ca.gov/faces/billNavClient.xhtml?bill_id=201720180AB523 (Accessed 10 February
2021].

Ferrar, K. 2019. *More Oil And Gas Under The Newsom Administration | Fractracker Alliance.*
FracTracker Alliance. Available at https://www.fractracker.org/2019/07/permitting
-more-oil-gas-newsom/ [Accessed 14 March 2020].

First People of Color Summit, Environmental Justice Principles. 1991. Available at
http://ejnet.org/ej/principles.html

Global Warming Solutions Act of 2006: Greenhouse Gas Reduction Fund. Available at
https://leginfo.legislature.ca.gov/faces/billNavClient.xhtml?bill_id=201120120SB
535 [Accessed 13 March 2020].

Hersher, R. 2019. U.S. Formally Begins To Leave The Paris Climate Agreement. *NPR.*
Available at https://www.npr.org/2019/11/04/773474657/u-s-formally-begins-to-l
eave-the-paris-climate- agreement [Accessed May 31, 2020].

Kohler, Brian. 1998. Just Transition-A Labour View of Sustainable Development. *CEP
Journal* 6(2).

Morgen, S. 2020. Once Financially Stable, Coronavirus Rocks Bakersfield and Kern
County Budgets. *The Bakersfield Californian.* Available at https://www.bakersfield.c
om/news/once-financially-stable-coronavirus-rocks-bakersfield-and-kern-county
-budgets/article_2f0bb37e-80fe-11ea-a78c-d3764676bd29.html [Accessed May 15,
2020].

Multifamily Affordable Housing Solar Roofs Program. Available at https://leginfo
.legislature.ca.gov/faces/billNavClient.xhtml?bill_id=201520160AB693   [Accessed
10 February 2021].

Rapier, Robert, R. & Advanced Green Innovations LLC, 2015. The Boom-Bust Cycle
- Five Stages of the Oil Industry. *Financial Sense.* Available at https://www.financia
lsense.com/contributors/robert-rapier/boom-bust-five-stages-oil [Accessed May 15,
2020].

State Air Resources Board: Greenhouse Gases: Regulations. Available at https://leginfo
.legislature.ca.gov/faces/billNavClient.xhtml?bill_id=201520160AB197.   [Accessed
13 March 2020].

Solis, N. 2019. Feds to Open Over a Million California Acres for Oil, Fracking. *CNS.*
Available at https://www.courthousenews.com/feds-to-open-over-a-million-califo
rnia-acres-for-oil-fracking/ [Accessed May 15, 2020].

SOMAH. 2019. *Solar On Multifamily Affordable Housing.* Available at https://calsomah
.org/ [Accessed 15 March 2020].

Stano, M., 2019. *Resilient And Equitable Communities Panel Remarks, EPIC Symposium
2019.* Greenlining Institute. Available at http://greenlining.org/wp-content/u
ploads/2019/02/2019-EPIC-Symposium-Just-Transition-testimony.pdf   [Accessed
15 March 2020].

Transformative Climate Communities Program. Available at https://leginfo.legislature
.ca.gov/faces/billNavClient.xhtml?bill_id=201520160AB2722 [Accessed 13 March
2020].

U.S. Census. 2019. *Quick Facts.* Available at https://www.census.gov/quickfacts/arvincit
ycalifornia [Accessed 12 March 2020].

U.S. Energy Information Administration. *California Field Production Of Crude Oil
(Thousand Barrels).* Available at https://www.eia.gov/dnav/pet/hist/LeafHandler
.ashx?n=pet&s=mcrfpca1&f=a [Accessed 16 March 2020].

16

CONTESTED SUBURBAN MOBILITIES

Towards a sustainable urbanism of justice and difference

Shimeng Zhou

Introduction

Mainstream understandings of sustainability are dominated by post-political discourses that tend to favor technological "win–win" solutions while overlooking social justice. Often characterized by attempts to "green" rather than reconstruct the capitalist political economy (Hajer 1995; Dryzek 2005; Hult 2015), these understandings reflect a post-political condition where tacit consensus eliminates contestation, while sustainability is in fact a deeply political affair that is easily hijacked by corporate capitalism (Swyngedouw 2007, 2010, 2011; Parr 2009; Hult 2015). By contrast, political ecology looks at socio-economic arrangements, power relations, and social (in)justice, highlighting the hypocrisy of advocating environmentalism while polluting elsewhere (Harvey 1996, 2008).

Furthermore, mainstream practices of sustainable urbanism are commonly regarded as a set of politically neutral technological solutions expressed through "best practice." Ecological citizenship is often seen as a value-free practice in which all are free to partake (Lister 1997; Marson and Mitchell 2004; MacGregor 2006), while conscientious automobility practices, such as cycling, are increasingly framed as the citizen's responsibility to the city (Green, Steinbeck, and Datta 2012). In this context, an urban political ecology urges a re-evaluation of norms, values, and social equity in planning and urban development (Keil 2007).

This chapter draws attention to the different and often uneven ways in which sustainable urban environments, and their associated practices of citizenship and mobility, are produced and contested. By combining critical approaches to sustainable urbanism, ecological citizenship, and mobility with social practice theory, this paper highlights the justice dimensions of green transitions through the case of a cycling-promoting initiative within Sustainable Järva, a sustainable regeneration project (2010–2014) in Järva, an ethnically diverse suburb outside

Stockholm, Sweden. The project's attempts at encouraging ecological citizenship through reconfigurations of the physical and socio-cultural landscape, and the promotion of associated practices like cycling, are useful for understanding the inclusionary and exclusionary mechanisms of citizenship (Lister 1997). As an embodied practice that requires a set of physical skills, cycling links to Bourdieu's (1977, 1980/1990) understanding of routinized practices and bodily movement as re-enacting of social norms and values.

"Eco-cities" and sustainable urban futures

"Eco-cities" are expressions of how mainstream sustainability discourse has influenced urban planning (Hult 2015). Combining modern technologies with environmental concern, eco-cities are increasingly framed as neoliberal marketplaces for green consumption, with a tendency to disproportionately favor technological advancement at the expense of social equity and alternative urban visions (Joss 2011; Caprotti 2014, 2015; Hult 2015). Originally stemming from the 1960s/1970s counterculture, contemporary eco-city projects are more likely to be large scale and technology driven (Porter 2009; Hult 2015).

The Swedish Social Democratic Party sought to make Sweden a world champion in sustainability in the 1990s and 2000s (Anshelm 2002; Lövgren 2002; Bradley 2009). Contemporary Swedish urban planning tends to favor ecological lifestyles, and the Swedish eco-city has become increasingly commodified under the "best practice" banner (Bradley 2009; Hult 2013, 2015). Made by being *branded* as "eco-," "sustainable," or "green" by the dominant discourse, eco-cities are performative in their (re)production being sustained by the repetition of certain practices (Butler 1993; Hult 2015).

A common approach often (implicitly or explicitly) undertaken in eco-cities is urban regeneration, the spatial economic restructuring of neighborhoods through reinvesting in disinvested spaces (Porter 2009). While retrofitting can be an alternative to privileged "eco-enclaves" (Hodson and Marvin 2010), planning frequently reflects how the culturally dominant majority uses space (Checker 2011; Sandberg 2014). This means that sustainability efforts can be a means of (or have the unintended consequence of) gentrification (Porter 2009). While regeneration seeks to correct the problems caused by past planning, rising costs and changing landscapes risk displacing the very residents that regeneration is purported to benefit, thus necessitating "just green enough" strategies (Wolch, Byrne, and Newell 2014). Even where gentrification has not yet resulted in physical displacement, the reshaping of social practices can engender a sense of socio-cultural displacement (Paton 2014; Flemsæter, Setten, and Brown 2014).

Urban futures are therefore deeply political. Who decides what the ideal "green urban future" looks like? By whom, and through what practices, are these futures performed? How is ecological citizenship, cycling citizenship, and sustainability in the Anthropocene commonly understood? And can environmental remediation be achieved without environmental gentrification? We explore these questions below.

A practice theory approach

Practicing sustainable mobility

With social theories of practice as a common foundation, social science disciplines are offering nuanced insights into agency, choice and change in sustainable practices, asking how social practices and material elements circulate and intersect, and how their reproduction sustains patterns of inequality (Shove 2010; Shove and Spurling 2013). Viewing social phenomena as bundles of practices and material arrangements, practice theory is not only concerned with what people do, but also what *practices* do, re-orienting analysis from individuals toward doing as a carrier of identity. Doing is therefore a performance of a practice, never reducible to individual choice (Staeheli 2010; Watson 2012; Hui 2013; Schatzki 2013). Practice theory understands people as carriers of practice, and journeys and destinations as the outcomes of specific organizations of practices – never as arbitrary expressions of individual choice. Promoting resource-efficient ways of life therefore requires the reconfiguration of key practices (Shove, Pantzar, and Watson 2012; Hui 2013).

Practicing (ecological) citizenship

Recent geographical research has deviated from traditional understandings of citizenship as a set of civil, social, and political rights and instead understood citizenship as a practice, or a set of "processual, performative and everyday relations between spaces, objects, citizens and non-citizens that ebbs and flows" (Lewis 2004, p. 3; Spinney, Aldred, and Brown 2015, p. 1), based on continual negotiation and more accurately constituted in relation to the city than the nation-state (Massey 2004, in Desforges, Jones, and Woods 2005, p. 443; Cresswell 2013). Instead of asking, "who is a citizen?," it asks how people do things *as citizens*, how practices *do and make citizens* (Luque 2005; Isin 2009), and how citizenship and identity are produced in ways of *doing* (Bourdieu 1990).

Ecological citizenship – a normative account of how citizens ought to live in order to reduce their environmental impact – is practiced through acts of ecological citizenship (Wolf, Brown, and Conway 2009; Hobson 2013), and an ecological citizen masters forms of conduct deemed appropriate to attain insider status (Isin 2009). Mobility practices contribute to certain forms of citizenship, e.g. the "ecological citizen," and constitute cultural identities, e.g. the "cyclist" (Spinney, Aldred, and Brown 2015). While some contexts portray urban cyclists as citizens meeting ecological responsibilities to the city (Green, Steinbeck, and Datta 2012), other places view walking and cycling as unbecoming of the citizen compared to driving and flying (Spinney, Aldred, and Brown 2015).

In Sweden, physical planning is commonly seen as capable of solving social problems and fostering "active, ecologically interested and engaged groups"

(Bradley 2009). Practicing active ecological citizenship links to the historic idea of how barren natural conditions have shaped a "durable Swedish character" (Hedrén 2002, p. 30). Another study in Järva (Bradley 2009) revealed how Swedish identity carries familiarity with nature, with links made between "Swedishness" and environmentally conscientious activities such as recycling.

Any central unit of belonging (e.g. the nation-state) is reproduced through beliefs, assumptions, habits, and everyday practices (Billig 1995; Shove, Pantzar, and Watson 2012). Belonging touches on aspects of citizenship that enable or prevent membership in the polity and social body. Therefore, understanding citizenship as a dynamic process where meanings change exposes its mechanisms of inclusion and exclusion (Lewis 2004).

Practice and inequality

The repetition of routines and bodily movement – the *habitus* – enact societal norms and values (Bourdieu 1977, 1980/1990), and power relations are sustained through the reproduction of dominant practices that orient how people prioritize their time (Pred 1981). Connections between elements and practices are rooted in past inequalities and constitutive of similar patterns in the future (Shove, Pantzar, and Watson 2012, pp. 135–136). Those with the means to engage in valued social practices can steer the direction of their development (Bourdieu 1984), while socially marginalized groups lack the means to become carriers of practices deemed necessary for societal participation (Shove, Pantzar, and Watson 2012, pp. 135–136).

Within these uneven landscapes of opportunity and access, new forms of ecological citizenship involve moral responsibilities to enact this citizenship; for instance, the cycling citizen needs to be a "knowledgeable and alert risk-assessor competent to travel in ways that maximize independence, efficiency and health," potentially reinforcing the marginal citizenship of less mobile individuals (Cass, Shove, and Urry 2005; Green, Steinbeck and Datta 2012; Shove, Pantzar, and Watson 2012; Spinney, Aldred, and Brown 2015). Seemingly apolitical practices like cycling are perceived differently by culturally diverse persons (Fang Law and Karnilowicz 2014); for instance, feminist scholarship has shown how formulations of ecological citizenship lack attention to structural barriers such as gender, class, and race, asking what kind of subject one would have to be (a universal, gender-neutral agent-citizen?) to practice this citizenship (Marson and Mitchell 2004; MacGregor 2006). When citizenship becomes solely about individual responsibility, as if everyone had an equal ability to accept it, the conditions under which citizenship may be meaningfully practiced are disregarded, and "uneducated" and 'irresponsible' individuals become framed as the root cause of environmental degradation (MacGregor 2006). Citizenship can therefore create non- or partial citizens, and the practice of cycling can expose the two sides of citizenship's membership coin (Lister 1997, p. 43).

Sustainable Järva: a case study

This chapter explores how sustainable suburban regeneration, ecological citizenship, and cycling have been understood within Sustainable Järva – a suburban regeneration project led by the City of Stockholm 2010–2014 – and how their promotion has been experienced by different stakeholders.

The research is based on 16 semi-structured interviews with stakeholders, including residents targeted by the project, activists, city officials, and cycling coaches. Other materials include official documents and attendance at a Sustainable Järva workshop in 2015.

Järva is a suburban area composed of six residential areas – Akalla, Husby, Kista, Hjulsta, Rinkeby, and Tensta (Figure 16.1) – with less than 10% of the population size of Stockholm. In all residential areas, the percentage of the population with a foreign background is much higher than in Stockholm (over 73% and 33% respectively) (Stockholms stad 2019a–e).

Most buildings in Järva were built 1965–75 as part of *Miljonprogrammet*, a government plan to combat housing shortage. *Miljonprogrammet* is a physical expression of the post-war Swedish welfare state and is nowadays often associated with monotonous suburban landscapes and ethnic segregation in media reporting (Hall and Vidén 2005).

Having been promoted as a blueprint for the regeneration of post-war suburbs in Europe (Stockholms stad 2019f), Sustainable Järva involved both technological refurbishments as well as the promotion of sustainable lifestyles. Sustainable Järva was also part of a wider ambition to eco-profile the *Miljonprogrammet* residential stock, as well as *Järvalyftet*, a government-led commitment to "upgrade" Järva (Stockholms stad 2015).

Sustainable mobility formed an important part of the project. Cycling infrastructure was improved (Stockholms stad 2014b), and three bicycle rental stations were set up (Figure 16.1). After the project, bicycle maintenance at Akalla by and Husby gård was transferred to host organizations (Interviewee 1); 150 adult participants attended the project's free cycling courses (Stockholms stad 2014a–c; Sweco 2014), which were run in collaboration with Kista Sports Club and The National Society for Road Safety, and promoted via advertisements and word-of-mouth (Interviewee 2). Most participants were women with a foreign background. Although many were satisfied with the course, few purchased bicycles or cycled regularly after the course (Stockholms stad 2014c). While there was a continued demand for cycling courses, it was unclear who would bear funding responsibilities after the project (Interviewee 3; Interviewee 4).

Normalization of the (Swedish) eco-city, or gentrification?

The emphasis on eco-profiling (Interviewee 3; Interviewee 5) in Sustainable Järva spoke to the performativity of the "eco-city." By contrast, several interviewees mentioned the short-termism of regeneration projects and "token"

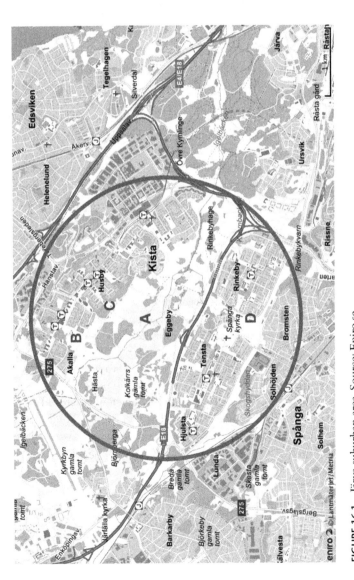

FIGURE 16.1 Järva suburban area. Source: Eniro.se

A. Järvafältet (a nature reserve)

B. Akalla by (a community center and bicycle rental station)

C. Husby gård (an arts and crafts organization and bicycle rental station)

D. Rinkebysvängen 22 (bicycle rental station managed by the City of Stockholm) interventions that "clear the conscience" of a white middle-class from the city center (Interviewee 6; Interviewee 7).

Sustainable Järva contributed to *Järvalyftet*, which sought to transform Järva into "an area to which people want to move and where people want to stay" (Stockholms stad 2012, p. 16).

> Normalizing Järva will solve some of the issues with integration. Then it becomes a place that anyone will move to. [...] If you make these areas more attractive, they will attract people from other neighborhoods, which will promote integration. [...] They say, 'You're changing the character of this neighborhood' – and yes, we are. That's how cities have always changed.
>
> *(Interviewee 5)*

This exemplifies the discourse of normalization in Sweden (Lövgren 2002; Bradley 2009), where regeneration is normalized by invoking its inevitability, and "normalization" – while believed to solve social problems – risks fostering integration at the expense of difference. The stated intention of cycling promotion was more along the lines of normalizing the sustainably regenerated suburb, yet cycling also seemed to work as a means of gentrification, and some perceived the promotion of eco-friendly lifestyles as value imposition.

> Cycling courses are great, but only if they exist everywhere, so it's not some sort of "Paralympics Special Edition" based on your address.
>
> *(Interviewee 8)*

Cycling thus became associated with "Swedishness" in the *manner* of promotion, when "a white person comes to instruct you," and there are intimate links between environmental gentrification and the hypocrisy of "white middle-class environmentalism" (Interviewee 9). Valued sustainable practices are neither affordable nor available for all.

> [It's about] the right person saying the right thing. Often, it's the wrong people saying the right things. That's not credible. I think it's hypocrisy to tell suburban kids to recycle when [the messenger] owns two cars.
>
> *(Interviewee 9)*

> Environmental issues are important, but in the suburbs, they're used as oppression. [...] Maybe people don't get recycling. But do they even need to recycle given how small their carbon footprint is? And if they *do* learn recycling – what should the middle-class do?
>
> *(Interviewee 9)*

> *Where* are you going to cycle? To work? You need a job for that. Where can you get a bike? You need money for that.
>
> *(Interviewee 9)*

There's already enough on your plate [...] My Dad says, 'I'd love to be eco-friendly, but it's not for me – it's not affordable'.

(Interviewee 8)

Given the discursive production of Järva as "deprived," ownership was crucial to reclaim the power to define the "problem."

We wanted to inform kids about environmental issues [...] and this should be done by a person who looks like them, can pronounce their names [...] We walked around *Järvafältet* and asked, "who is jogging here?" – again, mostly white middle-class. [...] We wanted them to reclaim that space.

(Interviewee 9)

Cycling is a good idea. But how it's being done is beneath contempt. [...] Just understand people. After that [...] if people want to cycle because it's practical, because you want stronger calves, that's great.

(Interviewee 9)

I hate the word [integration], but if I must use it, I think it should be a compromise. My traditions should be equally highlighted, so both parties gain insight into the other's world.

(Interviewee 8)

Cycling as "active ecological citizenship," or cycling as "Swedishness"?

Sustainable Järva was committed to "inform[ing] and educat[ing] residents on climate and environmental issues" (Stockholms stad 2010), in the spirit of ecological citizenship rooted in responsibility and enlightenment. The emphasis on "familiarity with nature" is distinctive; in places like London, cycling discourses tend to revolve around public health and obesity (Green, Steinbeck, and Datta 2012).

It's not just about cycling, it's about saying, "this is a nature reserve" [...] A lot of people are afraid of entering the woods.

(Interviewee 3)

Hansta is a 10-minute bike ride from here [...] it's like arriving in the 60s in Sweden. Flowers, trees, grazing cows [...] you could bring a basket and blanket, the kids could bathe in the lake [...] Cycling can create community [...] just doing something else than sitting by the computer.

(Interviewee 10)

Given the lack of cycling culture in Järva (Interviewee 4), especially "compared to more Swedish areas" (Interviewee 6), a city official stressed how "understanding the land" can be a "natural" route to integration. "Being outside" emerges as a way of being *on the inside* of citizenship – and a problematic and exclusionary understanding of Swedish identity.

> A lot of residents of foreign origin have never cycled. […] I can compromise with ice-skating, but everyone should learn cycling and swimming.
>
> *(Interviewee 3)*

> You're probably the first person in your family to ski, or anything like that. Doing "Swedish" things shouldn't be a requirement, but it should feel welcoming, if you're interested.
>
> *(Interviewee 8)*

> [Cycling] is something they should invest in […] so kids, instead of burning cars, can do something […] If there was a cycling school, [adults] could go there, instead of wasting their time, sitting on the couch […] So you use your time, do something important, that can help you in the future, forward.
>
> *(Interviewee 11)*

Cycling was framed as active and virtuous "Swedish" behavior, as opposed to the "passivity" and "idleness" of segregation and remaining indoors.

Several interviewees made links between cycling, "Swedish" identity and "cyclist" identity. Self-image and past experiences and all play a part, especially in Järva where many children may not see cycling as an option (Interviewee 4).

> I'm sure there's a widespread need [for cycling courses] in this neighborhood. I think almost all Swedes learn to cycle as children.
>
> *(Interviewee 12)*

> I was born here, but I've never cycled. My parents had to work day and night. Who was going to teach me? […] I wouldn't attend a cycling course as an adult […] in my mind, it's a white thing. It's not for me. […] There are activities that I've always felt excluded from, and that's why they're not attractive for me.
>
> *(Interviewee 8)*

Failing to master a physical competency makes one feel "unintelligent" (Interviewee 8) and requiring help as an adult can be "embarrassing" (Interviewee 2). This contrasted with the "pride" of finally mastering cycling (Interviewee 11). For some, "pride" was a problematic expression of the wish to "integrate."

> Immigrants who arrive as adults want to belong. It's like you're missing out on parts of the world you're in, because you don't feel welcome. And then you work hard to become part of it. But those of us who were born here

> [...] will notice that the things I'm excluded from are not a big deal. I can survive without them. If they exclude me, why should I fight? My world is just as good as theirs.
>
> *(Interviewee 8)*

> If people in Tensta don't want to cycle, you shouldn't try to fix the people – you should examine the bike and the people who use it normally.
>
> *(Interviewee 9)*

Cycling promotion in Järva was understood as a social sustainability initiative, as it provided the opportunity for women who were unable to cycle in their home countries to learn how. However, several interviewees mentioned the prejudices underpinning the idea of cycling as liberation *from* other cultures.

> She really struggles at the course. [...] She gets told by her family – they're from another country – that this is a scandal. [...] "No," she said, "I'm going to learn to cycle, I've set up goals, I want to feel free" [...] She was tough.
>
> *(Interviewee 3)*

> The problem is that they always pick the most controversial topic – women in Järva on bikes.
>
> *(Interviewee 7)*

Challenging the post-political: a sustainable urbanism of justice and difference

Having contrasted different understandings of sustainable suburban regeneration, ecological citizenship, and cycling in Järva, what may we conclude about the politics of sustainable urbanism in the Anthropocene?

Firstly, *the results challenge post-political understandings of sustainable urbanism* and the mainstream framing of best practice (e.g. the Swedish "eco-city") and regeneration as politically neutral. Instead, they reveal divergent understandings of suburban regeneration among different groups.

Secondly, *the results challenge post-political understandings of ecological citizenship and cycling citizenship* in the Anthropocene. In this case, these two citizenships were perceived as "white," "middle-class," and attached to norms and values linked to a "Swedish" identity associated with environmental responsibility, familiarity with nature, and active outdoor mobility. This risks the normative reproduction of power structures of class, gender, and race in the public opinion on desired forms of ecological citizenship and mobility. If attempts at achieving community or "integration" engender a sense of sustainability-led gentrification, issues such as class, gender, and race must be addressed.

Ecological citizenship in the Anthropocene should engage with how meanings embedded in citizenship practices link to identity and belonging, asking who has the means to perform the (seemingly neutral) "model ecological citizen" in the city, and why suburbs become sites of intense regeneration while the environmentally harmful practices of affluent communities remain unaddressed. Framing ecological citizenship as "active," "outdoors," and "mobile" – assuming that all citizens are equally capable of practicing this citizenship – also reinforces the marginal citizenship of those facing barriers to "activeness."

Thirdly, *the results challenge post-political understandings of sustainable mobility.* Cycling is not only a low-carbon way of getting from A to B, but a practice that constitutes cultural identities and creates both citizens and non-citizens. Here, cycling emerged as a deeply political practice where ecological citizenship and "Swedishness" seemed to overlap. The framing of valued social practices like cycling as tools for cultural integration can generate resistance against the *meanings* carried by these practices, and the power relations sustained by their reproduction.

This research hopes to contribute towards urban planning that makes societies more just and vibrant within our planetary boundaries. Rather than seeking conclusive answers or points of consensus, my intention has been to politicize the post-political by exposing sites of contestation and providing insight into the complexity of urban planning, regeneration, and ecological citizenship. I argue that we must address justice by acknowledging difference. Just approaches must seek equality without equivalence (Walker 2015), that is, to address justice without seeking uniformity, and to value singularity without seeking sameness, with "respect for group differences without oppression" (Young 1990, p. 47). Successful sustainability policies require that we consider justice as the recognition of difference: Who are the environmentalists and the messengers, what norms and values underpin the dominant discourse, and which practices does the discourse encourage, perhaps even impose? Similarly, when ecological citizenship is viewed as an individual and universal responsibility, as if everyone had an equal ability to accept it, the conditions under which citizenship may be meaningfully practiced are disregarded. Etymology is not insignificant; *Anthropocene* stems from *anthropos* – Ancient Greek for "human" – and we must ask who this "universal" *anthropos* is. Who has the means to shape our current geological epoch, and for whom are we framing and creating the future?

Planning for environmental regeneration should take the perspectives and experiences of different groups into account; the key to environmental remediation is not to obliterate difference by means of normalization, but to accommodate difference while avoiding treating regenerated areas as inherently different (Bradley 2009). This means being mindful of structural barriers to practicing sustainability without reinforcing the discursive production of places like Järva as "deprived" anomalies. This means understanding and incorporating aspects of local neighborhoods into Swedish eco-city planning as a potential solution for ensuring a more just green transition. This also means making cycling promotion more ubiquitous (rather than targeting Järva), more permanent and patient (therefore more reliable, embedded in everyday life and likely to generate long-term change), or more locally organized (therefore recognizing the skills of local communities, and supporting a knowledge exchange on equal terms). Cycling promotion alone cannot substitute structural change, yet can be part of the wider task of rethinking practices through which "sustainability," "urbanism," "ecological citizenship," "sustainable mobility," and "Swedishness" are performed, and of democratizing the power to shape these practices. We should enquire into where the core issue is situated: Is it a problem that some Järva residents lack the skills of the "model ecological citizen," or is this seemingly neutral citizen modeled in an excluding way? What kind of subject does one have to be to practice these practices and experience belonging in the city?

Sustainable urbanism is more than a set of technological solutions, ecological citizenship is more than a normative set of attitudes and behaviors, and cycling is more than getting from A to B. Academia can and should engage in progressive research that invites alternative urban visions. Just transitions to sustainable futures that ensure both the "green" and the "just" require environmentally progressive ontologies of sustainability, urbanism, ecological citizenship, and mobility, promoting ecologically sound transitions while accommodating difference, and addressing the joint environmental and social justice implications for diverse communities.

Acknowledgments

This chapter summarizes the key findings of my MSc thesis from the School of Geography and the Environment at the University of Oxford. I want to extend my gratitude to my interviewees, to whose wisdom I hope to have done justice, and to Professor Tim Schwanen, for invaluable guidance.

References

Anshelm, J. (2002) Det gröna folkhemmet: Striden om den ekologiska moderniseringen av Sverige. In: J. Hedrén, ed. *Naturen som brytpunkt – Om miljöfrågans mystifieringar, konflikter och motsägelser.* Stockholm: Brutus Östling Bokförlag Symposion.

Billig, M. (1995) *Banal Nationalism.* London: SAGE.

Bourdieu, P. (1977) *Outline of a Theory of Practice.* Translated by R. Nice. Cambridge: Cambridge University Press.

Bourdieu, P. (1984) *Distinction: A Social Critique of the Judgment of Taste.* London: Routledge.

Bourdieu, P. (1990) *The Logic of Practice.* Translated by R. Nice. Stanford: Stanford University Press. (Original work published 1980).

Bradley, K. (2009) Planning for eco-friendly living in diverse societies. *Local Environment,* 14(4), 347–363.

Butler, J. (1993) *Bodies That Matter: On the Discursive Limits of 'Sex'.* New York: Routledge.

Caprotti, F. (2014) Eco-urbanism and the Eco-city, or, Denying the Right to the City? *Antipode,* 46(5), 1285–1303.

Caprotti, F. (2015) *Eco-Cities and the Transition to Low Carbon Economies.* Basingstoke: Palgrave Macmillan.

Cass, N., Shove, E. and Urry, J. (2005) Social exclusion, mobility and access. *The Sociological Review*, 53(3), 539–555.

Checker, M. (2011) Wiped out by the 'Greenwave': Environmental Gentrification and the Paradoxical Politics of Urban Sustainability. *City and Society*, 23(2), 210–229.

Cresswell, T. (2013) Citizenship in Worlds of Mobility. In: O. Soderstrom, S. Randeria, G. D'Amato and F. Panese, eds. *Critical Mobilities*. Lausanne: EPFL Press, 81–100.

Desforges, L., Jones, R. and Woods, M. (2005) New Geographies of Citizenship. *Citizenship Studies*, 9(5), 439–451.

Dryzek, J. (2005) *The Politics of the Earth: Environmental Discourses*. 2nd ed. Oxford: Oxford University Press.

Fang Law, S. and Karnilowicz, W. (2014) 'In our country it's just poor people who ride a bike': Place, displacement and cycling in Australia. *Journal of Community & Applied Social Psychology*, 25(4), 296 – 309.

Flemsæter, F., Setten, G. and Brown, K.M. (2014) Morality, mobility and citizenship: Legitimising mobile subjectivities in a contested outdoors. *Geoforum*, 64, August 2015, 342–350.

Green, J., Steinbach, R. and Datta, J. (2012) The travelling citizen: Emergent discourses of moral mobility in a study of cycling in London. *Sociology*, 46(2), 272–289.

Hajer, M.A. (1995) *The Politics of Environmental Discourse: Ecological Modernization and the Policy Process*. Oxford: Clarendon Press.

Hall, T. and Vidén, S. (2005) The million homes programme: A review of the Great Swedish planning project. *Planning Perspectives*, 20(3), 301–328.

Harvey, D. (1996) *Justice, Nature and the Geography of Difference*. Cambridge, MA: Blackwell.

Harvey, D. (2008) The Right to the City. *New Left Review*, 53, 23–40.

Hedrén, J. (2002) *Naturen som brytpunkt – Om miljöfrågans mystifieringar, konflikter och motsägelser*. Stockholm: Brutus Östlings bokförlag Symposion.

Hobson, K. (2013) On the making of the environmental citizen. *Environmental Politics*, 22(1), 56–72.

Hodson, M. and Marvin, S. (2010) Urbanism in the Anthropocene: Ecological Urbanism or Premium Ecological Enclaves? *City*, 14(3), 298–313.

Hui, A. (2013) Practices, movement and circulation. In: E. Shove and N. Spurling, eds. *Sustainable Practices: Social Theory and Climate Change*. London: Routledge, 89–102.

Hult, A. (2013) Swedish Production of Sustainable Urban Imaginaries in China. *Journal of Urban Technology*, 20(1), 77–94.

Hult, A. (2015) The Circulation of Swedish Urban Sustainability Practices: To China and Back. *Environment and Planning. Part A*, 47, 537–553.

Isin, E. (2009) Citizenship in Flux: The Figure of the Activist Citizen. *Subjectivity*, 29, 367–388.

Joss, S. (2011) Eco-cities: The mainstreaming of urban sustainability; key characteristics and driving factors. *International Journal of Sustainable Development and Planning*, 6, 268–285.

Keil, R. (2007) Sustaining Modernity, Modernizing Nature: The Environmental Crisis and the Survival of Capitalism. In: R. Krueger and D. Gibbs, eds. *The Sustainable Development Paradox*. New York: Guilford Press, 41–65.

Lewis, G. (2004) *Citizenship: Personal Lives and Social Policy*. Milton Keynes: Open University Press.

Lister, R. (1997) *Citizenship: Feminist Perspectives*. New York: New York University Press.

Luque, E. (2005) Researching Environmental Citizenship and its Publics. In: A. Dobson and A. V Sáiz, eds. *Citizenship, Environmental Economy*. London: Routledge, 55–70.

Lövgren, S. (2002) *Att skapa ett framtidens folk – governmentality och miljödiskurs i modern svensk bostadspolitik*. Linköping: Tema Hälsa och samhälle, Linköping University.

MacGregor, S. (2006) No sustainability without justice: A feminist critique of environmental citizenship. In: A. Dobson and D. Bell, eds. *Environmental Citizenship*. Cambridge, MA: MIT Press, 101–126.

Marson, S.A. and Mitchell, J. (2004) Citizens and the State: Citizen Formations in Space and Time. In: C. Barnett and M. Low, eds. *Spaces of Democracy: Geographical Perspectives on Citizenship, Participation and Representation*. London: SAGE, 93–112.

Massey, D. (2004) *For Space*. London: SAGE. (Cited in Desforges, Jones and Woods, 2005: 443).

Parr, A. (2009) *Hijacking Sustainability*. Cambridge, MA: MIT Press.

Paton, K. (2014) *Gentrification: A Working-Class Perspective*. Farnham: Ashgate.

Porter, L. (2009) Whose Urban Renaissance? In: L. Porter and K. Shaw, eds. *Whose Urban Renaissance? An International Comparison of Urban Regeneration Strategies*. London: Routledge, 241–252.

Pred, A. (1981) Social Reproduction and the Time-Geography of Everyday Life. *Geografiska Annaler, Series B – Human Geography*, 63(1), 5–22.

Sandberg, L.A. (2014) Environmental gentrification in a post-industrial landscape: The case of the Limhamn quarry, Malmö, Sweden. *Local Environment*, 19(10), 1068–1085.

Schatzki, T. (2013) The edge of change: On the emergence, persistence and dissolution of practices. In: E. Shove and N. Spurling, eds. *Sustainable Practices: Social Theory and Climate Change*. London: Routledge, 31–46.

Shove, E. (2010) Beyond the ABC: Climate change policy and theories of social change. *Environment and Planning. Part A*, 42, 1273–1285.

Shove, E., Pantzar, M. and Watson, M. (2012) *The Dynamics of Social Practice: Everyday Life and How It Changes*. London: SAGE.

Shove, E. and Spurling, N. eds. (2013) *Sustainable Practices: Social Theory and Climate Change*. London: Routledge.

Spinney, J., Aldred, R. and Brown, K. (2015) Geographies of citizenship and everyday mobility. *Geoforum*, 64, 325–332.

Staeheli, L. (2010) Political geography: Where's citizenship? *Progress in Human Geography*, 35(3), 393–400.

Stockholms stad (2010) *Sustainable Järva*. [printed folder] Stockholm: Ekotryckredners.

Stockholms stad (2012) *Järva 2030 – A Future Vision Becomes Reality*. Available at: http: //international.stockholm.se/globalassets/rapporter/vision-jarva-2030---english. pdf

Stockholms stad (2014a) *Sustainable Järva!* Available at: http://www.stockholm.se/PageFi les/169740/SustainableJärva%2020140320%20Clue.pdf

Stockholms stad (2014b, September 24) *Hållbara Järva*. Available at: https://www.you tube.com/watch?v=jPMn6EWy0PY

Stockholms stad (2014c) *Slutrapport för Hållbara Järva projektet, 2010—2014*. Available at: https://insynsverige.se/documentHandler.ashx?did=1834194

Stockholms stad (2015) *Hållbara Järva!* Available at: http://www.stockholm.se/ hallbarajarva

Stockholms stad (2019a) *Områdesfakta: Akalla*. Available at: https://statistik.stockholm.se

Stockholms stad (2019b) *Områdesfakta: Husby*. Available at: https://statistik.stockholm.se

Stockholms stad (2019c) *Områdesfakta: Kista*. Available at: https://statistik.stockholm.se

Stockholms stad (2019d) *Områdesfakta: Rinkeby*. Available at: https://statistik.stockholm .se

Stockholms stad (2019e) *Områdesfakta: Tensta*. Available at: https://statistik.stockholm.se

Stockholms stad (2019f) *Hållbara Järva!* Available at: https://www.stockholm.se/hallbarajarva

Sweco (2014) *Cykelskola uppföljning.* Stockholm: Sweco.

Swyngedouw, E. (2007) Impossible/Undesirable Sustainability and the Post-Political Condition. In: J.R. Krueger and D. Gibbs, eds. *The Sustainable Development Paradox.* New York. Guilford Press.

Swyngedouw, E. (2010) Apocalypse forever? Post-political populism and the spectre of climate change. *Theory, Culture & Society,* 27(2–3), 213–232.

Swyngedouw, E. (2011) Depoliticized environments: The end of nature, climate change and the post-political condition. *Royal Institute of Philosophy Supplement,* 69, 253–274.

Walker, H. (speaker) (2015, May 28) *Equality Without Equivalence: An Anthropology of the Common* [audio podcast] Available at: http://www.lse.ac.uk/newsAndMedia/videoAndAudio/channels/publicLecturesAndEvents/player.aspx?id=3104 [Accessed 5 July 2015].

Watson, M. (2012) How theories of practice can inform transition to a decarbonised transport system. *Journal of Transport Geography,* 24, 488–496.

Wolch, J.R., Byrne, J. and Newell, J.P. (2014) Urban green space, public health, and environmental justice: The challenge of making cities 'just green enough'. *Landscape and Urban Planning,* 125, 234–244.

Wolf, J., Brown, K. and Conway, D. (2009) Ecological citizenship and climate change: Perceptions and practice. *Environmental Politics,* 18(4), 503–521.

Young, I.M. (1990) *Justice and the Politics of Difference.* Princeton: Princeton University Press.

17

SEEDS, CHEMICALS, AND STUFF

The agency of things in (un)just agriculture regimes

Matt Comi

Introduction

Both the tallgrass prairies of NE Kansas and the arid Yakima Valley in Washington are settler–colonial landscapes. The US Midwest has long used lands expropriated from Indigenous people to conduct a tilled, cash-cropped agriculture to produce commodities such as corn and soy. While the Yakima Valley still belongs to the Yakima nation, this high desert has been made arable by a series of irrigation canals which were built both by the Yakima nation and a variety of private US entities along with aid from the US government (Boening 1919). These canals channel meltwater from the nearby Cascade mountains throughout this L-shaped valley, forming a long, thin green belt in the otherwise arid south–central region of Washington state. Here, some of the largest berry farms, vineyards, and hop farms now employ vast numbers of agricultural workers to perform the labor-intensive tasks associated with growing these specialty goods. These human landscapes are conversely populated with numerous materials intimately involved in the co-production of the social and agricultural practices which inform environmental outcomes.

This chapter examines the social worlds of plant genetic resources (PGRs), the genetic code that informs crops' growth habits, in both corn/soy growing in the US Midwest and hop growing in the US Northwest. Drawing on qualitative empirical research gathered with seed sales agronomists in NE Kansas and NW Missouri in the corn and soy industry (n=12) along with hop growers operating in Washington (n=15), I compare these groups' diverging relationships with PGRs along with nearby materials (e.g. chemicals, soil, implements) to show how these socio-material worlds produce different environmental possibilities and outcomes. Particularly, I show how the large hop farmers in Yakima directly involve themselves in breeding plant material on-farm instead

of relying on off-farm input companies to conduct breeding. This unique practice not only demonstrates a direct collaboration between PGRs and farmers,
but also an indirect collaboration that includes the many environmental actors
which occur on-farm and act to improve environmental adaptive capacity in
Yakima hop growing contexts. I argue that this case example shows how hop
farmers' more collaborative stance with these material actors, what I call the
"stuff" of agriculture, incrementally destabilizes conventional agriculture's
input-driven power relationships and helps to make more just local agri-environmental futures possible. In the case of hops, I show how on-farm breeding,
as a human/material collaboration, produces the potential for incrementally
more sustainable, and therefore just, futures. Exploring both cases reveals how
environmental justice (EJ) scholarship and agricultural practice may benefit
from taking a more collaborative stance with the "stuff" that makes up agriculture and environments.

This inquiry responds to two open-ended questions: (1) (How) Do PGRs
along with the many materials and things involved in agriculture participate
as actors with agency in farming practices? And (2) How do human attitudes
toward these materials affect outcomes in large-scale agriculture? Exploring
these questions reconsiders the agency of the many things involved in agriculture
and how these things fill rural spaces with lively, contested social arrangements.
Drawing on assemblage-thinking approaches which identify materials as social
actors (Bennett 2010; Müller 2015; Roelvink 2015) I examine how "stuff," a
neologism I use to refer to the vast and diverse array of materials and organisms
in the agro-ecosystem, coproduces the social worlds of plant agriculture in the
Anthropocene. Using the case example of PGR treatment in each setting, I also
examine the degree to which "stuff" is constrained or freed by the social and
technological practices of these farming communities and the potential EJ outcomes of these practices.

As industrial-scale agriculture practices continue on a warming planet, it
is imperative that EJ scholars reconsider what democratic processes, on the
farm and in rural spaces, mean for the assemblages of people and things that
create and occupy rural places in the Anthropocene. These considerations
will have down-the-line consequences for environmental outcomes and for
human experiences of inequality. This paper argues that empirical social science research in environmental and agrifood contexts benefits from taking on
a collaborative and enlivened engagement with the more-than-human world.
Using the on-farm breeding programs of hop farmers as a contrasting case
example with corn and soy commodity agriculture, I show how farmers and
plants in this regime have marginally reduced chemical loads and significantly
increased local farm owner's profit and pricing power in the industry and therefore coproduced incrementally more just local environmental outcomes. This
imperfect, but more collaborative arrangement between the people and stuff
of agriculture demonstrates the potential for a generative transition toward a
better future.

Agriculture, the Anthropocene, and the "stuff" that makes both

Agriculture is a technique which involves the collaboration of human and non-human actors working toward particular environmental outcomes (Comi 2020). Socio-environmental research benefits from engagements that look beyond human action to understand the intersecting worlds of environmental problems. Environmental social science, and EJ scholarship in particular, has demonstrated that nonhumans are important participants in social landscapes (Bennett 2010; Carolan 2010; Catton 1980; Pellow 2017). EJ scholarship, like other environmental movements, embeds humans in a vast material network that precedes such activism or scholarship (Schlosberg and Coles 2016). This embeddedness delimits actors of all kinds, including humans, by clarifying their *sightedness* within, instead of above, the material flows which coproduce environmental outcomes, even in the human-driven context of the Anthropocene (Schlosberg 2016; Schlosberg and Craven 2019). Drawing on Schlosberg's emphasis on materials, I suggest that EJ scholarship and broader social science inquiry would benefit from a more robust inclusion of material actors in social science inquiry. EJ research has engaged meaningfully with human experiences of inequality stemming from, and causally impacting, environmental outcomes (Čapek 1993; Chiro 2008; Larkins 2018; Reed and George 2011). EJ has also taken on the inclusion of nonhumans, but as with much other environmental social science, EJ scholarship typically delimits agency or more-than-human status to animal actors (Bastian et al. 2017; Pellow 2017; Yarwood 2015). I mobilize assemblage-thinking approaches to show how material actors (e.g. soil, water, genetic material, chemicals, implements, etc.) may be studied as enlivened participants in social worlds and this may produce more democratic and inclusive outcomes in EJ and rural social science scholarship.

The tightly wound socio-material worlds of agriculture have been generatively studied as assemblages: processual networks between materials which can be observed in the relationships between actors (Müller 2015). Similarly to Schlosberg's notion that humans in the Anthropocene are limited by their *sightedness*, assemblages are a flat hierarchy, that operate as a flexible network of relationships (Bennett 2010; DeLanda 2016). Classes of materials, such as human or animal actors, do not exist above other materials, but within this vast, flat network of relationships. In the context of the human-driven Anthropocene, such assemblages reveal that human agency remains a function which is *distributed* between many material relationships within environments. Bennet's (2010) *vital materialism* suggests that socio-material relationships inform agency and power as not only a set of external relationships, but also a set of internal relationships: human bodies are themselves made up of many materials that inform many decisions that directly impact individual and community livelihoods. Social science inquiry, in this view, should see materials, however inert they may appear, as vital actors with agency in part of the large, flat network that makes up the environment in both local and global settings.

In the case of farming, one would study the socio-material world of the farm by considering how farmers, agronomists, seeds, implements, and soil (among many other materials) all interact with one another to coproduce the farm as an assemblage. In the case studies below, I focus on PGRs and how they relate to a variety of agricultural actors to produce diverging environmental outcomes stemming from the socio-material arrangements specific to each agricultural practice. Researchers who study agricultural and rural landscapes as relational assemblages have shown that such analyses are effective for better understanding the social–material interface for those populations who, like farmers, are uniquely responsible for land-use decisions and uniquely impacted by a wide range of environmental actors (Heley and Jones 2012; Legun 2015; Linke 2016). Put simply, a farmer's social world is uniquely co-constituted by climate, soil, weather, plants, and other materials and therefore understanding agriculture in the human-driven Anthropocene, ironically, hinges on understanding the diverse nonhuman social worlds on the farm. Research in this vein has the potential to reshape sociological discourse by more radically including a variety of material actors in the production and maintenance of social hierarchies and therefore in the analyses of environmental justice issues. Put simply, "stuff" participates in the making of power relationships as a collection of actors instead of as inert materials or tools.

I loosely categorize the wide array of materials that meaningfully act in agricultural assemblages as "stuff," a category which includes a variety of synthetics such as chemicals and implements, but also many organic units such as the PGRs often seen as a building block in eventual living plant material. Environmental movements and attention, including EJ, necessarily embed humans within the intricate material flows that produce environments (Schlosberg and Coles 2016). To explore this socio-material world I employ the broad neologism, "stuff," purposely to illustrate that, though an inquiry or example may be specific to one particular actor or material, one must keep in mind the tightly wound social relationships and flows that coproduce agri-environmental worlds. Put differently, while I explore PGRs and farmers as a case example, examining these two actors necessarily examines their embeddedness in a complex web of other materials: the "stuff"of farming.

By identifying the "stuff" of hops growing along with corn and soy agriculture practices in the United States, I draw out implications about the how the concept of the Anthropocene may be critically employed in assemblage-thinking scholarship and how this might better include nonhumans when studying (un) just transitions in the Anthropocene. This chapter considers PGRs as a comparative case example which reveals how human attitudes and local contexts shape environmental outcomes in the Anthropocene. PGRs refer to the genetic code contained in the material of a seed and the living plant it produces. It is both information technology and organic matter and while mutable, human control over PGRs following the green revolution has been a hallmark of the recent Anthropocene. In the following sections I explore how material and ontological changes about PGRs have variable outcomes depending on the many human and nonhuman actors involved in diverging agricultural practices. I comparatively examine how PGRs are mobilized in Midwestern corn/soy agriculture and Northwestern hops agriculture and draw insights about innovation in agricultural practices that remain possible in the Anthropocene and transitions toward a more sustainable future. While the Anthropocene is commonly used to refer to a global-scale shift where human activity dominates climatological outcomes (Crutzen 2002), EJ considerations in the Anthropocene are not just global in scale: how humans interact in local ecologies, especially agro-ecosystems reveals that human-centered attitudes and practices have local ecological and agricultural impacts. This chapter shows that anthropogenic change is observable on the genetic as well as climatic level. Modifying human attitudes toward specific materials, such as PGRs and the other "stuff" of agriculture has compounding socio-environmental impacts as these actors coproduce what is possible in farming practices. I use the following cases to describe the dominant treatment of PGRs in commodity agriculture exemplified in corn/soy agriculture followed by a contravening example exemplified by hop growers.

The "stuff" that makes a corn and soy farm

In the early twentieth century settler–colonial farms dotted much of the US landscape and were characterized by cash-crop economies that privileged grain and bean production, especially in the US Midwest. These farmers planted true-to-type seeds or propagated fruits and herbs with cuttings and grafts which were saved, shared, bought, and sold for reuse (Kloppenburg 1988). These farms were not intrinsically more *just* than contemporary agriculture, but were rather complex sociotechnical arrangements with contrasting outcomes: they were both family practices and colonial invasions depending on the theft of Indigenous lands; they were slow, and relatively adaptive, but they were also ecologically invasive and causally linked to significant negative agri-environmental outcomes (Hornbeck 2012). The transition to contemporary chemical agriculture began in the 1930s when the practice of planting first-generation hybrid corn seed became commonplace. This practice effectively required the annual purchasing of seed stock and it made seed and agrichemical production a profitable business in its own right instead of a farmer-driven enterprise.

Laboratories and test plots in land-grant universities and private companies began to produce new, more expensive hybrids and new fertilizers, pesticides, and herbicides to produce higher yield-per-acre on larger farms (Adams 2003; Goldschmidt 1978). This shift led to a series of now well-known legal changes made throughout the twentieth and early twenty-first centuries to the governance of genetically engineered (GE) seed stock (Aoki 2008). Because of landmark changes in the issuing of plant variety protection act (PVPA) certificates and utility patents, genetically engineered plants' genetic resources (PGRs) are legally protectable materials. These complex lineages of plants are now popularly considered static, ownable, and invented. This shift is integrally connected to the synthesis between chemicals and PGRs, most famously by Monsanto who first modified Corn PGRs to produce a resistance to the herbicide glyphosate (RoundUp™). Because Monsanto owned both the chemical and the PGR, two actors making up the "stuff" of this agricultural practice, the company was able to rigidly enroll these materials into a now commonplace agricultural assemblage known to limit farmer freedoms while coproducing deleterious local and global environmental outcomes.

While hybrid seed's genetic resources are legally considered fixed objects (Carolan 2010), research with those who sell these seeds to farmers reveals hybrids to be anything but static. Seed dealers are constantly engaged in the maintenance of on-farm systems which enable the continuation of hybrid commodity agriculture in the Midwest. Agronomists I spoke to sold for companies including Asgrow-Dekalb, Pioneer, Stine, and Channel. They live in the rural towns around which many of their clients farm and they often offer formal or informal on-farm consulting, or precision agriculture services in addition to their sales capacities. The meanings and assemblages surrounding genetically engineered PGRs are not maintained solely by the legal standing of patents and the material work of company labs. Rather these agronomists reproduce the onerous arrangement of Midwestern corn/soy agriculture: their work as consulting and sales agronomists involves continuously fixing the identity of active materials (PGRs and other "stuff") through their relationships with farmer clients (Comi 2019). According to one technical agronomists, David, corn and soy agriculture in the Midwest is a project of *systematic* techniques. Technical agronomists refer to their advisory capacity as being systematic thinkers for the farmers to which their companies are eventually selling seed and chemicals. Systematic thinking, I was told, is about producing a system of inputs and controls. For example, David considers PGRs as one part of a system including a fertilizer program that works in conjunction with a pesticide and herbicide program that also synchronizes with the particular PGR informing that hybrid's growth habit.

What lessons does this hold about the agency of things in such an agricultural regime? First, an ontological effort to fix the meaning of a seed does impact its materiality and its performance on the farm, but it does not negate the vibrancy of that thing. Bennet notes that even the most seemingly inert materials interact with others in a way which resists some meanings and enables others (Bennett 2010). For example, a hammer is a collection of materials that enables certain techniques while disabling or discouraging others. Assemblages like these self-stabilize their own relationships through the energetic relational inputs of their constituent actors (DeLanda 2016) and in this way assemblages are social worlds that resemble ecosystems (Morton 2016). Midwestern corn/soy agriculture requires material actors ("stuff") to persistently maintain specific relationships to other members in the farming assemblage. For such an assemblage to persist, even on a micro-level, hybrid seed stock's specific PGR must keep producing plant material that performs according to predicted ecological factors, and a collection of materials (agrochemicals) must be readily available to smooth out unpredictable outcomes like low fertility, high pest-load, etc. Further, human actors, agronomists, continue to discursively re-describe this system, helping to maintain the complex socio-environmental relationships of this practice by translating the meanings of seeds to those farmers who will plant them. This controlled, ploughed, farm alongside the controlled test-field settings where new hybrid seeds are developed, reproduces new material outcomes: the regeneration of such hybrid stock. The "stuff" of corn and soy agriculture may coproduce a farm that mimics a lab, but how would an agriculture of scale appear if farms were the location of innovation instead of the recipients of that innovation and what EJ lessons could be learned from examining such agricultures to encourage a more just Anthropocene?

The "stuff" that makes a hop farm

To respond to the above question, I turn to the unique practices of hop growers in the US Northwest. Hop farms in Yakima are unusual in the global hop-growing marketplace because of their large scale. This scale allows for a more robust comparison between these otherwise diverging agricultural techniques with vastly different approaches to innovation and PGRs. Comparing these case examples provides evidence that different material arrangements can result in different ontologies about environmental actors and, further, that the "stuff" of both agricultures, including PGRs, have significant agency in determining agri-environmental outcomes. In this case, seeing how hop farmers interact with plant genetics on their farms reveals differential outcomes for production, research, and the resulting plant material of the future. Put differently, within the wider context of the Anthropocene, different arrangements of the agricultural assemblage can produce more just outcomes even in the context of problematic, large-scale, industrial agriculture.

Hop bines are grown for their flowering strobili (what the industry refers to as "cones") which are used in beer production. Yakima hop producers are particularly well known for several proprietary varieties popular in the growing craft beer movement including Citra™, Simcoe™, and Amarillo™. The cones are harvested by cutting the bine in the field and taking the entire plant to a "picker" which is a large apparatus of mechanical arms, conveyer belts, and fans which separate the bines, shoots, and leaves from the hop-cone. Hop bines grown in the field are entirely female and are propagated from clonal root cuttings or tissue cultures. Hops, like many other agricultures, are an agriculture of control, where the various apparatuses are methods for maintaining and reproducing particular ecological outcomes. The most profitable hop farms are those which breed and own rights over desirable hop varieties. These farmers engage in an alternative biological marketplace of control and freedom with PGRs, but this marketplace is very different from the input- and yield-driven marketplace of corn and soy agriculture.

Hop farmers in Yakima have a unique relationship with PGRs. Unlike large commodity crops, genetic variation between hops is integral to the production and maintenance of particular flavors and aromas which are key considerations in the craft brewing industry which purchases a large amount of hops-per-barrel on average and is willing to pay a higher price for particular hops and lots within those varieties. For the hop farmers in Yakima who invested in breeding programs, and therefore have ownership stakes in the genetic resources of a popular varietal or group of varietals, the continuation and maintenance of these patents and their popularity with brewers is a key method for maintaining high profitability. Farmers I spoke to who are involved in breeding programs have extensive marketing and brewer outreach programs to produce interest in new varietals. For example, a new varietal Sabro™, is a unique cross between Yakima varieties and an uncommon wild hop bine from the American Southwest that the breeder/farmer was given by a friend a decade ago. Sabro has a unique flavor profile, a high alpha acid percentage (meaning greater antiseptic and bittering qualities) and is more heat hearty and drought tolerant than many previous varietals. Sabro™ is many things, but foremost it is an example of the intersecting agencies of plant material, human control, ecological factors, market demand, and incremental adjustments to changing environmental factors such as the high heat of summertime in Yakima.

The production of the hop varietal Sabr as a branded commodity is a collaborative technique, a work of both human intentionality and particular material agency involved in hop growth and the unpredictable crosses hops produce. Sabro comes to exist, by simplest explanation, by a human who crosses two genetic lineages. But to examine the entirety of that process, and the many participants involved in making these two lineages, the soil, climate, chemicals, and water that control the current hop-growing environment in Yakima, the many humans involved in making and maintaining Yakima's vast irrigation system, quickly distributes the responsibility among a variety of materials and people. This reveals what Schlosberg calls *sightedness*, but it also reveals that the materials that *make* agro-ecosystems, the "stuff" of hop agriculture, are directly and relationally involved in the co-production of Sabro as a PGR, an assemblage in which Sabro then participates by influencing and producing particular plant material in a given environmental assemblage.

These flat assemblages do still connect to human organizational apparatuses: YCH and Haas Inc. jointly own the rights to Sabro™ genetics and they are able to control profits by licensing only particular farms to grow the variety. While this program is based in problematic, profit-driven structures of control, the farmer-driven origins of hop breeding programs still produce a materiality that is more inclusive of the many ecological things involved in agriculture and this influences outcomes. For example, Sabro is bred on farms in the dry Yakima valley and it is reported that Sabro is incrementally more heat tolerant and requires lower chemical applications than many other varieties commonly produced in Yakima. This is not a perfectly just outcome, but it shows how materials are involved in social and environmental outcomes. Further, it shows how incorporating a study of the agency of things into EJ research offers unique insights into what pathways are possible for more environmentally just futures. This consideration leads to many novel questions integral to considerations of just transitions such as: What could Sabro and other farmer driven plants look like if they were bred in a program with more sustainable outcomes as a key goal? How could the incremental gains of these materials be more democratically shared? Rethinking materials and their involvements is both generative and necessary for more just transitions in the Anthropocene.

Seeds, plants, and localities in the Anthropocene: directions forward

These two case examples of Midwestern commodity agriculture and Northwestern specialty crop production reflect alternative assemblages by which farming is done and local environmental futures are (re)produced. The material flows of nonhumans in corn/soy agriculture are subject to rigorous controls both legally and in the obscured breeding process. Alternatively, the more open and collaborative breeding techniques in hop growing are more inclusive of many agri-ecosystem actors and the relational influence of this "stuff" impacts environmental outcomes. Comparatively examining both demonstrates the value of considering a more enlivened group of actors in the assemblage of agriculture. Both classes of farmers are motivated by financial stability and long-term profits, but in the latter case one engages with the environment and produces incrementally more adaptive and sustainable outcomes due to the differing material relationships. Put differently, looking to PGRs as actors in farming, we see that key differences between these two agricultural practices are actually coproduced results of unique demands of particular plants, and the ontologies that markets, buyers, and farmers all have in relation to the production of those plant and new varietals. Environmentally just futures in Yakima and in the US Midwest need to consider the many human intersections where inequality occurs, but they also ought to consider the inequalities and experiences of nonhuman actors involved in these assemblages. Not simply because this reflects a democratic approach in the widest sense, but also because free spaces help coproduce other free spaces, and the recognition of vibrant nonhuman actors down-the-line has the potential to better recognize and produce just outcomes for the many human actors involved in shared ecologies, be they agricultural or otherwise.

The relationship of PGRs in the particular practices of a farm represent an ontological–material relationship in the most micro-sense. While both hop farmers alongside corn and soy farmers seem to behave in anthropocentric ways, hop farmers reveal a more collaborative stance that sees local ecosystems as coproducers of the "stuff" that makes up hop farms, and if that "stuff" produces a profitable hop bine that makes pesticides less important, then that translates into greater financial and environmental sustainability. Conversely, corn/soy agriculture produces a tightly controlled system which can be translated to many different ecosystems, though this translation may result in long-term sustainability. These local practices of farmers reveal how the overarching logic of the Anthropocene is not only a macro-consideration of the earth system but a micro-consideration of local agroecosystems and the stuff which coproduces such systems.

The vibrant biological marketplace of hop genetics, while imperfect, reveals that robust farmer input into PGRs yields profitable and incrementally more environmentally just results in the Anthropocene. While onerous controls over plant-genetics do not equate to crimes against humans, the onerous controls on PGRs and the ontologies of control which arise from these material relations have rebounding impacts which affect outcomes for farmers. Hop growers show us that collaborative stances toward the "stuff" agriculture, including PGRs, can free these material actors and this more mobile material can help coproduce more sustainable outcomes. From an EJ perspective, just transitions can be encouraged by considering how human control over materials may be loosened. Such a notion confronts the logics that underly the Anthropocene, by asking humans scholars and practitioners to consider the agency instead of only the existence of other things. Beyond agricultural systems, this approach suggests that just transitions in the Anthropocene more generally hinge on the recognition of "stuff" as vital members of socio-environmental worlds. The "stuff" that makes up environments and the many socio-material relationships between people and this "stuff" are the arrangements by which new environmental futures will be co-constructed. Finding those just transitions within (or out of) the Anthropocene requires recognition and inclusion of the materials, animals, or plants involved in those same ecologies.

Acknowledgments

Part of this chapter is based on research supported by the National Science Foundation's Science, Technology and Society Program (NSF #1946941).

References

Adams, J. (Ed.), 2003. *Fighting for the Farm: Rural America Transformed.* University of Pennsylvania Press, Philadelphia, PA.

Aoki, K., 2008. *Seed Wars.* Carolina Academic Press, Durham, NC.

Bastian, M., Jones, O., Moore, N., Roe, E. (Eds.), 2017. *Participatory Research in More-Than-Human Worlds, Routledge Studies in Human Geography.* Routledge, Taylor & Francis Group, London.

Bennett, J., 2010. *Vibrant Matter : A Political Ecology of Things.* Duke University Press, Durham, NC.

Boening, R.M., 1919. History of Irrigation in the State of Washington: The State Epoch of Canal Building. *The Washington Historical Quarterly* 10, 21–45.

Čapek, S.M., 1993. The "Environmental Justice" Frame: A Conceptual Discussion and an Application. *Social Problems* 40, 5–24. https://doi.org/10.2307/3097023

Carolan, M., 2010. The Mutability of Biotechnology Patents: From Unwieldy Products of Nature to Independent "Object/s". *Theory, Culture & Society* 27, 110–129. https://doi.org/10.1177/0263276409350360

Catton, W.R., 1980. *Overshoot, the Ecological Basis of Revolutionary Change*. University of Illinois Press, Urbana.

Chiro, G.D., 2008. Living Environmentalisms: Coalition Politics, Social Reproduction, and Environmental Justice. *Environmental Politics* 17, 276–298. https://doi.org/10.1 080/09644010801936230

Comi, M., 2019. 'The Right Hybrid for Every Acre': Assembling the Social Worlds of Corn and Soy Seed-Selling in Conventional Agricultural Techniques. *Sociologia Ruralis* 59, 159–176. https://doi.org/10.1111/soru.12227

Comi, M., 2020. The Distributed Farmer: Rethinking US Midwestern Precision Agriculture Techniques. *Environmental Sociology* 1–13. https://doi.org/10.1080/2 3251042.2020.1794426

Crutzen, P.J., 2002. The Anthropocene: Geology of Mankind. *Nature* 415, 23.

DeLanda, M., 2016. *Assemblage Theory*. Edinburgh University Press, Edinburgh.

Goldschmidt, W., 1913–2010, 1978. *As You Sow*. Allanhead, Osmun, and Co., Montclair, NJ.

Heley, J., Jones, L., 2012. Relational Rurals: Some Thoughts on Relating Things and Theory in Rural Studies. *Journal of Rural Studies* 28, 208–217. https://doi.org/10.1016 /j.jrurstud.2012.01.011

Hornbeck, R., 2012. The Enduring Impact of the American Dust Bowl: Short- and Long-Run Adjustments to Environmental Catastrophe. *American Economic Review* 102, 1477–1507. https://doi.org/10.1257/aer.102.4.1477

Kloppenburg, J., 1988. *First The Seed: The Political Economy of Plant Biotechnology*. Cambridge University Press, New York.

Larkins, M.L., 2018. Complicating Communities: An Intersectional Approach to Women's Environmental Justice Narratives in the Rocky Mountain West. *Environmental Sociology* 4, 67–78. https://doi.org/10.1080/23251042.2017.1423011

Legun, K., 2015. Tiny Trees for Trendy Produce: Dwarfing Technologies as Assemblage Actors in Orchard Economies. *Geoforum* 65, 314–322. https://doi.org/10.1016/j.geof orum.2015.03.009

Linke, J., 2016. Re-Shaping "Soft Gold:" Fungal Agency and the Bioeconomy in The Caterpillar Fungus Market Assemblage. In: Heron, R.C.Hugh, Lewis, Nick, Carolan, Michael (Eds.), *Biological Economies*. Routledge, New York, 51–66.

Morton, T., 2016. *Dark Ecology: For a Logic of Future Coexistence, Wellek Library Lectures in Critical Theory*. Columbia University Press, New York.

Müller, M., 2015. Assemblages and Actor-Networks: Rethinking Socio-Material Power, Politics and Space. *Geography Compass* 9, 27–41.

Pellow, D.N., 2017. *What Is Critical Environmental Justice?* Polity Press, Newark.

Reed, M.G., George, C., 2011. Where in the World Is Environmental Justice? *Progress in Human Geography* 35, 835–842. https://doi.org/10.1177/0309132510388384

Roelvink, G., 2015. Performing Posthumanist Economies in The Anthropocene. In: Roelvink, G., St. Martin, K., Gibson-Graham, J.K. (Eds.), *Making Other Worlds Possible: Performing Diverse Economies*. University of Minnesota Press, Minneapolis.

Schlosberg, D., 2016. Environmental Management in the Anthropocene [WWW Document]. *The Oxford Handbook of Environmental Political Theory*. https://doi.org/10 .1093/oxfordhb/9780199685271.013.32

Schlosberg, D., Coles, R., 2016. The New Environmentalism of Everyday Life: Sustainability, Material Flows and Movements. *Contemp Polit Theory* 15, 160–181. https://doi.org/10.1057/cpt.2015.34

Schlosberg, D., Craven, L., 2019. *Sustainable Materialism: Environmental Movements and the Politics of Everyday Life*. Oxford University Press, Oxford.

Yarwood, R., 2015. Lost and Hound: The More-Than-Human Networks of Rural Policing. *Journal of Rural Studies* 39, 278–286. https://doi.org/10.1016/j.jrurstud.20 14.11.005

18

"TO HAVE A GARDEN IS AGAINST THIS SYSTEM"

The revolutionary subjectivity of convivial labor for home kitchen gardeners in San José, CA

Gabriel Valle

Introduction

The global coronavirus pandemic has illustrated the distinctive nature of uncertainty associated with life in the Anthropocene, but the global changes and cognitive shifts associated with uncertainty have differential impacts. This important topic has received little attention in the context of Anthropocene scholarship (Moore 2016, 2017). While the new norms of life in the Anthropocene may encourage a placeless, timeless world where individuals appear to be always at odds against their own existence, the so-called marginals make use of uncertainty to forge revolutionary subjectivities that enable new ways of being, seeing, and interacting with each other in the search for more just and sustainable worlds. In this chapter, I describe how a group of low-income and recent immigrant gardeners, those who are often more exposed and vulnerable to the uncertainty of life in the Anthropocene, cultivate new subjectivities that forge alternative pathways toward justice and reconfigure social interaction to better their quality of life.

This study began in the fall of 2012. Members of a San José, CA-based urban agriculture program called *La Mesa Verde* (LMV), which is a branch of Sacred Heart Community Services, invited me to co-produce a Community-Based Research (CBR) study with them. I worked in collaboration with the community of urban gardeners who were co-producers in the research objectives and design and helped to forge "research from, by, and with the margins" (Brown and Strega 2005). LMV is an urban agriculture program but differs from most urban agriculture or community garden programs because they do not have a "community garden" in the traditional sense (e.g., Kurtz 2001; Pudup 2008). Instead, they cultivate home–kitchen gardens in the back, front, side, or rooftop of individual family homes. Many LMV gardeners are recent immigrants from rural Mexico, Central and South America, as well as Southeast Asia and the Philippines. The neoliberal restructuring of the global South has ushered in a new era of diaspora immigrants from around the world who have tremendous traditional environmental and agroecological knowledge (McCune et al. 2017; Olsson 2017). As such, the urban cores of many cities in the global North have become repositories of self-provisioning knowledge. This multi-ethnic, multi-lingual group of gardeners ranges between traditional healers (or *curanderos*) and urban homesteaders who move beyond challenging the hegemonic industrial food system by fostering spaces of autonomy that allow for self- and communal-determination. Donna Haraway refers to this type of communal worldmaking as "sympoietic" (2016, p. 36) in nature. Through collective creation this group of home–kitchen gardeners create hybrid natures and multi-species communities within the city by making use of edges and marginality (also see Tsing 2015; Larmer 2016). This chapter highlights the transformative potential of garden subjectivities and the role of convivial labor in creating different modes of state intervention where cooperation and resistance are not rooted in the shared fate of others, but in the self-determination and self-constitution of community. These cultivated subjectivities reveal a "revolutionary subjectivity" as a non-compliant, defiant, innovative, community-oriented, subject (Negri 1991), which is a central part of the food–health nexus.

The gardens articulated here are "enacted spaces" (Rojas 1991) because they send a message of cooperation and resistance that hinges on relationships of trust. I argue that home–kitchen gardeners engage in "convivial labor" (Valle 2016), or labor as a form of cooperation and resistance, to address food insecurity, environmental injustice, and economic uncertainty. Convivial labor is the celebration of life in all its manifestations, and those who enact it, retool themselves to transform their worlds. This chapter draws upon the experiences of *La Mesa Verde* home–kitchen gardeners to demonstrate how the ability to grow food plays a vital role in the just transition to life in the Anthropocene by constructing a garden subjectivity that challenges the capitalist ordering of the world.

Convivial labor in the Anthropocene

The Anthropocene epoch situates human and non-human existence at the convergence of both an environmental and epistemological violence (Bryant 2011; Nixon 2011). Many marginalized populations are marked for erasure, and in some cases, an early death (see Pellow 2016). *La Mesa Verde* gardeners resist erasure and death through convivial labor. Their resistance is not just about the erasure or death of the human experience, but the erasure or death of the more-than-human worlds they inhabit. These home–kitchen gardens are assemblages of human and non-human agents and processes that hold together the biocultural fabric of the community (Callon 2007; Roelvink 2015). The continued practice of traditional agroecological knowledge ensures the continuity of cultural traditions and farming techniques that enable biological, cultural, and epistemological diversity. The inherently communal practice of convivial labor is a celebration of all our relationships, and it reminds us of our responsibility and indispensability of these elusive, clandestine, and even sacred spaces and actions.

Climate change occupies an unusual position in the human imagination. It exists as a "placeless place" because it is both an unreal utopia as my actions in one place may affect others in a different place utterly unknown to me, and it is also a heterotopia because climate change makes the place I occupy at the moment all the more real and connected to other places and times. Foucault referred to our current epoch as "the epoch of juxtaposition, the epoch of the near and far, of the side-by-side, of the dispersed" (1986, p. 22). The mythic and the real exist in juxtaposition in the Anthropocene, which makes climate change arduous to comprehend. The projections of climate change are so staggering that they have to be mythic, but the consequences of not addressing the effects of climate change have real effects that we can see and feel (as demonstrated by the 2019–20 Australian bush fires).

> The human-driven changes to the global environment will, at least, require societies to develop a multitude of creative responses and adaptation strategies. At worst, they may drive the Earth itself into a different state that may be much less hospitable to humans and other forms of life.
>
> *(Steffen et al. 2006, p. 299)*

The current epoch situates humans as both biological and geological agents, which forces us to contemplate how to make sense of this new world, and to question what new tools or "other spaces" may emerge to reinvent justice.

For the past several decades, environmental justice scholars have used social justice approaches to forge theories and social movements (e.g. Faber 1998; Agyeman, Bullard, and Evans 2003; Agyeman 2005; Bullard 2005; Schlosberg 2007). While this has generated large-scale social movements, policy proposals, and governmental laws that challenge environmental racism, the conditions imposed upon us today as the result of anthropogenic climate change will force different and innovative forms of resistance *and* cooperation. The convivial labor deployed by gardeners in this chapter challenges the drivers of social and ecological destruction by confronting gardener's relationships with the system of capitalism. Capitalism organizes nature in such a way that exclusion becomes the norm (Moore 2016). Under conditions of exclusion, everything and anything – land, water, air, food, bodies – are disconnected from the web of life and become commodities sold for a price.

One answer to the ideology of disconnection is relationality. As explained by Shawn Wilson, "Rather than viewing ourselves as being *in* relationship with other people or things, we *are* the relationships that we hold and are part of" (2008, p. 80). Rather than seeing oneself as an isolated individual who exists *in* relation to other people and places, we *are* mothers, fathers, sons, daughters, friends, neighbors, and we *are* from places. This worldview puts things into orientation and explains how individuals hold these relationships together. Convivial labor, similar to Illich's "tools of conviviality" (1973), works in a very similar manner because it exists in direct opposition to the ideology of disconnection of industrial capitalism and does not succumb to the same logic and norms of consumption, competition, progress, and development. Convivial labor exists prior to the emergence of alienated labor whereby capitalism produced workers made to feel foreign and removed from the products of their own labor. Tools of conviviality "are those which give each person who uses them the greatest opportunity to enrich the environment with the fruits of his own vision" (Illich 1973, p. 21). In a sense, convivial labor is enabled by the capabilities approach of social justice (Schlosberg 2007). Gardeners move beyond thinking about justice in distributive terms (i.e. equal allocation of resources) and begin enacting justice in ways influenced by collective wellbeing. LMV gardeners provide us with the context to understand how conviviality can inform the norms of a community and enrich their environment with their own vision while also holding each other accountable to their social relationships.

Cooperation: (re)learning how to trust

On a fall afternoon in 2013, an LMV gardener walked me through his garden and explained,

> Your garden is a reminder of how to live well. It's a reminder of your surroundings. Every day you greet the plants. When you share the food from your garden, you greet your family, your friends, your community. You greet life.

Greeting your garden is part of a garden subjectivity that embraces the relationships of food, family, and the human and nonhuman communities we are a part of – maintaining accountability to these relationships informs one how to live well. Growing food for family, friends, and community challenges the logic of "cheap nature" (Moore 2016) because such a garden subjectivity is rooted in the continuity of culture, tradition, and livelihoods that can only exist with awareness and accountability to our relationship with things, people, and places.

Traditional environmental knowledge (TEK) is "a cumulative body of knowledge, practice, and belief, evolving by adaptive processes and handed down through generation by cultural transmissions" (Berkes et al. 2000, p. 1252). When gardeners share traditional knowledge of how to cultivate a crop, especially an heirloom or landrace variety, they are ensuring both the continuity of agrobiodiversity and the ancestral knowledge of how to care for and nurture the crop. While many LMV members are new to gardening, many were also raised on farms and received traditional knowledge passed down from their elders. LMV provides the spaces needed to continue to pass that knowledge to the next generation. By sharing meals and recipes, gardeners are ensuring the longevity of heritage cuisines for healthy people and cultures. The convivial labor of sharing in these home–kitchen gardens encourages the continuity of traditional environmental and agroecological knowledge in the form of cultivation techniques (e.g., crop rotation, seed saving, watering) and self-provisioning (e.g., recipes, medicinal herbs, culinary techniques).

La Mesa Verde began as a simple gardening program in 2009. The goal was to create as many urban gardeners as possible to help alleviate the stresses of living in a food desert. The organization gives seeds, seedlings, and garden workshops to participating low-income families who expressed interest in learning how to grow their own food. In 2009, most of the LMV community lived in Washington-Alma, a small, predominately Latino immigrant neighborhood located just south of downtown San José, CA. Without a supermarket within walking distance, the community has been referred to as a food desert, and many living there without cars are forced to walk to nearby liquor stores and convenience marts for their daily supply of fruit and vegetables. These sorts of systemic inequalities are part of a broader pattern of environmental racism commonly found in the design of many cities. The overpriced and nutrient-deficient foods in these locations placed an amplifying burden on a community already seen as "expendable." Similar spaces of neoliberal neglect exist in countless cities across the world (see Davis 2006). The goal of the LMV program in 2009 was to provide a resource to the community that would improve self-sufficiency and reduce the need and reliance on convenience markets and food banks while also saving money.

Over time, the LMV community would learn to utilize pre-established workshops, cooking demonstrations, training, and advisory meetings to construct spaces of autonomy built on the practice of trust. The community would use the spaces provided at LMV events to resist erasure and continue the intergenerational sharing of traditional knowledge. As one gardener told me on a fall evening in 2013, "This program teaches us how to trust again." She did not mean that workshops, cooking demos, training, and advisory meetings were about learning to trust each other. Instead, how the act of gardening *in collaboration with others* provides opportunities to learn (and relearn) how to trust. This learning and relearning is part of a garden subjectivity that arises when people recognize their relationships with others. What this group understands and practices, is that autonomy is not a far-right, individualist, libertarian, "don't bother me" ideology, nor is it an idealized free from state censorship utopia. For LMV gardeners, the autonomy they cultivate is a delicate balance held together through relational accountability, not individual rights. In the gardens of LMV, this collective responsibility is carefully assembled through the practice of convivial labor.

New alliances of cooperation arise through convivial labor because they tend to contribute to what Gibson-Graham call "community economies" (2006), which can take on endless forms. Such spaces are perfect opportunities to envision and practice the "collective experimentation" (Latour 2004) of alternative food networks, and LMV is just one example of a trend that is occurring in places around the globe (e.g., Mougeot 2005; Wittman et al. 2010). By cultivating home–kitchen gardens, the LMV community is not asking for food justice or demanding more supermarkets in their communities; they are simply *doing justice*. They are not asking for recognition or saying "we exist, we matter," because they know they already exist, and they know they matter. Enacting justice strengthens their relationships with each other. Convivial labor establishes social norms that are part of a "knowledge-practice-belief-complex" (Berkes 1999) that are a source of right livelihoods and not "capital" (Valle 2016). Knowledge of how to grow food for the community produces practices that respect human and nonhuman sympoietic relationships, which then produce beliefs of how to live well. This reoccurring cycle generates new knowledge that enables ways of living that restructure the capitalist ordering of nature.

Framing their world through moral values allows gardeners to distance their engagements as acts of cultural capital, which is a concept informed by the logics of neoliberalism (Spies-Butcher 2002, 2003), and root them in the cultural norms of the community. Reintegrating conviviality and cooperation as a cultural practice of the community enables gardeners to confront the uncertainty of life in the Anthropocene by operating through moral values, and it may allow us to "remake our place in nature in a way that promises emancipation for all life" (Moore 2016, p. 114).

A defining aspect of convivial labor is cooperation. While LMV gardeners grow food and herbs in individual family homes, they do not rationalize their efforts as individual efforts. Their gardens enable the infrastructure of the commons, or are a "way of commoning" (Petrescu 2013, p. 267). LMV gardeners disrupt the very foundation of "private property" because it is through private property that gives them access to the common (also see Lang 2014). As a 35-year-old Chicano LMV gardener told me in the summer of 2014, "I don't like to wait on the government for anything. If I can do it myself, I will." At face value, this statement appears to represent the neoliberal ideology of self-help, whereby the government skirts accountability and places the burden of health and nutrition on individuals. As he explained to me, "Everyone in my neighborhood grows different things, and when we can, we share ... We're all just trying to survive." A closer look reveals a complex garden subjectivity that is held together through relational accountability. "Growing food doesn't complicate things; it simplifies them. It's the small things that matter ... you know, water, sun, soil, space, community, [and] life." For these gardeners, growing food offers opportunities to denaturalizes assumptions about the way things are by recognizing alternative ways of living that are not based on economic transactions and are rooted in our relationships with others (see Roelvink et al. 2015).

Organizations and social movements like LMV are more crucial than ever in our current world because of the diversity of ways growing food offers "escapes" from the capitalist ordering of nature (Valle 2016). When LMV gardeners plant an heirloom seed passed down from their ancestors, they are doing far more than planting a seed or "growing a garden." They are participating in the continuity of culture, knowledge, language, and even agrobiodiversity that is often marked for erasure.

At a recent LMV meeting, I sat with a group of English and Spanish speaking gardeners. I listened to them as they discussed why they continued to return to the LMV community year after year. While there are various reasons for members to remain in the program, the word that continued to surface was community. As one woman explained, "We could be anywhere right now, but we want to grow food, heal ourselves, our families, and our communities … [and we want to] be around others who also want to … *You're not just on your own here*." These comments resonate with a garden subjectivity that recognizes cooperation and conviviality as a social norm that informs community (*inter*)action. Such a norm allows gardeners to define and articulate their own situation based on the reframing of something as simple as the value of food.

Resistance: a labor of change

In 2014, a focus group of Spanish speaking gardeners discussed why they grow and share food. It was a small group made up of mostly females, many of whom had brought their children to the event and were seated with us at the table. As the conversation developed, one woman explained how growing food is about raising consciousness. Sharing their knowledge amongst each other and then spreading that knowledge on to their children, husbands, or neighbors is an essential aspect of LMV's cooperative resistance. "*Para tener una jardín es contra esta sistema* [to have a garden is against this system]," she explained. This profound garden subjectivity resonates with the understanding that something as simple as a vegetable garden in one's backyard has tremendous transformative potential.

La Mesa Verde gardeners are against "this system" because these gardens provide people affordable access to healthy food, and in the process, they reject overpriced processed foods. Gardens can restore relationships with food and the places people inhabit by connecting gardeners to the seasons and disrupting the capitalist ordering of the global food system. Gardeners also restore and reinvent the cultural practices of healing (also see Peña et al. 2017). Very similar to how Shava et al. (2010) argue that new immigrants revive traditional knowledge in New York City community gardens, new immigrants at LMV revived cultural norms of conviviality, trust, and sharing. By carrying forward key elements of subjectivities rooted in Mexican social history, LMV gardeners transform existing and create new forms of social relations anchored by food and eating that are part of their food geographies and knowledges of their dislocations.

Home–kitchen gardeners create "autotopographies" (Mares and Peña 2010, 2011), or places transformed by identity, history, and sense of place, that are clear examples of how knowledge is mobile and how people make practical uses of the tools and knowledge they have access to as a means to better their worlds. The sharing of traditional meals is not a simple act and should not go unnoticed because it roots one deep into the cultural and geographical history of a place. As explained by Nabhan et al., "recovering these species and restoring them to their 'rightful place' in the landscape is therefore seen as a spiritual and moral imperative" (2016, pp. 158–159). Traditional knowledge is very much alive, and when a community enacts "gardens of sabotage" (Valle 2015) against "this system," they are restoring and renewing their relationships with each other and with the land. As one gardener informed me on a bright San José afternoon in 2014, "My spirit lives in this garden, and I hope that I can pass it along to my neighbors and friends."

Conclusion

The gardeners in this chapter reveal a way of living that exists in sharp contrast to the hyper-individualism normalized in contemporary society. Fears about an uncertain future exposes a worldview comprised of rational egoists driven by cost–benefit analysis. Yet, despite current leadership of some prominent countries who are driven seemingly by self-interest, these remain not the norm but the exception. Throughout history, people have overcome adversity not as individuals, but as communities. LMV gardeners prompt us to consider how the relational approach of convivial labor may encourage a more just transition to alternative futures in the Anthropocene.

In this essay, I have argued that while the norms of life in the Anthropocene may encourage a lifestyle at odds against the very ecosystem services life depends on, the convivial labor practices of growing, sharing, and consuming food together allow gardeners to challenge the capitalist ordering of the world and to re-situate themselves, their families, and their communities in ways that matter. Throughout this chapter, I attempted to avoid the trap of the "suffering subject" by engaging in an "anthropology of good" (Robins 2013), which highlights how people imagine better worlds and how they work to enact them. The birth of the Anthropocene means goodbye to the relative stability of the Holocene, and hello to unpredictability and uncertainty (Davies 2016). Yet, the changing climate has always been a major catalyst for new opportunities. As the abrupt, and even violent social, economic, and environmental shifts disrupt local ecosystems and communities, new ways of living emerge. The "new normal" ushered in by the COVID-19 global pandemic makes it certain that our relational ties remain essential for working outside already existing social and economic systems, a much-needed move for more just transitions to life in the Anthropocene (Pellow 2018). This does not mean people "give up" or sit back and wait for a technological fix. Instead, this chapter shows how convivial labor challenges the alienating aspects of capitalism by celebrating our relationships we hold together with our food, communities, environments, and families.

An LMV gardener once told me, "The garden is the carrot. Once people get hooked, they're in it for life." While she was referring to the capacity building gardening encourages, it is also important to acknowledge the underlying neoliberal aspects of the "carrot and the stick" metaphor whereby urban agriculture creates a particular type of citizen–subject who succumbs to neoliberal logics (Pudup 2008). This is part of the contradictions inherent in urban agriculture and what makes this movement both radical and neoliberal (McClintock 2014). But groups like LMV overcome this contradiction by creating different models of state intervention to enact justice (Pellow, 2018). A garden is not an endpoint, but a means to an end; and as we transition to more just and sustainable futures in the Anthropocene, we must continue to remake systems and institutions that foster wellbeing and conviviality. Every day, gardeners around the world are finding new opportunities to share and celebrate the act of growing food (Winne 2010). We have even seen an increase in the availability of vegetables, fruit, and grain varieties in North America in the past years all because people are beginning to understand the importance of growing food (Nabhan 2016). The exciting thing about gardening is that it always "finds people where they are at," as a gardener told me, and in the process, it allows the opportunity for gardeners to enact their own version of liberation.

References

Agyeman, J. (2005) *Sustainable Communities and the Challenge of Environmental Studies*. New York: New York University Press.

Agyeman, J., Bullard, R. and Evans, B. (eds.) (2003) *Just Sustainabilities: Development in an Unequal World*. Boston: MIT Press.

Berkes, F. (1999) *Sacred Ecology: Traditional Ecological Knowledge and Resource Management*. Philadelphia: Taylor & Francis.

Berkes, F., Colding, J. and Folke, C. (2000) 'Rediscovery of Traditional Ecological Knowledge as Adaptive Management', *Ecological Applications*, 10(5), 1251–1262.

Brown, L. and Strega, S. (eds.) (2005) *Research as Resistance: Critical, Indigenous and Anti-Oppressive Approaches*. Toronto: Canadian Scholars' Press.

Bryant, B. (ed.) (2011) *Environmental Crisis: Working for Sustainable Knowledge and Environmental Justice*. New York: Morgan James Publishing.

Bullard, R. (ed.) (2005) *The Quest for Environmental Justice: Human Rights and the Politics of Pollution*. San Francisco: Sierra Club Books.

Callon, M. (2007) 'What Does It Mean to Say That Economics Is Performative?', in MacKenzie, D., Muniesa, F. and Sui, L. (eds.) *Do Economists Make Markets?* Princeton: Princeton University Press, 311–357.

Davies, J. (2016) *The Birth of the Anthropocene*. Berkeley: University of California Press.

Davis, M. (2006) *City of Quartz: Excavating the Future of Los Angeles*. 2nd Edition. New York: Verso.

Faber, D. (ed.) (1998) *The Struggle for Ecological Democracy: Environmental Justice Movements in the United States*. New York: Guilford Press.

Foucault, M. (1986) 'Of Other Spaces', *Diacritics*, 16(1), 22–27.

Gibson-Graham, J.K. (2006) *A Postcapitalist Politics*. Minneapolis: University of Minnesota Press.

Haraway, D.J. (2016) 'Staying with the Trouble: Anthropocene, Capitalocene, Chthulucene', in Moore, J.W. (ed.) *Anthropocene or Capitalocene? Nature, History, and the Crisis of Capitalism*. Oakland: PM Press, 34–76.

Illich, I. (1973) *Tools for Conviviality*. New York: Harper & Row.

Kurtz, H. (2001) 'Differentiating Multiple Meanings of Garden and Community', *Urban Geography*, 22(7), 656–670.

Lang, U. (2014) 'The Common Life of Yards', *Urban Geography*, 35(6), 852–869.

Larmer, M. (2016) 'Cultivating the Edge: An Ethnography of-First-Generation Women Farmers in the American Midwest', *Feminist Review*, 114(1), 91–111.

Latour, B. (2004) *Politics of Nature: How to Bring the Sciences into Democracy.* Cambridge: Harvard University Press.

Mares, T. and Peña, D.G. (2010) 'Urban Agriculture in the Making of Insurgent Spaces in Los Angeles and Seattle', in Hou, J. (ed.) *Insurgent Public Space: Guerrilla Urbanism and the Remaking of Contemporary Cities.* New York: Routledge, 253–267.

Mares, T. and Peña, D.G. (2011) 'Environmental and Food Justice: Toward Local, Slow, and Deep Food Systems', in Alkon, A.H. and Agyeman, J. (eds.) *Cultivating Food Justice: Race, Class, and Sustainability.* Cambridge: MIT Press, 197–219.

McClintock, N. (2014) 'Radical, Reformist, and Garden-variety Neoliberal: Coming to Terms with Urban Agriculture's Contradictions', *Local Environment*, 19(2), 147–171.

McCune, N., Rosset, P.M., Salazar, T.C., Morales, H. and Moreno, A.S. (2017) 'The Long Road: Rural Youth, Farming and Agroecological *Formación* in Central America', *Mind, Culture, and Activity*, 24(3), 183–198.

Moore, J.W. (ed.) (2016) *Anthropocene or Capitalocene? Nature, History, and the Crisis of Capitalism.* Oakland: PM Press.

Moore, J.W. (2017) 'The Capitalocene, Part I: On the Nature and Origins of our Ecological Crisis', *The Journal of Peasant Studies*, 44(3), 594–630.

Mougeot, L.J.A., (ed.) (2005) *Agropolis: The Social, Political, and Environmental Dimensions of Urban Agriculture.* Sterling: Earthscan.

Nabhan, G.P. (ed.) (2016) *Ethnobiology for the Future: Linking Cultural and Ecological Diversity.* Tucson: University of Arizona Press.

Nabhan, G.P., Walker, D. and Moreno, A.M. (2016) 'Biocultural and Ecogastronomic Restoration', in Nabhan, G.P. (ed.) *Ethnobiology for the Future: Linking Cultural and Ecological Diversity.* Tucson, AZ: University of Arizona Press, 156–183.

Negri, A. (1991) *Marx Beyond Marx: Lessons on the Grundrisse.* Brooklyn: Autonomedia.

Nixon, R. (2011) *Slow Violence and the Environmentalism of the Poor.* Cambridge: University of Harvard Press.

Olsson, T.C. (2017) *Agrarian Crossings: Reformers and the Remaking of the Mexican Countryside.* Princeton: Princeton University Press.

Pellow, D.N. (2016) 'Toward a Critical Environmental Justice Studies: Black Lives Matter as an Environmental Justice Challenge', *Du Bois Review*, 13(2), 221–236.

Pellow, D.N. (2018) *What Is Critical Environmental Justice?* Medford, MA: Polity Press.

Peña, D.G., Calvo, L., McFarland, P. and Valle, G.R. (eds.) (2017) *Mexican-Origin Foods, Foodways, and Social Movements: A Decolonial Reader.* Fayetteville: University of Arkansas Press.

Petrescu, D. (2013) 'Gardeners of Commons, for the Most Part Women', in Rawes, P. (ed.) *Relational Architectural Ecologies: Architecture, Nature, and Subjectivity.* New York: Routledge, 261–274.

Pudup, M.B. (2008) 'It Takes a Garden: Cultivating Citizen-Subjects in Organized Garden Projects', *Geoforum*, 39(3), 1228–1240.

Robbins, J. (2013) 'Beyond the Suffering Subject: Toward an Anthropology of the Good', *Journal of the Royal Anthropological Institute*, 19(3), 447–462.

Roelvink, Gerda. (2015) 'Performing Posthumanist Economies in the Anthropocene', in Roelvink, Gerda, St. Martin, Kevin and Gibson-Graham, J.K. (eds.) *Making Other*

Worlds Possible: Performing Diverse Economies. Minneapolis: University of Minnesota Press, 225–243.

Roelvink, G., St. Martin, K., Gibson-Graham, J. K., eds. (2015) *Making Other Worlds Possible. Performing Diverse Economies.* Minneapolis: University of Minnesota Press.

Rojas, J. (1991) 'The Enacted Environment: The Creation of "Place" by Mexican and Mexican Americans in East Los Angeles', Dissertation, MIT.

Schlosberg, D. (2007) *Defining Environmental Justice: Theories, Movements, and Nature.* New York: Oxford University Press.

Shava, S., Krasny, M.E., Tidball, K.G. and Zazu, C. (2010) 'Agricultural Knowledge in Urban and Resettled Communities: Application to Social-Ecological Resilience and Environmental Education', *Environmental Education Research,* 16(5–6), 575–589.

Spies-Butcher, B. (2002) 'Tracing the Rational Choice Origins of Social Capital: Is Social Capital a Neoliberal Trojan Horse?', *Australian Journal of Social Issues,* 37(2), 173–192.

Spies-Butcher, B. (2003) 'Social Capital in Economics: Why Social Capital Does Not Mean the End of Ideology', *The Drawing Board: An Australian Review of Public Affairs,* 3(3), 181–203.

Steffen, W., Sanderson, A., Tyson, P., Jäger, J., Matson, P., Moore III, B., Oldfield, F., Richardson, K., Schellnhuber, J.H., Turner, B.L. and Wasson, R.J. (2006) *Global Change and the Earth System: A Planet under Pressure.* New York: Springer Science+Business Media.

Tsing, A.L. (2015) *The Mushroom at the End of the World: On the Possibility of Life in Capitalist Ruins.* Princeton: Princeton University Press.

Valle, G.R. (2015) 'Gardens of Sabotage: Food, the Speed of Capitalism, and the Value of Work', *Aztlán: A Journal of Chicano Studies,* 40(1), 63–86.

Valle, G.R (2016) 'Cultivating Subjectivities: The Class Politics of Convivial Labor in the Interstitial Spaces of Neoliberal Neglect', Dissertation, University of Washington, Seattle.

Wilson, S. (2008) *Research is Ceremony: Indigenous Research Methods.* Black Point: Fernwood Publishers.

Winne, M. (2010) *Food Rebels, Guerrilla Gardeners, and Smart-Cookin' Mamas: Fighting Back in an Age of Industrial Agriculture.* Boston: Beacon Press.

Wittman, H., Desmarais, A. and Wiebe, N. (eds.) (2010) *Food Sovereignty: Reconnecting Food, Nature and Community.* Oakland: Food First Books.

PART IV

Just futures

INTRODUCTION

Looking forward: challenges and opportunities for a just future

Kathryn Powlen, Stacia Ryder, and Melinda Laituri

The term "Anthropocene" has been used to refer to our current geological epoch, though not undebated. The Anthropocene is best characterized by the widespread and largely irreversible impacts that humans have had on the planet (Lewis and Maslin 2015). As of 2019, it is estimated that 75% of terrestrial environments and 66% of marine environments have been significantly altered by human populations (IPBES, 2019). The alteration of these landscapes, under the strains of rising resource demands from industrialized capitalist societies, has led to a corresponding precipitous decline in global biodiversity. As much as seven million hectares of forest have been lost annually in the tropics since 2000 (FAO 2016), while almost 70% of wildlife populations have been lost since 1970 (WWF 2020).

We have seen an increase in the unpredictability and instability of the global climate. There has been a surge in the magnitude and frequency of extreme weather events, such as heatwaves, droughts, and heavy precipitation, across the globe (IPCC 2014, 2018). We have experienced a significant increase in the global average temperature since preindustrial times (IPCC 2018). These unpredictable weather events have damaging impacts on important resources, such as freshwater and food, and marginalized populations continue to experience the greatest health risk and be most vulnerable to physical displacement (Mirza 2003; McMichael et al. 2006). The impacts of climate change further complicate other global issues like the current COVID-19 pandemic, where shelter-in-place orders for virus safety stand at odds with evacuation orders in the face of disasters like wildfires and hurricanes.

Our response to climate change has major consequences on future generations, raising significant questions around intergenerational equity, including questions about comparable options, quality, and access for generations to come (Weiss 1992). These issues are addressed in two chapters in this section. First,

Motupalli identifies the crucial philosophical limitations for achieving intergenerational justice. After providing potential solutions to these limitations, he offers a framework for intergenerational justice which accounts for both the needs and interests of future generations and historic injustices perpetuated by generations of the past and present. Second, Vasconcellos Oliveira proposes a new framework linking sustainable development and climate justice, drawing on the concept of *conditional freedom*, or the idea that individual actions influence the freedom and capabilities of others. She argues that in order to ensure just opportunities for future generations, sustainable development must consider the conditionality of one's capability and freedom. In doing so, development could reinforce sustainable consumption and move towards more intergenerationally just outcomes.

The imperative to address climate change and secure a more just future for generations to come has seen decades of international mobilization around the issue. The first World Climate Conference was held in 1979, and was followed by the creation of the International Panel on Climate Change (IPCC; founded 1988), numerous World Climate Conferences (1979, 1990, 2009), as well as notable international agreements such as the Kyoto Protocol (1997) and Paris Agreement (2015). These events and arrangements have aimed to strengthen global response to climate change, as well as increase transparency and availability of climate related science for improved decision-making.

Despite this array of international climate change institutions and initiatives, mitigation efforts have fallen far short of expectations. One reason for this is the tendency of international climate negotiations to result in stalemates over how a transition to a healthier climate could be delivered in an equitable manner. Many argue that wealthier nations, responsible for the overwhelming majority of emissions to date, owe an "ecological debt" to countries in the global South, and should help to subsidize mitigation and adaptation efforts beyond their own countries (Roberts and Parks 2009; Parks and Roberts 2010). However, many of the richest nations have failed to even set sufficiently ambitious domestic emissions goals. Moreover, the United States, the largest CO_2 pollution emitter historically (Gillis and Popovich 2017), announced its withdrawal from the Paris Agreement in 2017 (Mulvaney 2019; Watson et al. 2019). A just solution to this political stalemate will require a major change from some of the world's largest polluters and should hold responsible nation-states accountable for their share of the problem, while also investing in measures that assist less-responsible countries in plans for climate change adaptation and resilience.

Grassroots movements have played a critical role in defending frontline communities from localized threats produced by fossil fuel industries (Schlosberg and Collins 2014). Powerful movements led by Indigenous peoples and people of color have mobilized across the globe, grounding the climate justice movements with first-hand experience of injustice. These grassroot movements are often argued to be more in line with original environmental justice principles compared to movements led by large NGOs and environmental organizations (Agyeman et al. 2016). Yet, creating solidarity among the multiple organizations and activists will strengthen the climate justice movement. How can we move forward more collectively, inclusively, and effectively in the fight for climate justice?

In his chapter, Goloff explores strategies to build a stronger, more inclusive climate justice movement, drawing on observations in two convergence spaces for climate politics, the National Convention of the Climate Justice Alliance (CJA) and the Annual Conference of US Climate Action Network (USCAN). Goloff highlights the multiple, and at times conflicting, needs, assumptions and issues at stake for a variety of climate activists, from well-funded NGO employees to frontline community members. To strengthen the climate justice movement, the author argues that there is a need for open and uncomfortable conversations, as well as space for diverse experiences and expertise. He highlights the important balance between acting with urgency in the face of a climate emergency, prioritizing accountability to people most impacted by extractive industries and climate impacts, and building authentic alignment across difference.

International climate agreements and climate change policy movements are not the only areas where marginalized voices are overlooked. These injustices occur in the production and distribution stages of meeting energy demands. Rowe and Finley draw on three case studies to highlight inconsistencies within the legal mechanisms used to protect cultural and environmental resources in the United States. The authors evaluate how the consultation processes of the National Environmental Policy Act (NEPA) and the National Historic Preservation Act differed in the level of communication and stakeholder involvement in planning and scoping, and how that resulted in just or unjust outcomes. The authors suggest policy changes for more meaningful and effective consultation processes.

Many of the international institutions and frameworks that seek to address environmental degradation and injustice are rooted in the same Euro-American capitalist systems that have historically been the primary drivers of the problems. The pursuit of more sustainable and equitable futures would benefit from considering alternative value systems and perspectives on the relationship between humans and nature.

Pandit and Purakayastha advocate for a plant- and nature-centric vision of the future where we move beyond the Anthropocene and its capitalistic, settler–colonial norms. They draw on Indigenous Indian approaches to advocate for a way of living as part of the environment and in stark contrast to the patterns of consumption which have brought on the current climate crisis. They call for Earth Democracy, or Earth-Justice, as a movement for peace, justice, and sustainability. From this perspective a just future entails re-envisioning how we as humans think, speak, and act in relation to non-human entities and the Earth.

Many chapters in this section complement and build upon existing approaches for achieving a more socially just and environmentally sustainable future. For example, Pandit and Purakayastha draw from post-growth approaches, specifically highlighting degrowth, which "calls for a democratically led redistributive downscaling of production and consumption—especially in industrialized countries—as a means to achieve environmental sustainability, social justice and well-being" (Gerber et al. 2020, p. 95). Vasconcellos Oliveira draws from the capabilities approach to climate justice, which recognizes humans' direct dependence on the environment for basic needs and functioning (Schlosberg 2012). We also acknowledge the vast body of literature and approaches not covered in this section that are just as critical for examining patterns of inequity at multiple scales. This includes planetary justice (e.g., Biermann and Kalfagianni 2020; Kashwan et al. 2020), multispecies justice (e.g., Celermajer et al. 2020), ecological justice (e.g., Davis et al. 2019), among others. As this body of literature continues to grow, it is critical that we find similarities across the various approaches to bridge and strengthen efforts rather than becoming siloed in our disciplines. Additionally, making sure research is available and accessible will help build coalitions across academics and practitioners, creating space for the convergence spaces that Goloff calls for.

Finally, we recognize that "just futures" are multidimensional, and that the issues addressed in this section are only a few of the threats that we face. A truly just future will require systemic change to our labor policies and practices, trends of incarceration and forgiveness, reparations for a long history of past settler–colonial injustices perpetuated against Indigenous peoples and across other marginalized racial and ethnic groups, among many other changes. We must also not forget that a just future will be embedded in future technologies that reshape environments and societies. McLean (2019) suggests that we must consider questions of environmental justice, including access, equity, and environmental harm, at the intersection of new technologies and digital spaces.

Where does this leave us when we think about cultivating a just future? Who defines how a just future looks and when have we achieved this goal? While daunting, there is still room for hope and for action. Chapters in this section highlight the range of future challenges we will face in efforts to combat climate change, environmental degradation, and the inequities arising from both, while also proposing practical, tangible, philosophical, and theoretical ways forward.

References

Agyeman, J. et al. (2016) 'Trends and Directions in Environmental Justice: From Inequity to Everyday Life, Community, and Just Sustainabilities', *Annual Review of Environment and Resources*, 41, pp. 321–340. doi: 10.1146/annurev-environ-110615-090052.

Biermann, F. and Kalfagianni, A. (2020) 'Planetary Justice: A Research Framework', *Earth System Governance*. doi: 10.1016/j.esg.2020.100049.

Celermajer, D. et al. (2020) 'Multispecies Justice: Theories, Challenges, and a Research Agenda for Environmental Politics', *Environmental Politics*. doi: 10.1080/09644016.2020.1827608

Davis, J., Moulton, A.A., Van Sant, L. and Williams, B. 2019. 'Anthropocene, Capitalocene,… Plantationocene?: A Manifesto for Ecological Justice in an Age of Global Crises', *Geography Compass*, 13(5), p. e12438.

FAO (2016) *State of the World's Forest.* Rome: Food and Agriculture Organization of the United Nations.

Gerber, J.F., Akbulut, B., Demaria, F. and Martínez-Alier, J. (2020) 'Degrowth and Environmental Justice: An Alliance between Two Movements?', in *Environmental Justice.* Edited by Brendan Coolseat. Abingdon, OX & New York, NY: Routledge, pp. 94–106.

Gillis, J. and Popovich, N. (2017) 'The U.S. Is the Biggest Carbon Polluter in History. It Just Walked Away from the Paris Climate Deal', *The New York Times.*

IPBES (2019) *Global Assessment Report on Biodiversity and Ecosystem Services of the Intergovernmental Science-Policy Platform of Biodiversity and Ecosystem Services.* Edited by E.S. Brondizio, S.D.J. Settele and H.T. Ngo. Bonn, Germany: IPBES secretariat.

IPCC (2014) *Climate Change 2014: Synthesis Report. Contribution of Working Groups I, II and III to the Fifth Assessment Report of the Intergovernmental Panel on Climate Change.* Edited by Core Writing Team R.K. Pachauri and L.A. Meyer. Geneva: IPCC.

IPCC (2018) *Global Warming of 1.5oC. An IPCC Special Report on the Impacts of Global Warming of 1.5°C above Pre-Industrial Levels and Related Global Greenhouse Gas Emission Pathways, in the Context of Strengthening the Global Response to the Threat of Climate Change.* Edited by V. Masson-Delmotte et al. Geneva, Switzerland: World Meteorological Organization.

Kashwan, P. et al. (2020) 'Planetary Justice: Prioritizing the Poor in Earth System Governance', in *Earth System Governance.* Elsevier Ltd. doi: 10.1016/j.esg.2020.100075.

Lewis, S.L. and Maslin, M.A. (2015) 'Defining the Anthropocene', *Nature.* Nature Publishing Group, 519. doi: 10.1038/nature14258.

McLean, J. (2019) *Changing Digital Geographies: Technologies, Environments, and People.* Switzerland: Springer Nature.

McMichael, A.J., Woodruff, R.E. and Hales, S. (2006) 'Climate Change and Human Health: Present and Future Risks', *Lancet,* 367, pp. 859–869. doi: 10.1016/S0140-6736(06)68079-3.

Mirza, M.M.Q. (2003) 'Climate Change and Extreme Weather Events: Can Developing Countries Adapt?', *Climate Policy,* 3(3), pp. 233–248. doi: 10.3763/cpol.2003.0330.

Mulvaney, K. (2019) *Climate Change Report Card: These Countries Are Reaching Targets.* https://www.nationalgeographic.com/environment/2019/09/climate-change-report-card-co2-emissions/.

Parks, B.C. and Roberts, J.T. (2010) 'Climate Change, Social Theory and Justice', *Theory, Culture & Society,* 27(2–3), pp. 134–166. doi: 10.1177/0263276409359018.

Roberts, J.T. and Parks, B.C. (2009) 'Ecologically Unequal Exchange, Ecological Debt, and Climate Justice', *International Journal of Comparative Sociology,* 503(3–4), pp. 385–409. doi: 10.1177/0020715209105147.

Schlosberg, D. (2012) 'Climate Justice and Capabilities: A Framework for Adaption Policy', *Ethnics & International Affairs,* 26(4), pp. 445–461. doi: 10.1017/S0892679412000615.

Schlosberg, D. and Collins, L.B. (2014) 'From Environmental to Climate Justice: Climate Change and the Discourse of Environmental Justice', *WIREs Climate Change,* 5, pp. 359–374. doi: 10.1002/wcc.275.

Watson, R. et al. (2019) *The Truth Behind the Climate Pledges.* FEU-US, https://feu-us.org/about-us/_.

Weiss, E.B. (1992) 'Intergenerational Equity: A Legal Framework for Global Environmental Change', in Weiss, E.B. (ed.) *Environmental Change and International Law: New Challenges and Dimensions.* Tokyo: United Nations University Press, pp. 1–24.

WWF (2020) *Living Planet Report −2020: Bending the Curve of Biodiversity Loss.* Edited by R.E.A. Almond, M. Grooten, and T. Petersen. Gland, Switzerland: WWF.

19

ENHANCING ENVIRONMENTAL AND CULTURAL JUSTICE OUTCOMES UNDER THE NATIONAL ENVIRONMENTAL POLICY ACT AND THE NATIONAL HISTORIC PRESERVATION ACT

Matthew J. Rowe and Judson B. Finley

Introduction

We encountered the Sarpy Bison Kill site in southeastern Montana during a field trip for the 2012 collaborative archaeological field school with the Apsáalooke (Crow) and Northern Cheyenne Nations (Rowe et al. 2014). Clearly something had gone horribly wrong. The meticulously brushed floors and walls associated with high-quality archaeological excavation at even the most mundane of sites were nonexistent. Lines of meter-and-a-half tall dirt piles sat in a hole the size of an Olympic swimming pool and a causeway for the backhoe separated a second, smaller hole from the main site. Cows stood defecating on a massive pile of 3,000-year-old bleached bison bones that had been thrown to the side during the excavation. A cursory walk through the devastation turned up artifacts overlooked during excavation, including a half dozen Pelican Lake spear points used in killing the animals that also confirmed the age of the site. We had just taught our students about how the National Environmental Policy Act 1969 (NEPA) and the National Historic Preservation Act 1966 (NHPA), the United States' so-called "Stop, Look, and Listen" laws (CEQ and ACHP 2013), help ensure cultural resources are evaluated and their significance to the nation's cultural heritage is considered before they are destroyed or impacted by developments under federal purview. These laws had failed to protect what might have qualified as a world heritage site (Jawort 2012; Macmillan 2012). Our students demanded to know how this happened.

The Sarpy Bison Kill Site destruction is another chapter in the ongoing, global conflict between Indigenous rights and demands for cheap energy to fuel the mass consumption of the Anthropocene. Examples like the *Shuar People vs Burlington Resources in Ecuador* (Figueroa 2006), the First Nations resistance in Canada to the development of the Athabasca Tar Sands (e.g. Deranger 2015), and applications for drilling leases near Chaco Canyon, New Mexico (e.g. Chamberlain 2019), continue to generate conflict between Indigenous Peoples, energy companies, and government agencies. The central complaint in many of these disputes is that Tribes were not adequately consulted, and the decision-making process did not incorporate their concerns. Tribes argue they are not being treated fairly or given the opportunity for meaningful involvement in the implementation of environmental and cultural protection laws.

In this chapter we elucidate the argument that cultural justice (CJ) and environmental justice (EJ) are inseparable, and that mechanisms are needed to ensure that underrepresented communities are not bearing disproportionate losses of their cultural heritage. We argue that consultation requirements are central to ensuring cultural and environmental justice, but variation in implementing consultation mandates and a lack of a consistent legal definition for "meaningful" consultation undermine the effectiveness of NEPA and NHPA as EJ and CJ instruments.

Cultural justice is environmental justice

Environmental justice and cultural justice are inseparable parts of the same issue linked by legal mechanisms and the potential impacts to underrepresented communities. Environmental justice is "the fair treatment, representation, and participation in the implementation of environmental preservation laws" (USEPA 2017). We employ a similar definition for cultural justice: "The fair treatment and meaningful involvement of all people with respect to the implementation of laws and policies intended to protect and preserve cultural artifacts, including archaeological resources and affiliated cultural sites" (Rowe et al. 2018: 7). Both terms incorporate procedural and recognition justice (Schlosberg 2012, 2013; Schlosberg and Carruthers 2010) and are linked by legislation and potential impacts to underrepresented communities. We recognize that the capabilities approach (Schlosberg and Carruthers 2010) connects many EJ concerns among Indigenous communities and intend our definition of cultural justice to be a complementary term that highlights the synergistic relationship between cultural and environmental preservation laws.

Environmental and cultural justice is also connected by a common Indigenous worldview that incorporates a holistic perspective of the natural world in which the environment cannot be neatly separated from cultural resources (e.g. King 2004; LaPier 2018; Parker and King 1990; Stoffle et al. 1997; Zedeño 2007). This inter-connection means losses to the natural environment can undermine efforts by Indigenous cultures to preserve traditional knowledge, histories, and customs for future generations. From a justice perspective, this means that the repercussions of destroying environmental and cultural resources have similarities in that loss of one or the other effectively erases people and their culture from their historic landscape (Atalay 2006; Ferguson 1996).

Consultation is poorly defined

NHPA and NEPA often work simultaneously to drive environmental and cultural resource preservation in the United States, which legally links EJ and CJ. Neither policy prohibits the destruction of cultural or environmental resources, but both demand that agencies weigh the benefits of a project against its impacts through a transparent review process that includes the public, other agencies, and Tribes to ensure transparency and the incorporation of stakeholder concerns. The consultation mandate can be a strong EJ and CJ mechanism because agencies and companies share information about potential impacts and benefits of the project, provide opportunities for stakeholders to ask questions and raise concerns, and help develop alternative proposals. Consultation is thought to mitigate EJ and CJ concerns because it provides opportunities for all stakeholders to communicate their concerns and alter projects accordingly, but much variability exists in the consultation process which can significantly undermine stakeholder participation.

Additionally, the mandate to consult with Tribes is well codified (see WH-IAEWG and CACAG 2009), but no standard definition for what constitutes "meaningful" consultation exists. In practice, each federal agency develops its own guidance on how to perform NEPA analysis, based on factors such as agency mission, past experience with NEPA and subsequent litigation, and agency interpretation of best practice (Stern et al. 2009). Whichever agency has greatest involvement, approval authority, and expertise typically serves as lead agency for the review process (40 CFR§1501.5),[1] and agencies have different approaches to reviews and consultation due to their missions, mandates, and legislation. Defining who is involved is also left to agency discretion. Furthermore, variation exists within different laws regarding who may be consulted and under what circumstances consultation should be initiated, which can affect the consultation process under NEPA and NHPA. For example, the Native American Graves Protection and Repatriation Act 1990 (NAGPRA) initiates consultation with Tribes during repatriation or discovery of human remains and objects of cultural patrimony, and the American Indian Religious Freedom Act 1979 (AIRFA) defines a consultation role for spiritual practitioners outside the formal Tribal government (Sebastian and Lipe 2009).

Agencies have significant discretion in how they fulfill the consultation mandate, and there are few avenues to relieve dissatisfaction with the consultation process outside of the federal courts. Courts have been reluctant to review the substance of an agency's decision, respecting the agency's technical expertise, and instead assess whether the decision was arbitrary and capricious (Jourdan and Gifford 2009). This stems from the Administrative Procedure Act 1946 (APA), which grants agencies significant freedom to interpret statutes and regulations because each agency holds specialized knowledge related to their purview and mission. Regarding consultation, this means courts have been reluctant to review whether the consultation was "meaningful" and instead look for evidence that the process met legal requirements. It is less clear whether agencies are subject matter experts in environmental and cultural review, which suggests that the courts' deference to agencies on these matters may be less appropriate.

Variation in consultation approaches affect outcomes

> It was a shrine or temple to us. We wanted to preserve the whole area. No amount of money in the world is enough to replace what has been lost here. The spirituality of our people has been broken.
>
> *Burton Pretty on Top, Apsáalooke (Crow) Elder and*
> *Spiritual Leader (Brown 2019)*

Analysis of three case studies found significant variation in consultation practices during the preparation of the Environmental Impact Statement (EIS) for the Sarpy Mine expansion on the Crow Reservation in Montana, the Tongue River Railroad on the Northern Cheyenne Reservation in Montana, and the Dakota Access Pipeline in the American Midwest (Rowe et al. 2018). Three areas of variation appear to impact the effectiveness of the consultation process and alter whether outcomes met both the spirit and letter of the law and contribute to procedural justice failures.

- Timing and extent of first contact
- Communication methods and information sharing
- Involvement in planning, scoping, and data collection

> Consultation was successful because an effort was made by all parties to be considered before anything took place. We worked from point 'A' through the whole process 'together' as a group.
>
> *Ms. Giiwegiizhigookway Martin, THPO, Lac Vieux*
> *Desert Band of Lake Superior Chippewa. (Hutt and*
> *Lavallee 2005: 16)*

Timing and extent of first contact: The lead agency has much discretion in when to initiate requests for consultation and contact stakeholders. Federal agencies should consult "early" with stakeholders, including "state and local agencies and Indian tribes and with interested private persons and organizations when its own involvement is reasonably foreseeable" (40CFR§1501.2(d)(2)). The lead agency holds responsibility for contacting potential stakeholders and "shall invite" stakeholders to participate during scoping process (40CFR§1501.7(a)(1)). The agency also has discretion in how they provide public notification under 40CFR§1506.6, which compels the agency to make a diligent effort to involve the public.

Timing of initial contact during the Sarpy Bison Kill Site EIS is uncertain. On November 28, 2006 a notice of intent to prepare an EIS and a notice of scoping was published in the Federal Register (WWC Engineering 2008). Records indicate public involvement was limited and relevant committees within the Crow Tribe were unaware of the proposed action (USDOI 2008). A total of eight citizens attended the first of two public meetings and the only written comments to the proposal were submitted by two private citizens and the Northern Cheyenne Air Quality Division. Three citizens and agency and tribal officials attended a single public hearing at the Big Horn county courthouse on April 23, 2008. The Crow tribal historic preservation officer (THPO) was a consulting party, but the Crow cultural committee and the Crow 107 committee of Elders, designated consulting parties for the NHPA, were excluded. Integration of stakeholders into the Sarpy EIS process was incomplete and the site was destroyed with little or no external input.

The Tongue River Railroad Expansion (TRRE) case was significantly different. The Tongue River Railroad Company (TRRC) initiated contact with Tribal consulting parties in January 2012, several months prior to applying for permits with the Surface Transportation Board. The Montana state historic preservation officer (SHPO) and other agencies were invited to the review process in October 2012. In contrast to the Sarpy EIS, contact was initiated before permits were requested and a broad range of stakeholders participated, commented, and contributed. Early, notification about the upcoming plans provided time to inform a broad coalition of stakeholders and resulted in a robust network of contributors to the preparation of the EIS.

The Dakota Access Pipeline Project (DAPL) is the most high-profile case due to widely distributed coverage of protests led by the Standing Rock Sioux (e.g., ARCA 2016; Sisk 2016). Unlike the other case studies, the review process for DAPL was adjudicated by the United States District Court, District of Columbia in *Standing Rock Sioux v. United States Army Corps of Engineers* (Civil Action 16-1534 JEB). Central to the dispute was the allegation that the United States Army Corps of Engineers (USACE) failed to fulfill their consultation obligations under NEPA and NHPA.

Exactly when the USACE initiated the consultation process is unclear, but court documents suggest that the North Dakota SHPO was contacted in August 2014 and the project was presented to the Standing Rock Sioux Tribal Council on September 30, 2014. Court documents also provide a timeline for contacts and attempts to contact the Tribe by both letter and email, and dates for several meetings not attended by tribal officials (see Rowe et al. 2018). Little information is provided about the Tribe's response in available documents, other than a letter from the Standing Rock THPO dated February 25, 2015 identifying cultural resources that could be impacted by the pipeline and requesting that a full EIS and cultural resource survey be conducted prior to construction. While the court found the consultation met the letter of the law, the apparently late notification of the Tribe and disjointed communication between the USACE, Dakota Access LLC, and the Standing Rock Sioux Tribe indicate a broken consultation process.

In each case the initial contact and request for consultation met the letter of the law, but different approaches, including the timing and extent of the agencies' efforts to engage stakeholders contributed to varied outcomes. The TRRE consultation built a broad network of stakeholders through early communication and contacted tribal stakeholders before they were legally obligated. The Sarpy Bison Kill Site consultation was limited and had extremely narrow public participation resulting in almost no knowledge of the process outside of the primary actors. The DAPL consultation displayed more effort but seemingly failed to recognize the ineffectiveness of their consultation approaches.

Communication methods and information sharing: Agencies shall "Make diligent efforts to involve the public in preparing and implementing their NEPA procedures" (40CFR§1506.6(a)). Agencies shall hold public hearings whenever appropriate or required by other statutory requirements applicable to specific agencies (40CFR§1506.6(c)). Additionally, hearings should be held in cases of substantial environmental controversy or when a request by another agency with jurisdiction requests and can support the benefit of a public meeting. Otherwise, agencies are compelled to provide information and notice through mail and publication in the Federal Register, but other methods of outreach at the local level, including newspapers and other local media are included under non-compelling "may" language.

In the case studies there are clear differences in the extent, approach, and location of public meetings, hearings, and information sharing. There is record of two, poorly attended public meetings and one public hearing during the Sarpy Bison Kill Site review process. Few public comments were received on the draft environmental impact statement (DEIS) and no comments were received from the professional archaeological community. The letter of the law was followed because the Notice of Intent to prepare an EIS was published in the Federal Register and the DEIS was posted for public review, but there is little evidence that additional approaches were taken to disseminate information about the project or the results of the environmental and cultural review.

In contrast, TRRE held multiple, well-attended meetings within the communities affected by the rail line expansion and court recorders attended every meeting to produce official transcripts. Some public meetings were held live online allowing potentially affected communities across the country to participate. Additionally, TRRE maintained a website where people could review plans, maps, and transcripts from the meetings. This approach allowed individuals that were unable to attend public meetings and hearings to review the plans and offer comments with full knowledge of the scope of the project. Employing what is now common information sharing technology engaged a broad network of stakeholders in a manner that respected the difficulties of attending public meetings in rural areas due to transportation limitations.

Records from the DAPL draft environmental assessment (DEA) document a more robust information sharing process that consisted of multiple mailings, hearings with the Tribe, and site visitations. In this case, conflict developed from a lack of agreement on what constitutes meaningful involvement and consultation rather than a lack of information sharing.

Involvement in planning, scoping, and data collection: Guidelines for participation in the NEPA scoping process is outlined in 40CFR§1501.7(a)(1), the EIS preparation and writing in 40CFR§1502.17, and in public commentary in 40CFR§1506.6. These implementation guidelines for the NEPA process direct the lead agency to contact other state and federal agencies, Indian tribes, and concerned public, but does not clearly outline a role for these stakeholders in the scoping process. It is unclear if "participation" is defined as an active role in defining the scope of the review or is more of an information providing or sharing role. Implementation guidelines explicitly require scientific rigor and quality with the assumption that qualified individuals or agencies will conduct the research and data analysis that contributes to the EIS, but stakeholder involvement in this stage is undefined. In comparison, stakeholder roles in commenting on the DEIS during the public review and comment period are well defined.

Of the three case studies, the TRRE review process was the only one in which Tribal members had significant and meaningful roles that went beyond consultation and information sharing. Inclusion of tribal members in the cultural and environmental surveys resulted in the addition of traditional cultural properties (TCPs) and other cultural resources that may have been missed or overlooked without their input. Additionally, inclusion of the tribal members also contributed to the overall transparency of the process. There was limited involvement of stakeholders during the Sarpy Bison Kill Site review process at any level, although a handful of tribal monitors were hired by the archaeological firm that conducted the excavation. There is little evidence for stakeholder involvement beyond information sharing and commentary during the DAPL review.

These variations share the common theme of increasing or decreasing the role and scope of stakeholder involvement in the review and planning process, which is a central issue in procedural and recognition justice discussions. Greater and consistent inclusion contributes to the overall transparency of the process and reduces the potential for conflict during the decision-making stages and helps avoid procedural equity violations. Greater and consistent inclusion also brings a broader perspective into the process and helps ensure that under-represented groups have a voice in all stages of the environmental and cultural review. Broader dissemination of knowledge also limits the opportunities for subversion of the NEPA process and more robust CJ and EJ protections.

Policy recommendations to enhance environmental and cultural justice outcomes

> I would consider any consultation successful in which there has been a collaborative effort and all parties acknowledge and respect the observations, comments and concerns of the other.
>
> *Dr. Richard L. Allen, Policy Analyst, Cherokee*
> *Nation. (Hutt and Lavallee 2005: 1)*

Based on lessons drawn from the case studies we present two policy changes that may help enhance the inclusivity and transparency of the review process and reinforce the effectiveness of NEPA and NHPA in ensuring cultural and environmental justice. Our first recommendation is for agencies to adopt a unified definition for cultural justice and shared standards for meaningful consultation practices. Our second recommendation is to institute a rating and review system for consultations conducted during the EIS/EA. The goals of these recommendations are to standardize and codify effective approaches to consultation and to create an oversight mechanism outside of the federal court system.

Our recommended standards are drawn from the National Association of Tribal Historic Preservation Officers (NATHPO) guidelines for best practices in tribal consultation within the historic preservation context (Hutt and Lavallee 2005) and models constructed by applied anthropologists (Stoffle et al. 2001). We identify shared principles from the perspectives of tribal representatives, agency officials, and cultural preservation practitioners that can form the foundation for codifying meaningful consultation.

- Consultation must go beyond information provision and seeking of approval or disapproval from tribal governments
- Contact and requests for consultation must happen before the official scoping process so tribal representatives can contribute to the initial scoping decisions
- Tribes must have clearly defined roles throughout the review process, including participation in research design, data collection, and preparation of the DEIS/DEA
- Regulations must ensure that environmental and cultural reviews maintain a high degree of transparency throughout the process

We also propose developing a mechanism for reviewing consultation processes outside of the federal court system to ensure that agency approaches meet both the letter and intent of the law. Establishment of standard evaluations of consultation proceedings at the agency level will help standardize best practices, encourage more detailed reporting of consultation activities, and ensure that agencies are meaningfully engaging under-represented communities. The review mechanism for consultation practices could reflect the Environmental Impact Statement Rating System that was established in 1984 (see Policy and Procedures for the Review of Federal Actions Impacting the Environment, chapter 4, Oct 3, 1984) and discontinued on October 22, 2018. This rating system gave an alphanumeric grade to each EIS based on the quality of the scientific review of the potential impact of the project and the adequacy of the investigation (USEPA 2018). A rating for the consultation process could include an evaluation of transparency based on the breadth of stakeholder involvement and a rating of information sharing based on types of outreach and frequency of communication between agencies and stakeholders. The combination of a definition for meaningful consultation and an established process for reviewing the consultation process should enhance the cultural and environmental justice outcomes under NEPA and NHPA.

Conclusion

The case studies in this chapter illustrate a range of consultation approaches acceptable under the strict letter of the law under NEPA and NHPA. Each project had a different outcome, and while much of the outcome may be attributed to broader global happenings (e.g., the global demand for coal), it is clear that the way stakeholders perceive and react to the review process is connected to the consultation process. TRRE demonstrates that consultation can be an effective mechanism for cultural and environmental justice, if the consultation is conducted thoughtfully, has specific elements designed to engage underrepresented communities, and brings stakeholders into the process early and with meaningful, well-defined roles. Without these elements, consultation becomes a box-checking mechanism where information primarily moves in one direction, if it is passed at all, and most stakeholders have little voice in the outcome of the review.

Effective consultation must recognize power and resource differentials between companies, agencies, and communities and be constructed and conducted in a manner that balances this power differential. Unfortunately, a lack of oversight and lack of an overarching legal definition of meaningful consultation undermine this understanding. While the extreme variability of projects that undergo cultural or environmental review complicate the establishment of formulaic consultation processes, some characteristics such as established roles for stakeholders in the planning, scoping, and data collection for a review could be better codified. Communication requirements should also be updated to move beyond form letters and public meetings.

Additionally, the primary avenue to address dissatisfaction with environmental and historic reviews and the consultation process sits in the court system. Courts have typically found agencies have met their legal requirements for consultation and continue to grant significant freedom to agencies to conduct consultations and reviews according to agency policies. We suggest establishing a review process for consultations similar to the mechanism that the EPA employed from 1984 to October 2018 to evaluate EAs and EISs for scientific quality could provide effective oversight and create avenues to address dissatisfaction outside of federal courts. We believe that this change could significantly improve NEPA and NHPA's effectiveness in mitigating environmental and cultural justice concerns.

Finally, while we focused on case studies in the United States it is important to recognize that the underlying source of these conflicts is the demand for cheap energy resources to fuel the mass consumption and population growth of the Anthropocene. Conflicts between Indigenous peoples, governments, and corporations are global issues that will continue as demand for energy, water, and other resources expand. Mitigating environmental and cultural justice abuses will require strong international policy approaches that recognize and respect holistic Indigenous worldviews. Those policies must move consultation beyond information sharing, mandate early contact and robust communication, create well-defined roles for stakeholders, and ensure transparency in the decision-making process.

Note

1 40 CFR§1501.5 refers to Title 40 of the United States' Code of Federal Regulations, Part 1501, Rule 5. Title 40 covers Protection of the Environment and guides the USEPA mission.

References

ACRA 2016, *American Cultural Resource Association: Statement on the Dakota Access Pipeline Controversy*, September 28, https://acra-crm.org/resources/Pictures/ACRADAPLSt atement_9_28_2016.pdf.

Atalay, S 2006, Archaeology as Decolonizing Practice. *American Indian Quarterly* 30(3/4):280–310.

Brown, M 2019, Montana Bison Killing Ground in Dispute. *Billings Gazette*, November 10, 2019, https://billingsgazette.com/news/local/tribe-members-ancient-bison-kil l-site-desecrated-by-mining/article_94334e0a-c4aa-5a5a-bf42-3157f6f08c0a.html.

CEQ and ACHP 2013, *NEPA and NHPA: A Handbook for Integrating NEPA and Section 106*, edited by Council on Environmental Quality and the Advisory Council on Historic Preservation, Office of NEPA Policy and Compliance, Washington D.C., https:// www.energy.gov/nepa/downloads/nepa-and-nhpa-handbook-integrating-nepa-and -section-106-ceq-and-achp-2013.

Chamberlain, K 2019, *Navajo Government Officials, Environmental Groups Want Review of BLM's Chaco Canyon Leases*. The NM Political Report, July 16.

Deranger, E 2015, Canada's Tar Sands Aren't Just Oil Fields. They're Sacred for my People. *The Guardian*, June 23.

Ferguson, TJ 1996, Native Americans and the Practice of Archaeology. *Annual Review of Anthropology* 25:63–79.

Figueroa, I 2006, Indigenous Peoples Versus Oil Companies: Constitutional Control Within Resistance. *International Journal of Human Rights* 4:51–80.

Hutt, S and Lavallee, J 2005, *Tribal Consultation: Best Practices in Historic Preservation*. National Park Service and the National Association of Tribal Historic Preservation Officers, Washinton D.C.

Jawort, A 2012, Native American Archaeological Site Disturbed. *The Outpost*, November 24.

Jourdan, D and Gifford, K 2009, Wal-Mart in the Garden District: Does the Arbitrary and Capricious Standard of Review in NEPA Cases Undermine Citizen Participation? *Journal of Affordable Housing & Community Development* 18(3):269–285.

King, T 2004, *Cultural Resource Laws and Practice (Heritage Resource Management Series)*. Alta Mira Press, Walnut Creek, CA

LaPier, R 2018, How Shrinking Bears Ears is an Attack on Native American's Religious Freedom. *Pacific Standard Magazine*, August 15.

Macmillan, L 2012, Bison Bones, a Backhoe, and a Crow Curse. Outside Online. *Outside Magazine*.

Parker, P and King, T 1990, *Guidelines for the Evaluation and Documentation of Traditional Cultural Properties*. National Register Bulletin 38, National Register of Historic Places and the National Park Service.

Rowe, M, Finley, J and Branam, K 2014, *Putting America's Cultural Resources to Work*, 14 SAA Archaeological Record 34.

Rowe, M, Finley, J and Baldwin, E 2018, Accountability or Merely "Good Words"? An Analysis of Tribal Consultation under the National Environmental Policy Act and the National Historic Preservation Act. *Arizona Journal of Environmental Law and Policy*, Spring.

Schlosberg, D 2012, Climate Justice and Capabilities: A Framework for Adaptation Policy. *Ethics and International Affairs* 26(4):445–461.

Schlosberg, D 2013, Theorising Environmental Justice: The Expanding Sphere of a Discourse. *Environmental Politics* 22(1):37–55.

Schlosberg, D and Carruthers, D 2010, Indigenous Struggles, Environmental Justice, and Community Capabilities. *Global Environmental Politics* 10(4):12–35.

Sebastian, L and Lipe, W 2009, *Archaeology and Cultural Resource Management: Visions for the Future*. School for Advanced Research Press, Sante Fe, NM

Sisk, A 2016, Tensions Escalate as Police Clear Protesters Near Dakota Access Pipeline. *All Things Considered*, October 28. National Public Radio.

Stern, M, Blahna, D, Cerveny, L and Mortimer, M 2009, Visions of Success and Achievement in Recreation-Related USDA Forest Service NEPA Processes. *Environmental Impact Assessment Review* 29(4):220–228.

Stoffle, R, Halmo, D and Austin, D 1997, Cultural Landscapes and Traditional Cultural Properties: A Southern Paiute View of the Grand Canyon and Colorado River. *American Indian Quarterly* 21(2):229–249.

Stoffle, R, Zedeño, M and Halmo, D 2001, *American Indians and the Nevada Test Site: A Model of Research and Consultation*. U.S. Government Printing Office, Washington, D.C..

USDOI 2008, *U.S. Dept. of the Interior Bureau of Indian Affairs*. Record of Decision, Absaloka Mine Crow Reservation South Extension, Bighorn County, Montana.

USEPA 2017, *United States Environmental Protection Agency: Environmental Justice Website*. https://www.epa.gov/environmentaljustice. Accessed 2017.

USEPA 2018, *United States Environmental Protection Agency: Environmental Impact Statement Rating System Criteria*. https://www.epa.gov/nepa/environmental-impact-statement-rating-system-criteria. Accessed 2018.

WH-IAEWG and CACAG 2009, *List of Federal Tribal Consultation Statutes, Orders, Regulation, Rules, Policies, Manuals, Protocols and Guidance*, edited by White House-Indian Affairs Executive Working Group (WH-IAEWG) and Consultation and Coordination Advisory Group (CACAG), https://projects.ecr.gov/mrbir/pdfs/List%20of%20Fedl%20Tribal%20Consultation%20Statutes%20Orders%20Regs%20Rules.pdf.

WWC Engineering 2008, *DRAFT Environmental Impact Statement for the Absaloka Mine Crow Reservation South Extension Coal Lease Approval*. Proposed Mine Development Plan, and Related Federal and State Permitting Actions.

Zedeño, M 2007, *Blackfeet Landscape Knowledge and the Badger-Two Medicine Traditional Cultural District*. Society for American Archaeology, Archaeological Record, March.

20

ONE EARTH, ONE SPECIES HISTORY, AND ONE FUTURE

Earth-Justice in the Anthropocene

Saptaparni Pandit and Anindya Sekhar Purakayastha

Introduction

The "permanent war economy" against the planet earth, unleashed by global corporate capital demands immediate measures for eco-justice; it entails our quest for alternative epistemes of economic or developmental "degrowth" (D'Alisa et al. 2015) or radical ways to "make peace with the Earth." Centuries of commodified and consumerist living patterns pushed dominant thinking away from a focus on a sustainable and just society, premised on principles of conviviality or *solidarity economy*, or *bio-economics*. In 1970, French intellectual André Gorz's question on whether "the earth's balance, for which no-growth – or even degrowth – of material production is a necessary condition, is compatible with the survival of the capitalist system?" (Gorz 1972, p. iv), remains crucial for any discussion today on the Anthropocene and eco-justice.

Ideas of *degrowth*, non-extraction, or non-violence towards everything, and "shared economy" are doing the rounds today as a means of survival in the Anthropocene. Similarly, global environmental movements are urging for a "convivial manifesto" (Adloff 2014, 5) of shared living or non-utilitarian living for all or for the "commons." In a similar vein, this chapter examines Indigenous eco-theologies of Indian tribal groups as existing models of "dematerialized" shared living with Nature or what we subsequently call "vegetal" living with the Earth. We show that traditional Indian philosophy of Nature manifests alternative epistemic templates of respect for the Earth and for all Non-human Earth Others. Human hubris, which all too often has led to complete technologization and sense of human supremacy is deconstructed in Indigenous philosophies of eco-justice and Earth-oriented living. We unpack a constellation of radical thought currents which promote a desire to retreat to the pure Earth Time of interconnectedness or conviviality as opposed to the technocratic human temporality of estrangement or violent plundering of the "Other." The Earth emerges in our vision as the primary signifier, housing all species, construing that real justice signifies Justice to the Earth – a perfect form of living democracy or what we refer to here as "Earth Democracy."

The Anthropocene is viewed as the geological epoch in which "mankind became the force of telluric amplitude" (Bonneuil and Fressoz 2016, p. 4). The "shock of the Anthropocene" (Bonneuil and Fressoz 2016) throws up both a geological and political crisis. The present epoch of industrial capital has promoted a life of thoughtless consumption, unleashing what scholars argue are vicious forms of *Carbon Capitalism* (Muzio 2015) or *Fossil Capital* (Malm 2016) – a condition of living in which capitalism and its plundering accumulative ideologies permeate and brutalize the ecology or the larger "web of life" through our toxic carbon footprints driven primarily by reckless fossil fuel consumption (Moore 2016). Human legacies – specifically European colonization of the Earth and the entire life-world – have generated a climate of injustice. In response, global environmental movements are looking for alternative imaginaries that script a different worldview of co-living or inter-species democracy or Earth Democracy.

We therefore argue for a post-carbon, post-anthropogenic parallax view for our survival in the Anthropocene that requires the conjoining of the natural world with our everyday epistemic universe without injustice to the planet Earth and to other non-human members. By *post-anthropogenic*, we mean new coordinates that shun our anthropocentric behavior and accumulative developmental practices. To elucidate, we shall initially discuss the fatal eco-ontological wounds inflicted by the Anthropocene and how newer counter-currents of post-Anthropocentric thoughts are offering new survival strategies. We draw on recent works such as *The Shock of the Anthropocene: The Earth, History and Us* (Bonneuil and Fressoz 2016); *Manifesto for Living in the Anthropocene* (Gibson et al. 2015); *Degrowth: A Vocabulary for a New Era* (D'Alisa et al. 2015), and *The Routledge Companion to Alternative Organization* (Martin, et al. 2014) to look for survival ethics that are premised on Earth-centric norms.

Subsequently we shall explore Indigenous models of thought and living as adopted in India – an alternative mode which, we argue, offers fresh insights on how to fashion new Earth-centric epistemes. Our direct references to Indigenous worldviews of eco-living and shared economies will be primarily the tribal life world of Odisha, an Indian state. Odisha houses many Indigenous population groups who live in the remote mountain regions surrounded by lush green forests. Odisha remains our source of inspiration since it offers rich anthropological insights as these tribal groups, primarily the *Dongria Kondh* tribes, maintain even today their Earth-centric lifestyles of eco-justice. Odisha came into the news both nationally and internationally during the late 1990s, as the Indian government opened the remote forests and mountain lands populated by these tribal groups to direct foreign investment by multinational mining companies. These companies invaded these pristine eco-systems and began digging the mountains for minerals. The conflict between the ruthless march of developmentalism and Indigenous philosophy of natural living premised on ideologies of eco-justice in Odisha has been extensively documented by Booker-winning author Arundhati Roy (Roy 2013).

India has a large population of multi-ethnic groups who have survived through centuries of Earth-centric worldviews. Our use of the term "Indian tribes" does not signify a homogenous block. We remain alive to their ethnic diversity and plurality of survival epistemes, but what draws them together is their largely nature-centric or "vegetal" (plant and nature-centric) ways of living that generally abhors modern development drives – a thinking pattern which we shall explicate in subsequent sections.

Species history, plant thinking, and convivial living

Across the globe, philosophers, ecological activists, and theological leaders have been urging for a departure from our highly technologized and profit-orient drives. Yet, such a departure will require a rejection of anthropocentric narrations of Earth's story which have to date tended to gloss over or tell incomplete stories of the Earth and Earth-others, in ways that centralize and separate out humans from the natural world and other living entities. Pope Francis' recent encyclical letter *Laudato Si': on Care for Our Common Home* (2015) emphasizes this issue of eco-governance and an Earth-governance that can do justice to our "common home," the planet Earth – such a view resonates with the tribal imagination of the Earth as their sacred home. We therefore widen the frame and look at similar alliances of theologico-cultural forms of eco-governance, something which Indian philosophy has advocated since its inception.

Drawing on Vandana Shiva's idea of "Earth Democracy" (2015), Michael Marder's theorization of "Plant Thinking" (2013), and Dipesh Chakrabarty's recent notion of non-human "species history" (2009) – trajectories which were foreseen and practiced in Indian traditional thoughts – we argue for a reversal of anthropocentrism challenged by ideas of planetary history or non-human history that perceives the category "human" as just another example of a species, co-sharing the planet earth with other non-human species. Chakrabarty defines this non-human attention in history as *planetary history* or *species history* – an epistemic shift, required to abjure doctrines of human accumulation at the cost of the Earth or planetary life.

Marder's idea of "vegetal life," relying on "plant-thinking," construes a non-domination of the target of its investigations, something which usually happens in human-thinking patterns (Marder 2013). Marder argues for a process of bringing human thought back to its roots and rendering it plant-like. Marder places non-human life at the forefront of our philosophical investigation, deconstructing in that process our exclusive human preoccupations. For Marder, plant behavior and the vegetal heritage of human thought resist the logic of totalization and transcend the confines of human instrumentality. Simply put, plant thinking metaphorizes convivial thinking or a vision of embedded ecology in which everything is viewed as intermeshed and interdependent. Many Indigenous communities have always relied on similar ontologies of "plant-thinking" or "eco-spirit" (Kearns and Keller 2007).

Anthropocene: concerns, anxieties, and posthuman thoughts

The ecological devastation of the Anthropocene demands new ways of living or, what Gibson et al. (2015) refer to as a new *Manifesto for Living in the Anthropocene*. This approach begins with reference to the Biosphere, the part of the air where the humans and non-human animals can survive along with the whole abiotic element of the natural world. The realities of the Anthropocene require listening to the Earth for a change that would engender the possibility of thinking "with" the world and not "for" it, looking at Nature not as an objective entity, or offering mere economy-driven solutions. The way ahead calls for strengthening the 'tentative connections' between ecological humanities and community economies of life.

The quest for Eco-justice demands a total reversal of epistemologies and ontologies which focus almost exclusively on human needs. This means pursuing a posthuman paradigm which replaces the category "human" with the Earth as the primary signifier, moving us toward a state of Earth-Justice.

In tune with these thoughts, one strategy visualized to salvage humanity in the Anthropocene by the new *Manifesto* (Gibson, 2015) is "Rethinking Being." This entails the abandonment of the concept of individual "being" or individual profit, promoting instead the idea of "being-in-common" that radically rethinks the narrow idea of the individual self. Like the concepts described above, this hints at planet-centric modes of economies or bio-economies that adopt bio-recycles as opposed to financial transactions aimed at human wealth accumulation. The penultimate strategy in *Manifesto* is "Ethical Coordinates for More-than Human Communities" which proposes the ways of conjoined livelihoods of humans and non-human others. The third idea is called, "Contact Improvisation," envisaging a form of dance positioned on the propinquity of the collaborators. The concept is to:

> explore further the eco-philosophical implications of Contact Improvisation, by considering what it might mean to dance with the "earth body" that we have. "Earth body" might be taken to signify my own body, understood as a thing of Earth, as is that of all creatures, human and otherwise, with whom I share an earthly existence in the "dance" of life.
>
> *(Gibson et al. 2015, pp. 44–45)*

This idea of the "dance of life" entails an ecology of "knotting" or intertwinement and conjoined living with everything around (Ingold 2015). The

"Earth–body" encompasses everything and weaves an entangled web of living – an idea which finds an echo in Indian author Sitakant Mahapatra's *Celebration of Life: The Tangled Web: Tribal Life and Culture of Orissa* (1993) and in *The Endless Weave: Tribal Songs and Tales of Orissa* (1991). These works further elaborate on how tribal living patterns in Odisha, the Indian state, are attuned to this rhythm of Nature or the dance of life.

The Hindu tradition and long history of environmental movements in India spearheaded by these tribal groups during the Chipko Movement, or the Anti-Posco or Anti-Vedanta Movement, demonstrate the core ecological ethics in their cosmic worldviews – a belief system that sees all creations as part of one sacred spirit that disallows any harm to be caused to the planet Earth. These mythological ideas of creation, cosmic time, and moral responsibility encapsulate alternative codes of values towards Nature and nonhuman entities living in this planet. Any counter-logic to obviate predominant trends of human bias demands a post-humanist conversation that enfolds all the nonhuman Others including the Earth, our common home for survival. Notions of eco-justice cannot perceive natural phenomena as objects to be colonized for exclusive human need and profiteering.

Typologies of Earth living: the Indian case

Indigenous Indian cosmologies of Nature have always given primacy to the Earth, exemplifying what Indian Environmental Scholar Vandana Shiva has called "Earth Citizenship" – or convivial living with Nature. Indigenous life practices in tribal lands of India forge similar bonds in Eco-living premised on community bio-economics or community. In other words, the slogan of making peace with the world is practiced by Indigenous tribes who live with the world, adopting models of degrowth and frugal living styles, sustaining them only through shared community works. Although rapid urbanization and massive inflow of industrial capital have made serious inroads in these ecological habits of urban India, these traditional worshipping of Nature and sustained norms of Earth-centric living are still pursued actively by many Indigenous tribal groups of India. In this section, we provide specific examples from Odisha of practices of eco-living.

The *Dongria Kondh* tribe of Odisha are practitioners of eco-living. They practice the idea of Earth Democracy (Shiva 2005) by resorting to authentic organic farming or "agroecology" (Shiva 2015, pp. 125–126). This tribal group actualizes the task of "reclaiming the Commons" in their everyday life as they believe in biodiversity, traditional knowledge, and in the "Rights of Mother Earth" (Shiva 2020). They mostly survive through agriculture and generally try to preserve their natural habitat.

In the Indian traditional art of living, one begins the day by greeting and showing respect to the shining rays of the morning sun and by acknowledging the supremacy of the cosmic elemental forces. Out of this sense of attachment with the Earth and interactive cognitive bonding arises the notion of *ahimsa* or nonviolence in Indian philosophy – an ethos that debars everyone from doing harm to the Earth. For example, Maitreyee Mishra, through her research on Orissa, has shown how the Indigenous tribes of Odisha maintain certain ecological numinous codes in their everyday approaches to Nature. They do not unnecessarily break branches of trees or pluck leaves as that, they believe, would hurt, particularly in the night as the tree/plant is asleep. Sun-worship and moon-worship were also prescribed in oral traditions, particularly for good harvests. Worshipping of rivers, plants, and animals is also common.

Odisha, like many parts of India, has rich Indigenous traditions of environmentalism. These traditions and knowledge systems, however, are varied and reflect the multitude of experiences within the state, between modern and traditional systems, between the "mainstream" and tribal (Indigenous) systems of knowledge. Indigenous knowledge (IK) is "a cumulative body of knowledge and beliefs, handed down through generations by cultural transmission, about the relationship of living beings (including humans) with one another and with their environment" (Mishra 2018, 54). IK may be useful to understand "the potential of certain adaptation strategies that are cost-effective, participatory and sustainable" (Mishra 2018, 56). Inspired by this Indigenous knowledge system, many tribal communities in India refused to adopt forceful adherence to modern market-oriented developmental ideologies. Their traditional knowledge of eco-living impelled them to fight for environmental justice and they have protested against the takeover of their lands and territories. For example, in 2010, the Dongria Kondh tribes of Odisha struggled to retain their sacred hills and forest homes from destruction by the mining activities of the UK-based Vedanta Resources, which ended in a legal victory for the tribes (Mishra 2018). Bookerwinning author Arundhati Roy has written extensively about the fierce struggles of these Indigenous tribes against multinational capital in her book, *Broken Republic* (2013).

The intrusion of neoliberal capital in South Asia has seriously brutalized this lasting Nature–Human co-habitation and evicted countless Indigenous populations from their natural habitats, turning dense forests and mountains into special economic zones (SEZs) (Roy 2013). This has also led to some traditional Indian approaches to Nature and its philosophic legacy of frugality or simple living losing grounds in urban consumerist and industrialized India. However, traditional practices continue to retain their full appeal among other Indigenous tribes in remote areas. For example, Odisha's Niyamgiri Hills witnessed stiff resistance against government's acquiring of tribal lands and resources. These tribes have been described as "Ecological Warriors" for their valiant attempt to save the environment (Krishnan and Naga 2017).

Resistance by Indigenous populations has been witnessed in other in parts of India. The *Bishnoi tribes* of the state of Rajasthan are also well-documented practitioners of eco-living. For example, the Chipko Movement spearheaded by the Indigenous Bishnoi community in Rajasthan prevented the cutting of trees planned to be cut by government workers for development (Jain 2016, 51). There are also accounts of how the Bishnoi community will save trees even by endangering their own lives (e.g., Jain 2016). Pankaj Jain's *Dharma and Ecology of Hindu Communities* (2016) is a product of his field survey of different Indigenous communities in India like the Bishnois and the Bhils and his translation of a Bishnoi community song clearly testifies to their priority for Nature over self:

> Heads lost, trees saved, consider it a good deal! It is better to sacrifice your head to save a tree. Accepting price for your sacrifice becomes a stigma on your sacrifice
>
> *(Jain 2011, p. 51)*

Indigenous dharmic traditions in India help Indians, Jain argues, to transcend the boundary of subject and object and this holistic attitude of Indians based on *dharma* can be used for wider environmental awareness.

Earth Dharma

The Swadhyaya community of India observes what Pankaj Jain describes as "Earth Dharma" (Jain 2011, 41). They regularly perform the *Bhumi Pūjan* or what can be translated as the "earth dharma." Thousands of Swadhyaya community members recite this verse every morning

> "Samudravasane devī, parvata stanamaṇḍale. Viṣṇupatni! Namastubhyaṃ pādasparśaṃ kṣamasva me!" [O ocean-clad goddess earth, with mountains as your nurturing-breasts. O wife of Viṣṇu! I bow to you and ask for forgiveness as I touch you with my feet]
>
> *(Jain 2011, p. 41)*

As with all other traditional Indian communities, the earth is perceived as the mother of every creature, providing shelter to all living creatures and dead substances. She takes care of everyone and Earth Dharma or Earth Ethics demands a reciprocation from our end towards the Earth, our common home as the present Pope describes in his new letter to his disciples.

Philosophies of Nature or different modes of bio-divinities as conceptualized in ancient India during the Vedic times resulted in multiple rituals and meditative practices which are attuned to natural living principles and Yoga. Indigenous rituals of Earth-worship, notions of sacred geographies and sacred groves and mountains have age-old philosophic sanctions in India. Yoga has become world famous today and the benefits of Indian Yogic practices are acting as healing powers for survival, even though yoga too is being commodified across the globe. Few realize that Yoga is not mere physical acrobatics, it emanates from the philosophy of *Yoga Sutra* of Patanjali, the Indian Saint, and Yoga references eco-merging with the world. Yoga emerges from the *Shramanic* (ascetic) tradition of Indian philosophy that include the core philosophical stipulations of the Jaina and Buddhist principles – nonviolence or *ahimsa* to everything (Thakkar 2008, pp. 163–193). These *Shramanic* traditions of austerity and nonviolence to Nature are continued today for achieving greater eco-justice.

Both traditional Indian philosophy and Indigenous cosmologies coalesce in their dharmic vision of cosmic unity or the entangled web of life in which humans, nonhumans and the planet Earth are weaved into one entity and none can be harmed as that would endanger the entire web of life. Ancient Indian thinkers, while conceptualizing the spiritual notion of the Cosmic *Mandala* in the Vedic Epiphany, thought of renunciation as the navel of creation. This pure asceticism goes against the very idea of modern combustive-developmentalism and reckless consumption. Jonardan Ganeri, a renowned Indian Philosophical scholar has recently written about the mystical and epistemic significance of the great Indian Banyan Tree (Ganeri 2017).

Trees are worshipped across India. In the *Bhagabat Gita*, the sacred book of India, Lord Krishna appears as the *avatara* of God and describes the Banyan tree as God himself. This connects us with our conceptual thread of "plant thinking" (Marder 2013), or "vegetal being" (Marder 2013), and the concept of "the plant contract" (Gibson 2018). All these were foreseen and practiced in Indian philosophy.

> "Stands an undying banyan tree," says Krishna in the *Bhagavad-Gita*, "with roots above and boughs beneath. Its leaves are the Vedic hymns: one who knows this tree knows the Vedas. Below, above, its well-nourished branches straggle out; sense objects are the twigs. Below its roots proliferate inseparably linked with works in the world of men."
>
> *(Ganeri 2017)*

These are glimpses of unalloyed plant thinking – an eco-phenomenology that has the ability to deconstruct the monolith of the materialist logos, a deconstructive exercise that obviates anthropocentric hostility to Earth others. Indigenous Earth Ethics or Earth Dharma demonstrates this eco-phenomenological respect for the Earth, hinting at a possible flowering of Earth democracy.

Earth Democracy, One Earth – the common home

Vandana Shiva, Indian ecological activist and theorist, postulates "Earth Democracy" as both "an ancient world view and an emergent political movement for peace, justice and sustainability." She quotes the 1848 speech attributed to Chief Seattle of the Suquamish tribe who said

> how can you buy or sell the sky, the warmth of the land? The idea is strange to us … The Earth does not belong to man; man belongs to the earth … all things are connected like the Blood which unites our family. All things are connected.
>
> *(Shiva 2005, p. 1)*

In contrast to the capitalist view of looking into the Earth as private property, alternative movements are defending the notion of the planet as "commons," a common living place for all creatures living on this planet, an idea that militates against exclusive corporate ownership on planetary spaces. Corporate globalization is based on new "enclosures of the commons" which is premised on the ideology of exclusion and colonization. Countering such trends, Vandana Shiva talks of a new future and new alternatives, a future

> based on inclusion, not exclusion; on non-violence, not violence, on reclaiming the commons, not their enclosure … I have named this project earth Democracy … Earth democracies' success concerns not just the fate and well-being of all humans, but all beings on the earth.
>
> *(Shiva 2005, p. 4)*

Earth Democracy therefore is not just a concept, it is shaped by the multiple and diverse practices of people reclaiming their commons. As an idea it throws up possibilities of resistance against all forms of carbon capitalism or the Capitalocene that vitiates the atmosphere with corporate-driven industrial usurpation of natural spaces. The Anthropocene has been seen by some scholars as the direct fall-out of capitalist consumption and therefore it can better be described as Capitalocene which encourages mindless carbonification of the climate through industrial greed and control over natural spaces.

Earth Democracy, through its Earth-centric coordinates, opens up the idea of Earth-Justice, a notion that posits one Earth as our common home that houses a shared history of all species of living organisms, erasing all distinctions of the human from the nonhuman or the Earth from the non-Earth. Any blueprint for survival in the Anthropocene must begin with this reinforcement of the idea of Earth Ethics as a means of resistance to the Anthropocene because mindless pursuit of anthropocentric capitalism

> leads not just to the death of democracy but to the democracy of death, in which exclusion, hate, and fear become the political means to mobilize votes and power. Earth Democracy enables us to envision and create living democracies … living democracies are based on the intrinsic worth of all species, all peoples, all cultures, and a just and equal sharing of the Earth's vital resources, and sharing the decisions about the use of the earth's resources.
>
> *(Shiva 2005, p. 6)*

The clear dialectic between the Earth System and the World System of capitalist expansion and the cataclysmic devastation of the Anthropocene requires us to forge a new politics of Earth System-oriented living, something that Indigenous populations in various parts of the world have been pursuing across generations and centuries. Vandana Shiva in her recent work, *Who Really Feeds the World?* (2015) argues

The planet's well-being, people's health, and societies' stability are severely threatened by an industrial, globalised agriculture, primarily driven by profit-making ... This crisis is not an accident; it has been built into the system's very design. At the heart of this paradigm is the Law of Exploitation, which sees the world as a machine and nature as a dead matter ... The industrial paradigm is in deep conflict with the ecological paradigm, and the law of exploitation is pitted against the law of return. These are paradigm wars of economics, culture and knowledge, and they frame the very basis of the food crisis we are facing today.

(Shiva 2015, pp. 1–4)

In the midst of the tussle between the "industrial" and "ecological" paradigms described above, one encounters the idea of the "Earth-citizen." The concept reiterates that for many of the Indigenous peoples of the world (particularly the Indian tribes discussed here), they see themselves as Earth-citizens who always take every means to make peace with the Earth, a practice which stands counter to all forms of industrialization. In their foundational work, *Indigenous Environmental Knowledge and Its Transformations: Critical Anthropological Perspectives* (2000), Roy Ellen, Peter Parkes, and Alan Bicker argue that "Indigenous knowledge" (IK); "Indigenous technical knowledge" (ITK); "ethnoecology"; "local knowledge"; "folk knowledge"; "traditional knowledge"; "traditional environmental (or ecological) knowledge"(TEK); "people's science"; or "rural people's knowledge" – are all multifaceted positions that have radical relevance for the future of convivial living of Earth-citizens and are essential for pragmatic strategies of sustainability. They call for a reverse journey back to Nature, possible to be achieved only through transfigured thinking or radical ruptures of post-humanist or non-anthropocentric thinking.

Conclusion: transfigured thinking for future

To summarize, the post-Anthropocene road map posits a radical transformation in thinking. In a capitalist world governed by "pyropolitics" (Greek *pyro* as fire) or combustion-oriented, ash-ridden optics that justify the burning of all earthly resources for acceleration of growth, the road map for a sustainable and just society lies in recognizing or incorporating deeper insights offered through alternative cosmologies or Earth-centric thinking. In our view this is how we can address the current energy and climate crisis and its resultant problems across the world. This interconnectedness with the vegetal nonhuman world is possible through transfigured perception or non-cognitive, non-ideational "plant thinking" in the Anthropocene.

These transversals of non-coercive, non-extractive thinking have configured Indigenous ways of living for centuries. They offer a dissident optic, establishing the fallacies of mechanistic materialism that induces extracting the secret of Nature and ferreting labor from human beings, promoting in that way the desire for limitless profit in the Anthropocene. Opposed to the ideology of capitalist extraction and subsequent destruction, Indigenous cosmologies of Earth Democracy and plant thinking stand as antidotes to this atomistic desire of human science to extract from matter the hidden energy. We reiterate Marder's thematization of the plant as ethically exemplary for our over-materialist life. Plants expand and exfoliate towards the Other, filiate with all and allow the space for us to unmake the current status quo as it consists of an anthropocentric, capitalist culture of self-enclosure and self-profit.

Plant thinking is transformative and convivial. When Indigenous tribes like the Bishnois and the Bhil communities practiced "bio-divinity" (Jain 2016, p. 1), and worshiped for centuries the plants or what they call the "sacred groves" and "dharmic sanctuaries" (Jain 2016, pp. 51–93), they prefigured in their daily eco-theologies this transversal of *becoming plant*, or to be plant-like in thinking. One recalls here Deleuze and Guattari's radical slogan of "Follow the plants" in their *A Thousand Plateaus* (1987). The fragility and weakness of plants, the worms and other natural phenomena constitute their philosophical strength; they offer a non-cognitive vegetal mode of phenomenology. Our human scale of over-cognition and rationalization have only ruined the Earth causing terrible injustices to the planet through activities where peoples' exploited labor has led to these earth injustices, such as over-farming and damming of waterways.

The rescue boats in the Anthropocene must sail in a radically different direction of phenomenological listening to the Earth rather than being exclusively beholden to human reason and cognitive closures. Indian tribal dances orchestrated regularly amidst their natural habitats, the dense forests and mountains, script this mytho-poetic hermeneutics of listening to the ants, the plants, the caterpillars, and the Earth God (the *Bhu-Devata*). They truly "follow the plants" or "vegetative life" and enlighten us of Earth reason, as opposed to extractive and colonizing human reason. The nimble, yet intense symbiotic art of living of the Indigenous communities is generally ridiculed by our doctrine of commodity fetishism and that is why Indigenous living patterns have mostly been museumized, only to be visited occasionally during our exotic tours, ignoring the fact that their Earth vision provides a survival strategy in the Anthropocene. They may appear archaic to our industrialized minds and yet their delicate, highly nuanced ethno-ecologies are the only gossamer horizons of extant Earth Ethics. One needs to revive these delicate counter-currents of Earth Dharma and vegetative living. Currently the Earth is the biggest subaltern and it has been weakened through the systemic and cognitive arrogance of the human species. In the Earth democracy, the weak is empowered to speak, that is real Earth Dharma or Earth Ethics.

We also imagine this as the Earth *Khora*, the Earth Womb Time of germination when everything was convivially intermeshed before being differentiated from each other by human logic. This pure "life itself" prior to human *techne* evoked in contact with vegetal Nature is a time before historical time. Being cut off from its natural source, the Earth has fallen prey to man's [sic] fabrication

(Irigaray and Marder 2016, 33), and thus to nihilistic forces. Tribal resistance and mobilization against cutting of forests in India and their fierce moves against construction of dams over rivers and mountainous jungles are their Indigenous ways of resisting man-made [sic] nihilism and technologization. Human ways of thinking are prone to colonize, whereas plant-thinking, Indigenous thinking, Earth Ethics believe in inter-subjectivity, in conviviality, in real co-living – a motto that can resist the Capitalocene and bring justice to the Earth.

References

Bonneuil, C. and Fressoz, J.B. 2016. *The Shock of the Anthropocene: The Earth, History and Us*, London: Verso.

Chakrabarty, D. 2009. "The Climate of History: Four Theses", *Critical Inquiry*, Vol. 35, 197–222.

D'Alisa, Demaria F. and Kallis, G. 2015. *Degrowth: A Vocabulary for a New Era*, London and New York: Routledge.

Fernbach, David, *The Shock of the Anthropocene: The Earth, History and Us*, New York, Verso Books, 2015.

Ganeri, J. 2017. "Why the Great Old Banyan Should Be the Tree of Knowledge", *Wire*, https://thewire.in/society/banyan-tree-of-knowledge

Gibson, K.D.B.R. and Fincher, R. eds. 2015. *Manifesto for Living in the Anthropocene*, Brooklyn, NY, Punctum Books.

Gorz, A. (M. Bosquet) (1972) Nouvel Observateur, Paris, 397, 19 June. Proceedings from a public debate organized in Paris by the Club du Nouvel Observateur.

Ingold, Tim, *The Life of Lines*, New York and London, Routledge, 2015.

Irigaray, L. and Marder, M. 2016. *Through Vegetal Being: Two Philosophical Perspectives*, New York, Columbia University Press.

Jain, P. 2011. *Dharma and Ecology of Hindu Communities: Sustenance and Sustainability*, Surrey, Ashgate.

Jain, P. (2016). *Dharma and Ecology of Hindu Communities: Sustenance and Sustainability*, New York, Routledge.

Kearns, Laurel and Keller, Catherine (2007). *Eco-Spirit: Religion, Philosophy and the Earth*, New York: Fordham University Press, 97–125.

Krishnan, R. and Naga, R. 2017. "'Ecological Warriors' versus 'Indigenous Performers': Understanding State Responses to Resistance Movements in Jagatsinghpur and Niyamgiri in Odisha", *South Asia: Journal of South Asian Studies*, Vol. 40 (4), 878–894.

Marder, M. 2013. *Plant-Thinking: A Philosophy of Vegetal Life*, New York, Columbia University Press.

Mishra, M. 2018. "Traditional Knowledge Systems, Culture and Environmental Sustainability: Concepts from Odisha", in Kiran Prasad, ed., *Communication, Culture and Ecology*, Rethinking Sustainable Development in Asia, Springer, 2018, 51–66.

Moore, J. 2016. *Anthropocene or Capitalocene? Nature, History, and the Crisis of Capitalism*. Binghamton University The Open Repository @ Binghamton (The ORB) Sociology Faculty Scholarship Sociology.

Muzio, T. 2015. *Carbon Capitalism: Energy, Social Reproduction and World Order*, London, Rowman and Littlefield.

Pope Francis. 2015. *Encyclical Letter Laudato Si of the Holy Father Francis On Care For Our Common Home*, Vatican Press.

Roy, A. 2013. *Broken Republic*, New Delhi, Penguin.

Shiva, V. 2005. *Earth Democracy: Justice, Sustainability and Peace*, Penang, Malaysia: Third World Network.

Shiva, V. 2015. *Who Really Feeds the World?* Milan: Giangiacomo Feltrinelli Editore.

Shiva, V. 2020. *Reclaiming the Commons: Biodiversity, Traditional Knowledge, and the Rights of Mother Earth*, Santa Fe and London, Synergetic Press.

Thakkar, V. 2008. *The Sahasranama Literature A Study*, Ch V, 163–193, http://hdl.handle .net/10603/60100.

21

A FRAMEWORK FOR INTERGENERATIONAL JUSTICE

Objections and principles

Chaitanya Motupalli

Introduction

Whether we agree that the name Anthropocene[1] best represents the current geological age or not, and regardless of the impact of scientific recognition of the Anthropocene on public perception and action, "The Anthropocene is now for better or worse humanity's chronic condition, a constant presence" (Dryzek and Pickering 2019, p. 11). While it is true that anthropogenic climate change is the major contributor to the "chronic condition" that we are now in, the implications of this condition are felt not just in the environmental sphere but in all other spheres of our society. Furthermore, the implications of the Anthropocene are felt severely by the most vulnerable populations of our times and will be felt by the generations that are yet to come. In that light, as much as it is important to figure out ways to respond effectively to the issues of the Anthropocene with the marginalized populations of the current generations in mind, it is crucial to consider future generations as well.

As a discipline offering theoretical grounding to guide praxis and vice versa, environmental justice addresses the present injustices in the Anthropocene and also provides a transformative vision for the future. In line with the aim of environmental justice to provide tools to envision an environmentally and ecologically just future that addresses the needs of future generations, I propose a framework for intergenerational justice in this chapter. Before I embark on that project, however, I will address three philosophical problems that are used to stall conversations on intergenerational justice and introduce possible solutions to address each of those problems in their respective sections. The three problems are: the problem of non-existence, the problem of nonidentity, and the problem of non-reciprocity.

Objections to intergenerational justice

The problem of non-existence

The problem of non-existence pertains to the existence of a thing or its lack thereof (i.e., being or non-being). If a thing exists, then one can either deny its existence or make truth claims about it. Likewise, if something doesn't exist, can one deny its existence or make claims about that thing? In the context of inter-generational justice, since future people do not exist now, it could be argued that we cannot make any claims about them. More importantly, based on the impli-cations of the problem of non-existence, some philosophers (e.g., Attfield 2003; DeGeorge 1981; Fienberg 1974) have argued that future generations cannot be conferred upon with rights.

One way of addressing the implications of the problem of non-existence in the context of the rights of future people is to consider their rights in a futur-istic sense. For example, Gosseries (2008) argues for *future rights of future people* as opposed to *present rights of future people*. In the same line of thought, Tremmel (2009) also argues that future people *will* have rights, just as they will have inter-ests. Similarly, Baier (1981, p. 171) maintains, "No one doubts that future gener-ations once they are present and actual, will have rights, if any of us have rights." She argues that the ontological precariousness of future generations is not that different from the future states of present people, and that it cannot be used to ignore the rights of future generations.

Another way to address the problem of non-existence is to resort to legal provisions that might undercut the argument of the problem of non-existence. Consider, for instance, Nelson's stance (2015, p. 90) that insists on having legal rights for future people in the present because they can legally exist in the present through the representation of a commissioner or an ombudsperson. It is not that Nelson doesn't understand the precarious position of the future generations. She does; yet she addresses the uncertainty surrounding future generations by differ-entiating between specific future individuals and the human race as a collective made up of indeterminate human beings. Ignoring the inevitable uncertainty that pertains to anything that has not yet happened, she thinks that the future generations, like current generations, will want to live in a healthy and clean environment. Therefore, upholding article 2 of the United Nations' *Universal Declaration of Human Rights* (1948), which states that human rights apply to eve-ryone, Nelson opines, "as soon as they [future generations] come into existence, they will have the same rights to life and health as current human beings" (ibid.).

In sum, there are at least two ways in which we can address the implications of the problem of non-existence. We can either recognize future people as a part of the human race that will come into existence with the same interests as the current generations and consider their interests and future rights just as we do those of the current generations. Or, resort to the binding documents that are produced by bodies like the United Nations and safeguard the rights and interests of future people.

The problem of nonidentity

The problem of nonidentity may be discussed under three propositions.

Proposition 1: Different future people can be brought into existence or their identities can be altered through our actions.

The problem of nonidentity rests upon the fact that we can change the identity (i.e., all aspects, including genetic makeup, that contribute to the understanding of who a person or a group is) of future people by our current actions. The ability to alter the identity of future people or decide who can be brought into existence doesn't seem like a problem from the outset. However, such ability leads to a moral impasse that we will address in the next proposition.

Proposition 2: If we can change the identity of future people through our actions, and if we consider morality of an act in person-affecting terms, then it could be argued that our actions might not harm anyone or make anyone's situation worse.

This proposition points to what is famously called "Parfit's Paradox," based on the name of the philosopher Derik Parfit, who is commonly associated with the problem of nonidentity. In order to understand this paradox, Parfit (1984, p. 358) gives the example of a young woman who gives birth at the age of 14. People may compare the chances in life of the baby that is born to the young woman to a baby that might be born to the same young woman at a more mature age in order to establish that the young woman's actions were morally wrong. From Parfit's perspective, however, we cannot say that the actions of the young woman are morally wrong because we cannot compare the wellbeing of the child that *is* already born to that of the child that *might be* born. In that sense, as Parfit argues, this young woman has not necessarily harmed the child that is born to her at 14.

The implications of this conclusion are troublesome, particularly in the context of intergenerational justice. For one, if our actions are not going to "harm" future generations, then all our actions or non-actions towards them are morally permissible. Sadly, then, our concern for future generations becomes irrelevant. This is an unwarranted conclusion that we are confronted with and we need to find a way to counter that conclusion.

Proposition 3: In situations where our actions are clearly harming someone and yet it could be argued that those actions are not making anyone's situation worse, then there is a need to find a way to judge that our actions are morally unacceptable.

In the example we've seen earlier, we have encountered a logical stalemate. How can we say that the 14-year-old's action is morally right, if she is deliberately going to give her newborn a hard start in life? Finding a solution to this apparent paradox is the problem of nonidentity. In the rest of this section, we will look into a couple of solutions to address the implications of the problem of nonidentity in the context of intergenerational justice.

While accepting the argument of the problem of nonidentity and its surprising conclusion, Page (2006) recognizes that the argument of the problem of nonidentity works well if it is set up in the context of an individual or a group of individuals and their rights. In the context of rights, when someone is harmed, their rights are compromised. To solve the problem, Page moves beyond the rights of individuals and proposes that we need to consider the rights of groups. More specifically, he proposes the *holistic* view of group rights[2] according to which a group is "viewed as bearing ethical status independently of its individual members" (ibid., p. 150).[3] According to Page, holistic rights of groups can avoid the problems of nonidentity because: (1) groups, unlike individual members, exist longer and are more fixed; and (2) the formation of groups does not depend on the union of a particular sperm or egg, which is a key aspect in the conception of the problem of nonidentity (ibid., p. 156). Therefore, future generations when considered as a group can bypass the obstacles posed by the problem of nonidentity.

Moving on, Harman (2004, p. 96) challenges the problem of nonidentity because it is based on a "worse off" argument, which states: "An action harms a person only if it makes the person worse off than she would otherwise have been if the action had not been performed." Given that the alternative is nonexistence of the child, in Parfit's case, it could be argued that the child that is born to the 14-year-old is not worse off. Harman doesn't agree with this argument. The alternative for comparison, according to Harman, should have been a healthy bodily state of a human person, rather than a state of non-existence.[4] In such context, Harman proposes (2004, p. 93) her *sufficient* condition for harm: An action harms a person if the action causes pain, early death, bodily damage, or deformity to her, even if she would not have existed if the action had not been performed.

If we consider Harman's *sufficient* condition for harm, the 14-year-old's actions could be deemed morally wrong. The same condition may be applied to resolve ethical dilemmas that the problem of nonidentity poses to the issues of intergenerational justice. These two solutions show that the problem of nonidentity cannot be unchallenged.

The problem of non-reciprocity

Another hurdle to cross before we discuss the principles of intergenerational justice is the problem of non-reciprocity. As Hiskes (2009, p. 226) points out, the problem of non-reciprocity in the context of intergenerational justice boils down to just relationships among those who can exchange:

> Reciprocity-based justice requires … that persons provide benefits for others, including members of different nations or generations, only if the

recipients are in a position to reciprocate. Persons belonging to later generations, however, can do little either to enhance or diminish the well-being of members of earlier generations. It would not seem just, on grounds of prudence or fairness, for earlier generations to sacrifice their well-being for the sake of their successors whom they will never meet or who cannot contribute to their well-being.

The seriousness of the problem of non-reciprocity in the context of intergenerational justice arises due to the fact that future generations are not in a position to reciprocate for the actions of the earlier generations. As a result, it could be argued that future generations do not have any claims against the earlier generations.

The first solution to the problem of non-reciprocity comes from Page (2007), who attempts to resolve the problem with his idea of *intergenerational stewardship*. It stands on the notion that reciprocity doesn't necessarily exist only between those persons who can interact with each other through some direct causal pathway. Rather, reciprocity can happen between people through an *indirect* causal pathway as well. By including the indirect causal pathway of reciprocity, Page opens the possibility of including persons that do not directly interact, e.g., the future generations. Given the indirect causal pathway, the current generation can discharge a duty to the next and expect that generation to benefit the generation that follows it. The idea of intergenerational stewardship is that "existing persons are bound by duties of indirect reciprocity to protect environmental and human resources for posterity in return for the benefits inherited from their ancestors" (Page 2007, p. 233).

Hiskes offers another solution to the problem through his idea of *reflexive reciprocity*. "If reciprocity is a defining characteristic of justice between individual members in a community," he maintains, "then we must ask what [the] present generation knows or can assume about future members for reciprocity to be possible with them" (Hiskes, 2009, p. 58). For that question, he proposes two things that we know about future generations: (1) they have moral and communal values, and (2) they share essential interests with each other and with us. Since those interests exist "simultaneously now *and* in the future in one and the same time" (ibid., p. 59), we are compelled to protect those interests for the sake of our own welfare as well as for the sake of the welfare of future generations (ibid., p. 60). The relationship of reciprocity between our environmental interests with the environmental interests of the future he calls reflexive reciprocity.

To bring this discussion on the objections to intergenerational justice to a close, we may say that there are problems on the path to intergenerational justice, yet they are not without solutions. Therefore, they should not come in the way of our discussion on intergenerational justice. With that in mind, we need to understand what we are concerned about when we are talking about intergenerational justice. As Page puts it, it is the *currency* of intergenerational justice that we need to discuss.

A framework for intergenerational justice

In order to figure out the *currency* of intergenerational justice, we need to know what future generations need. Schuppert (2011, p. 304) suggests:

> Justifying our moral concern for future generations we can appeal to the basic moral assumption that all persons share a set of fundamental interests and that the fundamental interests of future people weigh just as heavily as the fundamental interests of present people when we devise principles of intergenerational justice.

Considering fundamental interests as the currency of intergenerational justice, what Schuppert is proposing is a sufficientarian perspective of dealing with those interests of future people. So, instead of focusing on the inequality that future generations will have to face due to their place on the timeline of history, Schuppert aims at making sure that everyone – including the future people – has their fundamental interests fulfilled. If that is the case, two questions that need to be addressed are: (1) What are those fundamental interests? and (2) What are those principles of intergenerational justice?

Principles of basic needs and fundamental interests

Schuppert provides answers to both questions. To outline the fundamental interests of future people, he depends on the work of political theorist Simon Caney. According to Caney (as cited in Schuppert 2011, p. 316), global justice requires,

> in addition to meeting everybody's basic needs, i.e. food, water, clothing, shelter, basic health care, and physical security (which would be a baseline sufficientarianism) that every person receives the rights, liberties and goods necessary to form, revise and have the ability to fulfill their own conception of the good.

Based on that understanding of justice, Schuppert (2011, p. 316) proposes a person's basic interests as "a set of liberties, goods and things that give them equal opportunity to flourish."

Given these fundamental interests of a person, Schuppert (ibid.) offers three key requirements for achieving intergenerational justice:

> First, every person's basic needs must be met, which means that each person has an equal right to food, water, clothing, shelter, physical security and basic health care. Second, every person has a right to a healthy environment with functioning eco-systems as human life ultimately depends on nature, and thus a person's opportunity to realize her fundamental interests depend on it, too. Third, every person has a set of social, political and economic liberties and rights which cannot be restricted for the sake of

secondary concerns of intergenerational justice, such as the fair and equal distribution of climate change mitigation costs, for instance.

As noted, the first requirement pertains to the basic needs of a person, the second requirement goes beyond the person and covers the needs that a person has pertaining to the natural environment in which that person lives, and finally, the third requirement covers the social needs of that person. These three requirements do give a basic framework or a benchmark that needs to be reached for achieving intergenerational justice. Taking into the account the implications of Anthropocene on the environmental, social–economic and political spheres, it is pivotal that the requirements of intergenerational justice go beyond meeting the basic needs of a person, and Schuppert's conception does that. However, given the purpose of this essay is to provide tools to envision an environmentally and ecologically just future, we'll uplift the second requirement that Schuppert posits, which is concerned about the rights of every person to a healthy environment with functioning ecosystems, and move on to answer the question: How can we make sure that future generations enjoy at least the same kind of Earth and natural resources that the current generations are enjoying?

Principles of intergenerational ecological equity

In order to answer this question, we may depend on Brown Weiss' three principles of intergenerational ecological equity that are widely invoked in environmental literature (Page 2006; Weston 2007–2008; Westra 2006). In a summary fashion, intergenerational ecological equity is achieved through comparable options, comparable quality, and comparable access. Before we go any further, we need to understand that comparability is an important issue here and ecological equity cannot be achieved without this aspect of comparison. For instance, even to understand how climate changes, we need to depend on the aspect of comparison. Despite its importance, the concept of comparability has limits. Let's consider biodiversity, for example. The United Nations' Convention on Biodiversity (1992, p. 3) construed biodiversity as "the variability among living organisms from all sources including, *inter alia*, terrestrial, marine and other aquatic ecosystems and the ecological complexes of which they are part: this includes diversity within species, between species and of ecosystems." Understandably, comparing such a broad spectrum of organisms from various ecosystems across time poses a limitation. Yet, the aspect of comparability is significant for the purposes of achieving justice across generations, especially in the light of the implications of the Anthropocene that cut across generational lines.

The first principle of intergenerational ecological equity is that each generation must conserve options. By options, Brown Weiss means that there are the opportunities available to both solve the problems that future generations might face and to fulfill their values. The options are believed to be available in and through the diversity of natural and cultural resource base. So, the diversity of these resources needs to be conserved, since future generations are entitled to options available to them comparable to those that the previous generations have enjoyed.

Secondly, the principle of comparable quality: "[E]ach generation should be required to maintain the quality of the planet so that it is passed on in a condition no worse than that in which it was received" (Brown Weiss 1992, p. 22). It stresses the conservation of the quality of the earth that is passed on from one generation to the next. In other words, a generation cannot pass on the earth to the next generation in a condition or quality worse than it had received it. In addition to the diversity of natural and cultural resources, this principle recognizes that future generations are entitled to a comparable quality of those resources.

Finally, the principle of comparable access states, "[E]ach generation should provide its members with equitable rights of access to the legacy of past generations and conserve this access for future generations" (ibid., p. 23). This principle highlights the conservation of non-discriminatory access to the Earth and its resources. This is an important consideration because even though we maintain comparable options and comparable quality, it is futile unless the future generations have access to those resources.

These principles of ecological equity are widely discussed in environmental literature for various reasons. For one, as Weston (2007–2008, pp. 396–397) points out, these principles give "both the ethical rationales that give intergenerational justice moral purpose and the jurisprudential theories that give it legal standing." Further, Westra (2006, p. 136) observes that Brown Weiss' principles comprise both rights and duties, while also covering both *intra*generational and *inter*generational aspects. While the principles of comparable options, comparable quality, and comparable access cover the rights of future generations, as Westra (ibid.) notes, the duties that Brown Weiss proposal covers are:

1. to pass on the Earth to the next generation in as good a condition as it was when that generation first received it;
2. a duty to repair any damage caused by any failure of previous generations to do the same.

In addition to combining the rights and duties in her principles, the inclusion of the demands of intergenerational and intragenerational justice is significant. Often it is thought that the goals of intergenerational justice are in conflict with the goals of intragenerational justice, but Brown Weiss' proposal diffuses such an argument. The aspect of "comparability" in her principles gives the needed balance to address the needs of the current generations as well as the needs of the future generations.

Principles of non-violation and remedial justice

While Brown Weiss' principles of intergenerational justice have many attractive features and stipulate the minimum requirements of intergenerational justice, they do not set boundaries of the purview of justice between generations. In other words, how far can we go to fulfill the demands of justice for future generations? For that, the principles of international intergenerational justice that Thompson (2009, p. 163) proposes are critical:

> The first, and primary, principle is that polities, and other international agents, ought not to violate each other's entitlements, or the entitlement of communities within each other's borders, to maintain intergenerational relationships, practices and institutions which satisfy basic requirements of justice and to fulfill their intergenerational responsibilities within the framework of these relationships and institutions ....
>
> The second principle is a requirement of remedial justice. Polities and other international agents ought to make reparation for violations of the requirements of the first principle with the objective of bringing about a state of affairs in which both perpetrators and victims (or their successors) are no longer justified in regarding the violation as standing in the way of establishing or re-establishing just relationships.

The first principle may be referred to as the principle of non-violation. As much as there is a need for polities and international agents to fulfill their intergenerational responsibilities, they cannot violate each other's entitlements or the entitlements of communities within each other's borders. To put it differently, even though there is a need to protect the environment for future generations, polities such as international communities or international agents cannot violate the entitlements of communities within anyone's borders in the present. Applied generationally, this principle serves the purpose of safeguarding the entitlements of the present generations from being sacrificed for the sake of future generations. Yet, that doesn't mean that the present generations do not have intergenerational responsibilities. It only means that there are limits for how far polities and international agents can go to fulfill their intergenerational obligations.

The second principle may be referred to as the principle of remedial justice. This principle recognizes the need for reparative justice so that just relations may be established within a national or international setting. Similarly, this principle can be applied to establish just relationships intra-generationally or inter-generationally. Consider, for instance, an international institution S, in an attempt to make the future generations have clean water, jeopardized the ability of people at a particular time period in a country B to access a certain source of clean water. In such a case, the principle of remedial justice requires that S make reparations to the communities of B in the present. At any given point of time, this principle helps in rectifying the wrongs that might have been done before that point of time. This principle is in some ways similar to the second duty that Brown Weiss presents, where she talks about repairing the damage done by previous generations. As much as intergenerational justice is about protecting the options and quality of the Earth for future generations, it is also about taking responsibility of the past injustices. Without such provisions of repair and reparations, it is impossible to achieve a *just* future.

Altogether, the principles that we have discussed so far can provide an ethical framework for intergenerational justice. These principles can ensure that a proposed policy fosters a just future. For instance, when any policy pertaining to future generations is proposed, it needs to allow for the future generations to: (1) fulfill their fundamental interests, (2) enjoy a healthy environment with functioning ecosystems, and (3) enjoy their socio-economic and political liberties in a fair social environment. If an environmental policy relating to future generations is being proposed, it has to be specifically aimed at fulfilling the obligations of providing: (1) comparable options (natural and cultural resources) to those in the future to fulfill their fundamental interests, (2) comparable quality of the environment, and (3) comparable access to the Earth and its resources. Finally, it has to be ensured that all policies with regard to the future generations, environmental or otherwise, do not violate the rights of the vulnerable population of the current generations. Also, all policies need to be aimed at bringing about a just state of affairs and providing reparations for past injustices.

In the context of the severe injustices in the Anthropocene, this framework serves the purpose of fostering a just relationship with the future generations and also helps in addressing some of the historic injustices. It also sets limits on the requirements of intergenerational justice so that the needs of the current generations are not compromised for the sake of future generations and vice versa. Furthermore, this framework also supports the broader goals of environmental justice.

Conclusion

We are at a historic moment sandwiched between the blunders of the past and the possibilities of the future. The blunders of the past are way too many to count. Ignoring the signs of our times and the implications of the Anthropocene is one of the biggest mistakes of our times. If the implications of human activity on the environment and the Earth system are ignored and our state of affairs continues in a "business as usual" style, then the future remains bleak. Unfortunately, those that will be gravely impacted are the ones that would have contributed the least to the Anthropocene – the most vulnerable populations, the non-human beings, and future generations. The possibility of changing the course of the Earth's future (our future) by reimagining our role on this planet and how we relate to the non-human beings and the future generations is our biggest obligation. Envisioning a just future in that sense is pivotal in addressing the chronic condition that we are in now. The framework of intergenerational justice that we have discussed in this essay is a step in that direction.

Notes

1 Ellis defines Anthropocene as "human-induced shift in Earth's functioning as a system" (Ellis 2018, p. 130).
2 Page distinguishes between *holistic* view of group rights and *reductionist* view of group rights. According to the *reductionist* view of group rights the group itself has no ethical status above and beyond that possessed by its members (Page 2006, p. 150).
3 On a side note, Page thinks that it is more useful to think of cultural groups and their rights instead of generations when we are talking about intergenerational justice. It is because unlike a cultural group or nation, a generation is abstract, and it is hard to define a generation along with the overlap between one generation and the other. Also, in reality people do not act as if the generation they belong to possesses any independent value (Page 2006, p. 150, pp. 155–156).
4 Like Harman, Heyd (1992, p. 37) argues that the value attributed to the life of an actually existing person cannot be compared to that of non-existence. A couple of considerations that he proposes (ibid.), which will block the comparison between life and non-existence, are: "the valuelessness of nonexistence as such and the unattributability of its alleged value to individual subjects." He thinks that these two considerations are intricately connected. The reason why we cannot give value to nonexistence *of* people is because it cannot be attached *to* people.

References

Attfield, R., 2003. *Environmental Ethics: An Overview for the Twenty-First Century.* Cambridge: Polity Press.
Baier, A., 1981. 'The Rights of Past and Future Persons.' In Partridge, E. (ed.) *Responsibilities to Future Generations.* Buffalo: Prometheus Books, 171–183.
Brown Weiss, E., 1992. 'In Fairness to Future Generations and Sustainable Development.' *American University International Law Review,* 8(1), 19–26.
DeGeorge, R., 1981. 'The Environment, Rights, and Future Generations.' In Partridge, E. (ed.) *Responsibilities to Future Generations.* Buffalo: Prometheus Books, 157–166.
Dryzek, J. and Pickering, J., 2019. *The Politics of the Anthropocene.* Oxford: Oxford University Press.
Ellis, E., 2018. *Anthropocene: A Very Short Introduction.* Oxford: Oxford University Press.
Feinberg, J., 1974. 'The Rights of Animals and Unborn Generations.' In Blackstone, W. (ed.) *Philosophy and Environmental Crisis.* Athens: University of Georgia Press, 43–68.
Gosseries, A., 2008. 'On Future Generations' Future Rights.' *Journal of Political Philosophy,* 16(4), 446–474.
Harman, E., 2004. 'Can We Harm and Benefit in Creating?' *Philosophical Perspectives,* 18, 89–113. Available from: https://www.princeton.edu/~eharman/canweharm.pdf [Accessed 22 March 2020].
Heyd, D., 1992. *Genethics: Moral Issues in the Creation of People.* Berkeley: University of California.
Hiskes, R., 2009. *The Human Right to a Green Future: Environmental Rights and Intergenerational Justice.* New York: Cambridge University Press.
Nelson, G., 2015. 'Future Generations and Climate Change.' *International Social Science Journal,* 64(211–212), 89–97.
Page, E., 2006. *Climate Change, Justice and Future Generations.* Northampton, MA: Edward Elgar.
Page, E., 2007. 'Fairness on the Day after Tomorrow: Justice, Reciprocity, and Global Climate Change.' *Political Studies,* 55(1), 225–242.

Parfit, D., 1984. *Reasons and Persons*. Oxford: Clarendon Press.

Schuppert, F., 2011. 'Climate Change Mitigation and Intergenerational Justice.' *Environmental Politics*, 20(3), 303–321. Available from: http://dx.doi.org/10.1080 /09644016.2011.573351 [Accessed 20 March 2020].

Thompson, J., 2009. *Intergenerational Justice: Rights and Responsibilities in an Intergenerational Polity*. New York: Routledge.

Tremmel, J., 2009. *A Theory of Intergenerational Justice*. London: Earthscan.

United Nations' Convention on Biodiversity, 1992. Available from: https://www.cbd.int /doc/legal/cbd-en.pdf [Accessed 20 March 2020].

Weston, B., 2007–2008. 'Climate Change and Intergenerational Justice: Foundational Reflections.' *Vermont Journal of Environmental Law*, 9, 374–430. Available from: http:/ /vjel.vermontlaw.edu/files/2013/06/Climate-Change-and-Intergenerational-Justice -Foundational-Reflections.pdf [Accessed 19 March 2020].

Westra, L., 2006. *Environmental Justice and the Rights of Unborn and Future Generations: Law, Environmental Harm and the Right to Health*. London: Earthscan.

22

CONDITIONAL FREEDOM

A governance innovation for climate justice

Rita Vasconcellos Oliveira

Introduction

Climate change is a key issue in the overall effort for sustainable development (SD). Our generation is already living with climate change and the devastating consequences of the recrudescence of extreme weather events. This crisis is so relevant that it characterizes the era we live in – the Anthropocene. The negative impacts of climate change are being felt by millions of individuals, and often disproportionately impact the world's most vulnerable and marginalized communities. In the words of Secretary-General António Guterres, "climate change is happening now and to all of us ... And, as is always the case, the poor and vulnerable are the first to suffer and the worst hit" (United Nations 2019a). Climate change is a social and environmental justice issue at the core of climate justice (CJ) and by extension, is central to the very notion of Anthropocene.

International institutions have taken the lead in creating global strategies for climate action. The United Nations Framework Convention on Climate Change is the main international agreement on climate action, which includes among other agreements, the Kyoto Protocol and the Paris Agreement. Achieving the goals of these agreements in an equitable fashion requires more than what has been done so far. For overcoming the greatest challenges of the Anthropocene, it is crucial to anchor socio-political actions in an ethical frame that does not systematically ignore relevant normative traditions (Parks and Roberts 2006). In general, politicians have acknowledged this fact, but mostly in an ambiguous way. For example, the sustainable development goal of climate action (SDG 13) includes justice principles related to the distributive implications of global warming. However, as Vasconcellos Oliveira (2018) shows, these justice principles are frequently contradicting in objective and timeframe, creating additional tensions during strategy implementation. Thus, a new vision for climate justice is needed.

Utilitarianism has been the prevalent ethical theory for considering justice issues and framing climate change at large. However, it has fallen short in delivering justice especially for smaller and underprivileged societal groups (Vasconcellos Oliveira et al. 2018). To overcome the hegemony and the ethical limitations of utilitarianism in the CJ debate, this chapter proposes a less prevalent ethical perspective but with increased possibilities to promote environmental, climate and distributive justice (Schlosberg and Carruthers 2010). In this chapter, the capability approach (CA) is applied as an ethical guideline to climate change strategies, closely related to Schlosberg's work (Schlosberg and Collins 2014; Schlosberg 2009). However, the novelty of this work resides in the focus on the collective good as means of achieving meaningful freedom that, ultimately, changes consumption into a sustainable tool for CJ. The aim is to contribute to a much-needed shift in the socio-political framing of the Anthropocene, where climate justice is a key to finding transformative remedies for the current climate situation.

To establish this relation and to correctly apply the CA to the climate change debate, especially as a SD challenge and policy aimed at climate change mitigation and adaptation, it is necessary to revisit and elaborate on specific CA concepts such as well-being, freedom and responsibility. Thus, the chapter starts with a short description of how SD and climate change are to be framed under the CA. Afterwards, the CA notions of *well-being, freedom* and *agency* are revisited in the context of CJ. A reflection on the repercussions of the CJ principles of *avoiding harm* and *sharing burdens* in the CA conceptual framework follows. This theoretical development exposes the relevance of future generations' well-being for both the CA and CJ. The chapter then develops the concept of *conditional freedom* in connection to climate justice and related to the notion of responsibility. It also develops the concept of sustainable consumption under the CA and targeting CJ. Conclusions are drawn in the last part of the chapter.

Sustainable development based on human capabilities: implications for climate justice

The CA was originally formulated to improve the relationship between economics and development. Strictly speaking, it stems from Amartya Sen's critique of welfare economics (Sen 1997) and utilitarianism (Sen 1980). Sen claims that there are relevant shortcomings in considering goods as a measure for human development. According to Sen, well-being revolves around the freedom and opportunities to be and to do what each individual believes is worth valuing.

The CA holds two key concepts: functionings and capabilities. Functionings refer to all an individual is and does and is not the actual choice and associated freedom. Capability represents the different combinations of functionings, i.e., an opportunity set. Each person can choose from a set of available functionings. This act of choosing creates unique combinations that grant each person their own path (Sen 1993).

In the CA, freedom comprises both well-being and agency (Nussbaum et al. 1993). Well-being consists of the capacity of choice, while agency concerns the objectives each individual values for her/his well-being.

Probably due to the focus of the CA in developmental and poverty issues (Nussbaum 2007), the relevance of sustainability and SD was acknowledged rather late in relation to intergenerational justice (Anand and Sen 1994) and the economic sides of SD (Anand and Sen 2000). Anand and Sen (1994, 2000) argue that SD should be person- and freedom-oriented, which is in sharp contrast with (western) scientific approaches, traditionally centered on resources and processes.

Since the beginning, researchers have singled out potential limitations to the CA as a normative framework for SD (Schultz et al. 2013). For example, the CA runs the risk of ignoring how freedom of choice can overstretch the earth's limits, especially when considering greenhouse gas (GHG) emissions.

In response, Peeters et al. (2015) proposed the idea of constraining people's functionings consonantly to a personal budget, which consists of a fair share of environmental resources. In doing so, the authors point out the interdependency of individual's freedoms. They conceive individual's freedoms as relations in which a person deals with limitations, originating from potential functionings. The authors advocate for introducing constraints to functionings to protect intrapersonal freedom and future people's interests (also interpreted as freedoms).

Schultz et al. (2013) advanced another solution, based on the notions of *valuable functionings* and *evaluative space*. According to the authors, it is crucial to establish an integrated evaluative space to be able to discern what is actually good for people and the environment. The final objective is to determine *what* achieved functionings are worth because they are only valuable if they are sustainable.

Another important contribution to harmonize the CA and SD comes from Pelenc and colleagues who focus on *special responsibility* (towards nature) as a way to move from individual freedom towards "taking into account the potentially irreversible consequences of achieving a particular choice, or a particular set of capabilities, on other people's well-being or/and on the natural environment" collectively (Pelenc et al. 2015, p. 231).

In the case of climate change, there are (at least) two dimensions that need specific consideration and have not yet been mentioned. This includes the collective nature of the problem as the origin and as the means of mitigation (Rauschmayer and Lessmann 2013). This fact requires the recognition of collective responsibility in terms of its adverse effects on people and nature and of the justice implications for present and future generations. On this issue, it is defensible to follow Ballet et al.'s (2013) position that the CA is a worthy approach to comparative environmental justice. They propose applying the CA as a justice framework, in which climate change arrangements (e.g., social, institutional, or economic) are evaluated in terms of justice gradations. This possibility has a straightforward application in climate governance and policy.

For the sake of climate debate and action (e.g., climate treaties), it is vital to re-emphasize justice dimensions such as distributive and intergenerational.

Interestingly, they are also pivotal in the CA theory. The next section focuses on justice as the strategic point for articulation between the CA and SD and as a key issue in the Anthropocene.

Aligning climate justice with the capabilities approach

In the introduction, it was established that climate change has an undeniable justice dimension. As Lindley et al. (2011, p. 7) write, climate change generates "important losses in central dimensions of well-being." However, well-being does not cover the whole phenomenon of climate injustice. It is equally fundamental to recognition that those least responsible for climate change experience the greatest negative impacts on their well-being. CJ captures the equity aspects of climate change, seeks the reduction of disparities in development and power that drive climate change (Parks and Roberts 2006), and aims at a profound change in governance patterns (Ciplet et al. 2018).

In the context of the CA, CJ relates largely to the negative effect of global warming on well-being and capabilities. The focus is on how climate change threatens well-being in terms of opportunities to be and opportunities to do what individuals consider valuable.

That said, and since the CA and CJ have evolved separately, it is important to continue working on the moral alignment of the CA and CJ principles. As Caney (2014, pp. 125–126) refers, there are two main ways of thinking about CJ:

> One starts by focusing on how the burden of combating the problem should be shared fairly among the duty-bearers [...] *Burden-Sharing Justice.* [... And the] second perspective takes as its starting point the imperative to prevent climate change, and it works back from this to deduce who should do what [...] *Harm Avoidance Justice.*

Looking first to *burden-sharing justice*, climate change creates justice issues of how to fairly distribute its burdens to not decrease the present level of well-being, or in the CA terminology, how to make sure that the distribution of the encumbrances is fair enough not to exacerbate the damages in the capabilities of the most vulnerable?

While Sen did not advocate for any particular theory of resource or burden allocation, Nussbaum and Anderson have advocated for sufficiency, in the sense of guaranteeing that every person can develop fundamental capabilities (Anderson 1999, Nussbaum 2009). Therefore, it is reasonable to propose sufficientarianism as a distributive matrix based on CA's application of the capabilities thresholds (Nielsen and Axelsen 2017). Following this reasoning, agents emitting more than the minimum amount of GHG necessary for reaching a capabilities threshold are responsible (preferably in a proportional way) to ensure efforts towards mitigation and/or adaptation. As Steinberger and Roberts (2010) argue, energy sufficiency goals are reachable at low environmental costs. On a macroscale, authors like Ciplet et al. (2013) offer concrete proposals for fair(er) international climate negotiation agenda, especially on how to economically support the adaption effort.

Focusing on *harm avoidance justice*, one question arises. In terms of climate governance and development policies, what should society justly prioritize: climate change mitigation or climate change adaptation? The CA offers guidance to address this crucial interrogation in CJ.

Strategies that alleviate the negative effects of climate change (i.e., climate change adaptation) in the most vulnerable individuals are much in line with the CA as this theory stresses the need to change social arrangements to advance justice (Sen 2006). As Schlosberg (2012, p. 458) states, the CA is the best-equipped justice theory "to identify and physically map vulnerabilities caused by climate change," which makes it essential for new forms of governance for the Anthropocene.

Despite the crucial importance of climate change adaptation, we would prevent further or even reduce existent inequalities deriving from environmental constraints to capabilities by concentrating efforts on climate change mitigation (Robeyns 2005). Climate change mitigation efforts can also have positive side effects, or co-benefits, due to the intersection with other societal goals. As Vasconcellos Oliveira and Thorseth (2016) show, there is the possibility of achieving far more climate justice if co-benefits are framed by CA with a focus on capabilities instead of commodities as current climate change mitigation strategies do. Additionally, climate change mitigation efforts are absolutely justified and necessary for intergenerational reasons, mostly because different generations should have an adequate freedom-capabilities space, which can only be achieved if global warming is mitigated.

More importantly, intergenerational justice is a very robust justification for reinforcing SD principles in the CA, particularly in the climate change context. The argumentation takes a negative form: the need and action towards the expansion of freedom as capabilities (intragenerational justice) cannot be made at the expense of compromising those from future people. For example, expanding current energy availability (improving agency and well-being) should not be achieved through the investment and dissemination of fossil fuels because this option would exacerbate climate change, which will have nefarious consequences for the well-being and freedom of future generations.

Expanding the concept of conditional freedom

Individual capability sets include freedoms, regarded as capabilities, that are dependent on other people's choices and capability sets (i.e., there are freedoms which are conditional) (Basu 1987). For example, two commercial partners are individually free to pursue their ideas for their business but since they are in a partnership, their business-related functionings and well-being achievements are a product of both their individual freedom and the interaction of both capabilities' spheres. Hence, each individual's freedom is conditioned by their partner's capabilities and also by his/her functionings.

This demonstrates the inter-relational aspect of the CA notion of freedom, or capability. For example, being able to have pleasurable life experiences, depends on things that past and present individuals have contributed or not to produce a stable climate. More importantly, if some freedoms are enabled and/or conditional to others, there is an inherited relation of reciprocity. This relation of reciprocity evokes moral responsibility, i.e., if an individual "is given" something or in this case, a capability is enabled by other(s), then the same individual should "give back" or enable (at least) that capability in others.

Using Holland's argument of "meta-capability," or a capability that ultimately enables all others (Holland 2008), it can be argued that each individual should contribute to this capability because it enables additional capabilities for other individuals. Looking closer at climate change, Page (2007) establishes a safe and hospitable environment as a crucial capability and Holland (2008) stresses the fact that Nussbaum's list of capabilities is dependent upon a stable climate system. However, their acknowledgements miss the point that a safe and hospitable environment or climate is conditional to other's choices and behaviors, and that guaranteeing a stable climate system is dependent on and enabler of capabilities of people. Consequently, it is crucial to realize that, under the CA, there is an inherent obligation to contribute to a stable climate.

Similarly, this reciprocity originates a chain of obligations towards the maintenance of a stable climate system for future individuals. A "climate chain of reciprocity" creates situations where present individuals have to sacrifice and/ or constrain their freedom to be "fair" to their own generation and to future people. There will be a need for voluntary self-restraint to satisfy obligations towards others. Pelenc et al. (2013) refer to this as *ex-ante responsibility*. There may be cases, where ex-ante responsibility means exercising individual responsibility by considering the potential consequences of one's acts on others' capabilities, and at large on the environment and climate.

Having this in consideration, it is possible to extend the concept of conditional freedom(s) to include the requirement of an agent to adopt a prudent approach when the exercise of agency may affect the capabilities of others. In CJ, the integration of the precautionary principle, especially in decision-making processes, is recurrent. However, this is not the case in the traditional CA. Nevertheless, and as Pelenc et al. (2013) argue, the integration of the precautionary principle would make a significant difference in closing the gap between CA and SD.

It is relevant to make clear that ex-ante responsibility is not a limitation to an individual's freedom. It only narrows down what can be considered worth valuing by adding a clear intra- and inter-generational justice dimension to the evaluative space. Ex-ante responsibility molds the capability space, "which includes people's choice, ability, and opportunity to transform resources into achieved functionings" (Frediani 2010, p. 178), but does not diminish it.

In sum, the concept of conditional freedom can help in the integration of SD in CA and can be particularly helpful in the climate debate. The consideration of justice as a frame for the capability space directs individual choices to transform resources into achieved functionings. The recognition that some capabilities are conditional to the capabilities of others, mainly those related to the environment, creates a responsibility based on justice that will condition the evaluative space and generate functionings that are attainable sustainably. This might translate, for example, in not choosing certain resources (e.g., fossil fuels) even if they meant achieving desired functionings (e.g., mobility) because the stable climate system is necessary for others' capabilities.

Sustainable consumption: a governance issue

In the SDGs, the UN dedicated particular attention to the way resources are used and goods consumed, especially concerning energy governance (United Nations 2019b). Already in 1994, at the Oslo Symposium, consumption was conceived under the key idea of environmental and intergenerational justice. The participants urged society to "use services and related products which respond to basic needs and bring a better quality of life while minimizing the use of natural resources and toxic materials … so not to jeopardize the needs of further generations" (United Nations 2019c).

Unfortunately, this call for action did not make evident the intimate connection between consumption and climate, especially how the increase in consumption has fueled global warming. The population increase and the improvement of well-being worldwide, in combination with more lavish lifestyles, have led to the environmental and climate crises we live in today. This situation incited a global movement to transform present patterns of consumption while lifting people out of poverty, i.e., make sustainable consumption a reality for all.

It is relevant to understand that sustainable consumption is an umbrella term that extends beyond meeting peoples' needs and increasing the use of renewable energy sources, but includes equity and governance dimensions as well.

In the CA literature, the vision of consumption is traditional and relates to microeconomics consumer choice and marketable goods (Sen 1992). More recently, Leßmann and Masson (2015) proposed a richer definition and established an analogy between the budget set and the capability set, in the sense of consumption as achieving functionings.

With respect to the connection between sustainable consumption and climate, it is useful to consider Lessmann and Rauschmayer's (2013) claim that sustainable consumption presupposes the consideration of the capabilities-sets of future people. However, their position does not deliver a full account of how sustainable consumption could be under the CA framework.

Going back to the previous considerations on conditional freedom, sustainable consumption is an example where the principle of prudence, or "avoiding harm" in CJ jargon, in the context of ex-ante responsibility, could shape the capability space. In this sense, people's choice, ability, and opportunity to transform resources into achieved functionings would be oriented by achieving justice. Under such assumption, consumption would be sustainable under the CA if it follows two principles: individual choices should guarantee future generations' equal or minimal capabilities and implemented actions/strategies should improve the resource-use ability of individuals of the present generation. Both conditions are also part of the governance dimension of sustainable consumption.

It is relevant to make clear that governance is not just a set of institutions, but rather a practical activity that includes rationalities, programs, techniques, and subjectivities which underpin it and give it its form and effect (Walters 2012). In our contemporary societies, green governmentality translates in the notion that individuals should contribute to SD, and particularly to climate change mitigation by making minor adjustments in their daily livelihoods and, above all, they should be responsible consumers (Soneryd and Uggla 2015).

The CA framework, especially the second condition for sustainable consumption, goes beyond this personal sphere of responsibility and reinforces the role of policies and development strategies in the accomplishment of SD. As Evans et al. (2017) show in the case of food waste in the UK, it is possible to create practical actions to improve the resource-use ability of individuals (e.g., supermarket packages that keep food fresher). Additionally, and under the CA approach, it is critical to protect future generations' capabilities, which could be achieved, for example by making available smaller portions at the supermarket. This way it would decrease resource consumption and consequently, GHG emissions.

As climate treaties will be translated into concrete policies, there is a unique opportunity for institutions to change their approach to civil society and implement new visions that include transformative remedies emerging from those struggling for EJ. The CA to sustainable consumption can be one of the elements reshaping political-economic structures behind injustices because at its core stands personal and collective actions for improving the resource-use ability of individuals, particularly of the worst-off. Moreover, the CA has an intrinsic commitment to poverty alleviation.

Previous research has suggested that sustainable consumption can be achieved by either investing in the development of green eco-innovations or by promoting frugality, sufficiency, and localism. In response to these extreme governance views and closer to a CA viewpoint, it is here proposed an intermediate third position that advocates a transition from the current configuration of the socio-economic and technical systems so as to obtain substantial sustainability gains (Geels et al. 2015). This transition entails connections between new (e.g., packages for increased food shelf time) and existing elements (e.g., small portion packaging), with an original configuration having more sustainable consumption and production characteristics. For example, implementing national campaigns for "food literacy" would improve everyone's capabilities, while decreasing waste. More importantly, it would beneficiate more the ones who suffer from food injustice.

Conclusions

Climate change is a key problem in the Anthropocene era. It affects us all but is particularly brutal for underprivileged populations who have to cope with its negative impacts without proper capacities. The unfairness of this situation is at the core of climate justice. So far, the international treaties on climate have failed to deliver relevant results in the diminishing global GHG emissions and have been unsuccessful in tackling climate injustice.

Researchers and NGO leaders have been claiming that climate action needs strong ethical roots. Despite being lesser applied, the CA can be a viable ethical framework for climate change, especially in terms of justice.

The scientific and the ethical discourse on SD and climate change action are for the most part centered on resources, particularly on scarcity and access. The CA offers a new take on climate injustice by highlighting people and freedom as drivers of change.

In response to this, it is argued here that it is necessary to bring justice to the center of the CA, especially concerning SD and climate. This translates into giving far more relevance to the interests of future generations when addressing development. It is crucial to guarantee that future people will enjoy the same or at least minimum capabilities when compared to current individuals.

To strengthen SD considerations within CA and to respond to CJ objectives, it is proposed to expand the concept of conditional freedom to include the precautionary principle in the capability space. Individual freedom would not be curtailed but the functionings deemed valuable would be subjected to a valuation based on sustainable and intergenerational justice principles. The introduction of conditional freedom in the evaluative space would impact the capabilities-sets of people. In this respect, it would affect consumption by framing consumption as an achieved functioning. In this way, the evaluative space would have a justice dimension that includes people and the environment.

If the CA would frame policies concerning consumption governance, there would be relevant changes in the guiding principles. Strategies promoting sustainable consumption would be human-centered and focus would be on improving the resource-ability of people, or the access and operative use of goods, while safeguarding future generations' capabilities. Additionally, the inclusion of conditional freedom in this framing would compel individual and collective agents to adopt a prudent approach when the exercise of agency may affect the capabilities of others. Moreover, it would demand the re-conceptualization of personal "wishes" into capabilities, which in turn would accentuate the importance of collective intra- and inter-generational good.

Climate injustice is a fundamental issue in our era. Therefore, it is crucial to develop a justice framework that responds to the current climate problems and also limits future injustices. The CA and the conditional freedom concept can offer an EJ transformative remedy where people, especially those experiencing the greatest injustices, are at the center of concerns.

References

Anand, S. and Sen, A. 1994. *Sustainable Human Development: Concepts and Priorities.* Occasional Papers 8. UNDP Human Development Report Office.

Anand, S. and Sen, A. 2000. Human Development and Economic Sustainability. *World Development*, 28(12), 2029–2049.

Anderson, E.S. 1999. What is the Point of Equality? *Ethics*, 109(2), 287–337.

Ballet, J., Koffi, J.-M. and Pelenc, J. 2013. Environment, Justice and the Capability Approach. *Ecological Economics*, 85, 28–34.

Basu, K. 1987. Achievements, Capabilities and the Concept of Well-Being. *Social Choice and Welfare*, 4(1), 69–76.

Caney, S. 2014. Two Kinds of Climate Justice: Avoiding Harm and Sharing Burdens. *Journal of Political Philosophy*, 22(2), 125–149.

Ciplet, D. et al. 2018. The Transformative Capability of Transparency in Global Environmental Governance. *Global Environmental Politics*, 18(3), 130–150.

Ciplet, D., Roberts, J.T. and Khan, M. 2013. The Politics of International Climate Adaptation Funding: Justice and Divisions in the Greenhouse. *Global Environmental Politics*, 13(1), 49–68.

Evans, D., Welch, D. and Swaffield, J. 2017. Constructing and Mobilizing 'The Consumer': Responsibility, Consumption and the Politics of Sustainability. *Environment and Planning A: Economy and Space*, 49(6), 1396–1412.

Frediani, A.A. 2010. Sen's Capability Approach as a Framework to the Practice of Development. *Development in Practice*, 20(2), 173–187.

Geels, F.W. et al. 2015. A Critical Appraisal of Sustainable Consumption and Production Research: The Reformist, Revolutionary and Reconfiguration Positions. *Global Environmental Change*, 34, 1–12.

Holland, B. 2008. Justice and the Environment in Nussbaum's "Capabilities Approach" Why Sustainable Ecological Capacity Is a Meta-Capability. *Political Research Quarterly*, 61(2), 319–332.

Leßmann, O. and Masson, T. 2015. Sustainable Consumption in Capability Perspective: Operationalization and Empirical Illustration. *Journal of Behavioral and Experimental Economics*, 57, 64–72.

Lessmann, O. and Rauschmayer, F. 2013. Re-conceptualizing Sustainable Development on the Basis of the Capability Approach: A Model and Its Difficulties. *Journal of Human Development and Capabilities*, 14(1), 95–114.

Lindley, S. et al. 2011. *Climate Change, Justice and Vulnerability.* York: Joseph Rowntree Foundation.

Nielsen, L. and Axelsen, D.V. 2017. Capabilitarian Sufficiency: Capabilities and Social Justice. *Journal of Human Development and Capabilities*, 18(1), 46–59.

Nussbaum, M. 2007. Human Rights and Human Capabilities. *Harvard Law School Human Rights Journal*, 20, 21.

Nussbaum, M., Sen, A. and Sen, M.A. 1993. *The Quality of Life.* Oxford: Oxford University Press.

Nussbaum, M.C. 2009. *Frontiers of Justice: Disability, Nationality, Species Membership.* Cambridge, MA: Harvard University Press.

Page, E.A. 2007. *Climate Change, Justice and Future Generations.* Cheltenham: Edward Elgar Publishing.

Parks, B.C. and Roberts, J.T. 2006. Globalization, Vulnerability to Climate Change, and Perceived Injustice. *Society and Natural Resources*, 19(4), 337–355.

Peeters, W., Dirix, J. and Sterckx, S. 2015. The Capabilities Approach and Environmental Sustainability: The Case for Functioning Constraints. *Environmental Values*, 24(3), 367–389.

Pelenc, J. et al. 2013. Sustainable Human Development and the Capability Approach: Integrating Environment, Responsibility and Collective Agency. *Journal of Human Development and Capabilities*, 14(1), 77–94.

Pelenc, J., Bazile, D. and Ceruti, C. 2015. Collective Capability and Collective Agency for Sustainability: A Case Study. *Ecological Economics*, 118, 226–239.

Rauschmayer, F. and Lessmann, O. 2013. The Capability Approach and Sustainability. *Journal of Human Development and Capabilities*, 14(1), 1–5.

Robeyns, I. 2005. The Capability Approach: A Theoretical Survey. *Journal of Human Development*, 6(1), 93–117.

Schlosberg, D. 2009. Capacity and Capabilities: A Response to the Greenhouse Development Rights Framework. *Ethics, Place & Environment*, 12(3), 287–290.

Schlosberg, D. 2012. Climate Justice and Capabilities: A Framework for Adaptation Policy. *Ethics & International Affairs*, 26(4), 445–461.

Schlosberg, D. and Carruthers, D. 2010. Indigenous Struggles, Environmental Justice, and Community Capabilities. *Global Environmental Politics*, 10(4), 12–35.

Schlosberg, D. and Collins, L.B. 2014. From Environmental to Climate Justice: Climate Change and the Discourse of Environmental Justice. *WIREs Climate Change*, 5(3), 359–374.

Schultz, E. et al. 2013. A Sustainability-Fitting Interpretation of the Capability Approach: Integrating the Natural Dimension by Employing Feedback Loops. *Journal of Human Development and Capabilities*, 14(1), 115–133.

Sen, A. 1980. Equality of What? *The Tanner Lectures on Human Values*, 1, 197–220.

Sen, A. 1992. *Inequality Re-Examined* Oxford: Oxford University Press.

Sen, A. 1993. Capability and Well-Being. In: Nussbaum, M. and Sen, A. eds. *The Quality of Life*. Oxford: Clarendon Press.

Sen, A. 1997. *Choice, Welfare and Measurement*. Cambridge, MA: Harvard University Press.

Sen, A. 2006. What Do We Want from a Theory of Justice? *Journal of Philosophy*, 103(5), 215–238.

Soneryd, L. and Uggla, Y. 2015. Green Governmentality and Responsibilization: New Forms of Governance and Responses to 'Consumer Responsibility'. *Environmental Politics*, 24(6), 913–931.

Steinberger, J.K. and Roberts, J.T. 2010. From Constraint to Sufficiency: The Decoupling of Energy and Carbon from Human Needs, 1975–2005. *Ecological Economics*, 70(2), 425–433.

United Nations, U. 2019a. *Climate Justice*. Available from: https://www.un.org/sustainabledevelopment/blog/2019/05/climate-justice/ [Accessed 18 August 2019].

United Nations, U. 2019b. *Goal 12: Ensure Sustainable Consumption and Production Patterns*. Available from: https://www.un.org/sustainabledevelopment/sustainable-consumption-production/ [Accessed 22 August 2019].

United Nations, U. 2019c. *Sustainable Consumption and Production*. Available from: https://sustainabledevelopment.un.org/topics/sustainableconsumptionandproduction [Accessed 18 August 2019].

Vasconcellos Oliveira, R. 2018. Back to the Future: The Potential of Intergenerational Justice for the Achievement of the Sustainable Development Goals. *Sustainability*, 10(2), 1–16.

Vasconcellos Oliveira, R. and Thorseth, M. 2016. Ethical Implications of Co-Benefits Rationale within Climate Change Mitigation Strategy. *Etikk i Praksis: Nordic Journal of Applied Ethics*, 2, 141–170.

Vasconcellos Oliveira, R., Thorseth, M. and Brattebø, H. 2018. The Potential of Co-Benefits in Climate Change Mitigation Strategy: An Opportunity for Environmental and Social Justice. *Journal of Social Sciences*, Naresuan University, 14(1), 163–192.

Walters, W. 2012. *Governmentality: Critical Encounters*. Oxon: Routledge.

23

"BUILDING THE BIGGER WE" FOR CLIMATE JUSTICE

Benjamin Max Goloff

Introduction

The era of technocratic climate politics in the United States – iconized by white men addressing "the climate" narrowly as an environmental issue, communicated through slideshows of melting glaciers and drowning polar bears – is being usurped. In its place, climate justice (CJ) movements are reclaiming the politics of climate change through grassroots organizing led by Indigenous people, Black and Brown people, immigrants, workers, women, queer people, and people of different abilities on the frontlines of climate impacts and extractive industries. Following movements for environmental justice (Dawson 2010) and "alter-globalization" (Reitan and Gibson 2012) in the late twentieth century, US movements for CJ join two projects as co-dependent: organizing against extractive energy industries and linked systems of gendered and racialized colonization, militarism, economic exploitation, and ecological destruction; and organizing for a "just transition" to sustainable economies powered by relationships of care, deeply democratic governance, and decentralized renewable energy (Schlosberg and Collins 2014; Kilimanjaro 2015; Movement Generation 2016).

As storms rage, fires blaze, and calls for climate justice reverberate from the grassroots on up to Capitol Hill, the stakes have never been higher for re-thinking and reacting to CJ movements as vectors for justice and collective liberation (see Dixon 2014, p. 73). To those who take up CJ as a life-or-death fight for survival, its buzzword-ization risks extending a long history of white-led environmental organizations appropriating grassroots movements' language and practices without deep relationships and accountability to frontline communities (e.g., Walker 2009; Harrison 2015). In both anticipation and response, grassroots organizations working at the intersection of racial, economic, gender, and environmental justice have grown their power through establishing new networks and re-directing existing ones to define and advance CJ.

Organizers articulate an apparent paradox. On the one hand, CJ movements must be led by people and communities on the frontlines of climate change and the polluting industries driving it. On the other, the people power required for CJ movements to succeed as a deeply intersectional project of liberation will require rapidly scaling up by "Building the Bigger We" (Kilimanjaro 2015).

I carried out the action-research informing this chapter in the summer before the 2016 US presidential elections. Building on the Peoples Climate March in 2014, big-tent climate mobilizations were increasingly framing climate change as an intersectional justice crisis (Kilimanjaro 2015). The year 2016 ranked as the hottest on record at that time (Thompson 2017). Nevertheless, most of the larger US environmental organizations were just beginning to grapple with their history of marginalizing grassroots people of color-led movements for climate justice. And arguably without coincidence, action on climate change still rarely reached the political forefront in the United States.[1]

With this backdrop, I set out to document how CJ organizers have been building solidarities between people with deeply uneven, differently real urgencies for action to shift climate change politics toward potentialities of collective liberation. I engaged with CJ solidarity politics in practice in the summer of 2016 as they weaved between several US movement-building "convergence spaces" (Routledge 2003) interfacing grassroots CJ organizations and traditional Big Green efforts for climate action. I practiced qualitative, participatory action-research methodologies as both a researcher and a collaborator (Derickson and Routledge 2015), supported by 28 conversational interviews (see *Appendix: Cited Interviews* for details on the 11 interviews I refer to in-text). I center my analysis on two key convergence spaces: the National Convening of the Climate Justice Alliance (CJA),[2] an alliance of grassroots organizations led by people of color and formed explicitly to advance CJ; and the Annual Conference of US Climate Action Network (USCAN),[3] a more moneyed and historically conservative arena of climate politics with membership that spanned widely different theories of change.

At the CJA and USCAN convenings, CJ organizers engaged solidarity practices that met what I identify as the core ethos of CJ: commitment to acting now for intersectional justice even while making space and time (see Haiven and Khasnabish 2014) for accommodating radical difference and uncertainty. Organizers apply this ethos of CJ through prefigurative practices that open space for material and relational realignments among participants. In doing so, they transform modern configurations of politics, place, and time we are accustomed to in the Anthropocene (see Moore 2016). Through experimental but ethically grounded engagements of living otherwise, I will show how CJ solidarity practices enable aligning imaginaries, strategies, and tactics across difference. By doing so, these practices build movements more capable of enacting justice. I make a case that it is because, not in spite of the messiness and contingency of these ongoing (re)alignments that climate justice organizers are already transforming boundaries of the possible in climate politics.

An ethos of climate justice

Across the convergence spaces I engaged in 2016, movement collaborators suggested a need for practices steeped in an ethos (see Popke 2009) of CJ that demands *making time* for alignment across difference and *acting now* to support survival and justice for most-impacted groups.[4] Cindy Wiesner (who helped steer the 2016 CJA convening that I attended) and other convergence organizers suggested that building alignment through this two-pronged ethos demands practices that cut across traditional arenas of politics, place, and time:

> It means having ... that kind of *deeper political analysis, but then also act*. And I think, that those actions are in conjunction with organizing, and also are in the frame of, "let's not just push for what's possible, but *what political space do we create if we're able to push beyond that?*

Participants identified two registers that are necessary to convoke solidarities through this CJ ethos. First, Sean Estelle articulated what many expressed as the *material* necessity of a "movement ecosystem" approach for building CJ solidarities with people holding different experiences, strategies, and resources. At the same time, CJ organizers presented the *relational* need for a movement ecosystem as equally important for aligning through an ethos of CJ. Social movement geographers use the concept of affect to describe emotion experienced on a level that comes before or goes beyond our ability to represent it through reasoned thought (e.g., Bosco 2007). Ananda Lee Tan described the 2008 move to initiate what would become the Climate Justice Alliance through a multi-year process of "alignment" as critical to opening up spaces of affective encounter that cultivated "common cause" and deepened relationships.[5] Tan and others recognized that, to cultivate trust and empathy between collaborators, it was important to create safe space where people can be vulnerable, affective, and affected (Bosco 2007; Juris 2008). In doing so, they opened ripples for unsettling and realigning participants' experience of the urgencies at stake and realms of possibility for addressing them (Routledge and Derickson 2015).

Organizers thus suggested that, taken together, material and relational registers demand practices that transcend modern, capital-legitimated mindsets of *individual* responsibility (see Haraway 2016, p. 42) and position participants within the permeable borders of *collective* accountability to a greater "we" (Routledge and Derickson 2015). I turn now to the practices through which organizers engaged this CJ ethos to sow the seeds for Building the Bigger We.

Building solidarities in practice through contingent alignment

In recognizing CJ organizers' practices as explicitly "prefigurative," I highlight the way they insist on holding the daily means of the struggle accountable to the ends of justice, equity, and intersectional liberation (Maeckelbergh 2011). Thinking with Mouffe (2005), Routledge and Derickson recognize prefigurative practices as powerful tools for mobilizing "a constitutive 'we'" through "agonistic relationships ... that do not seek to eradicate or eliminate difference, but acknowledge and recognize it as different while still looking for promising, if partial, synergies to serve as the basis for solidaristic relationships" (2015, p. 392). These practical and dynamic solidarities, Routledge (2011) contends, "are crucial in order to construct meaningful translocal alliances" for CJ, mirroring CJ organizers' own call to Build the Bigger We.

I found a set of prefigurative practices threading unevenly across two of the movement-building "convergence spaces" (Routledge 2003) I attended in June 2016. The Climate Justice Alliance (CJA) National Convening is the direct product of the alignment process initiated by key CJ organizers in 2008, many of whom are also active in CJ organizing at the transnational level. Therefore, I treat practices and conversations from CJA's convening as a sort of baseline for comparative analysis.

US Climate Action Network (USCAN)'s Annual Conference, on the other hand, offered an ideal opportunity to follow CJ organizers into a space where they have historically been excluded. Many participants recognized that USCAN is going through a transformation after a long history of being dominated by white- and male-led Big Green groups focused on policy advocacy. With pressure below from CJ organizers – especially from Black women who also organize with CJA (Wiesner, email message to author, September 3, 2019) – and above from Executive Director Keya Chatterjee, USCAN has since been actively repositioning grassroots organizers at the core of its leadership and membership (Abdul-Rahman; Chatterjee; Patterson, interviews). Chatterjee conveyed her vision to reshape USCAN as a key vehicle for building solidarities centered on CJ in the United States, serving as a local counterpart to transnational CJ convergence spaces (engaged by Chatterton et al. 2013).

Following threads between each convening, I contend that CJ practices effectively build power through processes of alignment that push and pull between two features of a CJ ethos. On one hand, these practices are radically experimental, open to difference and potentialities (Stengers 2005; Whatmore 2009; Marres 2013). At the same time, they are grounded in unwavering attention to immediate urgencies for intersectional justice that make this work matter here and now (Kaijser and Kronsell 2014; Ryder 2018).

Making space and time for difference through "uncomfortable" situations

Attending to the first of these features, many of the CJ movement practices centered at CJA's convening and newly introduced at USCAN seemed to thrive rather than break down in the face of conflict and uncertainty. Wiesner noted the necessity of difference-confronting spaces that:

are deliberative, they're intentional, and they don't intend to diminish the different entry points, but in fact you build on that strength, and you build on that political diversity ... I think most people don't do [that] well, because either we have a politic that wants to erase those differences and/ or we have a politic that then is divisive around those differences.

Wiesner conveyed that these CJ movement-building spaces serve as critical arenas to align root-level conceptions of what exists (using philosophical terms, *ontologies*) in solidarity with communities most impacted by effects of climate change and the immediate pollution associated with extractive industries. In doing so, these convergence spaces invite shifts in understanding *what* problem is at stake and for whom, mirroring what Whatmore (2009) calls "ontological fluidity" and greeting "controversies" as "generative events" (Stengers 2005).

Many CJ movement practices I encountered both met Wiesner's criteria and exhibited characteristics of what Callon et al. call *hybrid forums* – "open spaces for discussing technical issues, with heterogeneous involvement of people and knowledge bases" (2009, p. 18). Hybrid forums are designed explicitly to engage grounded practices through which radically divergent but differently real "matters of concern" are made, contested, and remade (Latour 2004).

Focusing primarily on controversies of technoscience rather than movement-building, Callon et al. cling to what I take as both too little faith in the ability of political formations to self-organize, and too much faith in the ethical integrity of the state, the media, and other institutions as necessary sources of legitimization (2009, p. 181). Convergence practices at CJA "flipped the script" on the role of elite voices within *and* outside the convening (multiple participants, CJA convening; Kilimanjaro 2015), and I witnessed CJ organizers in leadership at USCAN actively working to implement a similar flip. Like hybrid forums, these convergences offered spaces for "intense, open, and quality" dialogical exchange between people with wide-ranging "expertise" (Callon et al. 2009, pp. 158–160), from combatting systemic environmental racism in East Michigan (Copeland, interview) to re-directing Western science to address sea-level rise in low-income communities of color in southeast Florida (Hernandez Hammer, interview). But these spaces were not conceived through academic theory, nor were they "competency groups" choreographed by researchers (c.f., Whatmore and Landström 2011). Rather, the convergences themselves formed through dialogical democracy *in practice* based on long-standing relationships of power – ranging from deep solidarity to open contention – that weave through political arenas, places, and times that participants have long traversed together (see Burke and Shear 2014; Shear 2014).

Growing through relationships in practice and attentive to power geometries from the start, CJA and USCAN eschewed engagement with traditional media for participant-led live tweeting and defy Callon et al.'s call for explicit validation by the state (2009, p. 181). CJA modeled an especially deep relationship-based politic of accountability by convening only core member groups and a handful of allies with whom they had cultivated deep trust over time. CJA organizers thus welcomed in some members of the larger movement ecosystem but took charge of authorizing *them* rather than asking to be authorized.

Denise Abdul-Rahman explained that USCAN Steering Committee members – including herself and several others who also work at CJA-member organizations – prioritized outreach to most-impacted groups in recruiting participants and presenters at USCAN. While the conference was still majority white and Big Green, many community organizers, people of color, and youth showed up, too. Discussion leaned so heavily toward topics of building grassroots power and justice that, noting the "tricky balance" required to open spaces for negotiating strategic difference between old and new factions of USCAN, Chatterjee admits they may have "lost people from this conference" from the old guard. But overall, Chatterjee expressed gratification, not regret, for the number of "uncomfortable conversations" enabled through these shifts.

Taken together, the democratized hybrid forum-like qualities that CJA's convening modeled and USCAN's convergence was beginning to explore configured them well to deal with "uncomfortable conversations" between people holding different motivating realities for being there. From the convening's start, Chatterjee emphasized that USCAN is driven by and for members holding radically different experiences and objectives. Organizers made clear that they considered nothing *a priori*; if USCAN "can't do anything useful … we'll shut it down" (Chatterjee, public address). The meeting was predominately structured around member-led "Open Space" sessions governed by four rules: "Whoever comes are the right people. Whatever happens is the only thing that could've happened. When it starts is the right time. When it's over, it's over."

Dramatically, USCAN featured a "Strategy Panel" meant to critically engage its membership's full political spread at the time. Two white, male, mid-career environmentalists from large NGOs defended the "virtuous cycle" of "incrementalism." Climate policy, they contended, should first attend to the bottom-line "irreversible effects" of greenhouse gas emissions; only then should advocates address "luxury" concerns like equity for disadvantaged communities. Three panelists rebutted this incremental vision: Reverend Leo Woodberry, a pastor and environmental justice organizer who supports grassroots CJ efforts across the US South under the banner of the "Justice First Tour"; Will Lawrence, who helped start the student fossil fuel divestment movement and would later co-found Sunrise Movement, chief popularizer of the Green New Deal; and Janet Redman, who at the time was director of the Climate Policy Program at the CJA member group Institute for Policy Studies and previously co-convened the transnational Climate Justice Now! network. Lawrence emphasized that grassroots, base-building strategies remain systemically undervalued and underfunded despite being essential for just and equitable climate policy. Woodberry and Redman articulated that equity must be a "bottom-line priority," inseparable from efforts to curb fossil fuel extraction and carbon emissions. As Redman put it, "people are being poisoned today" in environmental "sacrifice zones."

"Radical pragmatism," not "incrementalism," she argued, is the only solution for addressing the "different urgencies" experienced for CJ.

Backed by a screen projecting live tweets from the audience, few words were minced on the panel, and much of the room – myself included – expressed some level of surprise or discomfort. Yet it is precisely these kinds of comparatively safe, publicly accountable hybrid forums for negotiating tensions that Chatterjee hoped USCAN could create. Situations fostering what Chatterjee calls "uncomfortable conversations" exhibit features that Callon (1998) might recognize in particularly "hot" situations. On the USCAN Strategy Panel, every aspect of climate politics became open to uncertainty. Participants agreed little on where to look for expertise: communities confronting extraction or climate scientists? Even if experts could be found, there would have been no "stabilized knowledge base" to draw from (Callon 1998, p. 260). Panelists depicted apparently "mutually incompatible" bottom-line concerns (Callon 1998, p. 260): an "irreversible" biophysical tipping point, from the center-left environmentalists, and stopping people from being "poisoned today," from Woodberry, Lawrence, and Redman. For the remainder of the conference, attendees repeatedly referenced this frank exchange as *making space* for concrete projects of equitable finance, intersectionality, and grassroots power.

Chatterjee suggested that fostering these situations is vitally necessary for both their material and relational qualities. From one side, she sees a material disjunction: Big Greens have disproportionate access to funding and visibility in climate activism, while grassroots, base-building organizers practice strategies most needed to achieve rapid, justice-centered emissions reduction. Building alignment on root-level understandings of the problems at stake between D.C. lobbyists and CJ organizers practicing direct action is thus pivotal to building powerful movements for CJ. At the same time, Chatterjee recognized that creating "memorable" even if "uncomfortable" "common experiences," hot with emotion and uncertainty, is the only way to make these material conditions possible. The "affective solidarity" these experiences generate is strategic not for binding together collaborators already sharing common visions and practices (Juris 2008), but rather for catalyzing "empathetic agonism" between organizers who continue to hold radically different urgencies for pursuing CJ (Horowitz 2013). Rob Friedman frames the situation on "the metaphor of dance":

> I always love spaces like this because there's an opportunity to really build those relationships that I think are fundamental to this work … A lot of people are asking questions, though, about, "what does anything we're talking about mean for my work?" Are organizations actually going to shift course as "equity" and "justice" are centered in this work, particularly the big organizations? My belief is that they will take these ideas seriously only when they recognize that their very existence is being threatened … so we're dancing through how to do this work in a better, more just way, and it's going to be a salsa dance, with the frontline leading.

Friedman suggests these convergence spaces enable dialogical contention not just over strategy, but also over ontological questions of *what matter is at stake*. In doing so, the convergence spaces reflect Callon et al.'s "hybrid forums": opening channels not for closing down on "consensus," but rather dynamically negotiating different underlying urgencies and different capabilities for addressing them (2009; c.f., Habermas 1984). Through such an unsettling process, as Chatterjee noted, CJ organizers might lose some people. Yet by establishing publicly accountable, dialogically democratic arenas, people have an opportunity to "shift" not only strategies but also basic understandings of "the" issue at stake.

Enacting intersectional justice now

As Friedman acknowledged, experimental spaces of confrontation and openness to difference are risky – especially for those working from CJ urgencies of survival, not only recognition. To build alignment on the ethos of CJ, these practices needed to do more than make time and space for shifting underlining realities of the problem (see Whatmore 2009 on "ontological fluidity") and reach beyond an end goal of a "hybrid forum" for making meaning across difference (Callon et al. 2009, 189). They needed to do so while holding fast attention to *acting now* in solidarity with organizers defending survival in the face of intersectional injustice (Kaijser and Kronsell 2014).

As Kandi White unpacked, there are no external mediators in the climate crisis. Everybody is implicated in and affected by climate change through deeply uneven urgencies and experiences (see also Levin et al. 2012) – from white people grappling with legacies of colonizing and extracting to Native people carrying forward knowledges honoring relationships of mutual care with the earth:

> That's why it's so important for the Climate Justice Alliance to bring together groups that are like-minded – but [also] to push the envelope of who is working together. Regardless of our differences, we're going to have to work together, all of us as humanity.

This hottest and wildest of situations demands more radical democratization and "stronger" objectivity than the external mediators and internal systems of accountability Callon and colleagues envisioned for "hybrid forums" (Callon 1998; Callon and Rabeharisoa 2003; Callon et al. 2009, p. 171). Instead, they demand embodied objectivity, acting from positioned experiences of feeling and responding to the matters at hand (Haraway 1988; Harding 1992; Latour 2000). If prefigurative practices of CJ are to meet urgencies of people literally fighting for their and their communities' lives, and external mediators are non-existent, CJ solidarity practices must operate on "implementation criteria" (Callon et al. 2009, p. 163) that privilege people least responsible for and most affected by the struggle for CJ.

I found exactly these kinds of justice-centered, "strongly objective" implementation criteria taking shape through practices attentive to both material and relational dimensions of building solidarities. Rather than enlist "professional" mediators attempting neutrality, movement participants facilitated themselves. At USCAN and especially CJA, people with deep histories of leadership on the frontlines of disruptive fossil fuel extraction or exposure to toxic pollutants were granted first position in setting the terms of debate and changing the course of discussion.

To maintain this radically objective negotiation of expertise, organizers repeatedly invoked several practices. Some of these operate primarily through registers of relational, affect-heavy engagement. Storytelling, visual media, songs, chants, and prayers by spiritual leaders served an important role at both CJA's and USCAN's convenings, positioned as "grounding" for evoking and focusing emotional and spiritual gravity. For example, organizers at both CJA and USCAN created semi-structured spaces that explicitly encouraged vulnerability through sharing stories in small groups. As Ananda Lee Tan points out, there were differences in "how" stories were told in each of these spaces. Unlike at USCAN, CJA's relational activities were grounded in long histories of collaboration rooted in environmental justice principles and cultures of practice centered on reinforcing an explicit ethic of "collective empowerment and self-determination" (Tan, email message to author, September 7, 2019).

Nevertheless, participants at both convergence spaces repeatedly identified structured and unstructured moments of emotional encounter as the most potent offerings of the summit – facilitating what Juris (2008) calls "affective solidarity." Especially at CJA, organizers focused relational gravity on the leadership and material struggles of those most "objectively" confronting intersecting oppressions associated with climate injustice (see Latour 2000), and at the same time created space and time for all participants to (re)connect and reconsider *what* brings them to this work (Haiven and Khasnabish 2014). These affective solidarities opened channels for building trust and "empathetic agonism" by affecting and being affected together (Horowitz 2013). More than this, they enabled CJ actors to pointedly refract moments of emotional rawness toward alignment on centering the struggle of most-impacted people and communities, even in the face of radically different urgencies and open disagreement on strategies needed to address them (see de Vries and Rosenow 2015). CJ organizers thus share in an ethic of "becoming" through their articulation of a CJ ethos grounded in *process* rather than a predefined moral code (Popke 2009, p. 84; Connolly 2010).

Callon et al. recognize the need for accompanying accountability structures that guide and maintain alignments cultivated over the course of dialogical engagement (2009, p. 163). CJ organizers similarly invoked other practices primarily for their material importance for navigating the risks of making time for radical openness across difference even while doubling down on core urgencies to combat systemic intersectional injustice. The Jemez Principles for Democratic Organizing served a key role at CJA's and USCAN's convergence spaces in solidifying accountability to this CJ ethos without closing down generative potentialities of encounter. The Jemez Principles come from a landmark 1996 meeting of grassroots organizers and emphasize six guiding priorities for movement-building practice (Southwest Network for Environmental and Economic Justice 1996). As Ananda Lee Tan describes, "the Principles are part of CJA's DNA, defining our basic expectations, lines of accountability, and relational trust in collaboration" (Tan, email message to author, September 10, 2019). In contrast, USCAN had only recently adopted the Jemez Principles during the network's new engagement of CJ organizations led by people of color.

Within these different contexts, CJ organizers invoked the Jemez Principles frequently and effectively to either bring contestation out into the open or "call in" participants acting in ways that CJ organizers felt violated their core commitment to intersectional justice (e.g., Abdul-Rahman; Chatterjee, interviews). Chatterjee appreciated that since USCAN took up the Jemez Principles, CJ organizers have helped "one or two large member organizations agree to adopt those Principles … a good starting point if [they] can not just read them, but also figure out how to operationalize them." CJ organizers frequently flagged their limitations with the context of a big-tent network like USCAN and noted that Big Greens do not get credit for simply posting principles on their website. But provoked by events like the Strategy Panel, I did see participants figuring "out how to operationalize" the Jemez Principles. An older white man representing a Big Green wondered how he could "bring more people who don't look like me" into his organization. Invoking Jemez Principle 4 (Southwest Network for Environmental and Economic Justice 1996), several participants conveyed that rather than seek the "optics" of "getting minorities in," Big Greens must themselves meet urgencies of those most affected by intersections of climate injustice through their work. The next day, unprompted, the same man appreciated learning that "equity, justice, and climate change all have the same enemy." Convoked by USCAN's ratification of the Jemez Principles, this encounter and others like it appear to have helped shift some participants' ontological grounding closer in line with an ethos of CJ.

Organizers' deployment of practices facilitating affective encounter and material accountability created *space and time* that transformed the tenor of these convergences (see Haiven and Khasnabish 2014). Thus configured, CJA and USCAN created movement spaces at once open to difference and committed to intersectional justice. Attuned to this core ethos, CJ solidarity practices welcome *trans-political* multiplicity by leaning into rather than writing over tensions between strategies. These same practices created space for participants to connect across diverse geographical *places* of impact and struggle even while deepening translocal accountability and alignment on what matters and who is unevenly impacted. All the while, CJ solidarity practices engage *trans-temporal* urgencies demanded by living in the embodied, directly impacted "objective" present held by participants on the frontlines of injustice, rather than abstract future projections (Harding 1992; Latour 2000).

Taken together, trans-political, translocal, and trans-temporal potentialities opened by CJ solidarity practices at CJA and USCAN did more than prefigure an "alternative" system (c.f., Maeckelbergh 2011; Chatterton et al. 2013). CJ organizers' practices of alignment do not embody conventional temporalities of *revolution*, sparking sweeping shifts to the "next" economic–ecological system (c.f., Hardt and Negri 2000; Democracy Collaborative 2019). Aligning for CJ does not mean accepting climate politics as either *progressive* or "incremental" (e.g., Knaggård 2014); nor hopelessly concluding that building solidarities engaging multiple urgencies for CJ is futile (c.f., Rayner 2006). CJ organizers work through temporalities that are performative, experimental, and "radically pragmatic" (Redman, USCAN Strategy Panel and interview with the author; see also Gibson-Graham 2008; Barnett and Bridge 2012). Whether reaching between existing toolsets or making their own, CJ organizers build bigger, more powerful, and more just movements for collective liberation through prefiguring ongoing practices of alignment.

Conclusion

Grassroots movements for climate justice (CJ) are prefiguring practices of radical alignment across difference toward justice and collective liberation. Addressing whether and how CJ solidarity politics build power capable of shifting climate politics toward equity and justice, I have argued, requires recognizing CJ movement convergence spaces as hybrid sites of "ontological fluidity" (Whatmore 2009) – destabilizing assumed realities of what matters and for whom (Callon et al. 2009). Doing so enables attending to the ways CJ movements confront, rather than seek to contain, risks and opportunities inherent in working across conventional lines of politics, place, and time.

The CJ ethos I experienced – *making time* for alignment across difference while *acting now* in solidarity with those most impacted – offers a living roadmap for just transitions sought more broadly by movements for racial, economic, and environmental justice. To both "make time" and "act now," CJ organizers convened spaces of encounter that involved both relational and material practices. Relational practices enabled organizers to adjust their basic realities of what problems are at stake and what strategies are needed to address them. CJ organizers used storytelling, song, and ritual to create portals of emotional encounter between people with vastly different and uneven lived experiences of climate injustice. Through doing so, they were able to pull the collective closer into alignment with people directly struggling to survive. Material practices helped them address power dynamics and ensure accountability – for example, by centering leadership from most-impacted people, equitably shifting resources, and putting to use the Jemez Principles for Democratic Organizing. Organizers, educators, and policymakers seeking to cultivate just transitions in the Anthropocene have much to learn from CJ organizers' difference-confronting convenings and the relational and material technologies they engage therein.

In four years that have passed at time of writing since the 2016 CJA and USCAN convenings, US CJ organizers have relationally and materially transformed the "what" of climate politics to center justice now while preventing catastrophic climate futures. The "just transition" CJ organizers have been building power behind for decades is now a political hot topic from the community level on up to the 2020 US Democratic primary debates for President (Astor 2019; Climate Justice Alliance 2019a). Without question, the wider and more powerful CJ movement alignments grow, the more visible conflicts within CJ politics become. For example, CJA publicly contested US Representative Alexandra Ocasio-Cortez, Sunrise Movement, and other early advocates of the federal "Green New Deal" concept for failing initially to center meaningful leadership from and accountability to frontline communities and base-building organizations (Climate Justice Alliance 2019b). Yet, through constant work by CJ organizers to engage relational and material tools of accountability, these conflicts are increasingly transformed by the "salsa dance" that Friedman described – where the frontlines hold our movements accountable and build collective power toward justice.

By explicitly unsettling ontologies of "the" climate crisis, CJ movements in the United States are reshaping both the grounds and means of success in confronting climate change. Engaging a prefigurative ethos of CJ means giving up hope of treading a linear, technocratic path towards Progress, that ever-alluring modern specter of the Anthropocene (Haraway 2016, 50). Yet in exchange, CJ movements are building us footing in these contingent, ethically potent times where potentials abound and certitudes escape us.

Notes

1 For example, in stark contrast to the 2020 US presidential race, climate change barely came up in the 2016 presidential election cycle (see Stokes 2019).
2 June 24–26, 2016; University of Missouri, St. Louis, Missouri.
3 June 13–15, 2016; Intercontinental Hotel, Miami, Florida.
4 For another framework that synergies well with this CJ ethos, see Gross (2019) and Foran (2014).
5 Like Tan, Haraway envisions "alignment" as "a rich metaphor for wayfarers, for the Earthbound" that "does not as easily as 'decision' carry the tones of modernist liberal choice discourse, at least in the United States" (2016, 41–42).

References

Astor, M. 2019. Environmental justice was a climate forum theme: here's why. *The New York Times*, September 4. Available from: https://www.nytimes.com/2019/09/05/us/politics/environmental-justice-climate-town-hall.html [Accessed June 23, 2020].

Barnett, C. and Bridge, G. 2012. Geographies of radical democracy: agonistic pragmatism and the formation of affected interests. *Annals of the Association of American Geographers*, 103(4): 1022–1040.

Bosco, F.J. 2007. Emotions that build networks: geographies of human rights movements in Argentina and beyond. *Tijdschrift voor Economische en Sociale Geografie*, 98(5): 545–563.

Burke, B.J. and Shear, B.W. 2014. Introduction: engaged scholarship for non-capitalist political ecologies. In: Burke, B.J. and Shear, B.W. eds. Non-Capitalist Political Ecologies. Special Section of the *Journal of Political Ecology*, 21: 127–144, https://journals.uair.arizona.edu/index.php/JPE.

Callon, M. 1998. An essay on framing and overflowing: economic externalities revisited by sociology. In: Callon, M. ed. *The laws of markets*. Oxford: Blackwell, 244–269.

Callon, M. and Rabeharisoa, V. 2003. Research "in the wild" and the shaping of new social identities. *Technology in Society*, 25: 193–204.

Callon, M., Lascoumes, P. and Barthe, Y. 2009. *Acting in an uncertain world: an essay on technological democracy*. Translated by G. Burchell. Cambridge, MA: MIT Press.

Chatterton, P., Featherstone, D. and Routledge, P. 2013. Articulating climate justice in Copenhagen: antagonism, the commons, and solidarity. *Antipode*, 45(3): 602–620.

Climate Justice Alliance. 2019a. *2020 democratic primary*. Available from: https://climatejusticealliance.org/primary/ [Accessed September 13, 2019].

Climate Justice Alliance. 2019b. *A Green new deal must be rooted in a just transition for workers and communities most impacted by climate change*. Available from: https://climatejusticealliance.org/green-new-deal-must-rooted-just-transition-workers-communities-impacted-climate-change/ [Accessed December 11, 2019].

Connolly, W.E. 2010. *A world of becoming*. Durham, NC: Duke University Press.

Dawson, A. 2010. Climate justice: the emergent movement against capitalism. *South Atlantic Quarterly*, 109(2): 313–338.

Democracy Collaborative. 2019. *The next system project*. Available from: http://thenextsystem.org/ [Accessed September 13, 2019].

Derickson, K.D. and Routledge, P. 2015. Resourcing scholar-activism: collaboration, transformation, and the production of knowledge. *The Professional Geographer*, 67(1): 1–7.

de Vries, L.A. and Rosenow, D. 2015. Opposing the opposition? Binarity and complexity in political resistance. *Environment and Planning D: Society and Space*, 33(6): 1118–1134.

Dixon, C. 2014. *Another politics: talking across today's transformative movements*. Oakland, CA: University of California Press.

Foran, J. 2014. Beyond insurgency to radical social change: the new situation. *Social Justice Studies*, 8(1): 5–25.

Gibson-Graham, J.K. 2008. "Place-based globalism": a new imaginary of revolution. *Remarx, Rethinking Marxism*, 20(4): 659–664.

Gross, C. 2019. Climate justice movement building: values and cultures of creation in Santa Barbara, California. *Social Sciences*, 8(3): 1–26.

Habermas, J. 1984. *The theory of communicative action*. Translated by T. McCarthy. Boston: Beacon Press.

Haiven, M. and Khasnabish, A. 2014. *Radical imagination: social movement research in the age of austerity*. London: Zed Books.

Haraway, D.J. 1988. Situated knowledges: the science question in feminism and the privilege of partial perspective. *Feminist Studies*, 14(3): 575–599.

Haraway, D.J 2016. *Staying with the trouble: making kin in the Chthulucene*. Durham, NC: Duke University Press, 30–57.

Harding, S. 1992. Rethinking standpoint epistemology: what is "objectivity?" *Centennial Review*, 36(3): 437–470.

Hardt, M. and Negri, A. 2000. *Empire*. Cambridge, MA: Harvard University Press.

Harrison, J.L. 2015. Coopted environmental justice? Activists' roles in shaping EJ policy implementation. *Environmental Sociology*, 1(4): 241–255.

Horowitz, L.S. 2013. Toward empathic agonism: conflicting vulnerabilities in urban wetland governance. *Environment and Planning. Part A*, 45(10): 2344–2361.

Juris, J.S. 2008. Performing politics: image, embodiment, and affective solidarity during anti-corporate globalization protests. *Ethnography*, 9(1): 61–97.

Kaijser, A. and Kronsell, A. 2014. Climate change through the lens of intersectionality. *Environmental Politics*, 23(3): 417–433.

Kilimanjaro, I. 2015. *The people's climate March: a climate justice story.* Grassroots Global Justice Alliance. Available from: https://ggjalliance.org/resources/the-peoples-clim ate-march-2014-a-climate-justice-story/ [Accessed June 23, 2020].

Knaggård, Å. 2014. What do policy-makers do with scientific uncertainty? The incremental character of Swedish climate change policy-making. *Policy Studies*, 35(1): 22–39.

Latour, B. 2000. When things strike back: a possible contribution of "science studies" to the social sciences. *British Journal of Sociology*, 51(1): 107–123.

Latour, B. 2004. Why has critique run out of steam? From matters of fact to matters of concern. *Critical Inquiry*, 30: 225–48.

Levin, K., Cashore, B., Bernstein, S. and Auld, G. 2012. Overcoming the tragedy of super wicked problems: constraining our future selves to ameliorate global climate change. *Policy Sciences*, 45(2): 123–152.

Maeckelbergh, M. 2011. Doing is believing: prefiguration as strategic practice in the alterglobalization movement. *Social Movement Studies*, 10(1): 1–20.

Marres, N. 2013. Why political ontology must be experimentalized: on eco-show homes as devices of participation. *Social Studies of Science*, 43(3): 417–443.

Moore, J.W. 2016. Introduction. In: Moore, J.W. ed. *Anthropocene or capitalocene? Nature, history, and the crisis of capitalism.* Oakland, CA: PM Press, 1–11.

Mouffe, C. 2005. *On the political.* New York: Verso.

Movement Generation. 2016. *Movement generation just transition framework resources.* Movement Generation Justice & Ecology Project. Available from: http://mov ementgeneration.org/movement-generation-just-transition-framework-resources/ [Accessed April 14, 2017].

Popke, J. 2009. Geography and ethics: non-representational encounters, collective responsibility and economic difference. *Progress in Human Geography*, 33(1): 81–90.

Rayner, S. 2006. Wicked problems: clumsy solutions – diagnoses and prescriptions for environmental ills. In: *Jack Beale memorial lecture on global environment.* Sydney: University of New South Wales. Available from: http://eureka.sbs.ox.ac.uk/93/ [Accessed April 14, 2017].

Reitan, R. and Gibson, S. 2012. Climate change or social change? Environmental and leftist praxis and participatory action research. *Globalizations*, 9(3): 395–410.

Routledge, P. 2003. Convergence space: process geographies of grassroots globalization networks. *Transactions of the Institute of British Geographers*, 28(3): 333–349.

Routledge, P. 2011. Translocal climate justice solidarities. In: Dryzek, J.S., Norgaard, R.B. and Schlosberg, D. eds. *The Oxford handbook of climate change and society.* Oxford: Oxford University Press, 384–398.

Routledge, P. and Derickson, K.D. 2015. Situated solidarities and the practice of scholar-activism. *Environment and Planning D: Society and Space*, 33(3): 391–407.

Ryder, S.S. 2018. Developing an intersectionally-informed, multi-sited, critical policy ethnography to examine power and procedural justice in multi-scalar energy and climate change decision making processes. *Energy Research & Social Sciences*, 45: 266–275.

Schlosberg, D. and Collins, L.B. 2014. From environmental to climate justice: climate change and the discourse of environmental justice. *Wiley Interdisciplinary Reviews: Climate Change*, 5(3): 359–374.

Shear, B.W. 2014. Making the green economy: politics, desire, and economic possibility. In: Burke, B.J. and Shear, B.W. eds. Non-capitalist political ecologies. Special Section of the *Journal of Political Ecology*, 21: 193–209.

Southwest Network for Environmental and Economic Justice. 1996. The Jemez principles for democratic organizing. Reproduced by *Environmental Justice Network*. Available from: http://www.ejnet.org/ej/jemez.pdf [Accessed September 13, 2019].

Stengers, I. 2005. The cosmopolitical proposal. In: Latour, B. and Weibel, P. eds. *Making things public*. Cambridge, MA: MIT Press, 994–1003.

Stokes, L.C. 2019. With Hurricane Dorian looming, democratic candidates discuss their climate plans tonight. *The Washington Post*, September 5. Available from: https://www.washingtonpost.com/politics/2019/09/04/with-hurricane-dorian-looming-democratic-candidates-discuss-their-climate-plans-tuesday-night/ [Accessed June 23, 2020].

Thompson, A. 2017. 2016 officially declared hottest year on record. *Climate Central*, January 18. Available from: https://www.climatecentral.org/news/2016-declared-hottest-year-on-record-21070 [Accessed June 23, 2020].

Walker, G. 2009. Globalizing environmental justice: the geography and politics of frame contextualization and evolution. *Global Social Policy*, 9(3): 355–382.

Whatmore, S.J. 2009. Mapping knowledge controversies: science, democracy and the redistribution of expertise. *Progress in Human Geography*, 33(5): 587–598.

Whatmore, S.J. and Landström, C. 2011. Flood apprentices: an exercise in making things public. *Economy and Society*, 40(4): 582–610.

CONCLUSION

The quest for environmental justice

Melinda Laituri, Stacia Ryder, Kathryn Powlen,
Stephanie A. Malin, Joshua Sbicca, and Dimitris Stevis

The preparation of this volume has been bookended by two significant events: first, the US election of President Trump in 2016, an event which compounded the influence of authoritarianism and illiberalism across the global political spectrum, and then the global pandemic of 2020. The election of Donald Trump heralded a new age for the United States, full of changing and eroding commitments to global efforts to combat climate change and support for environmental regulation. The COVID-19 pandemic hit amid a year of upheaval that has included unprecedented disasters like the Australian bush fires and the global elevation of racial justice by the Black Lives Matter (BLM) movement. In the latter case, the Trump administration's white supremacist attitudes and efforts to further codify racism in contemporary US society have exacerbated the terror that Black, Indigenous, and people of color (BIPOC) experience in their daily lives. Following the murder of George Floyd, protests in support of BLM mobilized in at least 4,444 cities and across more than 60 countries (Creosote Maps 2020; Haddad 2020) – even in the midst of the global pandemic. Floyd's murder, and the patterned killing of unarmed Native and Black and Brown Americans without police accountability, such as the case of Breonna Taylor, are rooted in the same acts of state-backed violence that also create environmental injustices (see Pellow 2016).

As of this writing, we remain in the midst of the pandemic that has impacted our perspective on the Anthropocene and environmental justice. Early in the pandemic there were some positive environmental impacts. In Spring 2020, amid government lockdowns around the world, we experienced the Great Pause – or the Anthropause (Rutz et al. 2020). Though not everyone experienced it with the same degree of challenges and hardship, people did share a unique moment of collective slow-down exceeding anything we have experienced in the industrial age. The change was at first subtle, the silence of empty streets met with the sudden outburst of birdsong. Rather than a silent spring, we had a reawakened, re-emergent nature at our doorstep. Fewer cars and less airplane travel resulted in clearer skies. Venice canals became cleaner; the skies over Delhi and Los Angeles became bluer; wild animals forayed into urban streets around the world. Space and time intersected in unfamiliar ways, providing a period for reflection. The Anthropause gave crucial evidence of the much-contested term, the Anthropocene, this epoch of the dominance of human activity – but highlighted how climate crises relate to *industrial* activity and their scale under globalized capitalism. Though the Earth appeared to give a sigh of relief – it did not last for long.

The pandemic has had important environmental outcomes, even if temporary. This slow-down illustrated that the Capitalocene, with all its industrial production and focus on unending growth, created some of the most substantial environmental impacts. Ironically, the drop in global carbon emissions recorded during this time (reports range from 8.8 to 13%) is temporary and is ultimately unlikely to significantly impact CO_2 concentrations or climate change (Borunda 2020; Garcia and Culbertson 2020; Le Quéré et al. 2020; Liu et al. 2020). And the Anthropause hid enormous environmental cost as consumption at home meant an increase in deliveries with single-use packaging and growing waste streams of disposable personal protective equipment. We expect future research will reveal these social and environmental costs more clearly.

Some countries have successfully responded to the virus. This includes countries such as Senegal, Mozambique, Cameroon, Vietnam, South Korea, Taiwan, and New Zealand. This is attributed to a variety of factors, including preparedness and quick action, as well as effective leadership using public health data, which has incorporated lessons learned from contending with previous viral outbreaks (Ebola, SARS, HIV) (see Mormina and Nsofor 2020; Soy 2020). Other countries, such as the UK and US, have been challenged in managing the pandemic and the high numbers of preventable deaths (Robertson 2020; CDC 2020).

This moment of global collective experience starkly revealed how environmental injustices are everywhere. The virus has impacted vulnerable populations most significantly – those who are older, poorer, and BIPOC – and more substantially affected at-risk populations, such as frontline workers, significantly immigrants, refugees and BIPOC. Patterns reveal that BIPOC in Western industrial countries are disproportionately impacted by the pandemic as a result of a confluence of factors, including their overrepresentation in essential worker roles, discrimination, economic inequality, and inequality in healthcare access and quality (CDC 2020; Gould and Wilson 2020; Hawkins 2020). Further, for some, this period of time is associated with forced labor, where those deemed essential and those who were economically insecure were forced to put themselves at risk for the sake of their jobs, such as meatpackers and farm workers. The virus has been particularly brutal on Native American reservation populations in the United States (Schneider et al. 2020). The same disproportionate patterns recorded for Indigenous populations in Canada and Australia, are evident among Black, Asian and minority ethnic (BAME) backgrounds within the United Kingdom (Robertson 2020). Additionally, we have seen an increase in hate crimes committed against Chinese and Asian Americans due to anti-Chinese virus-related rhetoric (Gover et al. 2020).

The COVID-19 pandemic cannot be separated from deepening social and environmental justice crises; if anything, the pandemic has made these inequities more visible and pronounced. The current situation exposes inequity through the razor-thin margin between having, having less, and having nothing in the global economy. This is an important reminder that to truly address climate crises and all forms of environmental and social injustice, we must problematize and challenge power, the power elite, and the industrial production systems on which current capitalist economies depend. Though they are not about COVID-19 outcomes specifically, the chapters in this volume amply display these inequalities through temporal and spatial lenses of justice, which offer a means to evaluate and imagine just transitions and just futures.

The section on spatial justice demonstrates how powerful case studies with environmental justice approaches can be in exposing inequities across diverse landscapes. These case studies investigate the intersection of projects and policies, revealing struggles by local communities to resist and shift the balance of power away from industry and government in diverse environments that include mining in Chile (Baver), water insecurity in Nicaragua (Romano and LaVanchy), bioenergy in Mexico (Banerjee), and energy conflicts over pipeline locations in the United States (Lester). Power relationships are further embedded in policy arrangements between governments and donors, which can create inequitable outcomes for recipient countries on the front line of climate change (Tabassum). Other case studies emphasize the unequal distribution of environmental benefits in the form of access to critical resources such as housing in Vienna, Austria (Cucca and Friesenecker) and Budapest, Hungary (Antal), household energy supply in Mexico (Vera, Manrique, and Peña), and differential access to community environmental benefits as described by women leaders of a Latinx community in Colorado in the United States (Larkins).

Spatial justice represents a foundational concept, vital to just transitions, that authors analyze throughout the volume. Just transitions refers to spaces for the process and practice of solution-building – but they vary across different contexts and scales of action. There are parallels and patterns that help to forge spaces of change, which can lead humanity towards more just socio-environmental systems. When utilizing an EJ lens, people must be vigilant to remember and represent that just transitions aim to justly represent workers, unions, and frontline communities and extend beyond changes to energy systems and infrastructures. Just transitions include shifts away from industrial capitalism and toward regenerative energy and production systems adapted to planetary limits to create diverse energy communities (Burke); institutional innovation across multiple scales of governance and community collaboration as exemplified in rural communities in China (Mao, Zhang, and Weeks); and conceptualizations of ecological citizenship across diverse communities in urban and suburban spaces, such as in Stockholm, Sweden (Zhou). Just transitions can also attend to climate justice in spaces where historical and contemporary relations collide in the form of unjust landscapes, specifically where communities grapple with ways to extricate themselves from extractive practices that include deforestation (Omukuti) and oil and gas (Farrel and Stano). Transitions will be long-term, on-going, and multidimensional as evidenced by the lessons to be learned from the examples in this volume.

The volume's final section focuses on Just Futures – highlighting the need for a transformational moment to create a just world that prioritizes environmental equities across space and time. This is a tall order, multi-scalar and multidimensional. The themes of cultural justice (Rowe and Finley) and intergenerational justice (Motupalli; Vasconcellos Oliveira) identify the critical linkages to under-represented populations here and in the future. The central question becomes: How to accomplish procedural justice and include their voices? This volume has emphasized differential impacts, voices, and action across time and space. Yet, the solutions offered in this section are based on solidarity, which can be rooted in shared and differential experiences, alignment of purposes (Goloff), an overarching acceptance of limits (Vasconcellos Oliveira), and an existential acceptance of an earth-centric perspective (Pandit and Purakayastha).

Throughout the volume, we introduce several novel concepts to the EJ debate, and engage with rich debates within the field. Consequently, in this volume, an emerging lexicon provides a rich arena to further understand and address the complexity and holistic basis of environmental justice. Valle uses the term *convivial labor* in juxtaposition to capitalism, where labor is not a tool of capitalism but a form of celebration and cultural connectivity. Vasconcellos Oliveira suggests that *conditional freedom* includes the precautionary principle in decisions to limit effects upon others where working towards a stable climate has obligations and responsibilities that cascade across actions. Further, she postulates the need for *sustainable consumption* – seemingly an oxymoron – but situated within the context of limiting future injustices through accentuating intergenerational capabilities. Pandit and Purakayastha employ Shiva's *earth democracy* to illuminate the contributions of indigenous Indian cultures to furthering *vegetal living* of connectivity and conviviality.

Further, several chapters in this volume work to refine the term Anthropocene; other suggested names include Capitalocene, Age of Fossil Capital, Plantationocene, and the Pyrocene. These alternative terms invoke the economic and settler colonial injustices embedded in the histories of some of the places we analyze and examine in this volume's case studies (Malin). We recognize all of the ways in which Anthropocene is a contested and insufficient term. We suggest perhaps the use of the asterisked "Anthropo★cene," signifying the complexities of the term and problematizing it, to demonstrate the intersections of inequalities highlighted by the use of the other terms mentioned throughout this volume and beyond.

We solicited contributions from a cross-section of academics and practitioners to capture the broad landscape of environmental justice in the Anthropo*cene. The stories showcase the challenges inherent in creating a just future, where the necessary transformations must also address the conditions of vulnerability that result in environmental injustices. Vulnerability will always be a part of the landscape. However, societies and governments need effective and innovative ways to address vulnerability by creating spaces for participation and empowerment among those who are currently vulnerable, limiting those who may become vulnerable, and strongly regulating those in power. These steps are essential to realize just transitions and futures.

Globally, humanity finds itself on the threshold of an uncertain future of political change, environmental disruption, and an unprecedented infectious disease. The economic divide has been greatly exacerbated by all of these uncertainties – and vulnerable populations are increasing. Other species have also been driven to crisis because of the industrial activities of the dominant capitalist systems and racist societies. Engagement in state-sanctioned slow violence and necropolitics is on display more than ever before.

However, moments of great cataclysm often offer opportunities for change and transformation. And so, we offer an Environmental Justice Manifesto to consider how to marshal humanity's forces and engage in new ways to address this uncertain future. Uncertainty can be daunting, but it also provides for opportunity. Below, we offer some comprehensive steps forward, taken from the insights of this volume, to help create a more just and equitable future.

Advocates for science and democracy note objectivity and neutrality are not the same thing, and that as scientists we strive to be objective but are increasingly challenged to not be neutral. We believe these words hold true even more today than they did when we hosted the Symposium on which this edited volume is based. The resurgence of nativism and intolerance that have taken hold in the United States and many other parts of the world requires that all of us invested in environmental justice reflect, react, and re-engage for change. The range of topics covered during the Symposium and this volume reflects such commitments and we hope that you can all participate to further develop and implement this statement.

We cannot accept marginalization and exploitation as if, somehow, victims and victimizers are equally responsible. We must not accept the language that dresses power in a veneer of neutrality, while delegitimizing those who call for a more equitable, ecologically sound, and sustainable world. We must recognize that while our struggles are varied and different, they are intimately interconnected. To quote Audre Lorde, "I am not free while any woman is unfree, even when her shackles are very different from my own." The 1991 Principles of Environmental Justice, crafted by a number of popular organizations in the United States and considered as a foundational statement of the movement in the

United States and beyond, are more timely than ever in their recognition of the multiple sources of environmental injustice and the breadth and depth of their vision towards environmental justice.

Environmental justice is multidimensional. Moreover, as scholars and practitioners of environmental and ecological justice, our moral universe includes the environment not only as a resource or target of our philanthropy but as having inherent value and as setting the parameters of our social choices. The distributional divide between the haves and have-nots continues to grow, as does the number of people who are vulnerable and disenfranchised. But it is not only the growth of that divide that should attract our attention – it is its sheer existence and normalization. We think that EJ does and should address social inequalities and, in fact, should question the social rules that produce these inequalities – not only their manifestations.

As EJ researchers and practitioners, we are called upon to broaden our universe of recognition. But we must not only ask who is included and who is excluded amongst people. We must also ask whether we include or exclude the environment and what the implications may be as all life is intertwined. Increased sensibilities about just distribution and broader recognition will remain aspirational unless we continue to demand deeper and more inclusive participation – participation that is not exhausted in formulaic consultation and deliberation, but allows those hitherto marginalized to contest and change the rules and processes that marginalized them.

The multidimensionality of EJ requires that people must continually work to expand EJ research and practice in the direction of an ever more comprehensive and holistic vision of EJ. In moving toward this goal, researchers and practitioners of EJ face a range of specific challenges. Most immediately, we are called upon to recognize different worlds and types of knowledge without succumbing to "alternative facts." We need to listen and learn, particularly from those most likely to be affected by our practices and choices. Finally, building solidarity between societies and cultures and recognizing that incorporating differences into collective engagement can create stronger networks to meet the urgency of the moment and the challenge of the next century. In the words of Karl Polanyi, also written at a pivotal moment in our modern history, "Indeed, the secret of success lies rather in the measure in which the groups are able to represent – by including in their own – the interests of others than themselves" (Polanyi 1934, 188).

References

Borunda, A. (2020). Plunge in carbon emissions from lockdowns will not slow climate change. *National Geographic*, May 20. Available at: https://www.nationalgeographic .co.uk/environment-and-conservation/2020/05/plunge-in-carbon-emissions-from -lockdowns-will-not-slow (Accessed November 6, 2020).

CDC (Centers for Disease Control). 2020. Health Equity Considerations and Racial and Ethnic Minority Groups. 24 July 2020. https://www.cdc.gov/coronavirus/2019-nco v/community/health-equity/race-ethnicity.html.

Creosote Maps. (2020). *Black Lives Matters Protests 2020*. https://www.creosotemaps.com /blm2020/ (Accessed November 5, 2020).

Garcia, C.A. and Culbertson, A. (2020). Coronavirus: Why scientists have warned COVID lockdowns will not stop climate change. *Sky News*, October 16. Available at: https://ne ws.sky.com/story/coronavirus-why-scientists-have-warned-covid-lockdowns-will-not -stop-climate-change-12067396 (Accessed November 5, 2020).

Gould, E. and Wilson, V. (2020). Black workers face two of the most lethal preexisting conditions for coronavirus – racism and economic inequality. Economic Policy Institute, Washington DC. https://files.epi.org/pdf/193246.pdf

Gover, A.R., Harper, S.B. and Langton, L. (2020). Anti-Asian hate crime during the COVID-19 pandemic: Exploring the reproduction of inequality. *American Journal of Criminal Justice*, 45(4), 647–667.

Haddad, M. (2020). Mapping anti-racism solidarity protests around the world. *Al Jazeera*, June 7. Available at: https://www.aljazeera.com/news/2020/6/7/mapping-anti-ra cism-solidarity-protests-around-the-world (Accessed 5 November 2020).

Hawkins, D. (2020). The coronavirus burden is falling heavily on black Americans. Why? The Guardian. https://www.theguardian.com/commentisfree/2020/apr/16/b lack-workers-coronavirus-covid-19

Le Quéré, C., Jackson, R.B., Jones, M.W. et al. (2020). Temporary reduction in daily global CO2 emissions during the COVID-19 forced confinement. *Nature Climate Change*, 10, 647–653. https://doi.org/10.1038/s41558-020-0797-x

Liu, Z., Ciais, P., Deng, Z. et al. (2020). Near-real-time monitoring of global CO2 emissions reveals the effects of the COVID-19 pandemic. *Nature Communications* 11, 5172 https://doi.org/10.1038/s41467-020-18922-7

Mormina, M. and Nsofor, I. (2020) What developing countries can teach rich countries about how to respond to a pandemic. *Quartz Africa*, October 20. Available at: https:/ /qz.com/africa/1919785/what-africa-and-asia-teach-rich-countries-on-handling-a -pandemic/ (Accessed 5 November 2020).

Pellow, D.N. (2016). Toward a critical environmental justice studies: Black lives matter as an environmental justice challenge. *Du Bois Review: Social Science Research on Race*, 13(2), 221–236.

Polanyi, K. (1934). Marxism restated. *New Britain*, 187–188.

Robertson, G. (2020). COVID-19 and the continuous denial of indigenous rights in Canada. *LSE Blogs*, July 7. Available at: https://blogs.lse.ac.uk/humanrights/2020 /07/07/covid-19-and-the-continuous-denial-of-indigenous-rights-in-canada/ (Accessed 5 November 2020).

Rutz, C., Loretto, M., Bates, A., Davidson, S., Duarte, C., Jetz, W., Johnson, M., Kato, A., Kays, R., Mueller, T., Primack, R., Ropert-Coudert, Y., Tucker, M., Wikelski, M. and Cagnacci, F. (2020). COVID-19 lockdown allows researchers to quantify the effects of human activity on wildlife. *Nature Ecology & Evolution*, 4, 1156–1159. https ://doi.org/10.1038/s41559-020-1237-z

Schneider, L., Sbicca, J. and Malin, S. (2020). Native American tribes' pandemic response is hamstrung by many inequities. *The Conversation*, June 1. Available at: https://th econversation.com/native-american-tribes-pandemic-response-is-hamstrung-by-ma ny-inequities-136225 (Accessed 5 November 2020).

Soy, A. (2020). Coronavirus in Africa: Five reasons why COVID-19 has been less deadly than elsewhere. *BBC News*, October 7. Available at: https://www.bbc.co.uk/news/ world-africa-54418613 (Accessed 5 November 2020).

INDEX

Page numbers in **bold** denote tables, in *italic* denote figures

Printed in the United States
by Baker & Taylor Publisher Services